Craig Swan

Study Guide for

Macroeconomics
Principles and Policy
Sixth Edition

William J. Baumol
Alan S. Blinder

The Dryden Press
Harcourt Brace College Publishers
Fort Worth   Philadelphia   San Diego   New York   Orlando   Austin   San Antonio
Toronto   Montreal   London   Sydney   Tokyo

Cover Image: Tommy Lynn

Address for Editorial Correspondence
The Dryden Press, 301 Commerce Street, Suite 3700, Fort Worth, TX 76102

Address for Orders
The Dryden Press, 6277 Sea Harbor Drive, Orlando, FL 32887
1-800-782-4479, or 1-800-433-0001 (in Florida)

ISBN: 0-03-098607-9

Printed in the United States of America

4 5 6 7 8 9 0 1 2 3   018   9 8 7 6 5 4 3 2 1

The Dryden Press
Harcourt Brace College Publishers

Table of Contents

Introduction

This study guide is designed to be used with *Macroeconomics: Principles and Policy*, Sixth Edition, by William J. Baumol and Alan S. Blinder. This guide is not a substitute for the basic textbook; rather, experience has shown that conscientious use of a supplement such as this guide can lead to greater learning and understanding of the course material. It might also improve your grade.

The chapters in this book parallel those in *Macroeconomics: Principles and Policy*, Sixth Edition. Each chapter here is a review of the material covered in the textbook chapters. You should first read and study each chapter in the textbook and then use the corresponding chapter in this book. "Use" is the correct verb, as chapters in this book are designed for your *active* participation.

The material with which you will be working is organized into the following elements.

LEARNING OBJECTIVES

Each chapter starts with a set of behavioral learning objectives. These indicate the things you should be able to do upon completing each chapter.

IMPORTANT TERMS AND CONCEPTS

As one of the learning objectives for each chapter states, you should be able to define, understand, and use correctly the terms and concepts that are listed in this section. They parallel the important terms and concepts listed at the end of the text chapter. Being able to *define* these terms is likely to be important for your grade. But to really *understand* what they mean, rather than to temporarily memorize their definition, is even better. The ultimate test of your understanding will be your ability to *use correctly* the terms and concepts in real-life situations.

CHAPTER REVIEW

Each review section has a summary discussion of the major points of each chapter. The reviews are designed to be used actively. Frequently, you will need to supply the appropriate missing term or to choose between pairs of alternative words. Some of the missing words are quite specific and can be found in the list of important terms and concepts. At other times, the answers are less clear-cut, as the following hypothetical example illustrates: "If people expect inflation at higher rates than before, nominal interest rates are likely to _____." Any of the following would be correct answers: increase, rise, go up. In cases like this, do not get concerned if the answer you choose is different from the one in the back of the book.

IMPORTANT TERMS AND CONCEPTS QUIZ

Each chapter contains an important terms and concepts quiz to help you review important terms and concepts. Match each term with the most appropriate definition.

BASIC EXERCISE

Most chapters have one or more exercises that are designed for you to use as a check on your understanding of a basic principle discussed in the chapter. Many of the exercises use simple arithmetic or geometry. While getting the correct answers is one measure of understanding, do not mistake the arithmetic manipulations for the economic content of the problems. A hand calculator may make the arithmetic less burdensome.

SELF-TEST FOR UNDERSTANDING

Each chapter has a set of multiple choice and true-false questions for you to use as a further check on your understanding. It is important to know not only the correct answers but also why other answers are wrong. When considering the true-false questions especially, be sure you understand why the false statements are false. Answers for the Self-Tests are in the back of this guide and include page references to the textbook to help you understand correct choices.

APPENDIX

Many chapters in the text contain an appendix, which generally is designed to supplement the chapter content with material that is either a bit more difficult or offers further exposition of a particular economic concept. In some cases, the review material for the appendix parallels that for the chapter, including learning objectives, important terms and concepts, and so forth. In other cases, the appendix material is reviewed here in the form of an additional exercise designed to illustrate the principals discussed in the appendix.

SUPPLEMENTARY EXERCISE

Many chapters end with a supplementary exercise, which may be either an additional mathematical exercise or some suggestions that allow you to use what you have learned in real-world situations. Some exercises use more advanced mathematics. Since many of these exercises review Basic Exercise material, they illustrate how economists use mathematics and are included for students with appropriate training. Most importantly, understand the economic principles that underlie the Basic Exercise, something that does not depend upon advanced mathematics.

ECONOMICS IN ACTION

Most chapters include a brief example, mostly from recent newspapers or magazines. Each example has been chosen to show how economic concepts and ideas can help one understand real world problems and issues.

STUDY QUESTIONS

Each chapter ends with a short list of study questions. Working with friends on these questions is a useful way to review chapter material and should help on examinations.

Being introduced to economics for the first time should be exciting and fun. For many, it is likely to be hard work, but hard work does not have to be dull and uninteresting. Do not look for a pat set of answers with universal applicability. Economics does not offer answers but rather a way of looking at the world and thinking systematically about issues. As the English economist John Maynard Keynes said:

> The theory of economics does not furnish a body of settled conclusions immediately applicable to policy. It is a method rather than a doctrine, an apparatus of the mind, a technique of thinking, which helps its possessor to draw correct conclusions.

> Bertrand Russell, the distinguished British philosopher and mathematician, had considered studying economics but decided it was too easy. The Nobel prize-winning physicist, Max Planck, also considered studying economics but decided it was too hard. Whether, like Russell, you find economics easy or, like Planck, you find it hard, I trust that with the use of this guide you will find it relevant and exciting!

> The preparation of this guide would not have been possible without the help and contributions of others. I especially want to acknowledge the contributions of Dr. Marianne Felton of Indiana University, Southeast, Jack Stecher, and my wife, Janet.

Craig Swan

Chapter **1**

What Is Economics?

LEARNING OBJECTIVES

After completing this chapter, you should be able to:

- explain the role of abstraction, or simplification, in economic theory.
- explain the role of theory as a guide to understanding real-world phenomena.
- explain why correlation need not imply causation.
- explain why imperfect information and value judgments will always mean that economics cannot provide definitive answers to all social problems.

IMPORTANT TERMS AND CONCEPTS

Voluntary exchange
Comparative advantage
Productivity
Externalities
Marginal analysis
Marginal costs
Abstraction and generalization
Theory
Correlation versus causation
Economic model
Opportunity Cost

CHAPTER REVIEW

Chapter 1 has two objectives: It introduces the types of problems that concern economists, offering 12 important ideas for Beyond the Final Exam, and it discusses the methods of economic analysis, in particular the role of theory in economics.

Problems discussed in the first part of the chapter have been chosen to illustrate 12 basic economic issues to be remembered beyond the final exam. You should not only read this material now, but re–examine the list at the end of the course. Understanding the economic principles that underlie these 12 basic issues is the real final examination in economics.

The methods of economic inquiry are best described as "eclectic," meaning they are drawn from many sources according to their usefulness to the subject matter. Economists borrow from the social sciences to theorize about human behavior. They borrow from mathematics to express theories concisely. And they borrow from statistics to make inferences from real-world data about hypotheses suggested by economic theory.

Economists are interested in understanding human behavior not only for its own sake, but for the policy implications of this knowledge. How can we know what to expect from changes resulting from public policy or business decisions unless we understand why people behave the way they do? Consider the 12 ideas discussed in the first part of this chapter. Each derives from economic theory. As you will learn, each idea also offers insight into actual experience and is an important guide to evaluating future changes.

As in other scientific disciplines, theory in economics is an abstraction, or simplification, of innumerable complex relationships in the real world. When thinking about some aspects of behavior, say a family's spending decisions or why the price of wheat fluctuates so much, economists will develop a model that attempts to explain the behavior under examination. Elements of the model derive from economic theory. Economists study the model to see what hypotheses, or predictions, it suggests. These can then be checked against real-world data. An economist's model will typically be built not with hammer and nails, but with pencil, paper, and computers. The appropriate degree of abstraction for an economic model is determined, to a large extent, by the problem at hand and is not something that can be specified in advance for all problems.

Economists believe they can make a significant contribution to resolving many important social issues. It is hoped that by the time you finish this course, you will agree with this belief. At the same time, you should realize that economics offers a way of looking at questions rather than a comprehensive set of answers to all questions. Economists will (1) always have differences of opinion on final policy recommendations because of incomplete_____ and different _____ judgments.

IMPORTANT TERMS AND CONCEPTS

Choose the best definition for the following terms.

1. _____ Voluntary exchange
2. _____ Comparative advantage
3. _____ Productivity
4. _____ Externalities
5. _____ Marginal analysis
6. _____ Marginal costs
7. _____ Abstraction
8. _____ Theory
9. _____ Correlation
10. _____ Model
11. _____ Opportunity cost

a. Additional cost incurred by a one–unit increase in output.
b. Ability to produce a good less inefficiently than other goods.
c. Ignoring many details to focus on essential parts of a problem.
d. Situation in which the movements of two variables are linked, whether or not a causal relation exists.
e. Output produced by a unit of input.
f. Trade in which both parties are willing participants.
g. Effects on third parties that are not part of an economic transaction.
h. Cost per unit produced.
i. Deliberate simplification of relationships to explain how those relationships work.
j. Value of the next best alternative.
k. Simplified version of some aspect of the economy.
l. Evaluation of the impact of changes.

SELF-TESTS FOR UNDERSTANDING

Test A

Circle the most appropriate answer.

1. Most economists believe that policies to reduce inflation will
   a. permanently increase unemployment.
   b. never be adopted in democracies.
   c. increase unemployment for a time.
   d. have immediate and lasting impact.

2. In addition to interest rates, information about _____ is necessary to investigate the real cost of borrowing and lending.
   a. the inflation rate
   b. exchange rates
   c. the unemployment rate
   d. marginal cost

3. Economic analysis shows that federal budget deficits
    a. are a significant burden on future generations.
    b. are really of no concern.
    c. produce an impact that will depend on particular circumstances.
    d. are, in reality, usually beneficial.

4. Small differences in the productivity growth rate
    a. make little difference, even over periods as long as a century.
    b. can compound into significant differences.
    c. can be safely ignored by citizens and politicians.
    d. will lead only to small differences in the standard of living between countries.

5. Most economists believe that exchange
    a. is likely to be considered mutually advantageous to both parties when it is voluntary.
    b. only takes place when one side can extract a profit from the other.
    c. usually makes both parties worse off.
    d. is best when strictly regulated by the government.

6. With respect to international trade,
    a. a country can gain only if its neighbors lose.
    b. countries should try to be self–sufficient of all goods.
    c. only those countries with the highest productivity levels will gain.
    d. a country can gain by producing those goods in which it has a comparative advantage.

7. Most economists believe that attempts to set prices by decree
    a. will work best in the long run.
    b. are likely to create significant new problems.
    c. are the only way to establish fair prices.
    d. have a history of practical effectiveness.

8. When the actions of some economic agents impose cost on others, for example the polluting smoke of a factory or power plant,
    a. market mechanisms may exist that can help remedy the situation.
    b. the only answer is government regulation.
    c. there is very little one can do; such is the price of progress.
    d. it is always best to close down the offending action.

9. Economists define opportunity cost as
    a. the money price of goods and services.
    b. the lowest price you can bargain for.
    c. the value of the next best alternative.
    d. the time you must spend when shopping.

10. Marginal analysis is concerned with the study of
    a. buying stocks and bonds on credit.
    b. those groups that operate on the margins of the market economy.
    c. changes, such as the increase in cost when output increases.
    d. an engineer's fudge factor for possible errors.

11. The cost disease of personal services
    a. could be eliminated if only the government would regulate prices.
    b. would be eliminated if everyone practiced safe sex.
    c. is only an excuse for the government's inability to control its own spending.
    d. refers to the impact of differential rates of growth of productivity between the manufacturing and service sectors of the economy.

12. Economic analysis suggests that
    a. policies that promote the highest rate of economic growth unambiguously improve the distribution of income.
    b. policies to increase equality may reduce output.
    c. incentives for work and savings have almost no impact on people's behavior.
    d. there is no tradeoff between the size of the economic pie and how the pie is divided.

Test B

Circle T or F for true or false.

T F 1. Economic models are no good unless they include all of the detail that characterizes the real world.

T F 2. Material in this text will reveal the answer to many important social problems.

T F 3. Opportunity cost is measured by considering the best alternative foregone.

T F 4. Economists' policy prescriptions will always differ because of incomplete information and different value judgments.

T F 5. Theory and practical policy have nothing to do with each other.

T F 6. If two variables are correlated, we can be certain that one causes the other.

T F 7. The best economic models all use the same degree of abstraction.

T F 8. An economist tests a hypothesis when she deliberately simplifies the nature of relationships in order to explain cause and effect.

T F 9. No business should ever sell its output at a price that does not cover full cost.

T F 10. There is no tradeoff between policies that increase output and those that equalize income.

SUPPLEMENTARY EXERCISE

The following suggested readings offer an excellent introduction to the ideas and lives of economists past and present:

1. *The Worldly Philosophers: The Lives, Times & Ideas of the Great Economic Thinkers*, 6th ed., by Robert L. Heilbroner (Touchstone Books, 1987).

2. In recent years, *The Quarterly Review* of the Banca Nazionale del Lavoro and *The American Economist*, published by Omicron Delta Epsilon, the undergraduate economics honors society, have published recollections and reflections by distinguished economists. Read what these authors have to say about their lives as economists. The December 1983 issue of *The Quarterly Review* contains reflections by William Baumol.

3. *Lives of the Laureates: Ten Nobel Economists*, edited by William Breit and Roger W. Spencer (MIT Press, 1990). This is a collection of recollections by ten winners of the Nobel Prize in Economics.

STUDY QUESTIONS

1. Explain the relationships between theories, models, and hypotheses.

2. Why are theories necessary for understanding the causal links between economic variables? Why can't the facts speak for themselves?

3. Many trace the establishment of economics as a field of study to the publication of Adam Smith's *Wealth of Nations* in 1776. Why, after more than 200 years, do so many questions remain?

ECONOMICS IN ACTION
Play Ball

Are baseball players overpaid? Contracts worth $3 million to $5 million a year seemed common in the early 1990s. Even after adjusting for inflation, Babe Ruth's highest salary is estimated to have been less than $700,000. What accounts for the difference, and does it make economic sense?

Writing in *Scientific American*, Paul Wallich and Elizabeth Corcoran explain the difference through the concepts of opportunity cost and marginal analysis, ideas introduced in this chapter. Under the reserve clause, in effect from 1903 until the mid-1970s, a baseball player who did not like his contract had little choice other than retiring from baseball. Players were not free to bargain with other teams. After the introduction of free agency, baseball players could sell their services to the team with the best offer.

Gerald Scully, in his book *The Business of Major League Baseball*, uses statistical techniques to see how hitting and pitching help determine a team's winning percentage and how a team's revenue relates to its record and the size of the market in which it plays. He then estimates how adding a particular player might add to a team's performance and hence its revenue.

Using data from the late 1980s, Scully finds that the performance of selected superstars increased team revenues by $2 million to $3 million, numbers consistent with the highest salaries at the time. Using data from the late 1960s, he estimates that superstars increased team revenues by $600,000 to $1 million and notes that the highest salaries were only $100,000 to $125,000.

1. How does the concept of opportunity cost help explain baseball salaries while the reserve clause was in effect? What was the opportunity cost of a baseball player's time? How did free agency change the opportunity cost for a player deciding whether to stay with a team?

2. How would marginal analysis help a team determine how much it should offer a free agent?

SOURCES: Paul Wallich and Elizabeth Corcoran, "The MBAs of Summer," *Scientific American*, (June 1992): p. 120.
Gerald W. Scully, *The Business of Major League Baseball*, (Chicago: University of Chicago Press, 1989).

Appendix: The Graphs Used in Economic Analysis

LEARNING OBJECTIVES

After completing the material in this appendix, you should be able to:

♦ interpret various graphs:

use a two-variable graph to determine what combinations of variables go together.

use a three-variable graph to determine what combinations of the X and Y variables are consistent with the same value for the Z variable.

♦ construct two-variable and three-variable graphs.

♦ compute the slope of a straight line and explain what it measures.

♦ explain how to compute the slope of a curved line.

♦ explain how a 45–degree line can divide a graph into two regions, one in which the Y variable exceeds the X variable, and another in which the X variable exceeds the Y variable.

IMPORTANT TERMS AND CONCEPTS

Variable
Two-variable diagram
Horizontal and vertical axes
Origin (of a graph)
Slope of a straight (or curved) line
Negative, positive, zero, and infinite slope
Tangent to a curve
Y-intercept
Ray through the origin, or ray 45–degree line
Contour map

APPENDIX REVIEW

Economists like to draw pictures, primarily *graphs*. Your textbook and this study guide also make extensive use of graphs. There is nothing very difficult about graphs, but understanding them from the beginning will help you avoid mistakes later on.

(1) All the graphs we will use start with two straight lines, one on the bottom and one on the left side. These edges of the graph will usually have labels to indicate what is being measured in both the vertical and horizontal directions. The line on the bottom is called the (horizontal/vertical) axis, and the line running up the side is called the _____ axis. The point at which the two lines meet is called the _____. The variable measured along the horizontal axis is often called the *X* variable, while the term *Y* variable is often used to refer to the variable measured along the vertical axis.

Figure 1-1 is a two-variable diagram plotting expenditures on alcoholic beverages and ministers' salaries. Does this graph imply that wealthier clergymen drink more, or does it suggest that more drinking in general is increasing the demand for, and hence the salaries of, clergymen? Most likely neither interpretation is correct; just because you can plot two variables does not mean that one caused the other.

(2) Many two-variable diagrams encountered in introductory economics use *straight lines*, primarily for simplicity. An important characteristic of a straight line is its *slope*, measured by comparing differences between two points. To calculate the slope of a straight line, divide the (horizontal/vertical) change by the corresponding _____ change as you move to the right along the line. The change between any two points can be used to compute the slope because the slope of a straight line is _____. If the straight line shows that both the horizontal and vertical variables increase together, then the line is said to have a (positive/negative) slope; that is, as we move to the right, the line slopes (up/down). If one variable decreases as the other variable increases, the line is said to have a _____ slope. A line with a zero slope shows _____ change in the *Y* variable as the *X* variable changes.

(3)   A special type of straight line passes through the origin of a graph. This is called a _____ through the origin. Its slope is measured the same as the slope of any other straight line. A special type of ray is one that connects all points where the vertical and horizontal variables are equal. If the vertical and horizontal variables are measured in the same units, then this line has a slope of +1 and is called the _____ line.

Like straight lines, curved lines also have slopes, but the slope of a curved line is not constant. We measure the slope of a curved line at any point by the slope of the one straight **(4)** line that just touches, or is _____ to, the line at that point.

A third type of graph is used by economists as well as cartographers. Such a graph can **(5)** represent three dimensions on a diagram with only two axes by the use of _____ lines. A traditional application of such a graph in economics is a diagram that measures inputs along the horizontal and vertical axes and then uses contour lines to show what different combinations of inputs can be used to produced the same amount of output.

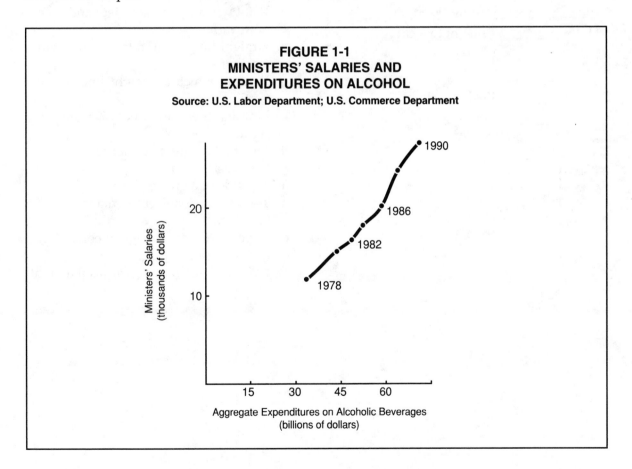

FIGURE 1-1
MINISTERS' SALARIES AND
EXPENDITURES ON ALCOHOL
Source: U.S. Labor Department; U.S. Commerce Department

TERMS AND CONCEPTS QUIZ

Choose the best definition for the following terms.

1. _____ Variable
2. _____ Two-variable diagram
3. _____ Horizontal axis
4. _____ Vertical axis
5. _____ Origin
6. _____ Slope
7. _____ Negative slope
8. _____ Positive slope
9. _____ Zero slope
10. _____ Infinite slope
11. _____ Tangent to a curve
12. _____ Y-intercept
13. _____ Ray
14. _____ 45–degree line
15. _____ Contour map

a. Graph of how a variable changes over time.
b. Vertical line segment.
c. Straight line, touching a curve at a point without cutting the curve.
d. The bottom line of a graph.
e. Straight line emanating from the origin.
f. Object whose magnitude is measured by a number.
g. Simultaneous representation of the magnitudes of two variables.
h. Point where both axes meet and where both variables are zero.
i. Straight line through the origin with a slope of +1.
j. Point at which a straight line cuts the vertical axis.
k. Line that goes down, moving from left to right.
l. Line that neither rises nor falls, moving from left to right.
m. The side of a graph.
n. Two-dimensional representation of three variables.
o. Ratio of vertical change to corresponding horizontal change.
p. Line that rises, moving from left to right.

BASIC EXERCISES
Reading Graphs

These exercises are designed to give practice working with two–variable diagrams.

1. **Understanding a Demand Curve**
    The demand curve in Figure 1-2 represents the demand for new Ph.D. economists.
    a. What quantity would colleges and universities demand if they have to pay a salary of $45,000? _____
    b. What does the graph indicate would happen to the quantity demanded if salaries fall to $35,000? The quantity demanded would (increase/decrease) to _____
    c. What would happen to the quantity demanded if salaries were $50,000? It would (increase/decrease) to _____
    d. What is the slope of the demand curve? _____
    e. Explain how the slope of the demand curve provides information about the change in the number of new Ph.D. economists demanded as salary changes.

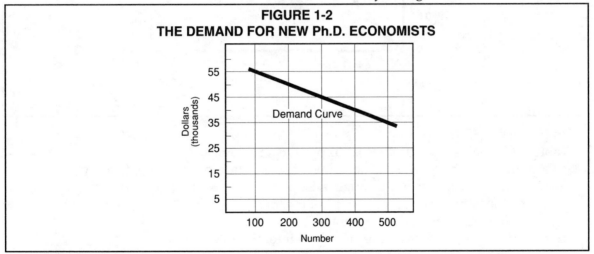

FIGURE 1-2
THE DEMAND FOR NEW Ph.D. ECONOMISTS

2. **Understanding a 45–degree Line**
    Figure 1-3 shows data on grade point averages for Valerie and her friends. Overall averages are measured along the horizontal axis while GPAs for courses in economics are measured along the vertical axis. Figure 1-3 also includes a 45–degree line.
    a. How many individuals have higher overall GPAs than economics GPAs?

    _____

    b. How many individuals do better in economics courses than in their other courses?

    _____

    c. If all of Valerie's friends had their best grades in economics courses, all of the points in Figure 1-3 would lie (above/below) the 45–degree line.
    d. If all of the points in Figure 1-3 were below the 45–degree line, we could conclude that Valerie and her friends did better in (economics/non-economics) courses.

FIGURE 1-3
GRADE POINT AVERAGES

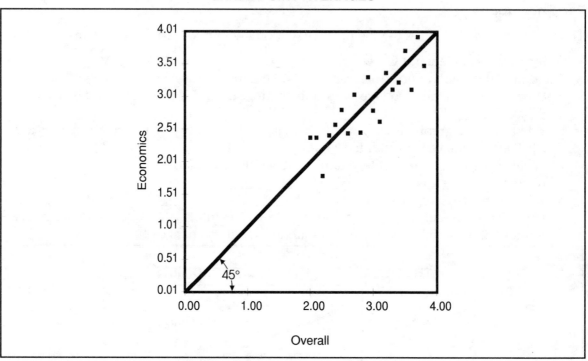

3. Understanding Slopes

Table 1-1 contains data on the cost of producing widgets.

a. Plot this data in Figure 1-4. The points appear to lie along a (<u>curved/straight</u>) line.

b. Draw the appropriate line through these points and extend it to the vertical axis. What is the mathematical value for the slope of the line? _____. Can you provide an economic meaning for this number?

c. What is the mathematical value for the Y–intercept of your line? _____.
Can you provide an economic meaning for this number?

d. Now consider Figure 1-5, which shows how the cost of producing gadgets varies with output. Describe how the slope of the curved line varies as output increases. Can you provide an economic interpretation for your answer?

TABLE 1-1

Output	Cost
0	$1,000
200	$2,000
400	$3,000
600	$4,000
800	$5,000
1,000	$6,000

FIGURE1-4
TOTAL COST AND OUTPUT: WIDGETS

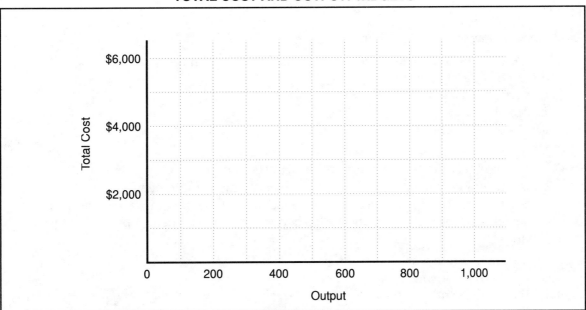

FIGURE 1-5
TOTAL COST AND OUTPUT: GADGETS

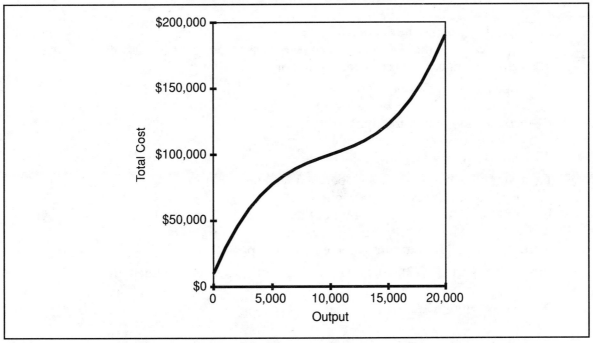

SELF-TESTS FOR UNDERSTANDING
Test A

Circle the most appropriate answer.

1. The vertical line on the left side of a two-variable diagram is called the
    a. ray through the origin.
    b. vertical axis.
    c. X axis.
    d. slope of the graph.

2. A two-variable diagram
    a. can only be drawn when one variable causes another.
    b. is a useful way to show how two variables change simultaneously.
    c. is a useful way of summarizing the influence of all factors that affect the Y variable.
    d. can only be used when relationships between variables can be represented by straight lines.

3. The origin of a two–variable graph is
    a. found in the lower right corner of a graph.
    b. the same as the Y–intercept.
    c. the intersection of the vertical and horizontal axes where both variables are equal to zero.
    d. found by following the slope to the point where it equals zero.

4. The slope of a straight line is found by dividing the
    a. Y variable by the X variable.
    b. vertical axis by the horizontal axis.
    c. largest value of the Y variable by the smallest value of the X variable.
    d. vertical change by the corresponding horizontal change.

5. The slope of a straight line
    a. is the same at all points.
    b. increases moving to the right.
    c. will be zero when the X variable equals to zero.
    d. is always positive.

6. If a straight line has a positive slope, then we know that
    a. it runs uphill, moving to the right.
    b. the slope of the line will be greater than that of a 45–degree line.
    c. it must also have a positive Y–intercept.
    d. it will reach its maximum value when its slope is zero.

7. Referring to parts (1), (2), (3), and (4) of Figure 1-6, determine which line has a(n)
    a. positive slope _____.
    b. negative slope _____.
    c. zero slope _____.
    d. infinite slope _____.

FIGURE 1-6

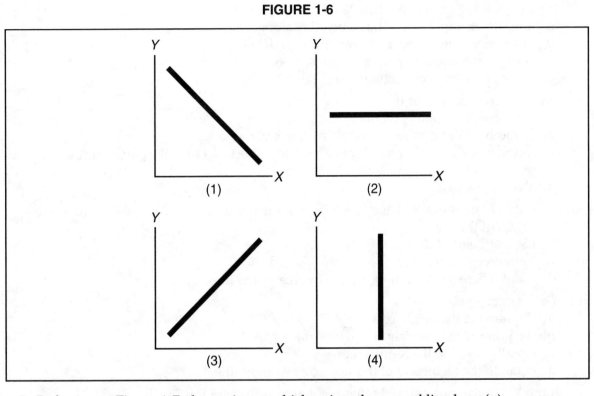

(1)   (2)   (3)   (4)

8. Referring to Figure 1-7, determine at which points the curved line has a(n)
   a. positive slope _____ _____ _____.
   b. negative slope _____ _____ _____.
   c. zero slope _____ _____ _____.
   d. infinite slope _____ _____ _____.

FIGURE 1-7

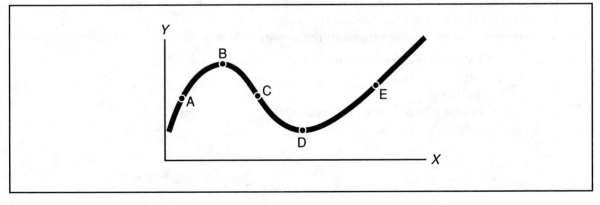

9. If when $X = 5$, $Y = 16$ and when $X = 8$, $Y = 10$, then the
    a. line connecting X and Y has a positive slope.
    b. line connecting X and Y is a ray through the origin.
    c. slope of the line connecting X and Y is +6.
    d. slope of the line connecting X and Y is –2.

10. The slope of a curved line is
    a. the same at all points on the line.
    b. found by dividing the Y variable by the X variable.
    c. found by determining the slope of a straight line tangent to the curved line at the point of interest.
    d. always positive.

11. If a curved line is in the shape of a hill, then the point of zero slope will occur at the
    a. origin of the line.
    b. highest point of the line.
    c. Y–intercept of the line.
    d. point where a ray from the origin intercepts the line.

12. The Y–intercept is
    a. the same as the origin of a graph.
    b. the point where a straight line cuts the Y axis.
    c. usually equal to the X–intercept.
    d. equal to the reciprocal of the slope of a straight line.

13. If the Y–intercept of a straight line is equal to zero, then this line is called
    a. the opportunity cost of a graph.
    b. a ray through the origin.
    c. the 45–degree line.
    d. the X axis.

14. A ray is
    a. any straight line with a slope of +1.
    b. any line, straight or curved, that passes through the origin of a graph.
    c. a straight line with a positive Y–intercept.
    d. a straight line that passes through the origin.

15. If the X and Y variables are measured in the same units, a 45–degree line will
    a. have a positive Y–intercept.
    b. have a negative slope.
    c. show all points where X and Y are equal.
    d. be steeper than the Y axis.

16. If X and Y are measured in the same units, and we consider a point that lies below a 45–degree line, then we know that for the X and Y combination associated with this point,
    a. the X variable is greater than the Y variable.
    b. a line from the origin through this point will be a ray and will have a slope greater than +1.
    c. the Y variable is greater than the X variable.
    d. the slope of the point is less than 1.

17. Referring to parts (1), (2), (3), and (4) of Figure 1-8, determine which part(s) show a ray through the origin.
    a. (2)
    b. (1) and (3)
    c. (1) and (4)
    d. (3) and (4)

FIGURE 1-8

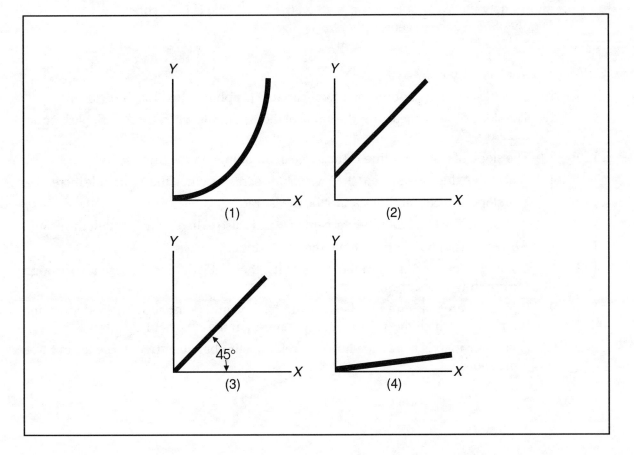

18. If in part (4) of Figure 1-8, the *Y* variable changes by 2 units when the *X* variable changes by 5 units, then the slope of the line is
    a. .4 ($2/5$).
    b. 2.5 ($5/2$).
    c. 10 (2x5).
    d. insufficient information to compute.

19. If two straight line have the same slope, then they
    a. must also have the same Y–intercept.
    b. will show the same change in Y for similar changes in X.
    c. will both pass through the origin.
    d. are said to be complements.

20. A contour map
    a. is always better than a two-variable diagram.
    b. is a way of collapsing three variables into a two-variable diagram.
    c. shows how the Y variable changes when the X variable is held constant.
    d. is only of relevance to geographers.

Test B

Circle T or F for true or false.

T F 1. The line along the bottom of a two–variable graph is called the vertical axis.

T F 2. The slope of a line measures the value of the *Y* variable when the *X* variable is equal to zero.

T F 3. The slope of a straight line is the same at all points on the line.

T F 4. A negative slope means that the *Y* variable decreases when the *X* variable increases.

T F 5. The slope of a curved line cannot be measured.

T F 6. A straight line that has a *Y*–intercept of zero is also called a ray through the origin.

T F 7. All rays through the origin have the same slope.

T F 8. If *X* and *Y* are measured in the same units, then a 45–degree line is a ray through the origin with a slope of +1.

T F 9. If *X* and *Y* are measured in the same units, then any point above a 45–degree line is a point at which the *Y* variable is greater than the *X* variable.

T F 10. A contour map is a way to show the relationship between two variables in three dimensions.

C h a p t e r **2**

A Profile of the
U.S. Economy

LEARNING OBJECTIVES

After completing this chapter, you should be able to:

♦ explain the difference between inputs and outputs.

♦ explain why total output of the American economy is larger than that of other nations.

♦ explain why real GDP per capita is a better measure of living standards than GDP.

♦ explain the difference between a closed and open economy.

♦ describe in general terms the growth experience of the American economy.

♦ describe the broad changes in American work experience: Who goes to work outside the home? What sorts of jobs do they hold? What sorts of goods and services do they produce?

♦ describe who gets what proportion of national income.

♦ describe the common forms of business organization.

♦ describe the role of government in the American economy.

♦ explain the implications of the pitfalls of time series graphs:
  • failure to adjust for changes in prices and/or population.
  • the use of short time periods with unique features.
  • omitting the origin.
  • the use of different units to measure the same variable.

IMPORTANT TERMS AND CONCEPTS

Economy
Inputs (factors of production)
Outputs
Gross domestic product (GDP)
Real GDP
Open economy
Closed economy
Inflation
Recession
Sole proprietorship
Partnership
Corporation
Transfer payments
Mixed economy

CHAPTER REVIEW

This chapter offers an introduction to and overview of the American economy. The money value of total output of the American economy is usually measured by something called
(1) gross_____ _____or _____for short. American GDP is so large because of the size of the work force and the productivity of American workers. Other countries, for example China and India, have larger populations, but the productivity of workers there does not compare with that of American workers.

Why is the American economy so productive? It is useful to view an economic system as a social mechanism that organizes (<u>inputs/outputs</u>) to produce _____.
(2) Many believe that the productivity of the American economy is a reflection of business competition fostered by the extensive use of_____ markets and _____ enterprise.

No economy is self–sufficient. All economies trade with each other, although their reliance on trade varies. The average of exports and imports as a percentage of GDP is often used as a measure of the degree to which an economy can be called _____ or
(3) _____. Compared to other industrialized countries, the United State would look like a(n) (<u>closed/open</u>) economy. While exports and imports have both increased since World War II, they are currently just a bit more than 10 percent of American GDP.

Because it uses money values to add up different types of outputs, i.e, food, clothes, cars, medical services, and new houses, GDP will increase when prices increase even if there is no change in production. A sustained increase in prices on average is referred to as
(4) _____. A time series graph of American GDP since World War II shows

significant growth. As with all time series graphs, one needs to be careful about exactly how the variable of interest is measured. If one is interested in consumption possibilities, it is best to correct for inflation by looking at GDP measured in dollars of constant purchasing power or _____ GDP. It may also be useful to adjust real GDP by the growth in population for a measure of GDP _____ _____. Adjusting for inflation and population growth still shows a doubling of per capita real GDP over the past 40 years.

(5) While the time series graph of real GDP for the United States shows significant growth since World War II, it has not been continual growth. There have been periods when total output declined. These periods are called _____. How the government should respond during or in anticipation of a period of recession continues to spark controversy. Material in chapters _____ to _____ has been designed to help you understand the issues and arguments of this debate.

(6) Organizing inputs, also called factors of _____, is a central issue that any economy must address. For the most part, output in the United States is produced by private firms that compete in free markets. Most economists believe that having to meet the competition is an important reason why the American economy is so productive. Inputs include labor, machinery, buildings, and natural resources. It is the revenue from selling output that creates income for these factors of production.

In the United States the largest share of income accrues to which factor of production?
(7) _____. The income earned by those who put up the money to buy buildings and machinery comes in the form of interest and profits. Together, these two forms of income receive about _____of each sales dollar. Most Americans work in (<u>manufacturing/service</u>) industries. One of the Basic Exercises to this chapter examines the issue of declining manufacturing employment.

(8) A business may be owned and operated by a single individual, in which case it is called a sole_____. If a business is run by a fixed number of individuals, it is called a _____. However, most output is produced by _____, fictitious legal entities that have the status of individuals. Most large corporations are owned by stockholders and run by managers. While almost 90 percent of output in the United States is produced by privately owned businesses, most observers would say that the American economy is best described as a (<u>laissez faire/mixed/socialistic</u>) economy. That is, there is important public influence over the private market along with a mixture of public and private ownership.

The discussion in the text lists five roles for government:

1) To provide certain goods and services.
2) To raise taxes to finance its operations.
3) To redistribute income.
4) To regulate business.
5) To enforce the rules of business and society, including property rights.

This or any other list does not say whether particular actions are best done by the government or by the private economy. Are there legitimate unmet needs that should be addressed by government, or is government already too big? Much of the material in subsequent chapters is designed to help you understand what markets do well and what they do poorly. It is hoped that a better understanding of the insights from economic analysis will help you decide where you would draw the line between markets and government.

Appendix

As illustrated in the text, economists make extensive use of time series graphs. These are two variable graphs with time measured along the (horizontal/vertical) axis and one or more
(9) variables of interest measured along the _____ axis. Time series graphs are an effective way to convey a lot of information, but they also can be misleading if misused either inadvertently or deliberately.

When making or interpreting time series graphs you should be aware of the following pitfalls:

- Failing to adjust for inflation or population growth can give a misleading impression of growth.
- Showing only a brief period of time and/or one with an atypical beginning or ending can give a distorted impression of actual experience.
- Omitting the origin can give an exaggerated impression of changes.
- Changing the units of measurement, say from pounds to ounces or dollars to pennies, can make a graph arbitrarily steeper or flatter.

IMPORTANT TERMS AND CONCEPTS QUIZ

Choose the most appropriate definition for the following terms.

1. _____ Economy
2. _____ Inputs (factors of production)
3. _____ Outputs
4. _____ Gross domestic product (GDP)
5. _____ Real GDP
6. _____ Open economy
7. _____ Closed economy
8. _____ Inflation
9. _____ Recession
10. _____ Sole proprietorship
11. _____ Partnership
12. _____ Corporation
13. _____ Transfer payments
14. _____ Mixed economy

a. Money value of all goods and services produced in a year.
b. A business owned by a fixed number of individuals.
c. A sustained increase in the average level of prices.
d. A collection of markets in a specified geographic area.
e. Economy in which exports and imports are small relative to GDP.
f. A measure of how prices today compare to prices during a specified base period.
g. Value of goods and services produced in a year measured by dollars of constant purchasing power.
h. A period when real GDP declines.
i. Labor, machinery, buildings, and natural resource used to produce goods and services.
j. A business owned by a single individual or family.
k. International trade is a large promotion of GDP.
l. Economy with public influence over the workings of free markets and a mix of public and private ownership.
m. Goods and services desired by consumers.
n. A business that has the legal status of a fictitious individual.
o. Money that individuals receive from the government as grants.

BASIC EXERCISES

These exercises are designed to introduce facts about the American economy and to offer practice working with graphs and economic data.

1. **Growth Trends**
   a. Look at Table 2-1, which has data on personal income after taxes. The data show that between 1960 and 1990 aggregate personal income after taxes increased more than eleven fold (4,042.9 ÷ 360.5 = 11.2). Do you agree that individuals in 1990 were eleven times richer than individuals in 1960? Could they buy eleven times as many goods and services as they could in 1960?
   b. For each year in Table 2-1 divide aggregate income by the corresponding population to compute income per capita rather than aggregate income. Rather than a twenty-five fold increase, per capita income in 1990 was only _____ times its 1960 level.
   c. For each year divide income per capita by the corresponding price level and multiply by 100 to compute income per capita in constant prices. The figures in the last column of Table 2-1 will tell us how per capita purchasing power, or real income, has changed since 1960. (The appendix to Chapter 6 contains more information about how a price index is constructed and what can be done with it.) In 1990, per capita purchasing power was _____ times its 1960 level.

TABLE 2-1
PERSONAL INCOME AFTER TAXES

Year	Aggregate Personal Income After Taxes (billions)	Population (millions)	Income per Capita	Price Index 1987 = 100	Real Income per Capita (1987 prices)
1960	$360.5	180,671	$_____	27.5	$_____
1970	$722.0	205,052	$_____	46.4	$_____
1980	$1,952.9	227,726	$_____	80.9	$_____
1990	$4,042.9	249,924	$_____	105.7	$_____

SOURCE: 1993 Economic Report of the President, Tables B-3, B-24, B-29

2. Rock Concerts: Adjusting for Inflation

Who paid more to attend their favorite rock concert, you or your parents? Table 2-2 has data on ticket prices of stadium rock concerts. Use the data on consumer prices to express ticket prices for earlier years in 1993 dollars. (Divide each ticket price by the value of the price index and multiply by 100.)

TABLE 2-2

Year	Concert	Ticket Price	Consumer Price Index (1993 = 100)	Ticket Price in 1993 Dollars
1965	Beatles	$3.50	21.9	$_____
1971	The Band, Muddy Waters, John Sebastian, Paul Butterfield Blues Band	$8.00	28.1	$_____
1976	Fleetwood Mac, Jeff Beck	$9.00	39.5	$_____
1978	Eagles, Steve Miller	$10.00	45.3	$_____
1982	The Who	$16.00	60.1	$_____
1983	Simon and Garfunkel	$20.00	69.2	$_____
1985	Bruce Springsteen	$17.50	74.7	$_____
1986	Bob Dylan, Grateful Dead	$20.00	76.1	$_____
1988	Pink Floyd	$22.50	82.2	$_____
1989	Rolling Stones	$28.50	86.1	$_____
1993	Paul McCartney	$32.50	100.0	$_____

SOURCE: Minneapolis StarTribune, May 21, 1993. 1993 Economic Report of the President

3. Dangers of Omitting the Origin

Table 2-3 contains data on gold prices during the late winter and early spring of 1993. Plot this data in Figures 2-1a and 2-1b. Which figure gives the more accurate representation of the increase in gold prices and why?

FIGURE 2-1A
Housing Starts: January-June, 1993

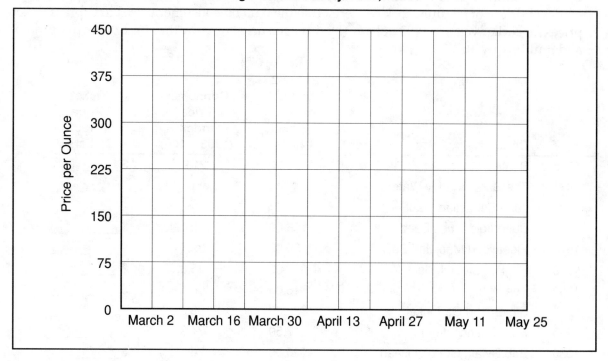

TABLE 2-3
The Price of Gold
March 2, 1993—May 25, 1993

Date	Dollars per Ounce
March 2	$328.95
March 9	$326.45
March 16	$328.75
March 23	$331.75
March 30	$336.15
April 6	$338.15
April 13	$337.15
April 20	$340.25
April 27	$350.55
May 4	$354.70
May 11	$356.45
May 18	$366.75
May 25	$374.45

SOURCE: *The Economist*, various issues

FIGURE 2-1B
Housing Starts: January–June, 1993

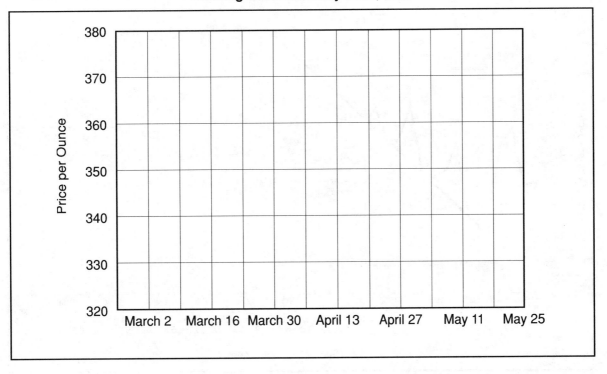

4. Choice of Time Periods

In 1960, John F. Kennedy campaigned on a promise to get the country moving, including more rapid economic expansion. When Kennedy was elected president the unemployment rate was rising and the economy was slipping into a recession. Many observers were claiming that for a variety of "structural" reasons the United States was entering an era of permanently higher unemployment. A major piece of evidence used to support this line of thinking was the rising succession of lowest unemployment rates in each postwar business expansion up to the early 1960s. The data are presented here, in Figure 2-2, together with a trend line connecting the succession of lowest unemployment rates. Use the data in Figure 2-2 to extend the time series graph and to check the accuracy of this argument. If the graph were restricted to data from 1968 to 1983, what would a similar trend line over this period show? What could one conclude from such a trend line?

FIGURE 2-2

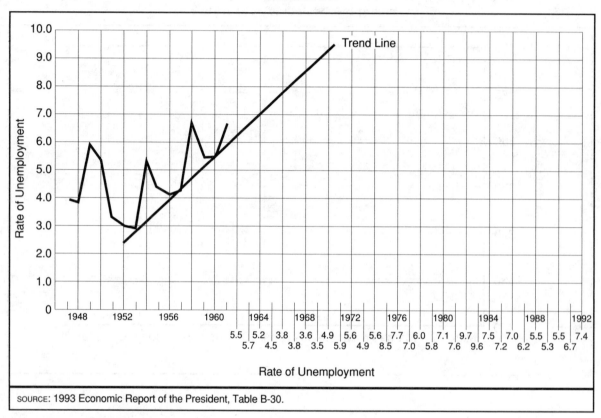

SOURCE: 1993 Economic Report of the President, Table B-30.

SELF-TESTS FOR UNDERSTANDING

Test A

Circle the most appropriate answer.

1. Which of the following help to explain why output of the American economy is as high as it is? (There may be more than one correct answer to this question.)
   a. The size of the labor force.
   b. The amount of money provided by the government.
   c. Business regulation.
   d. The productivity of American workers.

2. Total output of the United States economy
   a. is slightly less than that of Japan.
   b. is comparable to that of other industrialized countries.
   c. exceeds that of all other national economies.
   d. is among the lowest for industrialized countries.

3. Gross domestic product measures
   a. consumer spending.
   b. the vulgarness of many consumer goods.
   c. unpaid economic activity that takes place inside households.
   d. the money value of all the goods and services produced in an economy in a year.

4. Gross domestic product per capita refers to
   a. GDP per person (GDP/population).
   b. GDP times population (GDP x population).
   c. GDP per worker (GDP/employment).
   d. GDP measured in dollars of constant purchasing power.

5. The average standard of living over time is best measured by
   a. GDP.
   b. GDP per capita.
   c. real GDP.
   d. real GDP per capita.

6. If the price of everything increases, but the production of specific goods and services is unchanged,
   a. real GDP will actually decline.
   b. real GDP will remain unchanged.
   c. real GDP will increase as prices increase.

7. Inflation refers to
   a. an increase in the stock of money.
   b. an increase in the price of any single commodity.
   c. a sustained increase in the average level of prices.
   d. an increase in GDP.

8. The term *recession* refers to
   a. a period of inflation.
   b. a period of above–average economic growth.
   c. automatic reductions in government spending designed to reduce the deficit.
   d. a period when real GDP declines.

9. When referring to inputs, the term *capital* refers to
   a. money business firms need to borrow.
   b. the importance of a firm's head office.
   c. machines and buildings used to produce output.
   d. all of a firm's factors of production.

10. Which of the following would not be classified as an input?
    a. A farmer's time to grow wheat.
    b. The farmer's tractor.
    c. The farmer's land.
    d. The bread that is made from the wheat.

11. The majority of American workers work for
    a. manufacturing companies.
    b. the federal government.
    c. state and local governments.
    d. firms that produce a variety of services, including retail and wholesale trade.

12. Most business firms are
    a. corporations.
    b. partnerships.
    c. proprietorships.

13. Which business firms account for the greatest share of output?
    a. Corporations.
    b. Partnerships.
    c. Proprietorships.

14. The term *concentration ratio* refers to the
    a. purity of products produced by large consumer firms.
    b. proportion of output produced by the largest four firms in an industry.
    c. production process for reconstituted fruit juices.
    d. increasing power of the federal government.

15. When Americans buy goods produced abroad, _____increase.
    a. exports
    b. taxes
    c. transfer payments
    d. imports

16. When Americans are able to sell goods to foreigners, this adds to
    a. exports.
    b. taxes.
    c. transfer payments.
    d. imports.

17. Consumer spending accounts for _____ of American GDP.
    a. less than a fifth
    b. about a third
    c. about half
    d. about two–thirds
    e. about three–quarters

18. National defense accounts for _____ of federal government spending.
    a. less than a fifth
    b. about a third
    c. about half
    d. about two–thirds

19. For the most part, the United States has chosen to let markets determine pre–tax income and then uses taxes and _____ to reduce income inequalities.
    a. tariffs
    b. inflation
    c. transfer payments
    d. government production

20. Compared to other industrialized countries, taxes as a percent of GDP in the United States are
    a. among the lowest.
    b. about the same as most other industrialized countries.
    c. among the highest.

Test B

Circle T or F for true or false.

T F 1. An economic system is a social mechanism that organizes inputs to produce outputs.

T F 2. Since World War II American real GDP has increased every year without interruption.

T F 3. The American economy is a more open economy than other industrialized economies.

T F 4. The American economy relies on free markets and private enterprise to a greater extent than most other industrialized economies.

T F 5. During a recession, unemployment usually increases.

T F 6. Government production accounts for more than half of American GDP.

T F 7. Women hold more than half of the jobs outside the home.

T F 8. Most American workers still produce goods rather than services.

T F 9. Labor gets most of the income generated in the United States.

T F 10. Most businesses in the United States are sole proprietorships.

SUPPLEMENTARY EXERCISE

Table 2-4 reports data on tuition and required fees for four–year universities. How do increases in tuition and fees compare to the increase in prices in general and increases in income? You can adjust the data on nominal tuition and fees by dividing it by the price index from Table 2-1. An increase in real tuition and fees would indicate that this element of the cost of college has increased faster than prices in general. Once you have computed tuition and fees in terms of 1987 purchasing power, divide these figures by real per capita income calculated in Table 2-1 to see how tuition and fees have changed relative to real income per capita.

What has happened to tuition and fees at the college or university you attend? The appropriate office at your institution should be able to provide current and historical data on tuition and fees.

Information on prices and income can be found in the most recent *Economic Report of the President*.

TABLE 2-4
TUITION AND REQUIRED FEES
4-Year Universities

Year	Public	Private
1970-71	$478	$1,980
1980-81	$915	$4,275
1990-91	$2,159	$11,379

SOURCE: *Digest of Education Statistics*, 1992, National Center for Education Statistics, U.S. Department of Education, Table 301.

STUDY QUESTIONS

1. What is the difference between inputs and outputs? How would you categorize the steel used in new cars or home appliances?

2. How can output of the American economy be greater than that of countries like China and India with larger populations?

3. What measure(s) of economic activity would you use to compare living standards, either over time for a single country or between countries at a point in time? Why?

4. What does the historical record show regarding the growth in real GDP and real GDP per capita in the United States?

5. What is meant by a closed or open economy? How would you characterize the United States?

6. In the United States, who works outside the home for wages and salary and what types of jobs do they hold?

7. How is income in the United States distributed among factors of production?

8. What are the common forms of business organization? Which tend to be larger? Which smaller? Why?

9. How does the role of government in the American economy compare with that of other industrialized countries?

10. What are some of the common pitfalls of time series graphs and how can you avoid them?

ECONOMICS IN ACTION
The Proper Role for Government

How far should the government go when regulating business? If the government is to provide some goods and services, what principles determine which goods and services? How far should the government go in redistributing income?

Noted economist Milton Friedman has consistently argued for a limited role for government. In a widely publicized PBS series, Friedman and his wife, Rose, advocated four principles as tests of the appropriate business of government. National defense, domestic police and justice, the provision of goods and services in the limited cases where markets do not work well, and protection for citizens who cannot protect themselves, (e.g., children) define the Friedmans' four principles. These principles, especially the third, could be seen as justifying a range of government action. The Friedmans are as concerned with government failures as with market failures. They note that once started, government initiatives are rarely stopped. In their view the burden of proof should be on the proponents of government action.

The Friedmans see government as created by the citizenry. They argue that government should be organized to maximize individual "freedom to choose as individuals, as families, as members of voluntary groups." They endorse the view of Adam Smith that as long as individuals do not violate the laws of justice, they should be free to pursue their own interests and that competitive markets rather than government regulation are usually the most effective forms of social organization. "We can shape our institutions. Physical and human characteristics limit the alternatives available to us. But none prevents us, if we will, from building a society that relies primarily on voluntary cooperation to organize both economic and other activity, a society that preserves and expands human freedom, that keeps government in its place, keeping it our servant and not letting it become our master."[1]

The equally renowned John Kenneth Galbraith, on the other hand, argues that increasing affluence has led to an imbalance between private and public goods. Goods and services that are marketable to individuals allow private producers to accumulate the financial resources that give them control of labor, capital, and raw materials. Sophisticated advertising creates and sustains demand for private goods, generating more income and profits. This affluence of the private sector is in marked contrast to the poverty of the public sector. Galbraith argues that society needs a balance between private and public goods but that the pernicious effects of advertising that creates the demand that sustains the production of private goods gives rise to a serious imbalance. One result is an increasing demand for private goods and services to protect individuals from the poverty of public goods and services, such as elaborate alarm systems and private guards to counteract the lack of police.

How much increase in public spending is necessary to redress the balance? Galbraith will only say that the distance is considerable. "When we arrive, the opulence of our private

---

[1]Milton and Rose Friedman, *Free to Choose: A Personal Statement*, Harcourt Brace Jovanovich, 1980.

consumption will no longer be in contrast with the poverty of our schools, the unloveliness and congestion of our cities, our inability to get to work without a struggle, and the social disorder that is associated with imbalance. . . the precise point of balance will never be defined. This will be of comfort only to those who believe that any failure of definition can be made to score decisively against the larger idea."[2]

1. How would you define the proper role of government? Where would you draw the line between those activities best left to individual initiative and markets and those that are the appropriate business of government?

---

[2] John Kenneth Galbraith, *The Affluent Society*, Houghton Mifflin, 1958.

Chapter **3**

Scarcity and Choice:
The Economic Problem

LEARNING OBJECTIVES

After completing this chapter, you should be able to:

♦ explain why the true cost of any decision is its opportunity cost.

♦ explain the link between market prices and opportunity costs.

♦ explain why the scarcity of goods and services (outputs) must be attributed to a scarcity of resources, or inputs, used in production processes.

♦ draw a production possibilities frontier for a firm or for the economy.

♦ explain how the production possibility frontier contains information about the opportunity cost of changing output combinations.

♦ explain why specialized resources mean that a firm's or economy's production possibilities frontier is likely to bow outward.

♦ explain how an economy can shift its production possibilities frontier.

♦ explain why production efficiency requires that an economy produce on, rather than inside, its production possibilities frontier.

♦ describe the three coordination tasks that every economy must confront.

♦ explain why specialization and division of labor are likely to require the use of markets.

♦ describe how a market economy solves the three coordination tasks.

IMPORTANT TERMS AND CONCEPTS

Resources
Scarcity
Choice
Rational decision
Opportunity cost
Outputs
Inputs (means of production)
Production possibilities frontier
Allocation of resources
Principle of increasing costs
Economic growth
Consumption goods
Capital goods
Efficiency
Specialization
Division of labor
Exchange
Market system
Three coordination tasks

CHAPTER REVIEW

"You can't always get what you want" Mike Jesqer

Scarcity and the resulting necessity to make choices are fundamental concerns of economics. This chapter is an introduction to these issues, although they have already been implicitly introduced in many of the 12 ideas for Beyond the Final Exam, and will reappear throughout the text.

The importance of *choice* starts with the fact that virtually all resources are _____. Most people's desires exceed their incomes, and, thus, ev-
(1) eryone makes buying choices all the time. Similarly, firms, educational institutions, and government agencies make choices between what kinds of outputs to produce and what combination of inputs to use. An economist studying the use of inputs for the overall economy is studying the allocation of resources.

What is a good way to make choices? The obvious answer is to consider the alternatives. Economists call these forgone alternatives the _____ _____
(2) of a decision. Imagine it is the night before the first midterm in Introductory Economics, which will cover Chapters 1-6, and here you are only on Chapter 3. A friend suggests a night at the movies and even offers to buy your ticket so "it won't cost you anything." Do you agree that the evening out won't cost anything? What will you be giving up?

At first the idea of choices for the economy may sound strange. It may be easiest to imagine such choices being made by bureaucrats in a centrally planned economy. Even though there is no central planning bureau for the U.S. economy, it is useful to think of opportunities available to the American economy. The opportunities selected result from the combined spending and production decisions of all citizens, firms, and governmental units, decisions coordinated by our reliance on markets.

The *production possibilities frontier* is a useful diagram for representing the choices available to a firm or an economy. The frontier will tend to slope downward to the right because

(3) resources are (<u>scarce/specialized</u>). The frontier will tend to bow out because most resources are _____. For any one year the resources available to an economy—the number of workers, factories, and machines, and the state of technology—are essentially fixed. Over time, an economy can increase its resources if it produces (<u>more/fewer</u>) consumption goods and _____ capital goods. Similarly, technological advancements are more likely if an economy devotes (<u>more/fewer</u>) resources to research and development. In terms of a frontier showing possible combinations of consumption and capital goods, the true cost of faster economic growth is given by the foregone output of _____ goods.

Opportunity cost is the best measure of the true cost of any decision. For a single firm or an economy as a whole, with choices represented by a production possibilities frontier,

(4) the opportunity cost of changing the composition of output can be measured by the_____ of the production possibilities frontier.

(5) As an economy produces more and more of one good, say automobiles, the opportunity cost of further increases is likely to (<u>increase/decrease</u>). This change in opportunity cost illustrates the principle of_____ cost and is a result of the fact that most resources are (<u>scarce/specialized</u>).

For given amounts of all but one good, the production possibilities frontier for an economy measures the maximum amount of the remaining good that can be produced. Thus the production possibilities frontier defines maximum outputs or efficient production. There is, of course, no guarantee that the economy will operate on its frontier. If there is unemploy-

(6) ment, then the economy is operating (<u>on/inside</u>) the frontier. If a firm or economy operates inside its production possibilities frontier, it is said to be _____ that is, with the same resources the firm or the economy could have produced more of some commodities.

All economies must answer three questions:
1. How can we use resources efficiently to operate on the production possibilities frontier?
2. What combinations of output shall we produce: that is, where on the frontier shall we produce?
3. To whom shall we distribute what is produced?

The American economy answers these questions through the use of markets and prices.

(7) If markets are functioning well, then money prices (<u>will/will not</u>) be a reliable guide to opportunity costs. Problems arise when markets do not function well and when items do not have explicit price tags.

IMPORTANT TERMS AND CONCEPTS QUIZ

Choose the letter that is the most appropriate definition for each of the following terms.

1. _____ Resources
2. _____ Scarcity
3. _____ Choice
4. _____ Rational decision
5. _____ Opportunity cost
6. _____ Outputs
7. _____ Inputs
8. _____ Production possibilities frontier
9. _____ Allocation of resources
10. _____ Principle of increasing costs
11. _____ Consumption goods
12. _____ Capital goods
13. _____ Economic growth
14. _____ Efficiency
15. _____ Specialization
16. _____ Division of labor
17. _____ Exchange
18. _____ Market system
19. _____ Three coordination tasks

a. Resources used in production process.
b. Produced goods used to produce other goods in the future.
c. System in which allocation decisions are made in accordance with centralized direction.
d. Breaking tasks into smaller jobs.
e. Outward shift of the production possibilities frontier.

f. Decision on how to divide scarce resources among different uses.
g. Instruments used to create the goods and services people desire.
h. Process whereby a worker becomes more adept at a particular job.
i. Situation in which the amount of an item available is less than people want.
j. Goods and services that firms produce.
k. System in which decisions on resource allocation come from independent decisions of consumers and producers.
l. Absence of waste.
m. Foregone value of the next best alternative.
n. Decision made from a set of alternatives.
o. System in which people can trade with others.
p. Item available for immediate use by households.
q. Tendency for the opportunity cost of an additional unit of output to rise as production increases.
r. A decision that best serves the decision maker's objectives.
s. Graph of combinations of goods that can be produced with available inputs and technology.
t. Decisions on what goods to produce, how to produce them, and how to distribute them.

BASIC EXERCISES

These exercises are designed to explore more fully some of the implications of the production possibilities frontier for an economy.

1. Figure 3-1 shows the production possibilities frontier (PPF) for the economy of Adirondack, which produces consumption and capital goods, here called bread and computers.

   a. If all resources are devoted to the production of bread, Adirondack can produce _____ loaves of bread. In order to produce 1000 computers, the opportunity cost in terms of bread is _____ loaves. To produce another 1000 computers, the opportunity cost (rises/falls) to _____ loaves. As long as the PPF continues to curve downward, the opportunity costs of increased computer output will (continue to rise/start to fall). These changes are the result, not of scarce resources per se, but of _____ resources. (You might try drawing a PPF on the assumption that all resources are equally productive in the production of both outputs. Can you convince yourself that it should be a straight line?)

   b. Find the output combination of 2500 computers and 320,000 loaves on Figure 3-1. Label this point *A*. Is it an attainable combination for Adirondack? Label the output combination 1500 computers and 400,000 loaves *B*. Is this combination attainable? Finally, label the output combination 1000 computers and 520,000 loaves *C*. Is this combination attainable? We can conclude that the attainable output combinations for Adirondack are (on/inside/outside) the production possibilities frontier.

   c. An output combination is inefficient if it is possible to produce more of one or both goods. Which, if any, of the output combinations identified in question b is an inefficient combination? _____. Show that this point is inefficient by shading in all attainable points indicating more of one or both goods.

FIGURE 3-1

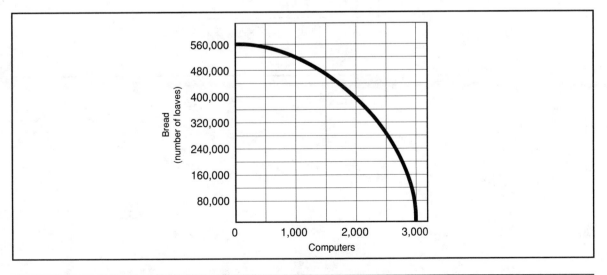

2. Figure 3-2 shows a PPF is applicable for two identical economies Catskill and Adirondack. The only difference is that Catskill produces 2,500 computers and 280,000 loaves of bread, point D, and Adirondack produces 2,000 computers and 400,000 loaves of bread, point E. Remember that computers stand for all capital goods and that the production of capital goods adds to the productive resources of an economy.

   a. The production of capital goods this year should cause the PPF for both economies to shift out next year. Figure 3-3 shows the new and initial PPFs for Adirondack following the production of 2,000 computers. Note that the new PPF lies outside the initial PPF. Draw the new PPF for Catskill. Has the PPF for Catskill shifted by more or less than that of Adirondack? Why?

   b. Describe how you would measure the cost of growth for the economy with the higher rate of economic growth?

FIGURE 3-2

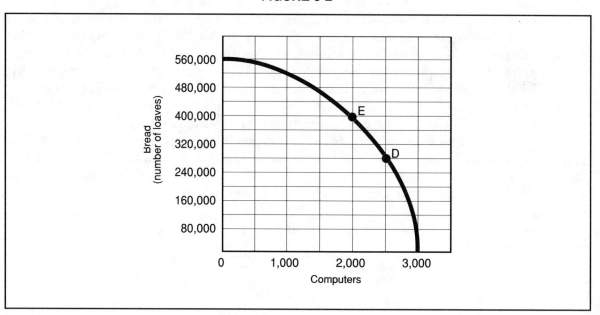

FIGURE 3-3

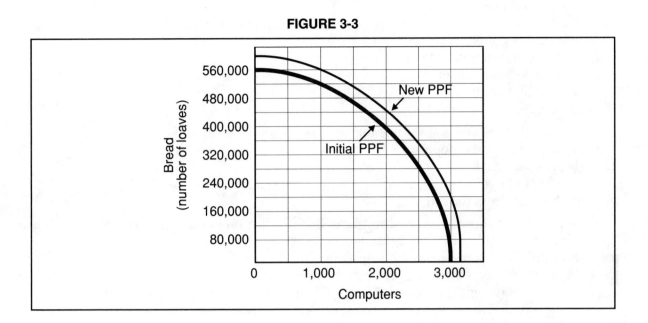

SELF-TESTS FOR UNDERSTANDING

Test A

Circle the most appropriate answer.

1. Economists define opportunity cost as
    a. the dollar price of goods and services.
    b. the hidden cost imposed by inflation.
    c. the value of the next best alternative use that is not chosen.
    d. the *time* spent shopping.

2. The position of an economy's production possibilities frontier is determined by all but which one of the following?
    a. The size of the labor force.
    b. Labor skills and training.
    c. The amount of consumption goods the economy can produce.
    d. Current technology.

3. A firm's production possibilities frontier shows
    a. the best combination of output for a firm to produce.
    b. its plans for increasing production over time.
    c. the architectural drawings of its most productive plant.
    d. different combinations of goods it can produce with a designated quantity of resources and available technology.

4. An efficient economy utilizes all available resources and produces the _____
   output its technology permits.
   a. minimum amount of
   b. best combination of
   c. one combination of
   d. maximum amount of

5. The fact that resources are scarce implies that the production possibility frontier will
   a. have a negative slope.
   b. be a straight line.
   c. shift out over time.
   d. bow out from the origin.

6. Which of the following statements imply that production possibilities frontiers are likely
   to be curved, rather than straightlines?
   a. Ultimately all resources are scarce.
   b. Most resources are more productive in certain uses than in others.
   c. Unemployment is a more serious problem for some social groups than for others.
   d. Economists are notoriously poor at drawing straight lines.

7. The set of attainable points for a firm that produces two goods is given by
   a. all points on the production possibilities frontier.
   b. all points inside the production possibilities frontier.
   c. all points on or inside the production possibilities frontier.
   d. none of the above.

8. If an economy is operating efficiently, it will be producing
   a. inside its production possibilities frontier.
   b. on its production possibilities frontier.
   c. outside its production possibilities frontier.
   d. the maximum amount of necessities and the minimum amount of luxuries.

9. The principle of increasing cost is consistent with a _____
   production possibilities frontier.
   a. straight–line
   b. bowed–in
   c. shifting
   d. bowed–out

10. The inability of the economy to produce as much as everyone would like is ultimately a
    reflection of
    a. a lack of money in the economy.
    b. congressional gridlock.
    c. the inability of a market economy to perform the necessary coordination tasks.
    d. a limited amount of productive resources.

11. The process of economic growth will be accompanied by
    a. a steeper production possibilities frontier.
    b. a production possibilities frontier that has shifted out.
    c. a smaller share of output devoted to government spending.
    d. an increase in the birth rate.

12. When, in Figure 3-1, the production of bread is increased from 280,000 loaves to 400,000 loaves, the opportunity cost in terms of reduced output of computers is
    a. 0
    b. 500
    c. 2,000
    d. 2,500

13. Which of the following implies a shift in the production possibilities frontier for a shoe firm?
    a. Raising all prices by 10 percent.
    b. Borrowing money to hire more workers and buying more machines.
    c. Changing the composition output toward more women's shoes and fewer men's shoes.
    d. Expanding the advertising budget.

14. Consider a production possibility frontier showing alternative combinations of corn and computers that can be produced in Cimonoce, a small island in the South Pacific. The opportunity cost of more computers can be measured by
    a. the slope of the production possibility frontier.
    b. the X-intercept of the production possibility frontier.
    c. the Y-intercept of the production possibility frontier
    d. the area under the production possibility frontier.

15. Which one of the following situations reflects a shift of the economy's production possibilities frontier?
    a. The proportion of labor devoted to the production of agricultural products has declined from 21 percent in 1929 to less than 3 percent in 1990.
    b. Total real output for the U.S. economy in 1990 was about six times greater than in 1929.
    c. Between 1990 and 1991 total real output of the U.S. economy declined by $35 billion as the unemployment rate rose from 5.5 to 6.7 percent.
    d. From 1979 to 1980 the inflation rate was about 13.5 percent.

16. Which of the following would not shift an economy's production possibilities frontier?
    a. A doubling of the labor force.
    b. A doubling of the number of machines.
    c. A doubling of the money supply.
    d. More advanced technology.

17. A rational decision is one that
    a. will win a majority if put to a vote.
    b. is supported unanimously.
    c. best serves the objectives of the decision maker.
    d. is supported by *The New York Times*.

18. If exchange is voluntary,
    a. there can be mutual gain even if no new goods are produced.
    b. one party will always get the better of the other.
    c. there can be mutual gain only if new goods are produced as a result of the trade.
    d. there can be mutual gain only if government oversees the trade.

19. All but which one of the following are examples of waste and inefficiency?
    a. Employment discrimination against women and people of color.
    b. Operating on an economy's production possibilities frontier.
    c. High levels of unemployment.
    d. Quotas that limit the educational opportunities of particular ethnic groups.

20. The three coordination tasks that all economies must perform
    a. can only be done by a central planning bureau.
    b. can only be done by markets.
    c. can only be done inefficiently.
    d. can be done by planning bureaus or markets.

Test B

Circle T or F for true or false.

T F 1. There can never be any real scarcity of manufactured goods, as we can always produce more.

T F 2. Market prices are always a good measure of opportunity cost.

T F 3. The principle of increasing costs is a reflection of the fact that most productive resources tend to be best at producing a limited number of things.

T F 4. An economy can shift its production possibilities frontier outward by the process of economic growth.

T F 5. Because they have the power to tax, governments do not need to make choices.

T F 6. The existence of specialized resources means that a firm's production possibilities frontier will be a straight line.

T F 7. The existence of widespread unemployment means that an economy is operating inside its production possibilities frontier.

T F 8. An economy using its resources efficiently is operating on its production possibilities frontier.

T F 9. Because they are nonprofit organizations, colleges and universities do not have to make choices.

T F 10. A sudden increase in the number of dollar bills will shift the economy's production possibilities frontier.

SUPPLEMENTARY EXERCISES

1. **The Cost of College**

   Those of you paying your way through college may not need to be reminded that the opportunity cost of lost wages is an important part of the cost of education. You can estimate the cost of your education as follows: Estimate what you could earn if instead of attending classes and studying you used those hours to work. Add in the direct outlays on tuition, books, and any differential living expenses incurred because you go to school. (Why only differential living expenses?)

2. **The Cost of Children**

   Bob and Jane both took Sociology 1 last year. As part of the course they were asked to compute the cost of raising a child. Bob estimated the cost at $184,000, an average of $5,000 a year in increased family expenditures for the first 12 years, then $6000 a year for the next six years, and finally four years of college at $22,000 per year. Jane also was enrolled in Economics 1. She estimated the cost at $300,000. She started with all the same outlays that Bob did but also included $29,000 a year for four years as the opportunity cost of the parent who stayed at home to care for the child. Which calculation better reflects the cost of raising a child? What would be the cost of a second child?

3. Consider an economy with a production possibilities frontier between cars (C) and tanks (T) given by

$$C = 6L^{.5}K^{.5} - 0.3T^2$$

   where L is the size of the labor force (50,000 people) and K is the number of machines, also 50,000.

   a. What is the maximum number of cars that can be produced? Call this number of cars C*. The maximum number of tanks? Call this number of tanks T*.
   b. Draw a PPF graph.
   c. Is this frontier consistent with the principle of increasing costs?
   d. Is the output combination ($1/2 C^*$, $1/2 T^*$) attainable? Is the output combination ($1/2 C^*$, $1/2 T^*$) efficient? Why or why not?
   e. What is the opportunity cost of more tanks when 10 tanks are produced? 50 tanks? 200 tanks?
   f. Find a mathematical expression for the opportunity cost of tanks in terms of cars. Is this mathematical expression consistent with the principle of increasing cost?
   g. Draw the new PPF if the labor force and the number of machines both increase by 10 percent. Where does this frontier lie relative to the original frontier?

4. **The Cost of Economic Growth**

If you have access to a microcomputer, you might try programming this small recursive model to investigate the cost of economic growth. You could either try writing your own program in BASIC or some other programming language, or you could use a spreadsheet program. Some programming hints are given at the end of the problem.

Imagine an economy that produces bundles of consumption goods. C, and investment goods, I, with the help of labor, L, and machines, M, that exist at the beginning of the year. The production of consumption and investment goods is described by equation (1)

$$(1) \qquad C + I = (L)^{.75} \bullet (M)^{.25}$$

Some machines wear out each year. The number of machines at the beginning of the next year is equal to 92 percent of the machines at the beginning of the year plus investment during the year, or $.92 \bullet M + I$. The number of machines will be constant when investment is sufficient to replace the 8 percent that wear out. If investment is greater, then the number of machines will increase, and the economy's production possibilities frontier will shift out.

This economy has 10,000 laborers, $L = 10,000$, and originally there are 20,000 machines, $M = 20,000$.

a. Verify that if $I = 1,600$, output and consumption will be constant.

b. What happens to output and consumption over time if I increases by 25 percent to 2,000?

c. In question b you should find that consumption initially declines as some output is diverted from consumption to investment. However, over time, the output of consumption goods should increase and surpass its earlier value found in a. If an increase in investment from 1,600 to 2,000 is a good thing, what about an increase from 2,000 to 2,400? How does the eventual increase in consumption following this increase compare with what you found in b?

d. Can there ever be too much investment? Try additional increases in investment and watch what happens to the eventual level of consumption. Can you explain what is going on?

Programming Hints   Columns in a spreadsheet would correspond to the following equations where subscripts refer to time periods. Note that equations for I and C are the same for all periods. Following the initial period you will need to be sure that your expression for the number of machines incorporates the subtraction of machines that have worn out and the addition of new machines from the production of investment goods. You will probably want to set your program or spreadsheet to run for about 100 periods.

$$M_t = 20,000 \qquad\qquad t = 1$$
$$I_t = 1,600 \qquad\qquad t = 1, 2, \dots$$
$$C_t = (10,000)^{.75} \bullet (M_t)^{.25} - I_t \qquad t = 1, 2, \dots$$
$$M_t = .92 \bullet M_{t-1} + I_t \qquad t = 2, 3, \dots$$

ECONOMICS IN ACTION

In 1971 the Brookings Institution published the first of a sequence of studies of the President's budget proposal called <u>Setting National Priorities</u>. The following is from the introduction to the first study.

The United States budget is not the document of an executive whose decisions are law, nor of a prime minister whose party must support him or bring down the government. It is, rather, a set of proposals to the Congress for action on appropriations and tax measures. Precisely because it must advocate the course recommended by the President, the budget cannot emphasize the difficulty of the choices made. It records the President's decisions, but it does not identify the close ones. Alternatives that were serious contenders for adoption but were finally rejected are seldom if ever mentioned. In some cases, programs generally recognized as ineffective or of low priority are debated but finally left unchanged because all participants in the debate realize how few are the lances a President can afford to break against politically impregnable targets. Thus, the budget is a document designed to persuade an independent Congress rather than to analyze policy alternatives.

The following pages seek to illuminate some of the President's budgetary choices for 1971. The study will (1) identify the major choices in fiscal policy and in specific expenditure programs; (2) consider some of the available alternatives and the reasoning behind the choices actually proposed; (3) discuss, by way of example, several federal programs that continue to be supported despite attempts by several administrations to alter or eliminate them; and (4) project to fiscal 1975 the revenue yield of existing tax laws and the expenditure consequences of current and proposed programs in order to estimate the likely size of the "fiscal dividends" over the next four years. The 1971 budget is the first in history to present longer-term projections. The projections offered in this study are spelled out in somewhat greater detail than those presented in the budget and include a range of alternatives that would depend on budgetary policies adopted in coming years.

The purpose of the study is to contribute to informed discussion of the budget, not to propose a different budget. It *examines* alternatives; it does not *recommend* alternatives. Its aim is to show the difficulty of making choices in a complex and uncertain world, not to criticize those who had to make them.

1. What sort of information would you need if you had to make decisions about defense spending or the structure of a national health insurance plan?

2. Are you likely to find the information for these and other decisions in the President's budget?

3. If not, what is the role of the President's budget?

SOURCE: From *Setting National Priorities. The 1971 Budget*, Charles L. Schultze, et. al., The Brookings Institution et. al. (Washington, D.C. 1970): p. 4.

STUDY QUESTIONS

1. How do markets help an economy address the three coordination tasks of deciding "how," "what," and "to whom"?

2. Explain when market prices are likely to be a good measure of opportunity cost and when they are not.

3. How do specialization and the division of labor enhance economic efficiency? Why do they require a system of exchange?

4. How can an economy choose to grow faster, and how can you use a production possibilities frontier to measure the cost of faster growth?

5. What is the difference between attainable points of production and efficient points of production? (It may be easiest to illustrate your answer using a diagram of a production possibilities frontier. Be sure that you can define and identify those points that are attainable and those points that are efficient.)

6. What is the difference between resources being scarce and resources being specialized? What are the implications of scarcity and specialization for the production possibilities frontier?

Chapter **4**

Supply and Demand:
An Initial Look

LEARNING OBJECTIVES

After completing this chapter, you should be able to:

- ♦ draw a demand curve, given appropriate information from a demand schedule of possible prices and the associated quantity demanded.

- ♦ draw a supply curve, given appropriate information from a supply schedule of possible prices and the associated quantity supplied.

- ♦ explain why demand curves usually slope downward and supply curves usually slope upward.

- ♦ determine the equilibrium price and quantity, given a demand and supply curve.

- ♦ explain what forces tend to move market prices and quantities toward their equilibrium values.

- ♦ analyze the impact on prices and quantities of shifts in the demand curve, supply curve, or both.

- ♦ distinguish between a shift in and a movement along either the demand or supply curve.

- ♦ distinguish between price ceilings and price floors.

- ♦ explain the likely consequences of government interference with market-determined prices.

IMPORTANT TERMS AND CONCEPTS

Quantity demanded
Demand schedule
Demand curve
Quantity supplied
Supply schedule
Supply curve
Supply-demand diagram
Shortage
Surplus
Equilibrium
Equilibrium price and quantity
Law of supply and demand
Shifts in (versus) movements along supply and demand curves
Price ceiling
Price floor

CHAPTER REVIEW

Along with scarcity and the need for choice, *demand* and *supply analysis* is a fundamental idea that pervades all of economics. After studying this chapter, look back at the 12 ideas for Beyond the Final Exam in Chapter 1 and see how many concern the "law" of supply and demand.

(1) Economists use a *demand curve* as a summary of the factors influencing people's demand for different commodities. A demand curve shows how, during a specified period, the quantity demanded of some good changes as the _____ of that good changes, holding all other determinants of demand constant. A demand curve usually has a (<u>negative/positive</u>) slope, indicating that as the price of a good declines, people will demand (<u>more/less</u>) of it. A particular quantity demanded is represented by a point on the demand curve. The change in the quantity demanded as price changes is a (<u>shift in/movement along</u>) the demand curve. Quantity demanded is also influenced by other factors, such as consumer incomes and tastes, population and the prices of related goods. Changes in any of these factors will result in a (<u>shift in/movement along</u>) the demand curve. Remember, a demand curve is defined for a particular period—a week, a month, or a year.

Economists use a *supply curve* to summarize the factors influencing producers' decisions. Like the demand curve, the supply curve is a relationship between quantity and _____.

(2) Supply curves usually have a (<u>negative/positive</u>) slope, indicating that at higher prices producers will be willing to supply (<u>more/less</u>) of the good in question. Like quantity demanded, quantity supplied is also influenced by factors other than price. The size of the industry, the state of technology, the prices of inputs, and the price of related outputs are important determinants.

Changes in any of these factors will change the quantity supplied and can be represented by a (shift in/movement along) the supply curve.

Demand and supply curves are hypothetical constructs that answer what-if questions. For example, the supply curve answers the question, "What quantity of milk would be supplied if its price were $10 a gallon?" At this point it is not fair to ask whether anyone would buy milk at that price. Information about the quantity demanded is given by the _____

(3) curve, which answers the question, "What quantity would be demanded if its price were $10 a gallon?" The viability of a price of $10 will be determined when we consider both curves simultaneously.

Figure 4-1 shows a demand and supply curve for stereo sets. The market outcome will be a

(4) price of $_____ and a quantity of_____. If the price is $400, then the quantity demanded will be (less/more) than the quantity supplied. In particular, from Figure 4-1 we can see that at a price of $400, producers will supply _____ sets _____ while consumers will demand _____ sets. This imbalance is a (shortage/surplus) and will lead to a(n) (increase/reduction) in price as inventories start piling up and suppliers compete for sales. If, instead, the price of stereo sets is only $200, there will be a (shortage/surplus) as the quantity (demanded/supplied) exceeds the quantity _____. Price is apt to (decrease/increase) as consumers scramble for a limited number of stereos at what appear to be bargain prices.

FIGURE 4-1

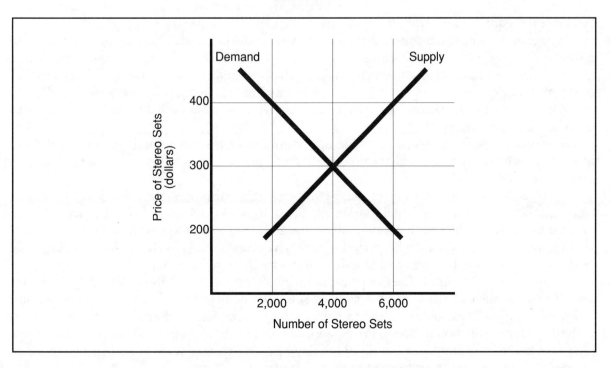

(5) These forces working to raise or lower prices will continue until price and quantity settle down at values given by the_____ of the demand and supply curves. At this point, barring outside changes that would shift either curve, there will be no further tendency for change. Market-determined price and quantity are then said to be in _____. This price and quantity combination is the only one in which consumers demand exactly what suppliers produce. There are no frustrated consumers or producers. However, equilibrium price and quantity will change if anything happens to shift either the demand or supply curves. The Basic Exercise in this chapter asks you to examine a number of shifts in demand and supply curves.

(6) Often factors affect demand but not supply, and vice versa. For example, changes in consumer incomes and tastes will shift the (demand/supply) curve but not the _____ curve. Following a shift in the demand curve, price must change to re–establish equilibrium. The change in price will lead to a (shift in/movement along) the supply curve until equilibrium is re–established at the intersection of the new demand curve and the original supply curve. Similarly a change in technology or the price of inputs will shift the _____ curve but not the _____ curve. Equilibrium will be re–established as the price change induced by the shift in the supply curve leads to a movement along the _____ curve to the new intersection.

(7) In many cases the government intervenes in the market mechanism in an attempt to control prices. Some price controls dictate a particular price; other controls set maximum or minimum prices. A *price ceiling* is a (maximum/minimum) legal price, typically below the market-determined equilibrium price. Examples of price ceilings include rent controls and usury laws. A *price floor* sets a _____ legal price. To be effective, the price floor would have to be above the equilibrium price. Price floors are often used in agricultural programs.

(8) In general, economists argue that interferences with the market mechanism are likely to have a number of undesirable features. Price controls will almost surely lead to a misallocation of resources, as it is unlikely legislated prices will equal opportunity cost. If there are a large number of suppliers, price controls will be (hard/easy) to monitor and evasion will be hard to police. In order to prevent the breakdown of price controls, governments quite likely find it necessary to introduce a large number of _____ _____. The enforcement of price controls can provide opportunities for favoritism and corruption. If all of this is not enough, price controls are almost certain to produce groups with a monetary stake in preserving controls.

(9) Price ceilings have a history of persistent (shortages/surpluses) and the development of black markets. Prices in the illegal market are likely to be greater than those that would have prevailed in a free market, with substantial income going to those whose only business is circumventing the controls. Over a longer period of time new investment is likely to (decrease/increase) as controlled prices reduce the profitability of investment in the industry.

(10) Firms try to get around effective price floors by offering nonprice inducements for consumers to buy from them rather than from someone else. (Remember that effective price floors result in excess supply.) These nonprice inducements are apt to be less preferred by consumers than would a general reduction in prices. Price floors will also result in inefficiencies as high-cost firms are protected from failing by artificially (high/low) prices. Another form of inefficiency involves the use of time and resources to evade effective controls.

IMPORTANT TERMS AND CONCEPTS QUIZ

Choose the best definition for the following terms.

1. _____ Quantity supplied
2. _____ Quantity demanded
3. _____ Demand schedule
4. _____ Demand curve
5. _____ Supply schedule
6. _____ Supply curve
7. _____ Supply-demand diagram
8. _____ Shortage
9. _____ Surplus
10. _____ Equilibrium
11. _____ Equilibrium price and quantity
12. _____ Shifts in supply or demand curves
13. _____ Movement along a supply or demand curve
14. _____ Price ceiling
15. _____ Price floor
16. _____ Law of supply and demand

a. Observation that in a free market, price tends to level where quantity supplied equals quantity demanded.
b. Legal minimum price that may be charged.
c. Graph depicting how quantity demanded changes as price changes.
d. Change in price causing a change in quantity supplied or demanded.
e. Number of units consumers want to buy at a given price.
f. Price/quantity pair at which quantity demanded equals quantity supplied.
g. Table depicting how the quantity demanded changes as price changes.
h. Situation in which there are no inherent forces producing change.
i. Table depicting how quantity supplied changes as price changes.
j. Legal maximum price that may be charged.
k. Number of units producers want to sell at a given price.
l. Table depicting the changes in both quantity demanded and quantity supplied as price changes.
m. Change in a variable other than price that affects quantity supplied or demanded.
n. Excess of quantity supplied over quantity demanded.
o. Graph depicting the changes in both quantity supplied and quantity demanded as price changes.
p. Excess of quantity demanded over quantity supplied.
q. Graph depicting how quantity supplied changes as price changes.

BASIC EXERCISES

These exercises ask you to analyze the impact of changes in factors that affect demand and supply.

1. a. Table 4-1 has data on the quantity of candy bars that would be demanded and supplied at various prices. Use the data to draw the demand curve and the supply curve for candy bars in Figure 4-2.

    b. From the information given in Table 4-1 and represented in Figure 4-2, the equilibrium price is _____ cents and the equilibrium quantity is

    _____.

TABLE 4-1
DEMAND AND SUPPLY SCHEDULES
FOR CANDY BARS

Quantity Demanded (millions)	Price per Bar (cents)	Quantity Supplied (millions)
1200	35	1050
1100	40	1100
900	50	1200
800	55	1250
700	60	1300

FIGURE 4-2

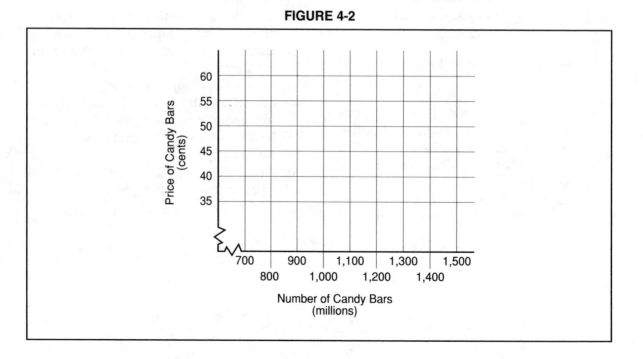

c. Now assume that increases in income and population mean the demand curve has shifted. Assume the shift is such that, at each price, the quantity demanded has increased by 300 candy bars. Draw the new demand curve. At the new equilibrium, price has (<u>increased/decreased</u>) to _____ cents, and quantity has (<u>increased/decreased</u>) to _____ million candy bars.

d. Next assume that an increase in the price of sugar has shifted the supply curve. Specifically, assume that, at each price, the quantity supplied has been reduced by 150 candy bars. Draw the new supply curve. The shift in the supply curve following the increase in the price of sugar will (<u>increase/decrease</u>) equilibrium price and _____ the equilibrium quantity. Using the demand curve you drew in part c, above, the new equilibrium price following the increase in the price of sugar will be _____ cents and the equilibrium quantity will be _____ million candy bars.

2. Figure 4-3 shows the demand and supply of chicken. Fill in Table 4-2 to trace the effects of various events on the equilibrium price and quantity.

3. Figure 4-4 shows the demand and supply of compact discs. Complete Table 4-3 to examine the impact of price ceilings and price floors. What conclusion can you draw about when ceilings and floors will affect market outcomes?

FIGURE 4-3
THE DEMAND AND SUPPLY OF CHICKEN

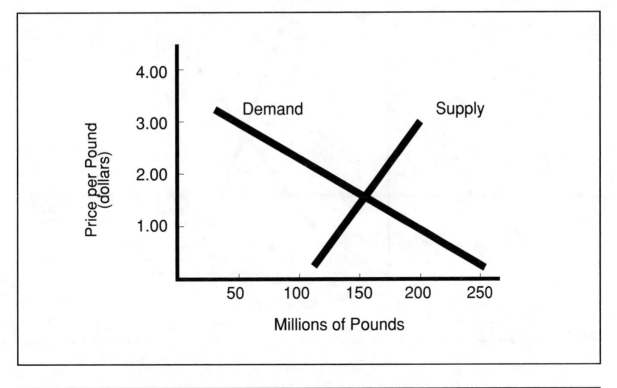

TABLE 4-2

Event	Which curve shifts?	Is the direction left or right?	Does the equilibrium price rise or fall?	Does the equilibrium quantity rise or fall?
a. A sharp increase in the price of beef leads many consumers to switch from beef to chicken.				
b. A bumper grain crop cuts the cost of chicken feed in half.				
c. Extraordinarily cold weather destroys a significant number of chickens.				
d. A sudden interest in eastern religions converts many chicken eaters to vegetarians.				

FIGURE 4-4
THE DEMAND AND SUPPLY OF DISCS

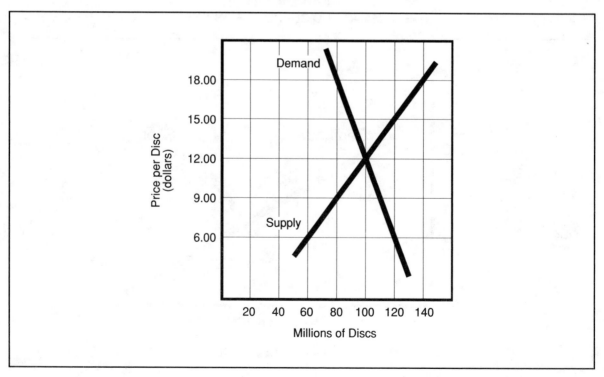

TABLE 4-3

	Quantity Demanded	Quantity Supplied	Shortage or Surplus
a. Price ceiling = $18			
b. Price ceiling = $9			
c. Price floor = $15			
d. Price floor = $6			

SELF-TESTS FOR UNDERSTANDING

Test A

Circle the most appropriate answer.

1. A demand curve is a graph showing how the quantity demanded changes when _____ changes.
   a. consumer income
   b. population
   c. price
   d. the price of closely related goods

2. The slope of a demand curve is usually _____, indicating that as price declines the quantity demanded increases.
   a. negative
   b. positive
   c. infinite
   d. zero

3. If price decreases, the quantity supplied usually
   a. increases.
   b. is unchanged.
   c. decreases.
   d. goes to zero.

4. Quantity demanded is likely to depend upon all but which one of the following?
   a. Consumer tastes.
   b. Consumer income.
   c. Price.
   d. The size of the industry producing the good in question.

5. A supply curve is a graphical representation of information in a(n)
   a. demand schedule.
   b. equilibrium.
   c. supply schedule.
   d. balance sheet.

6. The entire supply curve is likely to shift when all but which one of the following change?
   a. The size of the industry.
   b. Price.
   c. The price of important inputs.
   d. Technology that reduces the production cost.

7. There will likely be a movement along a fixed supply curve if which one of the following changes?
   a. Price.
   b. Technology that reduces the production cost.
   c. The price of important inputs.
   d. The size of the industry.

8. There will be a movement along the demand curve when which one of the following changes?
   a. The size of the industry producing the good.
   b. Population.
   c. Consumer incomes.
   d. The price of related goods.

9. Graphically, the equilibrium price and quantity in a free market will be given by
   a. the Y axis–intercept of the demand curve.
   b. the X axis–intercept of the supply curve.
   c. the point of maximum vertical difference between the demand and supply curves.
   d. the intersection of the demand and supply curves.

10. When the demand curve shifts to the right, which of the following is likely to occur?
    a. equilibrium price rises and equilibrium quantity declines.
    b. equilibrium price rises and equilibrium quantity rises.
    c. equilibrium price declines and equilibrium quantity rises.
    d. equilibrium price declines and equilibrium quantity declines.

11. If equilibrium price and quantity both decrease, it is likely that
    a. the supply curve has shifted to the right.
    b. the demand curve has shifted to the right.
    c. the demand curve has shifted to the left.
    d. the supply curve has shifted to the left.

12. A shift in the demand curve for sailboats resulting from a general increase in incomes will lead to
    a. higher prices.
    b. lower prices.
    c. a shift in the supply curve.
    d. lower output.

13. A shift in the supply curve of bicycles resulting from higher steel prices will lead to
    a. higher prices.
    b. lower prices.
    c. a shift in the demand curve.
    d. larger output.

14. Which of the following is likely to result in a shift in the supply curve for dresses? (There may be more than one correct answer.)
    a. An increase in consumer incomes.
    b. An increase in tariffs that forces manufacturers to import cotton cloth at higher prices.
    c. An increase in dress prices.
    d. Higher prices for skirts, pants, and blouses.

15. From an initial equilibrium, which of the following changes will lead to a shift in the supply curve for Chevrolets?
    a. Import restrictions on Japanese cars.
    b. New environmental protection measures that raise the cost of producing steel.
    c. A decrease in the price of Fords.
    d. Increases in the cost of gasoline.

16. If the price of oil, a close substitute for coal, increases, then
    a. the supply curve for coal will shift to the right.
    b. the demand curve for coal will shift to the right.
    c. the equilibrium price and quantity of coal will not change.
    d. the quantity of coal demanded will decline.

17. If the price of shoes is initially above the equilibrium value, which of the following is likely to occur?
    a. Stores inventories will decrease as consumers buy more shoes than shoe companies produce.
    b. The demand curve for shoes will shift in response to higher prices.
    c. Shoe stores and companies likely will reduce prices in order to increase sales, leading to a lower equilibrium price.
    d. Equilibrium will be re–established at the original price as the supply curve shifts to the left.

18. Price floors are likely to
    a. lead to a reduction in the volume of transactions, as we move along the demand curve, above the equilibrium price to the higher price floor.
    b. result in increased sales as suppliers react to higher prices.
    c. lead to shortages.
    d. be effective only if they are set at levels below the market equilibrium level.

19. Effective price ceilings are likely to
    a. result in surpluses.
    b. increase the volume of transactions as we move along the demand curve.
    c. increase production as producers respond to higher consumer demand at the low ceiling price.
    d. result in the development of black markets.

20. A surplus results when
    a. the quantity demanded exceeds the quantity supplied.
    b. the quantity supplied exceeds the quantity demanded.
    c. the demand curve shifts to the right.
    d. effective price ceilings are imposed.

Test B

Circle T or F for true or false.

T F 1. The Law of Supply and Demand was passed by Congress in 1776.

T F 2. The demand curve for hamburgers is a graph showing the quantity of hamburgers that would be demanded during a specified period at each possible price.

T F 3. The slope of the supply curve indicates the increase in price necessary to get producers to increase output.

T F 4. An increase in consumer income will shift both the supply and demand curves.

T F 5. Both demand and supply curves usually have positive slopes.

T F 6. If at a particular price the quantity supplied exceeds the quantity demanded, then price is likely to fall as suppliers compete.

T F 7. Equilibrium price and quantity are determined by the intersection of the demand and supply curves.

T F 8. Since equilibrium is defined as a situation with no inherent forces producing change, the equilibrium price and quantity will not change following an increase in consumer income.

T F 9. A change in the price of important inputs will change the quantity supplied but will not shift the supply curve.

T F 10. Price ceilings likely will result in the development of black markets.

T F 11.   Price controls, whether floors or ceilings, likely will increase the volume of transactions from what it would be without controls.

T F 12.   An effective price ceiling is normally accompanied by shortages.

T F 13.   An effective price floor is normally accompanied by shortages.

T F 14.   An increase in both the market price and quantity of beef following an increase in consumer incomes proves that demand curves do not always have a negative slope.

STUDY QUESTIONS

1. Why do economists argue that neither quantity demanded nor quantity supplied is likely to be a fixed number?

2. What adjustment mechanisms are likely to ensure that free–market prices move toward their equilibrium values given by the intersection of the demand and supply curves?

3. Why are changes in all of the supply determinants, except price, said to shift the entire supply curve while changes in price are said to give rise to a movement along a fixed supply curve?

4. How do factors that shift the entire supply curve usually give rise to a movement along a given demand curve?

5. If price cannot adjust, say due to an effective price ceiling, what factors will likely allocate the quantity supplied among consumers?

6. Consider the demand for a necessity (for example, food), and the demand for a luxury (for example, home hot tubs). For which good would you expect the quantity demanded to show a greater response to changes in price? Why? For which good would you expect the demand curve to be steeper? Why? For which good would you expect the demand curve to show a greater shift in response to changes in consumer income? Why?

ECONOMICS IN ACTION

1. **Energy Policy—The Mix of Politics and Economics**

The following quotation, written in the spring of 1977, is by Robert E. Hall and Robert S. Pindyck. As you read it, try to understand Hall's and Pindyck's argument in terms of simple demand and supply analysis.

National energy policy faces a deep conflict in objectives, which has been a major reason for the failure to adopt rational measures: Consumers want cheap energy, but producers need high prices to justify expanded production. So far the goal of low prices has dominated. Through a combination of measures, some longstanding and some thrown together quickly during the energy crisis of 1974, the price of energy to consumers in the United States has been held far below the world level. Domestic producers have been prohibited from taking advantage of the higher world price, and in the case of oil, a heavy tax has been imposed on domestic production to finance the subsidization of imports. These steps have caused demand to increase more rapidly than production, and energy imports have risen to fill the gap. If recent policies are continued, imports will continue to grow. Some painful choices regarding the objectives of energy policy will force themselves upon the United States in the next few years.

The economics of the nation's energy problem involves little more than the principle that higher prices result in less demand and more supply. The exact size and timing of the effects of price on demand and supply are still open to debate, but a summary of recent evidence indicates that demand falls by about one per cent for each four-percent increase in price, and supply rises by about one percent for each five-percent increase in price. Of course several years must pass before demand and supply fully respond to changes in price, and there is some uncertainty over the magnitude and speed of the supply response, but these numbers provide a reasonable basis for an initial description of the energy market in the United States. Policies in effect today have depressed the domestic price of energy, on the average, by about 30 percent below the world price. Consumption, then, is about eight-percent higher than it would be otherwise, and supply is about six-percent lower. Stated in oil-equivalents, the total consumption of energy in the United States is about 38 million barrels per day: 31 million barrels are filled by domestically produced oil, natural gas, and coal, and the rest is imported. Eight percent of consumption is just over three million barrels per day, and six percent of domestic production is just under two million barrels, so the policy of depressing prices has the net effect of increasing imports by about five million barrels. But current imports are around seven million barrels per day, so a striking conclusion emerges from these simple calculations *The problem of rising imports is largely of our own making.* Imports might well be much lower had our energy policy not been based on maintaining low prices.[1]

Table 4-3 presents data on U.S. demand for energy in oil equivalents and domestic U.S. supply, consistent with Hall's and Pindyck's argument.

  a. From the data in Table 4-3, plot the demand and domestic supply curves. In 1977 the controlled U.S. price was $8.75 a barrel. What was the domestic demand for energy and what was the domestic supply? What was the demand for imports (the difference between demand and domestic supply)?

---

[1] E. Hall and Robert S. Pindyck, "The Conflicting Goals of National Energy Policy." Reprinted with the permission of the authors from: *The Public Interest*, No. 47 (Spring 1977), pages 3–4, 977 by National Affairs, Inc.

b. Hall and Pindyck indicate that the world price of energy in 1977 was $12.50 a barrel. What would have happened to demand, domestic supply, and imports if the price of energy in the United States had been permitted to rise to the world price?

c. What would have happened to energy prices and consumption if we had banned all imports and allowed domestic supply and demand to determine the equilibrium price and quantity?

d. Some people have argued that the demand and supply curves are actually much steeper. They contend that higher prices will not reduce demand by as much as Hall and Pindyck estimate and neither will higher prices increase supply by as much. Draw new, steeper demand and supply curves and examine the impacts of a market solution to the energy problem. (The new curves should intersect the original curves at a price of $8.75)

TABLE 4-3

Demand Quantity of Energy (millions of oil barrel equivalents	Price per Barrel (dollars)	Domestic Supply Quantity of Energy (millions of oil barrel equivalents)
33.2	15	34.5
35.1	12	33.0
37.7	9	31.2
41.8	6	28.7

2. Hey, Buddy...

Scalping tickets—selling tickets at whatever the market will bear rather than at face value—is illegal in a number of states, including New York, where the high demand for tickets to a retrospective exhibition of Henri Matisse at the Museum of Modern Art in late 1992 prompted renewed interest in the economic effects of scalping. Admission was by special ticket. By the time the exhibit opened, all advance sale tickets had been sold. A limited number of tickets were available each day. Art lovers typically had to wait in line for up to two hours early in the morning to purchase these tickets at $12.50 each. Tickets also were available without the wait at $20 to $50 from scalpers who evaded the police.

Some economists view scalpers as providing a service to those who have not planned ahead or do not wish to stand in line. They point out that other businesses, such as airlines, charge a hefty price for last–minute purchases.

Scalpers also do a lively business at the Super Bowl and the Final Four of the NCAA basketball playoffs. Why doesn't the National Football League and the NCAA simply raise the price of tickets? Some would argue that they, along with other businesses, are concerned with "goodwill." Even if higher profits could be earned from higher ticket prices, it might come by sacrificing profits over the long run as goodwill is replaced by ill will and a growing lack of consumer interest.

Some argue that scalping should be illegal, as it makes events unaffordable for the average person. Others wonder whether the average person ever gets tickets to such events and, if he does, whether he might not prefer the option of selling his tickets at a handsome profit.

Some economists have proposed a two-tier system. First a limited number of tickets would be sold at lower prices to those willing to stand in line or enter a lottery. Then the remaining tickets would be sold at whatever price the market will bear.

1. Who is harmed when scalping is illegal?
2. Would you expect legalizing scalping to affect the price of tickets from scalpers? Why?
3. Evaluate the pros and cons of a two-tier system.

SOURCE: "Tickets: Supply Meets Demand on Sidewalk," *New York Times*, December 26, 1992.

SUPPLEMENTARY EXERCISE

Imagine that the demand curve for tomatoes can be represented as

$$Q = 1000 - 250\, P.$$

The supply curve is a bit trickier. Farmers must make planting decisions on what they anticipate prices to be. Once they have made these decisions, there is little room for increases or decreases in the quantity supplied. Except for disastrously low prices, it will almost certainly pay a farmer to harvest and market his tomatoes. Assuming that farmers forecast price on the basis of the price last period, we can represent the supply curve for tomatoes as

$$Q = 200 + 150\, P_{-1,}$$

where P_{-1} refers to price in the previous period. Initial equilibrium price and quantity of tomatoes are $2 and 500, respectively. Verify that at this price the quantity supplied is equal to the quantity demanded. (Equilibrium implies the same price in each period.)

Now assume that an increase in income has shifted the demand curve to

$$Q = 1,400 - 250\, P.$$

Starting with the initial equilibrium price, trace the evolution of price and quantity over time. Do prices and quantities seem to be approaching some sort of equilibrium? If so, what? You might try programming this example on a microcomputer or simulating it with a spreadsheet program. What happens if the slope of the demand and/or supply curve changes?

Ask your instructor about cobweb models. Do you think looking at last period's price is a good way to forecast prices?

Chapter **5**

The Realm of
Macroeconomics

LEARNING OBJECTIVES

After completing this chapter you should be able to:

♦ explain the difference between microeconomics and macroeconomics.

♦ determine whether particular problems are within the realm of microeconomics or macroeconomics.

♦ describe the role of economic aggregates in macroeconomics.

♦ explain how supply-demand analysis can be used to study inflation, recessions, and stabilization policy.

♦ distinguish between real and nominal GDP.

♦ explain how GDP is a measure of economic production, not economic well-being.

♦ characterize, in general terms, the movement in prices and output over the last 100 years.

♦ use aggregate demand and supply curves to explain how stabilization policy addresses problems of unemployment and inflation.

IMPORTANT TERMS AND CONCEPTS

Microeconomics
Macroeconomics
Domestic product
Aggregation
Aggregate demand and aggregate supply curves
Inflation
Deflation
Recession
Gross domestic product (GDP)
Nominal versus real GDP
Final goods and services
Intermediate goods
Stagflation
Stabilization policy

CHAPTER REVIEW

Economic theory is traditionally split into two parts, microeconomics and macroeconomics. If one studies the behavior of individual decision-making units, one is studying
(1) _____. If one studies the behavior of entire economies, one is studying _____. This chapter is an introduction to macroeconomics.

The American economy is made up of tens of millions of firms, hundreds of millions of individuals, and innumerable different goods and services. Since it would be impossible to list each of these firms, individuals, and commodities, economists have found it useful to use certain overall averages or aggregates. The concept of *domestic product* is an example. If we concentrate on macroeconomic aggregates, we ignore much of the micro detail; whereas by concentrating on the micro detail, we may ignore much of the overall picture. The two forms of analysis are not substitutes; rather, they can be usefully employed together. (Remember the map example in Chapter 1 of the text.) It has been argued that only successful macroeconomic policy leads to a situation in which the study of microeconomics is important, and vice versa.

Supply and demand analysis is a fundamental tool of both micro and macro theory. In microeconomics one looks at the supply and demand for individual commodities, while in macroeconomics one studies aggregate supply and aggregate demand. The intersection of the
(2) demand and supply curves in microeconomics determines equilibrium _____ and _____. In macroeconomics the intersection of the aggregate demand

and supply curves determines the cost of living, or the price level, and aggregate output, or the gross _____ _____.

(3) A sustained increase in the price level would be called _____, whereas a sustained decrease would be called _____. Domestic product in the U.S. economy usually increases every year for reasons that will be discussed in Chapters 17 and 21. Periods when domestic product declines are referred to as _____. With an unchanged aggregate supply curve, an outward (rightward) shift of the aggregate demand curve would lead to (higher/lower) prices and (higher/lower) output. Higher prices would also result if the aggregate supply curve shifted to the (left/right), but, this time, higher prices would be associated with a(n) (increase/decrease) in output. Such a combination of rising prices and declining output is called _____. If both curves shift to the right at the same rate, then it is possible to have increased output with constant prices.

(4) Gross domestic product is defined as the sum of the _____ values of all _____ goods and services produced in the domestic economy during a year. Economists and national income statisticians use prices to add up the different kinds of output. If one uses today's prices, the result is (nominal/real) GDP. If one values output by prices from some base period, one gets _____ GDP. Which is the better measure of changes in output? (Nominal/Real) GDP. If all prices rise and all outputs are unchanged, (nominal/real) GDP will increase while _____ GDP will not. It is important to remember that GDP is a measure of production; it (is/is not) a measure of economic well-being.

If you look at a long period of American history, you will see that there have been periods when both output and prices have risen and fallen. The long-term trend for output **(5)** is (up/down). The overall trend for prices (depends/does not depend) upon the period you are reviewing. Up until World War II, prices rose and fell whereas since 1945, prices seem only to have _____.

The government would like to keep output growing, thus avoiding recession; at the **(6)** same time, it would like to keep prices from rising, thus avoiding (inflation/deflation). Attempts to do just this are called _____ policy. The American government has been formally committed to such policies only since the end of World War II. A look at Figures 5-3 and 5-4 on text pages 113 and 114 suggests that since 1950 stabilization policy has done a good job avoiding _____ but not of avoiding _____. Chapter 16 discusses why this result is not surprising; that is, why, if one concentrates on maintaining high levels of employment and output, the result is likely to be higher prices.

IMPORTANT TERMS AND CONCEPTS QUIZ

Choose the best definition for the following terms.

1. _____ Microeconomics
2. _____ Macroeconomics
3. _____ Domestic product
4. _____ Aggregation
5. _____ Aggregate demand curve
6. _____ Aggregate supply curve
7. _____ Inflation
8. _____ Deflation
9. _____ Recession
10. _____ Gross domestic product
11. _____ Nominal GDP
12. _____ Real GDP
13. _____ Final goods and services
14. _____ Intermediate goods
15. _____ Stagflation
16. _____ Stabilization policy

a. Period of expansion in an economy's total output.
b. Period of decline in an economy's total output.
c. Inflation occurring while the economy is growing slowly or in a recession.

d. Gross domestic product calculated at current price levels.
e. Total production of a nation's economy.
f. Government programs designed to prevent or shorten recessions and to counteract inflation.
g. Products purchased by their ultimate users.
h. Study of behavior of an entire economy.
i. Combining individual markets into a single, overall market.
j. Gross domestic product calculated using prices from some agreed-upon year.
k. Products purchased for resale or for their use in producing other products.
l. Sustained decrease in general price level.
m. Graph of quantity of domestic product demanded at each possible price level.
n. Sum of money values of all final goods and services produced in the domestic economy within the year.
o. Graph of quantity of domestic product produced at each possible price level.
p. Study of behavior of individual decision-making units.
q. Sustained increase in general price level.

BASIC EXERCISES

These exercises use the aggregate demand–aggregate supply diagram to review a few basic concepts.

1. Figure 5-1 has four panels. The solid lines indicate the initial situation, and the dashed lines indicate a shift in one or both curves.
   a. Which diagram(s) suggests a period, or periods, of inflation? _____
   b. Which diagram(s) suggests a period, or periods, of deflation? _____
      (Have prices in the U.S. economy ever declined in the twentieth century? _____
      If so, when? _____)
   c. Which diagram(s) illustrates growth in real output with stable prices? _____
   d. Which diagram(s) illustrates stagflation? _____

FIGURE 5-1

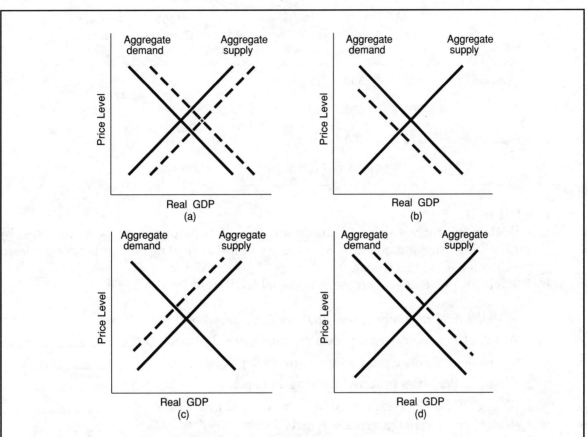

2. Stabilization policy involves changes in government policies designed to shorten recessions and stabilize prices. For reasons explored in Chapters 11 through 16, stabilization policies have their primary effect on the aggregate demand curve. For the cases listed below explain how stabilization policy can reestablish the initial levels of output and prices. Do this by indicating the appropriate shift in the aggregate demand curve. (The exact policies that will achieve these shifts will be described in detail in Chapters 11 through 16.)
   a. Inflation [diagram (d)]
   b. Recession [diagram (b)]
   c. Consider diagram (c), the case of stagflation. If the government is restricted to policies that shift the aggregate demand curve, what will happen to output if the government adopts policies to combat inflation and restore the original price level? What happens to prices if the government is committed to maintaining the original level of output?
3. Table 5-1 contains data on output and prices in a hypothetical economy that produces

TABLE 5-1

	Price (1)	1992 Quantity (2)	Money Value (3)	Price (4)	1993 Quantity (5)	Money Value (6)
Hamburgers	$2.00	300	_____	$2.80	310	_____
Shakes	1.00	300	_____	1.30	320	_____
Fries	0.75	300	_____	0.90	330	_____
		Nominal GDP	_____		Nominal GDP	_____

only fast food.

a. Calculate the money value of the production of hamburgers, shakes, and fries by multiplying price and quantity. Sum these results to calculate nominal gross domestic product (GDP) for each year.

b. What is the percentage increase in nominal GDP from 1992 to 1993?

_____

c. Use 1992 prices to compute real GDP for 1993 based on 1992 prices.

Value of 1993 hamburger production using 1992 prices _____

Value of 1993 shake production using 1992 prices _____

Value of 1993 fries production using 1992 prices _____

Real GDP for 1993 (expressed in terms of 1992 prices) _____

d. Calculate the percentage increase in real GDP from 1992 to 1993. _____

e. How does this figure compare to the increase in nominal GDP calculated in question b? Which is the better measure of the increase in production?_____

_____

SELF-TESTS FOR UNDERSTANDING

Test A

Circle the most appropriate answer.

1. Microeconomics is concerned with
    a. economic aggregates.
    b. the actions of individual economic decision-making units.
    c. small people.
    d. small countries.

2. The study of macroeconomics focuses on
    a. the economic actions of large people.
    b. decisions by the largest 500 industrial companies.
    c. the prices and output of all firms in an industry.
    d. the behavior of entire economies.

3. Which of the following is an example of a macroeconomic aggregate?
    a. The national output of Haiti.
    b. The total output of General Motors.
    c. Employment at Sears.
    d. The price Exxon charges for unleaded gas.

4. The aggregate demand curve shows
    a. the history of real GDP over the recent past.
    b. alternative levels of domestic output that policy makers might choose.
    c. how the quantity of domestic product demanded changes with changes in the price level.
    d. the demand for goods and services by the federal government.

5. The graph showing how the quantity of output produced by all firms depends upon the price level is called the
    a. aggregate supply curve.
    b. Phillips curve.
    c. production possibilities frontier.
    d. economy's aggregate indifference curve.

6. GDP measures the sum of money values of
    a. all goods sold in the domestic economy during the past year.
    b. all final goods and services produced in the domestic economy during the past year.
    c. attendance at all the worst movies during the past year.
    d. all payments to household domestic help during the past year.

7. GDP is designed to be a measure of
    a. economic activity conducted through organized markets.
    b. national well-being.
    c. all economic activity during the preceding year.
    d. all economic transactions involving checks or cash during the preceding year.

8. Using today's prices to aggregate all final output in the economy will yield
    a. nominal GDP.
    b. real GDP.
    c. the cost of living.
    d. GDP in constant dollars.

9. Real GDP is computed by valuing output by
    a. manufacturers' costs.
    b. current prices.
    c. some fixed set of prices.
    d. last year's rate of inflation.

10. Which of the following would not be included in GDP for 1994?
    a. The production of refrigerators in 1994.
    b. The government's purchase of paper clips in 1994.
    c. Consumer expenditures on haircuts in 1994.
    d. General Motors' expenditures on steel for producing Cadillacs in 1994.

11. Which of the following would not be part of GDP for 1994?
    a. Stacey's purchase of a 1994 Pontiac.
    b. Tanya's purchase of the latest microcomputer produced by Apple.
    c. Ramon's expenditures on new furniture for his apartment.
    d. Jamal's purchase of a guitar originally used by John Lennon in 1965.

12. Which of the following is measured by the GDP statisticians?
    a. Jerita's purchase of Boeing stock from Walter.
    b. Your spending on tuition and fees for this year.
    c. Durwood's winnings from his bookie.
    d. The value of Yvonne's volunteer time at her daughter's school.

13. Which of the following will be measured as an increase in GDP but need not reflect an increase in economic well-being?
    a. Expenditures to clean up a major oil spill in Prince William Sound.
    b. The value of the time Roland spends painting his own house.
    c. The cost of new medical care that reduces infant mortality.
    d. Earnings of numbers runners in Chicago.

14. In 1974 nominal GDP was $1.459 trillion. In 1975 nominal GDP increased to $1.768 trillion. On the basis of just this information, which of the following statements is true?
    a. Total output of the American economy was greater in 1975 than in 1974.
    b. The whole increase in nominal GDP was the result of inflation.
    c. Actual output increased by 8.50 percent.
       $[(1.598 - 1.473) \div (1.473)] \times 100$.
    d. It is impossible to determine what happened to prices and output from data on nominal GDP alone.

15. A recession is likely to occur if
    a. unemployment is falling.
    b. the aggregate supply curve shifts to the right.
    c. the increase in nominal GDP exceeds the increase in real GDP.
    d. the aggregate demand curve shifts to the left.

16. Inflation is defined as a period of
    a. rising nominal GDP.
    b. generally rising prices.
    c. falling real GDP.
    d. falling unemployment.

17. Which of the following conditions will result in stagflation?
    a. The aggregate demand curve shifts to the right.
    b. The aggregate demand curve shifts to the left.
    c. The aggregate supply curve shifts to the right.
    d. The aggregate supply curve shifts to the left.

18. Stabilization policy refers to actions by the government to
    a. keep real GDP from rising.
    b. minimize changes in government regulation.
    c. prevent recessions and fight inflation.
    d. equalize the rate of unemployment and inflation.

19. In the period following World War II, the historical record shows
    a. more frequent and more severe recessionary dips in real output than before World War II.
    b. an almost continuous increase in prices.
    c. little if any increase in real GDP.
    d. relatively little inflation.

20. Successful stabilization policy to reduce unemployment would shift
    a. the aggregate supply curve to the left.
    b. the burden of taxes from individuals to corporations.
    c. the aggregate demand curve to the right.
    d. decision making about monetary policy to the Congress.

Test B

Circle T or F for true or false.

T F   1.   A study of the economy of Luxembourg would be an example of microeconomics.

T F   2.   GDP is an example of a macroeconomic aggregate.

T F   3.   A decrease in nominal GDP necessarily implies a recession.

T F   4.   Real GDP is a better measure of national output than is nominal GDP.

T F   5.   Deflation can occur only as a result of shifts in the aggregate supply curve.

T F   6.   Even during the Great Depression of the 1930s prices did not decline.

T F   7.   On the eve of World War II, national output, or real GDP, was not much greater than at the end of the Civil War.

T F   8.   Stagflation refers to the simultaneous occurrence of rising prices and little if any increase in output.

T F   9.   Stabilization policy refers to attempts by the government to influence both prices and output by shifting the aggregate demand curve.

T F 10.   Stabilization policy to combat a recession would call for policies that shift the aggregate demand curve to the left.

STUDY QUESTIONS

1. Why is GDP, a measure of domestic production, not a good measure of national well-being?

2. Why does GDP exclude the sales of existing goods and assets such as used college textbooks and existing homes?

3. Which is the better measure of the change in domestic output, nominal GDP or real GDP? Why?

4. Why does GDP include only final goods and exclude intermediate goods?

5. Should measures of GDP include estimates of non-market economic activity? Why?

6. How can stabilization policy help to reduce unemployment? Inflation?

7. If stabilization policy has the strongest and most immediate impact on aggregate demand, what are the implications for prices when the government wants to reduce unemployment? What are the implications for unemployment when the government wants to reduce prices?

8. What might account for the differences in the American economy's record of economic growth and inflation after 1950 as compared with the period before World War II?

ECONOMICS IN ACTION

The text describes recessions as a period of decline in GDP. This is also the definition that is used by many media commentators. The beginnings and ends of recessions are actually determined by a group of economists associated with the National Bureau of Economic Research. They look at a broader range of measures of economic activity than just GDP. Much controversy surrounded the dating of the 1990-91 recession. The following is taken from a report by Professor Robert Hall, Stanford University, chairman of the NBER Business Cycle Dating Committee, written after data through October 1991 were available. Using Figure 5-2 can you date the beginning and end of the recession? The Committee's decisions are reported in the answers section of the Study Guide, but make your own determination before looking at their decision.

In April 1991, the NBER's Business Cycle Dating Committee determined that a recession had started _____. Figure 1 [5-2] shows the data that most strongly influenced the committee: real personal income less transfers, real sales in manufacturing and trade, nonagricultural employment (because 1990 was a census year, the committee looked at private nonagricultural employment, and nonagricultural employment minus Census workers), and industrial production. The figure shows the basic problem of dating a business cycle: that different cyclical indicators have different turning points.

FIGURE 5-2

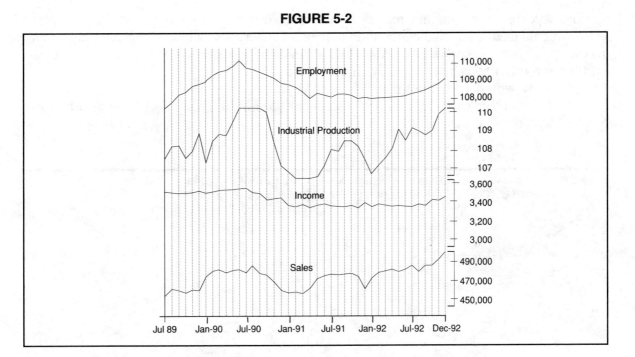

The U.S. economy in 1990 reflected the combined influence of two different forces. One was a very broad slowdown starting in the spring. The other was a sharp contraction in industries (automobile and others) following the spike in oil prices in August. The result was an unusual combination of leading employment and lagging industrial production. The peak date was a reasonable compromise. It embodied the notion that breadth, or dispersion, is an important characteristic of a recession. When measures that span all sectors of the economy—income and employment—peak earlier, the fact that goods production stayed strong for _____ added months should not control the date of the recession.

Figure 1 [Figure 5-1] also shows some of the challenges that will face the NBER Business Cycle Dating Committee in determining the date of the trough in economic activity. First, the figure makes it completely clear that any such determination in the near future would be quite premature. Should the economy begin to contract again, it is a distinct possibility that the trough would occur in late 1991 or 1992. A trough date cannot be assigned until activity has reached a sufficiently high level that a contraction would be a new recession, not a continuation of the existing one.

Economist James Tobin has argued that the traditional approach to dating business cycles is misguided in that it assumes that any increase in economic activity signals the end of a recession. Tobin argues that in a growing economy, output and employment have to increase simply to keep pace with a growing population. He would prefer growth-oriented dating and definitions of business cycles, recoveries, and recessions. On this view, anytime the growth of output and employment failed to match the growth in the potential output would be candidates to be called recession or growth-recession. According to Tobin's definition, periods of recession begin earlier and last somewhat longer than those defined by the NBER.

1. How would you date the recession? Why?
2. Do you think the definition of recessions should be growth-oriented as advocated by Tobin? Why?

SOURCES: *NBER Reporter*, (National Bureau of Economic Research, Winter 1991/92), pp. 1-3.

James Tobin, "Comments," *Brookings Papers on Economic Activity*, 1993:1, pp. 200-208.

C h a p t e r **6**

Unemployment and Inflation: The Twin Evils of Macroeconomics

LEARNING OBJECTIVES

After completing this chapter you should be able to:

- describe how the Bureau of Labor Statistics measures the number of unemployed and in what ways this number may be an overestimate or an underestimate of the unemployment level.

- explain the differences between frictional, structural, and cyclical unemployment.

- explain why unemployment insurance only spreads the financial burden of unemployment that individuals would otherwise face, but does not eliminate the economic cost of unemployment.

- summarize the debate over how much unemployment is consistent with full employment.

- distinguish between real and mythical costs of inflation.

- explain how the concept of real wages suggests that inflation has not systematically eroded the purchasing power of wages.

- distinguish between changes in prices that reflect a change in relative prices and changes that reflect general inflation.

- distinguish between real and nominal rates of interest.

- describe how the difference between real and nominal rates of interest is related to expectations about the rate of inflation.

- explain how the taxation of nominal interest income can mean that, during a period of inflation, savers will receive a reduced real return after taxes.

♦ explain why and how usury ceilings, based on nominal interest rates, can have undesirable impacts during periods of rapid inflation.

♦ distinguish between creeping and galloping inflation.

♦ explain why the variability of inflation is important to an understanding of the cost of inflation.

IMPORTANT TERMS AND CONCEPTS

Unemployment rate
Potential GDP
Labor force
Discouraged workers
Frictional unemployment
Structural unemployment
Cyclical unemployment
Full employment
Unemployment insurance
Purchasing power
Real wage
Relative prices

Redistribution by inflation
Real rate of interest
Nominal rate of interest
Expected rate of inflation
Inflation and the tax system
Usury laws
Creeping inflation
Galloping inflation

CHAPTER REVIEW

Ever since the Employment Act of 1946 committed the federal government to deliberate macroeconomic policy, policymakers have been facing the choice between the twin evils of
(1) macroeconomics. Attempts to lower unemployment have usually meant (<u>more/less</u>) inflation and attempts to fight inflation have usually meant _____
unemployment. How is one to make the choice? Economics cannot provide a definitive answer to this question, but the material in this chapter will help you understand the issues and enable you to make a more informed choice.

Unemployment has two sorts of costs. The personal costs include not only the lost income for individuals out of work, but also the loss of work experience and the psychic costs of involuntary idleness. The economic costs for the nation as a whole can be measured by the output of goods and services that might have been produced by those who are unemployed.

Unemployment insurance can help ease the burden of unemployment for individual fami-
(2) lies, but it (<u>can/cannot</u>) protect society against the lost output that the unemployed might have produced. Employing these people in the future does not bring back the hours of employment that have already been missed. Unemployment compensation provides (<u>complete/partial</u>) protection for (<u>all/some</u>) unemployed workers.

Economists have attempted to measure the economic cost of unemployment by estimating what output would have been at full employment. These figures are estimates of
(3) (potential/actual) GDP. The economic cost of unemployment is the difference between potential GDP and _____.

(4)   Full employment (is/is not) the same as zero unemployment. Some unemployment occurs naturally from the normal workings of labor markets, as people initially look for jobs, improve their own skills, look for better jobs, move to new locations, and so forth. Such unemployment is called _____ unemployment and involves people who are temporarily without a job more or less voluntarily. Full employment would not eliminate this kind of unemployment. Full employment would eliminate unemployment that is due to a decline in the economy's total production; that is, at full employment there would be no _____ unemployment. Unemployment may also occur because people's skills are no longer in demand due to automation or massive changes in production. This type of unemployment is called _____ unemployment.

Unemployment statistics come from a monthly survey by the Bureau of Labor Statistics. People are asked if they have a job. If they answer no, they are asked if they are laid off from a job they expect to return to, are actively looking for work, or are not looking for work. From these answers government statisticians derive estimates of employment, unemployment, and the labor force. These numbers are not above criticism. When unemployment rates are high, some people give up looking for work because they believe that looking for
(5) work is not worth the effort. These people are called _____ workers. An increase in the number of people who have given up looking for work means a(n) (increase/decrease) in the amount of statistical unemployment and is an important reason why some observers feel that the official unemployment statistics (understate/overstate) the problem of unemployment. Part-time workers are counted as employed. If part-time work is involuntary and these individuals would prefer full-time work, official unemployment statistics will (understate/overstate) the problem of unemployment.

In the 1970s it was argued that the increased importance of young workers in the
(6) labor force increased the percentage of (cyclical/frictional/structural) unemployment and (decreased/increased) the full employment rate of unemployment. Young workers have naturally higher rates of unemployment because they more frequently enter and leave the labor force, and because they change jobs more often. If liberal unemployment compensation induces people to call themselves unemployed even if they have no intention of looking for work then official statistics will (overstate/understate) unemployment.

There are important and valid reasons why people are concerned about continuing inflation. Nevertheless, quite a few popular arguments against inflation turn out to be based on misunderstandings. Many people worry that a high rate of inflation reduces their stan-
(7) dard of living, or their (real/nominal) income. But the facts show that periods of high inflation are usually accompanied by equally large if not larger increases in wages. For most workers, the real standard of living, or the change in wages adjusted for the change in prices, continues to increase, even during periods of rapid inflation. A worker whose wages double when prices double is able to consume (more/less/the same) goods and

services (<u>than/as</u>) before the rise in prices and wages. In this case one would say that real wages (<u>increased/were unchanged/decreased</u>).

(8)   During inflationary periods most prices increase at (<u>the same/different</u>) rates. As a result, goods and services with smaller than average price increases become relatively (<u>more/less</u>) expensive than they were before. Analogously, goods and services with larger than average price increases become relatively _____ expensive. Relative prices change all the time, during both inflationary and noninflationary periods. Changes in relative prices usually reflect shifts in demand and/or supply curves or various forms of government interventions. It is inaccurate to blame inflation for an increase in relative prices.

But inflation does have real effects. One important effect is the redistribution of wealth between borrowers and lenders in inflationary periods. If lenders expect higher prices in the
(9) future they will demand (<u>higher/lower</u>) interest rates to compensate them for the loss of purchasing power of the future dollars used to repay loans. Economists have thus found it useful to distinguish between nominal and real interest rates. If one looks at interest rates only in terms of the dollars that borrowers must pay lenders, one is looking at _____ interest rates. If one looks at interest rates in terms of the expected purchasing power the borrower will pay the lender, one is looking at _____ interest rates. The difference between these two measures of interest rate is related to expectations of _____. Real rates are often measured as the difference between the nominal rate and the rate of inflation.

If a change in the rate of inflation is accurately foreseen, and if nominal interest rates are correctly adjusted to reflect the change in expected inflation, then nominal interest rates
(10) (<u>will/will not</u>) change while real interest rates will (<u>also change/be unchanged</u>). More typically, expectations of inflation are incorrect, in which case inflation will result in a redistribution of wealth between borrowers and lenders. Who gains and who loses will depend on whether the adjustment of nominal interest rates is too large or too small. The tax treatment of interest payments can have a substantial impact on the real after-tax rate of return. Problems here reflect the fact that the tax system, originally designed for a world of no inflation, focuses on (<u>nominal/real</u>) interest rates.

(11)   Legal ceilings on interest charges for different types of loans are called _____ ceilings. These ceilings are almost universally written in terms of (<u>nominal/real</u>) interest rates rather than _____ interest rates. During periods of rapid inflation, (<u>nominal/real</u>) interest rates may rise, bumping into usury ceilings, while _____ interest rates may show little if any change. The result will be frustrated borrowers and lenders and reduced levels of economic activity in the affected areas.

Over the long run, small unexpected differences in the rate of inflation can compound to create large differences in profits and losses. Since most business investments depend on long-term contracts, this area of economic activity may suffer during periods of high inflation. The difficulty of making long-term contracts is a real cost of inflation.

Long-term inflation that proceeds at a fairly moderate and steady pace is referred to as
(12) _____ inflation. Inflation that progresses at exceptionally high

and, often, accelerating rates, if only for brief periods of time, is called _____ inflation. There is no simple borderline between the two. In different countries or in different periods of time, the dividing line will vary considerably.

IMPORTANT TERMS AND CONCEPTS QUIZ

Choose the best definition for the following terms.

1. _____ Unemployment rate
2. _____ Potential GDP
3. _____ Labor force
4. _____ Discouraged workers
5. _____ Frictional unemployment
6. _____ Structural unemployment
7. _____ Cyclical unemployment
8. _____ Unemployment insurance
9. _____ Purchasing power
10. _____ Real wage
11. _____ Relative prices
12. _____ Real rate of interest
13. _____ Nominal rate of interest
14. _____ Usury laws
15. _____ Creeping inflation
16. _____ Galloping inflation

a. Government transfer payments to eligible workers if unemployed.
b. Percentage of labor force unemployed.
c. Interest payments, in percentage terms, measured in dollars.
d. Number of people holding or seeking jobs.
e. Prices increasing at exceptionally high rate.
f. Unemployed people who cease looking for work, believing that no jobs are available.
g. Unemployment attributable to decline in economy's total production.
h. Unemployment due to normal workings of the labor market.
i. Legal maximum interest rate.
j. Interest payment, in percentage terms, measured on purchasing power.
k. Volume of goods and services that money wage will buy.
l. Unemployment due to changes in nature of economy.
m. Automatic adjustment of nominal interest rates during periods of inflation.
n. Price of an item in terms of some other item.
o. Prices rising for a long time at a moderate rate.
p. Volume of goods and services that a sum of money will buy.
q. Level of real output attainable if all resources were fully employed.

BASIC EXERCISES

These exercises are designed to illustrate the difference between real and nominal interest rates.

1. When Are High Interest Rates Really Low?

Let R = nominal interest rate,

π = actual rate of inflation, and

ρ = real rate of interest.

It is usual to estimate actual real interest rates as $\rho = R - \pi$. Consider the data in Table 6-1. Column 1 shows data on nominal interest rates on one-year government securities issued in December of each year from 1970 through 1990. Column 2 shows the rate of inflation from December to December as measured by the consumer price index. Note that for 1970 the rate of inflation is from December 1970 to December 1971, the same period for which a holder of the government security earned interest.

a. Complete column 3 by computing real interest rates.

b. The nominal interest rates from column 1 are plotted in Figure 6-1.
   Plot the real interest rates you calculated in column 3 in Figure 6-1.

c. How can actual real rates be negative?

d. When were interest rates higher, 1980 or 1987?

FIGURE 6-1

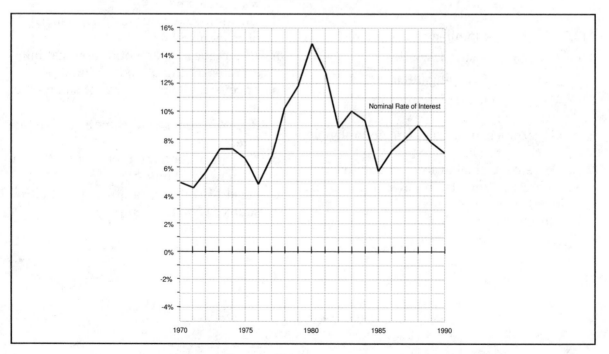

This exercise has made use of data on actual inflation to estimate actual real interest rates. Remember that when individuals decide to borrow or lend they typically know the nominal interest rate they will receive or have to pay, but they cannot know what the real interest rate will turn out to be, as that will depend upon future inflation. At the same time, economists argue that decisions to borrow and lend will be strongly influenced by expectations of inflation and the corresponding expectations for real interest rates.

TABLE 6-1
NOMINAL INTEREST RATES AND INFLATION

	Nominal Interest Rate on 1 Year Government Securities (December)	Rate of Inflation (December to December)	Real Interest Rate
1970	5.00%	5.70%	_____ %
1971	4.61%	4.40%	_____ %
1972	5.52%	3.20%	_____ %
1973	7.27%	6.20%	_____ %
1974	7.31%	11.00%	_____ %
1975	6.60%	9.10%	_____ %
1976	4.89%	5.80%	_____ %
1977	6.96%	6.50%	_____ %
1978	10.30%	7.60%	_____ %
1979	11.98%	11.30%	_____ %
1980	14.88%	13.50%	_____ %
1981	12.85%	10.30%	_____ %
1982	8.91%	6.20%	_____ %
1983	10.11%	3.20%	_____ %
1984	9.33%	4.30%	_____ %
1985	7.67%	3.60%	_____ %
1986	5.87%	1.90%	_____ %
1987	7.17%	3.60%	_____ %
1988	8.99%	4.10%	_____ %
1989	7.72%	4.80%	_____ %
1990	7.05%	5.40%	_____ %

SOURCES: Federal Reserve, Bureau of Labor Statistics

2. Who Gains and Loses from an Adjustment of Nominal Interest Rates?

This problem is designed to illustrate how the adjustment of nominal interest rates, when it is an accurate reflection of future inflation, can leave the real costs and returns to borrowers and lenders unchanged. For simplicity the exercise ignores taxes.

Angela Abbott has a manufacturing firm. After paying other costs she expects a cash flow of $10 million, out of which she must pay the principal and interest on a $5 million loan. If prices are unchanged and if the interest rate is 5 percent, Angela expects a nominal and real profit of $4,750,000. This result is shown in the first column of Table 6-2.

The next three columns reflect three possible alternatives. The second column shows the consequences of unexpected inflation of 10 percent. In the third column, nominal interest rates have adjusted in expectation of an inflation of 10 percent, which actually occurs. And in the last column, nominal interest rates reflect the consequences of expecting a higher rate of inflation than actually occurs.

a. Fill in the missing figures in the second column. Compare the real returns to both Angela and her lender with those of the noninflationary situation in column 1. Who gains and who loses when there is unexpected inflation?

b. Fill in the missing figures in the third column. This is the case in which nominal interest rates have adjusted appropriately. (The approximation is to add the rate of inflation, 10 percent, to the rate of interest in the noninflationary situation, 5 percent. The extra 0.5 percent comes from a more complex and complete adjustment.) Compare the real returns in rows 7 and 9 with the comparable figures in column 1. Who gains and who loses now?

c. Fill in the missing figures in column 4, where interest rates have adjusted in anticipation of a rate of inflation higher than the rate that actually occurs. Who gains and who loses when inflation turns out to be less than expected?

TABLE 6-2

	(1)	(2)	(3)	(4)
1. Price level	1.00	1.10	1.10	1.10
2. Sales revenue minus labor and materials costs *	10,000,000	11,000,000	11,000,000	11,000,000
3. Principal repayment	5,000,000	5,000,000	5,000,000	5,000,000
4. Interest rate	0.05	0.05	0.155	0.20
5. Interest payment [(4) × (3)]	250,000	_____	_____	_____
6. Total nominal payment to lender [(3) + (5)]	5,250,000	_____	_____	_____
7. Real payment to lender [(6) ÷ (1)]	5,250,000	_____	_____	_____
8. Nominal profits [(2) − (6)]	4,750,000	_____	_____	_____
9. Real profits[(8) ÷ (1)]	4,750,000	_____	_____	_____

* Inflation of 10 percent is assumed to increase sales revenue, labor costs, and materials costs by 10 percent each. As a result, the difference between sales revenue and labor plus material costs also increases by 10 percent in column 2, 3, and 4.

SELF-TESTS FOR UNDERSTANDING

Test A

Circle the most appropriate answer.

1. Indicate which examples go with which concepts.
   a. An older, unemployed telephone operator replaced by new, computerized switching machines.
   b. An unemployed college senior looking for her first job.
   c. An ex-construction worker who has given up looking for work because of a belief that no one is hiring.
   d. An unemployed retail clerk who is laid off because of declining sales associated with a general business recession.

frictional unemployment	_____
structural unemployment	_____
cyclical unemployment	_____
discouraged worker	_____

2. Which of the following factors implies that official statistics may understate the magnitude of the problem of unemployment? (There may be more than one correct answer.)
   a. Discouraged workers.
   b. The loss of expected overtime work.
   c. Generous unemployment benefits.
   d. Involuntary part-time work.

3. Which of the following people are eligible for unemployment compensation?
   a. A mechanic for Ford Motor Company laid off because of declining auto sales.
   b. A housewife seeking paid work after six years spent at home with two small children.
   c. A college senior looking for his first job.
   d. An engineer who quits to find a better job.

4. Which one of the following groups experiences the highest rate of unemployment?
   a. Married men.
   b. College graduates.
   c. Teenage workers.
   d. Non-white workers.

5. The measure of output that the economy could produce with the full employment of all people and factories is called
   a. real GDP.
   b. potential GDP.
   c. nominal GDP.
   d. expected GDP.

6. The difference between potential GDP and actual GDP is a reflection of
    a. frictional unemployment.
    b. cyclical unemployment.
    c. galloping inflation.
    d. nominal interest rates.

7. In 1992 unemployment insurance provided benefits to about _____ of the unemployed.
    a. one-quarter
    b. one-third
    c. one-half
    d. all

8. In 1992 unemployment insurance replaced a bit less than _____ of lost income for those who were insured.
    a. one-quarter
    b. one-third
    c. one-half
    d. all

9. Unemployment insurance
    a. eliminates the cost of unemployment to the economy as a whole.
    b. means that no unemployed worker need suffer a decline in his or her standard of living.
    c. helps to protect insured individuals by spreading the cost.
    d. must be paid back by the unemployed once they find a new job.

10. The real rate of interest relevant for a lender about to lend money is measured as the
    a. nominal interest rate divided by the rate of inflation.
    b. nominal interest rate minus the expected rate of inflation.
    c. rate of inflation minus the nominal interest rate.
    d. the increase in nominal GDP divided by the rate of increase in prices.

11. A nominal interest rate of 10 percent and inflationary expectations of 4 percent imply a real interest rate of about _____ percent.
    a. 4
    b. 6
    c. 10
    d. 14

12. Nominal interest rates of 9 percent are consistent with real interest rates of 4 percent if expectations of inflation are equal to
    a. 4 percent.
    b. 5 percent.
    c. 9 percent.
    d. 14 percent.

13. If suddenly everyone expects a higher rate of inflation, economists would expect nominal interest rates to
    a. rise.
    b. fall.
    c. stay unchanged.

14. In a world with no inflation and no taxes, nominal interest rates of 5 percent offer a real return of 5 percent. If suddenly it is expected that prices will rise by 6 percent, what increase in nominal interest rates is necessary if the expected real interest rate is to remain unchanged at 5 percent?
    a. 1 percent.
    b. 5 percent.
    c. 6 percent.
    d. 11 percent.

15. If inflation is unexpected, there is apt to be a redistribution of wealth from
    a. borrowers to lenders.
    b. lenders to borrowers.
    c. rich to poor.
    d. poor to rich.

16. Usury laws are designed to limit
    a. increases in nominal wages.
    b. real interest rates.
    c. the rate of inflation.
    d. nominal interest rates.

17. With overall inflation at 5 percent, if the price of jeans increases by 7 percent and the price of hand calculators declines by 3 percent, we would say that
    a. the relative price of jeans has increased.
    b. calculators are now less expensive in terms of jeans.
    c. both a and b are correct.
    d. only a is correct.

18. The dividing line between creeping and galloping inflation
    a. is 10 percent.
    b. is 50 percent.
    c. is 100 percent.
    d. will depend upon the particular country and historical circumstances.

19. If your wages go up by 10 percent when prices go up by 7 percent, the increase in your real wage is about _____ percent.
    a. 3
    b. 7
    c. 10
    d. 17

20. The historical evidence suggests that in periods with high rates of inflation, nominal wages
   a. increase at about the same rate as before.
   b. increase at much lower rates than inflation.
   c. also increase at high rates.
   d. remain unchanged.

Test B

Circle T or F for true or false.

T F 1. In periods of high unemployment the only people whose incomes are reduced are those who are out of work.

T F 2. The official unemployment statistics are adjusted to include those people with part-time jobs who are looking for full-time work.

T F 3. All major social groupings, young–old, men–women, blacks–whites, have essentially the same rate of unemployment.

T F 4. Unemployment insurance protects society against lost output from unemployment.

T F 5. Anyone who is officially counted as unemployed can collect unemployment benefits.

T F 6. Potential GDP is an estimate of the maximum possible output our economy could produce under conditions similar to wartime.

T F 7. The definition of full-employment is an unemployment rate of zero.

T F 8. Inflation does not redistribute wealth between borrowers and lenders because nominal interest rates are automatically adjusted to reflect actual inflation.

T F 9. The historical record shows that creeping inflation will always lead to galloping inflation.

T F 10. Predictable inflation is likely to impose less cost than unpredictable inflation.

Appendix:
How Statisticians Measure Inflation

LEARNING OBJECTIVES

After completing this appendix you should be able to:

♦ construct a price index from data on prices and the composition of the market basket in the base year.

♦ use a price index to compute real measures of economic activity by deflating the corresponding nominal measures.

♦ use a price index to compute the rate of inflation from one period to the next.

♦ explain how the market baskets differ for the Consumer Price Index and the GDP deflator.

IMPORTANT TERMS AND CONCEPTS

Index number
Index number problem
Consumer Price Index
Deflating by a price index
GDP deflator

IMPORTANT TERMS AND CONCEPTS QUIZ

Choose the best definition for the following terms.

1. _____ Index number

2. _____ Consumer Price Index

3. _____ Deflating

4. _____ GDP deflator

5. _____ Index number problem

a. Dividing a nominal magnitude by a price index to express the magnitude in constant purchasing power.

b. Magnitude of some variable relative to its magnitude in base periods.

c. Price index obtained by dividing nominal GDP by real GDP.

d. Measure of price level based on typical urban household's spending.

e. Average change in consumer prices.

f. Differences between consumption patterns of actual families and the market basket used for a price index.

BASIC EXERCISE

The following exercise should help you review the material on price indexes presented in the appendix to Chapter 6.

Table 6-3 presents data on expenditures and prices for a hypothetical family that buys only food and clothing. We see that in 1990 this family spent $5,000 on food at $2 per unit of food, and $10,000 on clothing at $25 per unit. Note that between 1990 and 1991, dollar expenditures by this family increased by 15.65 percent, rising from $15,000 to $17,348. Is this family able to consume 15.65 percent more of everything? Clearly not, since prices have risen. How much inflation has there been on average? What is the increase in real income for this family? These are the sorts of questions that a good price index can help you answer.

TABLE 6-3
HYPOTHETICAL PRICES AND EXPENDITURES

Year	Food		Clothing		
	Price	Expenditures	Price	Expenditures	Total Expenditures
1990	$2.00	$5,000	$25.00	$10,000	$15,000
1991	$2.36	$5,900	$26.50	$11,448	$17,348

1. Use the data in Table 6-3 to construct a family price index (FPI) using 1990 as the base year.
   a. Divide expenditures by price to find the quantities of each good purchased in 1990. This is the base-period market basket.

      Quantity of food   _____

      Quantity of clothing   _____
   b. Use 1991 prices to find out how much the base-period market basket would cost at 1991 prices.

      1991 cost of 1990 market basket _____
   c. Divide the 1991 cost of the base-period market basket by the 1990 cost of the same market basket and multiply by 100 to compute the value of the FPI for 1991.

      FPI for 1991 _____
   d. Convince yourself that if you repeat steps b and c using 1990 prices you will get an answer of 100 for the value of the FPI for 1990.
   e. Measure the increase in the cost of living by computing the percentage change in your price index from 1990 to 1991.

      Inflation between 1990 and 1991 _____
   f. Divide total dollar expenditures in 1991 by the 1991 FPI and multiply by 100 to get a measure of real expenditures for 1991.

      Real expenditures in 1991 (1990 prices)   _____

      Percentage change in real expenditures 1990 to 1991   _____

   Remember the following points about price indexes:
   - Most price indexes, like the Consumer Price Index, are computed by pricing a standard market basket of goods in subsequent periods.
   - A price index can be used to measure inflation and to deflate nominal values to adjust for inflation.
   - Different price indexes, such as the Consumer Price Index and the GDP deflator, will show slightly different measures of inflation because they use different market baskets.

2. (Optional) Compute a new FPI using 1991 as the base period rather than 1990. Now the value of your price index for 1991 will be 100 and the price index for 1990 will be something less than 100. Does this index give the same measure of inflation as the index with 1990 as the base period? Do not be surprised if it does not. Can you explain why they differ?

SUPPLEMENTARY EXERCISES

1. Table 6-4 contains data on consumer prices for seven countries. Try to answer each of the following questions or explain why the information in Table 6-4 is insufficient to answer the question.
   a. In 1970 which country had the lowest prices?
   b. In 1990 which country had the highest prices?

TABLE 6-4
INDEX OF CONSUMER PRICES (1982–1984 = 100)

	Canada	France	Italy	Japan	United Kingdom	United States	Germany
1970	35.1	28.7	16.8	38.5	21.8	38.8	52.9
1975	50.1	43.9	28.8	66.0	40.2	53.8	71.2
1980	76.1	72.2	63.2	91.0	78.5	82.4	86.8
1985	108.9	114.3	121.1	104.1	111.1	107.6	104.8
1990	135.5	133.2	159.6	111.4	148.2	130.7	112.1

Source: 1993 Economic Report of the President, Table B-105.

    c. Over the period 1970 to 1990, which country experienced the most inflation as measured by the percentage change in the consumer price index? Which country experienced the least inflation?

2. Go to the library to document the current unemployment situation of different workers. *Employment and Earnings* is published monthly by the Bureau of Labor Statistics. It contains detailed data on employment and unemployment by age, sex, and race of workers. The *Survey of Current Business* is another good source, although less detailed than *Employment and Earnings*. The *Economic Report of the President*, issued annually, is a good source for historic data.

3. Learn more about the composition of the market basket for the Consumer Price Index. A good place to start is "New basket of goods and services being priced in revised CPI," Charles Mason and Clifford Butler, *Monthly Labor Review*, January 1987, pages 3-22.

ECONOMICS IN ACTION

There is general agreement that inflation at a constant rate imposes less cost than inflation that fluctuates widely around a similar mean. Some argue that it does not matter what the rate of inflation is as long as it does not vary too much. If inflation could actually be held constant at a given rate, then borrowers and lenders, consumers, and producers would all come to expect this unchanged rate of inflation, and they could devise contracts for borrowing, lending, and wages that incorporated simple inflationary expectations. Using this line of reasoning it does not matter whether inflation averages 0 percent or 10 percent. Inflation that averaged 0 percent but fluctuated between plus 5 percent and minus 5 percent would be as bad as inflation that averaged 10 percent while fluctuating between 5 percent and 15 percent. Based on this view, policy should focus more on the stabilization of the rate of inflation and less on the average rate of inflation.

Others are skeptical that it is possible to stabilize inflation when the average rate is high and wonder whether higher rates of inflation are not necessarily associated with more variable rates. *The Economist*, in its November 7, 1992 issue, examined the question of what rate of inflation countries should aim for. Part of their investigation looked at historical data on the variability of inflation for a number of industrialized countries. Similar data for 22 countries* is shown in Figure 6-2, which plots the average rate of inflation over the period 1961 to 1991 on the horizontal axis and the standard deviation in the rate of inflation over the same period on the vertical axis. (The standard deviation is a statistical measure of variability. Larger numbers are associated with greater variability.)

1. What does Figure 6-2 suggest about the link between the average rate of inflation and the variability of inflation?
2. If higher rates of inflation mean greater variability, how low a rate of inflation should countries strive for? Is an average rate of zero possible? Would it be desirable?

You might want to consult the article in *The Economist*, "Zero Inflation: How Low is Low Enough?," November 7, 1992, pp. 23-26.

---

*Australia, Austria, Belgium, Canada, Denmark, Finland, France, Germany, Greece, Ireland, Italy, Japan, Luxembourg, Netherlands, New Zealand, Norway, Portugal, Spain, Sweden, Switzerland, United Kingdom, and United States.

FIGURE 6-2

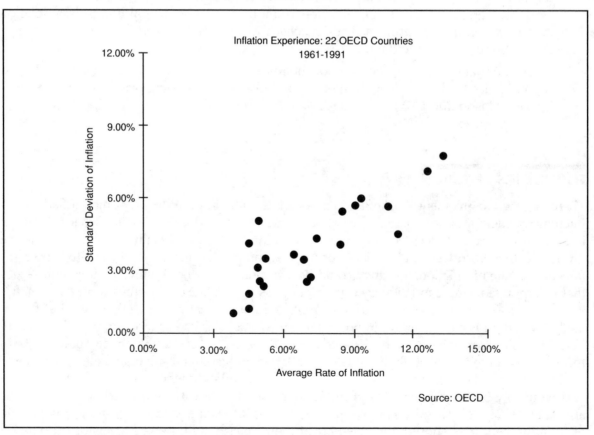

STUDY QUESTIONS

1. Why doesn't unemployment insurance eliminate the cost of unemployment for the economy as a whole?

2. Consider the following numbers for two hypothetical months:

	Month 1	Month 2
Employed	92	91
Unemployed	8	7
Not in the Labor Force	60	62
Rate of Unemployment	8.0%	7.1%

How might the concept of discouraged workers be relevant for explaining why the decline in employment is associated with a decline in the unemployment rate?

3. Do you believe the official rate of unemployment overstates or understates the seriousness of unemployment? Why?

4. Which concepts of unemployment—frictional, structural, and cyclical—are relevant when considering the full employment rate of unemployment? Why?

5. When does an increase in the price of textbooks reflect a change in relative prices and when does it reflect inflation?

6. During a period of inflation which is likely to be higher, nominal or real interest rates? Why?

7. Do you agree or disagree with the argument that the taxation of interest and capital gains should be based on real returns rather than nominal returns? Why?

8. Which is likely to have more adverse effects, steady or variable inflation? Why?

C h a p t e r **7**

Income and Spending:
The Powerful Consumer

LEARNING OBJECTIVES

After completing this chapter you should be able to:

- distinguish between spending, output, and income.
- describe what spending categories make up aggregate demand.
- distinguish between investment spending as a part of aggregate demand and financial investment.
- explain why, except for some technical complications, national product and national income are necessarily equal.
- explain how disposable income differs from national income.
- derive a consumption function given data on consumption and disposable income and compute the marginal propensity to consume at various levels of income.
- explain why the marginal propensity to consume is equal to the slope of the consumption function.
- distinguish between factors that result in a *movement along* the consumption function and factors that result in a *shift of* the function.
- explain why consumption spending is affected by a change in the level of prices even if real income is unchanged.
- describe why permanent and temporary changes in taxes of the same magnitude would be expected to have different impacts on consumption spending.

IMPORTANT TERMS AND CONCEPTS

Aggregate demand
Consumer expenditure (C)
Investment spending (I)
Government purchases (G)
Net exports (X – IM)
C + I + G + X – IM
National income
Disposable income (DI)
Circular flow diagram

Transfer payments
Scatter diagram
Consumption function
Marginal propensity to consume (MPC)
Movements along versus shifts of the
    consumption function
Money fixed assets
Temporary versus permanent tax changes

CHAPTER REVIEW

This chapter introduces two key concepts that economists use when discussing the determination of an economy's output: *aggregate demand* and the *consumption function*. These basic
concepts will be fundamental to the material in later chapters.

(1) The total amount that all consumers, business firms, government agencies, and foreigners are willing to spend on goods and services is called aggregate _____.
Economists typically divide this sum into four components: consumption expenditures, investment spending, government purchases, and net exports. Food, clothing, movies, and
hamburgers are examples of (consumption/investment/government) expenditures. Factories, office buildings, machinery, and houses would be examples of _____
spending. Red tape, bombers, filing cabinets, and the services of bureaucrats are examples of
_____ purchases. American wheat and tractors sold abroad are ex-
amples of (exports/imports), and American purchases of French wines, Canadian paper,
and Mexican oil are examples of _____. The difference between exports
and imports is called _____ _____. Economists use national income
accounts to keep track of these components of demand. Appendix B to this chapter provides
an introduction to these accounts.

There is a close analogy between the demand for a single product and aggregate demand.
As seen in the study of consumer demand in microeconomics, economists argue that demand
should be seen as a schedule showing how the quantity demanded depends upon a number of
factor, including price. In later chapters we will see that aggregate demand is also a schedule
showing how the demand by everyone for newly produced goods and services is affected by a
variety of factor, including the overall level of prices or, for short, the price level.

Two other concepts that are closely related to aggregate demand are *national product*
and *national income*. National product is simply the output of the economy. National income
(2) is the (before/after)-tax income of all the individuals in the economy. Disposable income is
the income of individuals after _____ have been paid and any
_____ payments from the government have been counted. The circular
flow diagram shows that national product and national income are two ways of measuring

the same thing: Producing goods and selling them results in income for the owners and employees of firms.

Economists use the concept of a *consumption function* to organize the determinants of consumption expenditures. Specifically, the consumption function is the relation between aggregate real consumption expenditures and aggregate real disposable income, holding all other **(3)** determinants of consumer spending constant. Higher disposable income leads to (more/less) consumption spending. A change in disposable income leads to a (shift in/movement along) the consumption function. A change in one of the other factors that affect consumer spending, such as wealth, the level of prices, the rate of inflation, or interest rates, leads to a _____ _____ the consumption function. (Two, more technical, aspects of the consumption function, the *marginal propensity to consume* and the *average propensity to consume*, are considered more fully in the Basic Exercise section of this chapter.)

An increase in the price level affects consumption spending and is an important reason **(4)** why aggregate demand, _____ + _____ + _____ + _____ – _____, is a schedule. If prices are higher we expect (more/less) consumption spending. Consumption spending changes because the value of many consumer assets is fixed in money terms, and an increase in the price level will (increase/decrease) the purchasing power of these assets. It is important to remember that higher prices will lead to lower real consumption expenditures even if real disposable income is constant. A doubling of *all* prices will also double wages—the price for an hour of labor services. If wages and prices both double, there is no change in the purchasing power of labor income, but there is a loss to consumers from the decline in the purchasing power of their money fixed assets. It is this latter decline that leads to a shift in the consumption function in response to a change in the price level.

Separately from the level of prices, the rate of inflation may also affect consumption spending. On the one hand, the notion that one should buy now, before prices increase still further, suggests that inflation stimulates consumption spending. On the other hand, the notion that one may have to save more in order to meet higher prices tomorrow, suggests that inflation depresses consumption spending. For rates of inflation experienced in the United States there is no clear evidence as to which tendency is greater. Economists have also found it difficult to detect a large impact on consumption spending from changes in interest rates. While a higher real interest rate provides an increased incentive to consume less and save more, it also means that one can reach a given dollar target with less savings.

A change in income taxes immediately changes disposable income. The consumption function, then, tells us how a change in disposable income will affect consumption spend- **(5)** ing. For example, a reduction in income taxes would (increase/decrease) disposable income. After computing the change in disposable income, one could estimate the initial impact on consumption spending by multiplying the change in disposable income by the (marginal/average) propensity to consume. A permanent increase in taxes would be expected to have a (larger/smaller) effect on consumption expenditures than a temporary tax increase of the same magnitude because the permanent increase changes consumers' long-run income prospects by (more/less) than the temporary increase. The same argument works in reverse and implies that temporary tax changes have a (larger/smaller) impact on consumption expenditures than do permanent tax changes.

IMPORTANT TERMS AND CONCEPTS QUIZ

Choose the best definition for the following terms.

1. _____ Aggregate demand
2. _____ Consumer expenditure (C)
3. _____ Investment spending (I)
4. _____ Government purchases (G)
5. _____ Net exports (X–IM)
6. _____ National income
7. _____ Disposable income (DI)
8. _____ Transfer payments
9. _____ Consumption function
10. _____ Marginal propensity to consume
11. _____ Movement along the consumption function
12. _____ Shift of the consumption function
13. _____ Money fixed asset

a. Relation between aggregate real consumption expenditures and aggregate real disposable income.
b. Income of individuals after taxes and transfer payments.
c. Purchases of newly produced goods and services by all levels of government.
d. Total amount spent by consumers on newly produced goods and services.
e. Change in consumption due to a change in disposable income.
f. Gross national product divided by price level.
g. Total amount consumers, firms, government agencies and foreigners are willing to spend on final goods.
h. Total spending by firms on new plants and equipment and by consumers on new homes.
i. Change in consumption divided by change in disposable income.
j. Item whose value is fixed in terms of dollars.
k. Exports minus imports.
l. Total earnings of all individuals in economy.
m. Change in consumption due to a change in any factor affecting consumption other than disposable income.
n. Government grants to individuals.

BASIC EXERCISES

Note that the first three problems are based on income and consumption data for individual families rather than aggregate income and consumption. Along with the fourth problem, they will give you practice using and understanding the MPC.

1. Table 7-1 reports some data on disposable income and consumption.
    a. For each change in income compute the marginal propensity to consume.
    b. The average propensity to consume is defined as the ratio of consumption expenditures to disposable income or $APC = C \div DI$. For the income of $10,000 the average propensity to consume is $.90 = \$9,000 \div \$10,000$. Use the data on income and consumption to fill in the column for the APC.
    c. Are the average and marginal propensities equal? Do the differences surprise you? Can you explain them? Perhaps steps d to f will help.

d. Use the graph of Figure 7-1 to draw the consumption function consistent with the data in Table 7-1. (Locate each income–consumption data pair and then draw a line connecting the points.)

e. The MPC is represented by what part of your graph?

FIGURE 7-1

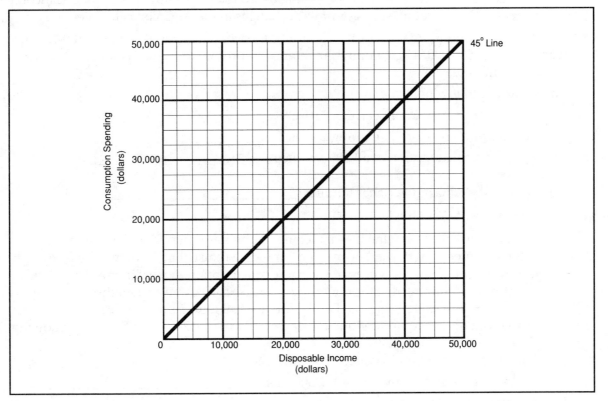

TABLE 7-1

Average Propensity to Consume	Disposable Income	Change in Disposable Income to	Marginal Propensity Consume	Change in Consumption Expenditures	Consumption Expenditures
_____	$10,000				$9,000
		$10,000	_____	$7,500	
_____	$20,000				$16,500
		$10,000	_____	$7,500	
_____	$30,000				$24,000
		$10,000	_____	$7,500	
_____	$40,000				$31,500
		$10,000	_____	$7,500	
_____	$50,000				$39,000

f. The APC can be represented by the slope of a ray from the origin to a point on the consumption function. Remember the slope of any straight line, including a ray, is the vertical change over the horizontal change. When measured from the origin, the vertical change of a ray to a point on the consumption function is C and the horizontal change is DI. Thus the slope of the ray, $(C \div DI)$, is the APC. Draw rays to represent the APC for incomes of $10,000 and $50,000. How does the slope of your rays change as income increases? Is this change consistent with changes in the APC you calculated in step c?

2. Imagine an economy made up of 100 families, each earning $10,000 and 100 families each earning $50,000. Each family consumes according to the consumption function described in Table 7-1.

   a. Fill in the following:

   Consumption of a family earning $10,000 _____

   Consumption of a family earning $50,000 _____

   Aggregate consumption of all 200 families _____

   b. What is the APC of the richer families? _____

   What is the APC of the poorer families? _____

   c. Randy argues that since the lower-income families are spending a greater proportion of their income than the higher-income families, a redistribution of income from high- to low-income families will increase total consumption expenditures. Test Randy's assertion by assuming that the government takes $5,000 from each high-income family and gives it to each low-income family, and that all families adjust their consumption in line with the consumption function described in Table 7-1. Then fill in the following:

   Consumption of a family with $15,000 income _____

   Consumption of a family with $45,000 income _____

   Aggregate consumption of all 200 families _____

   d. Explain why in this example aggregate consumption is unaffected by the redistribution of income.

3. (Optional) Use the data in Table 7-1 to compute an algebraic expression for the consumption function.

   Consumption = _____ + 0._____ × (disposable income)

4. The lower line in Figure 7-2 shows the location of the consumption function of Baulmovia in 1992. In 1992 Baulmovian disposable income was $4.0 trillion and consumption spending was $3.6 trillion. In 1993 there was a significant surge in consumer confidence that shifted the consumption function to the higher line in Figure 7-2. in 1993 Baulmovian disposable income was $4.4 trillion and consumption spending was $3.96 trillion.

FIGURE 7-2
CONSUMPTION FUNCTIONS FOR 1992 AND 1993

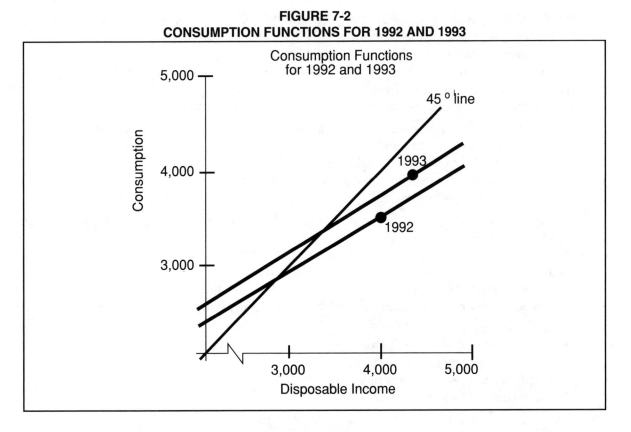

Consider an estimate of MPC by looking at the change in consumption spending and the change in disposable income from 1992 to 1993.

a. What is this estimate of MPC? _____
b. How does this estimate of MPC compare to the slope of either consumption function? Explain any differences.

SELF-TESTS FOR UNDERSTANDING

Test A

Circle the most appropriate answer.

1. Which of the following is not a part of aggregate demand?
    a. Consumption expenditures.
    b. National income.
    c. Net exports.
    d. Investment expenditures.

2. When thinking about aggregate demand, economists use the term investment to refer to all except which one of the following?
   a. The newly built house that Roberta just bought.
   b. The stock in General Electric that Ralph bought with his summer earnings.
   c. The new factory that is being built on the edge of town.
   d. The new machinery that Sherry bought to start her own company.

3. Which of the following would be an example of a government transfer payment?
   a. Wages paid to government bureaucrats.
   b. A tax refund for excess withholding.
   c. The purchase of paperclips by a government agency.
   d. Social security payments.

4. In a circular flow diagram all but which one of the following would be depicted as an injection into the stream of spending?
   a. The Defense Department's purchase of a new airplane.
   b. Joyce and Jim's purchase of an existing house.
   c. Alice's spending to rebuild her restaurant after the fire.
   d. The set of new micro-computers that Elaine's company bought for all its top management.

5. National income refers to
   a. the income of consumers before taxes.
   b. the sum of everyone's before-tax income.
   c. employee wage and salary payments.
   d. the income of federal government employees only.

6. Disposable income is equal to the income of individuals after
   a. subtracting taxes.
   b. adding transfer payments.
   c. adding taxes to transfer payments.
   d. subtracting taxes and adding transfer payments.

7. A graphical representation of how consumption spending varies with changes in disposable income is called the
   a. aggregate demand curve.
   b. income-expenditure schedule.
   c. consumption function.
   d. Phillips curve.

8. A change in which one of the following would be associated with a movement along the consumption function?
   a. Current disposable income.
   b. Wealth.
   c. The price level.
   d. Expected future incomes.

9. A change in all but which one of the following would be associated with a shift in the consumption function?
   a. Wealth.
   b. Interest rates.
   c. Current disposable income.
   d. The price level.

10. A consumption function is an example of a
    a. time series graph.
    b. two-variable diagram.
    c. contour diagram.

11. If an increase in prices is matched by an increase in wages and salaries such that there is no change in real disposable income, then
    a. there should be no effect on consumption spending.
    b. the increase in prices will lead to a movement along the consumption function.
    c. one should expect MPC to decline.
    d. the impact of the change in prices on the purchasing power of money fixed assets should lead to a shift in the consumption function.

12. The impact of a change in real disposable income on consumption spending can be represented as a
    a. movement along a given consumption function.
    b. a shift in the consumption function.
    c. a shift in MPC.
    d. a change in the price level.

13. MPC refers to
    a. Y-axis is intercept of the consumption function.
    b. the slope of the consumption function.
    c. the ratio of consumption spending to income.
    d. the slope of a ray from the origin to a point on the consumption function.

14. If MPC is 0.7, then a $100 billion change in disposable income will be associated with what change in consumption spending?
    a. $20 billion.
    b. $30 billion.
    c. $70 billion.
    d. $100 billion.

15. If a $100 billion increase in disposable income results in a $75 billion increase in consumption spending, then MPC is
    a. 0.25
    b. 0.50
    c. 0.75
    d. 1.0

16. If MPC is 0.80, what decrease in taxes will initially increase consumption spending by $16 billion?
    a. $12.8 billion.
    b. $16 billion.
    c. $20 billion.
    d. $64 billion.

17. If consumption spending declines by $45 billion when disposable income declines by $50 billion, what is MPC?
    a. 0.9
    b. 0.1
    c. –0.1
    d. –0.9

18. If MPC is .8, a $100 billion change in the wealth of consumers will lead to
    a. a $100 billion change in consumption spending.
    b. an $80 billion change in consumption spending.
    c. a movement along the consumption function.
    d. a shift in the entire consumption function.

19. An increase in interest rates
    a. always leads to a decrease in consumption spending as it provides an increased incentive for greater saving.
    b. can be modeled as a movement along the consumption function.
    c. always leads to an increase in consumption spending as the higher interest rate allows savers to reach fixed objectives with smaller savings.
    d. does not appear to have influenced consumption spending very much one way or the other.

20. Which type of tax change would be expected to have the largest impact on consumption spending?
    a. The tax rebate of 1975.
    b. The tax surcharge of 1969.
    c. The permanent reduction in tax rates of 1964.
    d. The reduction in tax withholding announced by President Bush in 1992.

Test B

Circle T or F for true or false.

T F 1. Aggregate demand is the aggregate of individual household consumption decisions.

T F 2. The consumption function reflects the close relationship between consumption spending and national output.

T F 3. The U.S. government has often used changes in income tax rates as a way of influencing consumer spending.

T F 4. A change in consumption divided by the change in disposable income that produced the change in consumption is called the marginal propensity to consume.

T F 5. An increase in the level of prices is likely to reduce consumption expenditures.

T F 6. The effect of a change in the level of prices on consumption would be viewed graphically as a shift in the consumption function.

T F 7. By increasing household wealth, a big increase in the stock market is likely to lead to a movement along the consumption function.

T F 8. The magnitude of the impact of a change in taxes on consumption expenditures is likely to depend on whether consumers view the change in taxes as permanent or temporary.

T F 9. A temporary decrease in taxes is likely to have a smaller impact on consumption than will a permanent decrease.

T F 10. The initial impact of a change in income taxes on consumption spending can be calculated by multiplying the change in disposable income by MPC.

Appendix A: The Saving Function and the Marginal Propensity to Save

LEARNING OBJECTIVES

Working through the exercise below should help you understand the basic message of Appendix A to Chapter 7: *We could just as easily have used the saving function instead of the consumption function.* When you have completed the exercise you should be able to

- compute savings, given data on disposable income and consumption.
- compute the marginal propensity to save.
- show that the MPC and the MPS sum to 1.0.

IMPORTANT TERMS AND CONCEPTS

Aggregate saving
Saving function
Marginal propensity to save (MPS)

IMPORTANT TERMS AND CONCEPTS QUIZ

Choose the best definition for the following terms.

1. _____ Aggregate saving
2. _____ Saving function
3. _____ Marginal propensity to save

a. Change in consumer savings divided by change in disposable income.

b. Consumer savings divided by disposable income.

c. Schedule relating consumer saving to disposable income.

d. Disposable income minus consumption.

BASIC EXERCICES

1. Table 7-2 reproduces the income and consumption data from Table 7-1. Use the data in Table 7-2 to compute the amount of saving at each level of income. Remember that saving is just the difference between disposable income and consumption, that is $S = DI - C$.

2. For each change in income, compute MPS. (You will first need to compute the change in savings.)

3. Using results from Tables 7-1 and 7-2, show that the sum of MPC and MPC for each change in income is 1.0.

4. Use the data on income and saving to compute the average propensity to save.

5. Again, using results from Tables 7-1 and 7-2, show that the sum of the APC and the APS at each level of income is 1.0.

6. It is because APC plus APS always equals 1.0 and MPC plus MPS always equals 1.0 that we can use the saving or consumption factor interchangeably.

TABLE 7-2

Average Propensity to save	Savings	Consumption Expenditures	Disposable Income	Change in Disposable Income	Change in Savings	Marginal Propensity to Save
_____	_____	$9,000	$10,000			
				$10,000	_____	_____
_____	_____	$16,500	$20,000			
				$10,000	_____	_____
_____	_____	$24,000	$30,000			
				$10,000	_____	_____
_____	_____	$31,500	$40,000			
				$10,000	_____	_____
_____	_____	$39,000	$50,000			

Some simple algebra also gives the same result. Start with the identity:

$$DI = C + S.$$

Now divide both sides of the equation by DI and interpret your results in terms of APC and APS.

We also know that since any change in income must be spent or saved

$$\Delta DI = \Delta C + \Delta S.$$

where Δ means change. Now divide both sides of the equation by ΔDI and interpret your results in terms of MPC and MPS.

Appendix B:
National Income Accounting

LEARNING OBJECTIVES

After completing this appendix you should be able to:

- describe the three alternative ways of measuring GDP and explain why, except for bookkeeping or statistical errors, they give the same answer.

- explain why national income accounting treats government purchases of goods and services differently from government transfer payments.

- explain the difference in theory and practice between the following macro measurements: GDP, NDP, national income, personal income, and disposable income.

IMPORTANT TERMS AND CONCEPTS

National income accounting
Gross National Product (GNP)
Gross Domestic Product (GDP)
Gross private domestic investment
Investment
Government purchases
Transfer payments
Net exports

National Income
Net Domestic Product (NDP)
Net National Product (NNP)
Depreciation
Value added
Personal income
Disposable Income (*DI*)

APPENDIX REVIEW

Although included in an appendix, this material on national income accounting deserves special treatment. When working through this material, do not lose sight of the forest for the trees. The forest is composed of broad income concepts, such as gross domestic product (GDP), net domestic product (NDP), and national income, what each of these concepts measures and how they relate to one another. This appendix is an introduction to the forest rather than to each individual tree.

The *national income accounts* measure economic activity: the production of goods and services and the incomes that are simultaneously generated. Accurate measurement of production and income is an important prerequisite to attempts to understand and control the economy. National income accounts are centered around measurement of the gross domestic product. Consumption (C), investment (I), government purchases of goods and services (G), and net exports (X – IM) are parts of GDP. Other concepts, such as *net domestic product* (NDP) and *national income*, are alternative measures of total economic activity.

(1)   GDP is defined as the sum of the money values of all _____
goods and services that are (produced/sold) during a specified period of time. Economists use money values or market prices to add up the very different types of output that make up GDP. Two of the three exceptions mentioned in Appendix B—government output and inventories—arise because some production is not sold on markets.

The emphasis on *final* goods and services is important, because it avoids double counting of intermediate goods. (The need to avoid double counting is also the key to why the three alternative ways of measuring GDP are conceptually equivalent.) The third part of the definition says that GDP is a statement of production, not sales. It is only production that creates new goods available for consumption or investment. Thus GDP, as a measure of production, is the appropriate measure of how much new consumption or investment our economy can enjoy.

There are three ways to measure GDP. Perhaps the simplest way to measure GDP is to add up the purchases of newly produced final goods and services by private individuals and firms-for consumption and investment—and by the government. For the United States in 1992, this sum of C + I + G + X – IM was estimated to be about $5.7 trillion.

(2)   Net exports are (imports/exports) minus _____. We must add exports to C + I + G because, even though bought by foreigners, exports are American products and GDP is a measure of total U.S. production. We subtract imports because C and I and G are measures of total spending, including spending on imports, and we want a measure that reflects only those goods and services (purchased/produced) in the United States.

All of a firm's sales receipts eventually end up as income for someone, directly in the case of workers, creditors, and firm owners, and indirectly in the case of payments to suppliers, who in turn use this money to pay their workers, creditors, and so forth. Thus, instead of measuring GDP as purchases of final goods and services, we could equivalently add up all incomes earned in the production of goods and services. This sum of factor
(3) incomes is also called national _____ and is the second way to

measure GDP. It is conceptually similar to GDP but differs for U.S. national income accounts because of three items. Indirect business taxes are included in market prices paid by consumers but (do/do not) result in income for any factor of production as they are immediately collected by the government. National income plus indirect business taxes is equal to NDP or _____ _____ product, which is almost, but not quite, equal to GDP. Adjusting for income that Americans receive for working abroad and for income that foreigners receive while working in the United States gives us net domestic income. The difference between NDP and GDP is _____ and, conceptually, refers to the portion of current total production that is used to replace those parts of the capital stock that have deteriorated as a result of current production. If GDP were all one edible good, we could eat NDP while maintaining our productive capacity. Eating GDP would reduce our productive capacity as we would not be replacing worn-out plants and machines.

To measure GDP as the money value of final goods and services, one would start by collecting sales data for final goods. The second way of measuring GDP, total factor incomes, would start with the collection of income data from firms and individuals. The third way of measuring GDP looks at the difference between a firm's sales receipts and its purchases

(4) from other firms. This difference, also called a firm's _____ _____, is the amount of money a firm has to pay the factors of production that it has employed, including the profits firm owners pay themselves. Thus, the sum of total value added in the economy is the third way to measure GDP.

Two other income concepts should be noted. The first, personal income, is just that, income received by persons. As such, starting from national income, we subtract income that is kept by corporations and payroll taxes, that are never received by persons, e.g. social security. We must add transfer payments, as these payments, while not remuneration for work are clearly income for the persons receiving them. Our last income concept, disposable

(5) personal income, is equal to personal income after _____.

In this discussion of national income accounting, the important lesson is the close link between income and production or output, the upper and lower halves of the circular flow diagram.

IMPORTANT TERMS AND CONCEPTS QUIZ

Choose the best definition for the following terms.

1. _____ National income accounting
2. _____ Net domestic product
3. _____ Depreciation
4. _____ Value added

a. Bookkeeping and measurement system for national economic data.

b. Value of an economy's capital used up during a year.

c. Revenue from sale of product minus amount paid for goods and services purchased from other firms.

d. Loss on value of business assets from inflation.

e. GDP minus depreciation.

BASIC EXERCISES

These problems are designed to give you practice in understanding alternative ways of measuring GDP.

1. Consider the following two-firm economy. Firm A is a mining company that does not make purchases from firm B. Firm A sells all its output to firm B, which in turn sells all its output to consumers.

	Firm A	Firm B
Total sales	$500	$1,700
Wages	400	800
Profits	100	400
Purchases from other firms	0	500

   a. What are the total sales for the economy? $_____

   b. What is the total value of sales for final uses? $_____

   c. What is the total of all factor incomes? $_____

   d. What is value added for firm A? $_____

   e. What is value added for firm B? $_____

   f. What is the total value added of both firms? $_____

   g. What is GDP? $_____

   h. What is national income? $_____

2. Table 7-3 contains information on a three-firm economy. Firm A sells only to other firms. Firm B has both an industrial and a household division. Firm C sells only to final consumers. Note also that production by firm C was greater than sales, thus the entry showing the addition to inventories. Simple addition shows that the sum of factor incomes, in this case wages and profits, is equal to $4,700. Answer the following questions to see if the two other ways of measuring GDP give the same answer. The tricky part of this question is the treatment of production that has not been sold, but added to inventories. You may want to review the discussion of inventories in Appendix B before answering the following questions.

   a. Calculate value added for each firm and the sum of value added for all firms.

     Value Added, firm A   _____

     Value Added, firm B   _____

     Value Added, firm C   _____

     Sum   _____

TABLE 7-3

	Firm A	Firm B	Firm C
TOTAL SALES	$1,000	$2,500	$3,000
Sales to firm B	$400		
Sales to firm C	$600	$1,000	
Sales to consumers		$1,500	$3,000
Change in inventories			$200
Wages	$750	$1,800	$1,200
Profits	$250	$300	$400

b. GDP is defined as the production of newly produced final goods and services. It is typically calculated by summing sales of newly produced final goods and services. Calculate sales for final use for each firm and the sum for all firms.

Sales for final use, firm A   _____

Sales for final use, firm B   _____

Sales for final use, firm C   _____

Sum   _____

SELF-TESTS FOR UNDERSTANDING

Test A

Circle the most appropriate answers.

1. GDP is
   a. the sum of all sales in the economy.
   b. the sum of all purchases in the economy.
   c. the sum of money value of all newly produced final goods and services produced during a year.
   d. equal to $C + I + G + X + IM$.

2. Conceptually, GDP can be measured by all but which one of the following:
   a. Add up all factor payments by firms in the economy.
   b. Add up all purchases of final goods and services, $C + I + G + (X - IM)$.
   c. Add up total sales of all firms in the economy.
   d. Add up value added for all firms in the economy.

3. When measuring GDP, money values are for the most part determined by
   a. the cost of production.
   b. market prices.
   c. estimates prepared by national income accountants who work for the U.S. Commerce Department.
   d. banks and eastern money interests.

4. Which of the following is not valued at market prices when computing GDP?
   a. Imports.
   b. Investment.
   c. Government output.
   d. Exports.

5. Which of the following would add to this year's GDP?
   a. Jim purchases a new copy of the Baumol Blinder textbook for this course.
   b. Jill purchases a used copy of the Baumol Blinder textbook for this course.
   c. Susan purchases 100 shares of GM stock.
   d. Steve sells his three year old car.

6. Which of the following transactions represents the sale of a final good as opposed to sale of an intermediate good?
   a. Farmer Jones sells her peaches to the Good Food Packing and Canning Company.
   b. Good Food sells a load of canned peaches to Smith Brothers Distributors.
   c. Smith Brothers sells the load of canned peaches to Irving's Supermarket.
   d. You buy a can of peaches at Irving's.

7. Which of the following events results in an addition to gross private domestic investment?
   a. Managers of the Good Earth, a newly formed food co-op, buy a used refrigerator case for their store.
   b. Sony's office in Tokyo buys a new IBM computer.
   c. The U.S. Air Force purchases a new plane for the president.
   d. United Airlines purchases 20 new planes so it can expand its service.

8. Gross private domestic investment includes all but which one of the following?
   a. The new home purchased by Kimberly and Jason.
   b. The new Japanese computer purchased by Acme Manufacturing to automate their production line.
   c. The increase in the inventory of newly produced but unsold cars.
   d. The construction of a new plant to manufacture micro computers for IBM.

9. When measuring GDP, government purchases include all but which one of the following:
   a. Salaries paid to members of Congress.
   b. Newly produced red tape purchased by government agencies.
   c. Social security payments to older Americans.
   d. Concrete for new highway construction.

10. If net exports are negative it means that
    a. the national income accountant made a mistake.
    b. exports are greater than imports.
    c. Americans are consuming too many foreign goods.
    d. imports are greater than exports.

11. Which accounts for the largest proportion of national income?
    a. Profits.
    b. Employee compensation.
    c. Rents.
    d. Interest.

12. In the national income accounts, transfer payments are
    a. counted twice, once as part of government purchases and again when spent by consumers.
    b. counted as part of government purchases.
    c. included in personal and disposable income.
    d. not included anywhere.

13. The difference between personal income and disposable personal income is given by
    a. depreciation.
    b. personal income taxes.
    c. social security taxes.
    d. government transfer payments.

14. Which of the following is not part of the difference between GDP and national income?
    a. Depreciation.
    b. Indirect business taxes.
    c. Transfer payments from the government.
    d. Income earned by Americans working abroad.

15. Depreciation explains the difference between
    a. GDP and NDP.
    b. NDP and National Income.
    c. National Income and Personal Income.

16. Value added by a single firm is measured as total sales revenue
    a. minus factor payments.
    b. plus indirect business taxes.
    c. plus depreciation.
    d. minus the purchase of intermediate goods.

17. An increase in government transfer payments to individuals will lead to an initial increase in which one of the following?
    a. GDP.
    b. NDP.
    c. Government purchases of goods and services.
    d. Disposable income.

18. In measuring GDP, government outputs are
    a. appropriately valued at zero.
    b. valued by estimates of their market prices.
    c. valued at the cost of inputs needed to produce them.

19. If net domestic product equals $5 trillion and indirect business taxes are $300 billion, then national income would equal
    a. $5.3 trillion.
    b. $5 trillion.
    c. $4.7 trillion.
    d. Insufficient information to determine national income.

20. NDP is
    a. always greater than GDP.
    b. considered by many economists to be a more meaningful measure of the nation's economic output than is GDP.
    c. conceptually superior to GDP because it excludes the output of environmental "bads."
    d. measured by subtracting indirect business taxes from GDP.

Test B

Circle T or F for true or false.

T F 1. GDP is designed to be a measure of economic well-being, not a measure of economic production.

T F 2. If you measured GDP by adding up total sales in the economy, you would be double or triple counting many intermediate goods.

T F 3. Production that is not sold but is instead added to inventories is not counted in GDP.

T F 4. If GM started its own steel company rather than continuing to buy steel from independent steel companies, GDP would be lower because intrafirm transfers are not part of GDP but all interfirm sales are.

T F 5. Since the output of government agencies is not sold on markets, it is not included in GDP.

T F 6. Value added is the difference between what a firm sells its output for and the cost of its own purchases from other firms.

T F 7. The difference between GDP and NDP is net exports.

T F 8. Disposable income is usually greater than net NDP.

T F 9. Corporate profits are the largest component of national income.

T F 10. The sum of value added for all firms in the economy is equal to the sum of all factor incomes—wages, interest, rents, and profits.

SUPPLEMENTARY EXERCISE

1. Consider the following nonlinear, consumption function.

$$C = 100 \sqrt{DI}.$$

Restricting yourself to positive values for disposable income, graph this function. What happens to MPC as income increases? Can you find an explicit expression for MPC as a function of income? (A knowledge of simple calculus will be helpful.) Use this new consumption function to re-answer Basic Exercise question 2 about income redistribution. Does your answer change? If so, why?

What is the savings function that goes with this consumption function? Does MPC + MPS = 1? Does APC + APS = 1?

STUDY QUESTIONS

1. What are the four major components of GDP? (Why are imports subtracted when everything else is added?)
2. What is the difference between national income and disposable income?
3. How is MPC different from the proportion of disposable income that is spent on consumption?
4. MPC can be represented by what part of the consumption function?
5. Why would a change in the price level or in expected future incomes lead to shift in the consumption function rather than a movement along the function?
6. If planning a reduction in income taxes to increase consumption spending by $200 billion, what difference would it make if MPC were 0.75 or 0.90? Would you expect any differences if the reduction in taxes were to be permanent or temporary? Why?
7. Why is knowledge of the consumption function sufficient for one to be able to describe the savings function for an economy?
8. What are the different ways one can measure GDP?
9. Economists often use national income or GDP interchangeably as a measure of the level of aggregate economic activity. What is the difference between national income and GDP?

ECONOMICS IN ACTION

Do Tax Incentives Increase Savings?

During the 1980s a number of specialized programs to increase household savings were introduced. One of the most controversial was the Individual Retirement Account or IRA. Under rules adopted in 1981, all employees could make a tax-deductible $2,000 contribution to an IRA. Previously, IRAs had been limited to individuals without an employer-provided pension plan. Not only did the contribution reduce one's immediate taxable income by $2,000 but interest earnings on IRAs were tax free until the time of withdrawal.[1] In exchange for these advantages, withdrawals before the age of 59-1/2 were subject to substantial tax penalties. Since regular savings can only be done with after-tax, not pre-tax, dollars and the interest earnings of regular savings are taxed on a year by year basis, IRAs offered taxpayers significant advantages and were heavily promoted by banks and other financial institutions. It was hoped that IRAs would lead to a significant increase in household savings.

Why were IRA accounts controversial? There were several reasons. For one, the advantages of an IRA depended upon one's marginal tax rate. An IRA postponed rather than reduced taxes, but being able to use that money until taxes were due could offer a significant benefit, especially to wealthy taxpayers with high marginal tax rates. For example, a $2,000 IRA contribution in 1982 by the wealthiest taxpayers reduced 1982 income taxes by $1,000, while the same contribution by a low-income family would have reduced 1982 taxes by only $220. A second area of controversy was whether IRAs would actually increase savings or only lead households to change the way they saved. That is, were people being given tax breaks for doing what they would have done anyway or would people save more? A related concern was that the money for opening an IRA could come from an existing, taxable savings account. If so, there might be only a shuffling of financial assets for tax advantages rather than any increase in savings. These concerns plus the continuing decline in personal savings as a proportion of disposable income led Congress to restructure and limit the tax advantages of IRAs in 1986.

What does the evidence show about the effectiveness of IRAs? Work by economists Harvey Galper and Charles Byce showed that wealthier taxpayers were more likely to make an IRA contribution and were more likely to make the largest possible contribution. At the same time, a substantial proportion of moderate-income taxpayers making IRA contributions were making the maximum possible contribution. In a series of papers, economists Steven Venti and David Wise used detailed microeconomic data to examine the savings behavior of individual households. They found a great deal of variability. Some households are thrifty while others appear to be spendthrifts. With regard to IRAs, Venti and Wise found that by 1985 two-thirds of IRAs were held by families with incomes less than $50,000. Venti and Wise also considered whether IRAs increased savings. They found little evidence of asset or saving switching and concluded that the introduction of IRAs resulted in a net increase in saving. Venti and Wise argue that the restrictions on IRAs, and the special feelings many people have about retirement savings made them poor substitutes for other forms of savings.

1. Should the United States use expanded tax incentives to induce households to increase their own savings? If so, how would should such a program be structured? How does your program provide incentives for new savings and not just an advantage for asset adjustments in pursuit of tax advantages?

---

[1]Each wage earner could contribute up to $2,000. There was also a provision for a $250 contribution for a non-working spouse. Taxes on the $2,000 contribution and accumulated interest earnings would be due at the time of withdrawal.
SOURCES: Galper, Harvey, and Charles Byce, "IRAs: Facts and Figures," *Tax Notes*, June 2, 1986.
 Venti, Steven F., and David A. Wise, "Government Policy and Personal Retirement Saving," in *Tax Policy and the Economy*, 6, (National Bureau of Economic Research, MIT Press, 1992) pp. 1-41.

Chapter **8**

Demand-Side Equilibrium: Unemployment or Inflation?

LEARNING OBJECTIVES

After completing this chapter you should be able to:

♦ describe some of the major determinants of investment spending by firms and explain which of these determinants can be directly affected by government action.

♦ describe how income and prices, both American and foreign, affect exports and imports.

♦ draw an expenditure schedule, given information about consumption spending, investment spending, and net exports.

♦ determine the equilibrium level of income and explain why the level of income tends toward its equilibrium value.

♦ describe how a change in the price level affects the expenditure schedule and the equilibrium level of income.

♦ describe how the impact of a change in prices on the expenditure schedule and the equilibrium level of income can be used to derive the aggregate demand curve.

♦ explain why equilibrium GDP can be above or below the full employment level of GDP.

IMPORTANT TERMS AND CONCEPTS

Investment tax credit
Equilibrium level of GDP
Expenditure schedule
Induced investment
$Y = C + I + G + (X - IM)$
Income–expenditure (or 45–degree line) diagram
Aggregate demand curve
Full-employment level of GDP (or potential GDP)
Recessionary gap
Inflationary gap
Coordination of saving and investment

CHAPTER REVIEW

This chapter is the introduction to explicit models of income determination. The model discussed in this chapter is relatively simple and is not meant to be taken literally. Do not be put off by the simplicity of the model or its lack of realism. Careful study now will pay future dividends in terms of easier understanding of later chapters, in which both the mechanics and policy implications of more complicated models are described,

The central focus of this chapter is on the concept of the *equilibrium level of income and output*. (You may want to review the material in Chapter 7 on the equality of national income and national output.) The models discussed in this chapter show us how spending decisions are reconciled with production decisions of firms to determine the equilibrium level of GDP.

When considering the determination of the equilibrium level of GDP, it is important to distinguish between output and income on the one hand and total spending on the other hand. If total spending exceeds current production, firms will find that their inventories are **(1)** decreasing. They are then likely to take steps to (decrease/increase) production and output. Analogously, if total spending is less than current output, firms are likely to find their inventories _____, and they are likely to take steps to _____ production.

The concept of equilibrium refers to a situation in which producers and consumers are satisfied with things the way they are and see no reason to change their behavior. Thus the equilibrium level of GDP must be a level of GDP at which firms have no reason to increase or decrease output; that is, at the equilibrium level of GDP, total spending and output will be equal. The determination of the equilibrium level of output thus reduces to

    1. describing how total spending changes as output (and income) changes, and
    2. finding the one level of output (and income) at which total spending equals output.

In the simplified model discussed in this chapter, there are three components to total spending: consumption, investment, and net exports. Chapter 7 discussed the important role that income plays as a determinant of consumption expenditures. There is no such central factor influencing investment expenditures. Instead, investment expenditures are influenced by a variety of factors, including business people's expectations about the future, the rate of growth of demand as measured against existing capacity, technology and product innovation, interest rates, and tax factors. If any of these factors change, investment spending is likely to change.

(2)   Net exports are the difference between exports and imports, specifically _____ minus _____. Exports reflect foreign demand for American production and imports come from American demand for foreign goods and services. It should not be surprising that both are influenced by income and prices. The tricky part is keeping straight whose income influences which demand and how changes in American and foreign prices influence net exports.

     The income-expenditure diagram is a useful tool for analyzing the determination of the equilibrium level of output. To find the equilibrium level of output and income we need to know how total spending changes as income and output change, and we need to know where total spending equals income. The relationship between total spending, $C + I + G + (X - IM)$, and income is given by the *expenditure schedule*. The 45-degree line shows all combinations of spending and income that are equal. The one place where spending is equal to

(3) income is given by the _____ of the expenditure schedule and the 45–degree line. This is the equilibrium level of output because it is the only level of output where total spending is equal to output. At any other level of output, total spending will not be equal to output. (You should be sure that you understand why the economy tends to move to the equilibrium level of output rather than getting stuck at a level of income and output at which total spending is either larger or smaller than output. Consider what happens to business inventories when spending is greater or less than output. Do not get confused between this automatic tendency to move to the equilibrium level of output and the lack, sometimes, of an automatic mechanism to ensure full employment.)

     Any particular expenditure schedule relates total spending to income for a given level of prices. If prices change, total spending will change, even for the same level of real income.

(4) In particular, a higher price level is apt to mean (more/less) consumption spending because of the decline in the purchasing power of the money assets of consumers. This effect of prices on consumption will lead to a (downward/upward) shift in the expenditure schedule and a new equilibrium of income that is (higher/lower) than before. In the opposite case, a lower price level would mean _____ consumption spending and a new, (higher/lower) equilibrium level of income. The relationship between the price level and the equilibrium level of income on the income–expenditure diagram is called the *aggregate demand curve*. As our model of income determination becomes more realistic we will see that a change in the price level affects more than consumption spending. The simplified introductory model of this chapter is sufficient to illustrate the principle behind deriving the aggregate demand curve.

The aggregate demand curve is derived from the income–expenditure diagram and, from the viewpoint of demand, shows how the equilibrium level of income changes when

(5) the _____ _____ changes. The qualifier "from the viewpoint of demand" is important. Complete determination of the equilibrium level of income/output and the equilibrium price level comes from the interaction of the aggregate demand and aggregate supply curves.

In Chapter 10 we will see how equilibrium depends upon aggregate demand and aggregate supply. At this point we are considering only the demand side of the economy. Nothing that has been said so far implies that, with regard to demand, the equilibrium level of output must equal the full-employment level of output. It may be larger or it may be smaller. It all depends upon the strength of aggregate demand. Appendix A shows how statements about the strength of aggregate demand relative to the full-employment level of output have an alternative and equivalent interpretation in terms of the amount of savings or leakages that would occur at full-employment relative to the strength of investment demand or injections at full-employment. If the equilibrium level of output exceeds the full-

(6) employment level of output, the difference is called the _____ gap. In a case where the equilibrium level of output is less than the full-employment level of output, the difference is called the _____ gap.

IMPORTANT TERMS AND CONCEPTS QUIZ

Choose the best definition for the following terms.

1. _____ Investment tax credit
2. _____ Equilibrium level of GDP
3. _____ Expenditure schedule
4. _____ Induced investment
5. _____ Income-expenditure diagram
6. _____ Aggregate demand curve
7. _____ Recessionary gap
8. _____ Inflationary gap
9. _____ Potential GDP

a. Graph of quantity of national product demanded at each possible price level.
b. Line showing relationship between GDP and total spending.
c. Full-employment level of GDP.
d. Reduction in tax liability proportional to business investment spending.
e. Amount by which GDP exceeds full-employment GDP.
f. Level of output where aggregate demand equals total production.
g. Investment spending that changes with changes in GDP.
h. Table or graph showing how saving depends on consumption.
i. Amount by which full-employment GDP exceeds GDP.
j. Two variable graph that allows plotting of total real expenditures against real income.

BASIC EXERCISES

These exercises are designed to give you practice with manipulations on the income–expenditure diagram. They are based on data for income (output), consumption spending, investment spending, and net exports given in Table 8-1.

1. This exercise shows you how the expenditure schedule is derived and how it helps to determine the equilibrium level of income. For this exercise it is assumed that prices are constant with the price level having a value of 100.

   a. Use the data on consumption spending and income to show how consumption spending varies with income in Figure 8-1.

   b. Add investment spending to the line drawn in Figure 8-1 to show how consumption plus investment spending vary with income.

   c. Now draw the expenditure schedule, $C + I + G + (X - IM)$ in Figure 8-1.

   d. Next, draw a line representing all the points where total spending and income could be equal. (This is the 45–degree line. Do you know why?)

   e. The 45–degree line represents all the points that *could be* the equilibrium level of income. Now circle the one point that *is* the equilibrium level of income. What is the equilibrium level of income on your graph?

FIGURE 8-1

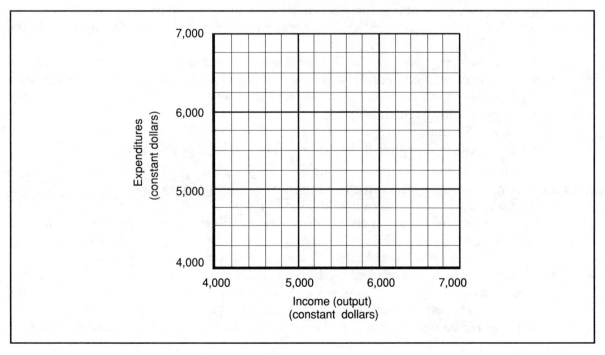

TABLE 8-1

Income (Output) Y	Taxes T	Disposable Income DI	Consumption Spending C	Investment Spending I	Government Purchases G	Exports X	Imports IM	Total Spending
5,600	700	4,900	4,300	900	800	500	600	_____
5,800	700	5,100	4,400	900	800	500	600	_____
6,000	700	5,300	4,500	900	800	500	600	_____
6,200	700	5,500	4,600	900	800	500	600	_____
6,400	700	5,700	4,700	900	800	500	600	_____
6,600	700	5,900	4,800	900	800	500	600	_____

    f. Check your answer by filling in the Total Spending column in Table 8-1 to see where total spending equals income. You should get the same answer from Table 8-1 as you do from the graph.

    g. Why isn't the equilibrium level of output $5,800 billion? If for some reason national output and income started out at $5,800 billion, what forces would tend to move the economy toward the equilibrium you determined in Questions e and f?

    h. Using the data in Table 8-1 and assuming that the full-employment level of output income is $6,000 billion, is there an inflationary or recessionary gap? How large is the gap? If the full-employment level of income were $6,500 billion, how large would the inflationary or recessionary gap be?

    i. Assume now that an increase in business confidence leads to an increased level of investment spending. Specifically, assume that investment spending rises to $1,000 billion at all levels of national income. As a result of this shift, what happens to each of the following?
- The expenditure schedule.
- The equilibrium level of income.
- Consumption spending at the new equilibrium level of income.

2. This exercise explores the implications of changes in the price level. It is designed to show how a change in the price level implies a shift in the expenditure schedule and can be used to derive the aggregate demand curve.

    a. The data in Table 8-1 assumed that prices were constant with the price level at a value of 100. Mark the point in Figure 8-2 that shows the price level of 100 and the equilibrium level of income you found when answering questions e and f of Exercise 1.

    b. Economic research has determined that if prices rose to 110, consumption spending would decline by $100 billion at every level of real income. Table 8-2 shows the relevant information. Each entry in the column for a price level of 110 should be 100 less than the values you calculated for total spending in question 1.f. What is the new

FIGURE 8-2

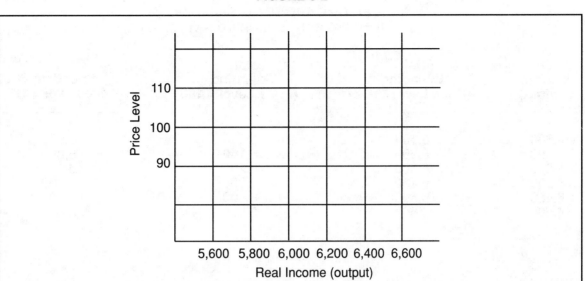

TABLE 8-2

Real Income (Output)	Total Spending (Price Level = 90)	Total Spending (Price Level = 110)
5,600	6,000	5,800
5,800	6,100	5,900
6,000	6,200	6,000
6,200	6,300	6,100
6,400	6,400	6,200
6,600	6,500	6,300

equilibrium level of income on the income-expenditure diagram with this higher price level? Mark the point in Figure 8-2 that show the price level of 110 and this new equilibrium level of income.

c. This same research determined that if prices fell to 90, real consumption spending would increase over amounts shown in Table 8-1 by $100 billion at every level of real income. What is the new equilibrium level of income on the income–expenditure diagram for this lower price level? Mark the point in Figure 8-2 that shows the price level of 90 and his new equilibrium level of income.

d. The points you have marked in Figure 8-2 help to trace what curve?

e. Connect these points to verify that your curve has a (<u>negative/positive</u>) slope.

TABLE 8-3
REAL INCOME AND TOTAL SPENDING
WHEN INVESTMENT SPENDING = $1,000

Real Income (Output)	Total Spending (Price Level = 90)	Total Spending (Price Level = 100)	Total Spending (Price Level = 110)
5,600	6,100	6,000	5,900
5,800	6,200	6,100	6,000
6,000	6,300	6,200	6,100
6,200	6,400	6,300	6,200
6,400	6,500	6,400	6,300
6,600	6,600	6,500	6,400

3. Question 1.i. asked you to consider the impact of an increase in investment spending. We saw then that an increase in investment spending shifts the expenditure schedule and leads to a new equilibrium on the income–expenditure diagram. What about the aggregate demand curve? Assume that the increase in business confidence means that investment spending rises to $1,000 regardless of the level of income or the price level. Table 8-3 contains information on total spending that includes the increase in investment spending. Use this information to plot the aggregate demand curve in Figure 8-2 following the increase in investment spending. How does this curve compare to the one you derived in question 2?

SELF-TESTS FOR UNDERSTANDING

Test A

Circle the most appropriate answer.

1. Government policies can directly affect all but which one of the following determinants of investment spending?
   a. Interest rates.
   b. The state of business confidence.
   c. Tax incentives.
   d. The overall state of aggregate demand.

2. The demand for imports into the United States is affected by all but which one of the following?
   a. American GDP
   b. American prices
   c. Foreign GDP
   d. Foreign prices

3. The demand for American exports is affected by all but which one of the following?
   a. American GDP
   b. American prices
   c. Foreign GDP
   d. Foreign prices

4. On balance, net exports are likely to _____ when domestic income increases.
   a. decrease
   b. remain unchanged
   c. increase

5. Of production, income and spending, _____ and _____ are always equal while _____ equals the other two only in equilibrium.
   a. spending and income; production
   b. production and spending; income
   c. income and production; spending

6. The expenditure schedule is a relationship between
   a. the equilibrium level of income and prices.
   b. consumption spending and income.
   c. total spending and income.
   d. consumption spending and prices.

7. The expenditure schedule is derived by showing how which of the following vary with income? (There may be more than one correct answer.)
   a. C - consumption
   b. Dl - disposable income
   c. G - government purchases
   d. I   - investment spending
   e. IM - imports
   f. T - taxes
   g. X - exports
   h. Y - GDP

8. If investment spending increased at all levels of income, the expenditure schedule would _____.
   a. shift down
   b. show no change
   c. shift up

9. An increase in the demand for exports will cause
    a. the expenditure schedule to shift up.
    b. no change in the expenditure schedule.
    c. the expenditure schedule to shift down.

10. A reduction in purchases of goods and services by the government will cause
    a. the expenditure schedule to shift up.
    b. no change in the expenditure schedule.
    c. the expenditure schedule to shift down.

11. In the income–expenditure diagram, the equilibrium level of output is given by the intersection of the expenditure schedule and the
    a. consumption function.
    b. aggregate demand curve.
    c. 45–degree line.
    d. level of full-employment output.

12. When total spending is less than output
    a. inventories are likely to be increasing.
    b. inventories are likely to be decreasing.
    c. there will be a shift in the expenditure schedule.
    d. firms are likely to raise prices.

13. From an initial position of equilibrium, consider an increase in investment spending that shifts the expenditure schedule up. If there were no change in the level of output, what would happen to inventories?
    a. Inventories would increase.
    b. Inventories would decrease.
    c. Inventories would not be affected.

14. When total spending is equal to output,
    a. the resulting level of output is called the full-employment level of output.
    b. the level of income is given by the intersection of the expenditure schedule and the 45–degree line.
    c. there is never an inflationary gap.
    d. the expenditure schedule and the aggregate demand curve coincide.

15. At the equilibrium level of income which one of the following is not necessarily true?
    a. The expenditure schedule will intersect the 45–degree line.
    b. There will be no unexpected changes in business inventories.
    c. There will be no unemployment.
    d. The equilibrium level of output and the price level will together determine one point on the aggregate demand curve.

16. If, at the full-employment level of income, consumers' savings plans are equal to firms' investment plans, then
    a. the equilibrium level of income will be equal to the full-employment level of income.
    b. there will be an inflationary gap.
    c. firms will find their inventories increasing.
    d. the economy will be producing less than potential output.

17. There is a recessionary gap when the equilibrium level of income
    a. is less than potential GDP.
    b. equal to the full-employment level of GDP.
    c. is greater than potential GDP.
    d. imports exceed exports.

18. A lower price level will _____ the equilibrium level of income on the income-expenditure diagram.
    a. decrease
    b. not affect
    c. increase

19. The aggregate demand curve is a relationship between the price level and
    a. consumption spending.
    b. the equilibrium level of income on the income-expenditure diagram.
    c. full-employment GDP.
    d. the interest rate.

20. A lower price level will lead to which of the following? (There may be more than one correct answer.)
    a. An increase in exports.
    b. A shift in the consumption function.
    c. A shift in the expenditure schedule.
    d. A shift in the aggregate demand curve.

Test B

Circle T or F for true or false.

T F 1. It is an easy task for government policymakers to influence the state of business confidence.

T F 2. The expenditure schedule refers to a relationship between total spending and the level of output (and income).

T F 3. The equilibrium level of GDP never equals the full-employment level of GDP.

T F 4. If total spending exceeds national output, the resulting decrease in inventories will lead firms to reduce the level of output and production.

T F 5. The intersection of the expenditure schedule and the 45–degree line determines one point on the aggregate demand curve.

T F   6.   The vertical difference between the 45–degree line and the aggregate demand curve is called the inflationary gap.

T F   7.   The term recessionary gap refers to a situation in which the equilibrium level of GDP is less than the full-employment level of GDP.

T F   8.   Because consumers usually invest their savings at financial institutions, there can be no difference between desired savings and desired investment for the economy.

T F   9.   An increase in the level of prices, through its impact on consumption spending and net exports, will lead to a movement along the expenditure schedule.

T F 10.   The aggregate demand curve refers to a relationship between the equilibrium level of income and the price level.

Appendix A: The "Leakages" and "Injections" Approach

LEARNING OBJECTIVES

The exercise below is intended to illustrate the basic content of Appendix A to Chapter 8: *The condition for the equilibrium level of income can be stated as $Y = C + I + G + (X - IM)$ or it can be stated as $S + T + IM = I + G + X$.* Both statements lead to the same result.

IMPORTANT TERMS AND CONCEPTS

$S + T + IM = I + G + X$
Saving schedule
Leakages schedule
Injections schedule
Induced investment

BASIC EXERCISE

Table 8-4 reproduces some data from Table 8-1.

1. Using the definition of saving, $S = DI - C$, determine the level of consumer saving at each level of national income.

2. At what level of income is the sum of injections, $I + G + X$, equal to the sum of leakages, $S + T + IM$? How does this level of income compare with the equilibrium level of income you computed in question e of the first Basic Exercise to this chapter?

---

3. Just as tabular results on spending have a graphical representation in the income–expenditure diagram, there is a graphical representation of the leakages and injections formulation. Use the data from Table 8-4 to draw schedules for leakages and injections in Figure 8-3. Using Figure 8-3, equilibrium is determined by_____

_____

_____

What is the equilibrium level of income in Figure 8-3? _____.

TABLE 8-4
(PRICE LEVEL = 100)

Income (Output) Y	Savings S	Taxes T	Imports IM	Total Leakages	Investment Spending I	Government Purchases G	Exports X	Total Injections
5,600	_____	700	600	_____	900	800	500	2,200
5,800	_____	700	600	_____	900	800	500	2,200
6,000	_____	700	600	_____	900	800	500	2,200
6,200	_____	700	600	_____	900	800	500	2,200
6,400	_____	700	600	_____	900	800	500	2,200
6,600	_____	700	600	_____	900	800	500	2,200

FIGURE 8-3

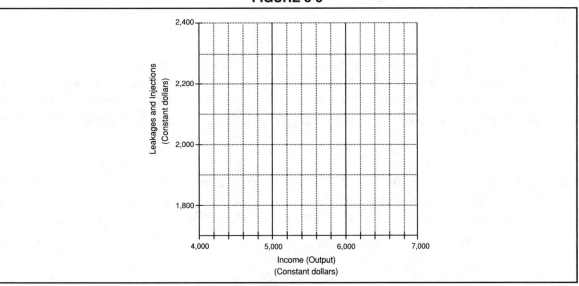

132

TABLE 8-5

	Expenditure Schedule	Leakages Schedule	Injections Schedule
Investment spending increases with income	_____	_____	_____
Imports increase with income	_____	_____	_____

4. In this example, only savings varied with income. What would happen if investment, imports or taxes varied with income? There would be no change in the principle that is used to determine the equilibrium level of income. In the income-expenditure diagram, the equilibrium level of income is determined by the intersection of the expenditure schedule and the 45–degree line. In the diagram of leakages and injections, equilibrium is the level of income leakages equal injections. The difference is that the expenditure schedule, the schedule for leakages, or the schedule for injections may be steeper or flatter. Complete Table 8-5 by indicating whether various schedules get steeper, flatter or show no change. Be sure you can explain why in each case. (Government purchases and taxes will be discussed in Chapter 11. Why doesn't it make sense to think of exports varying with income?)

5. We can also show the equivalence of the leakage/injection approach using a little high school algebra. Equilibrium on the income–expenditure diagram is the one level of national income where

$$Y = C + I + G + (X - IM).$$

In this economy the only difference between national income (Y) and disposable income (DI) is taxes. Represented symbolically: $Y = T + DI$. We also know that consumers either spend or save their income, that is $DI = C + S$. Using this last expression for disposable income we can rewrite our expression for Y as $Y = T + C + S$. Substituting this expression for national income into the equation for equilibrium gives

$$T + C + S = C + I + G + (X - IM)$$

Subtracting C from both sides of this expression, putting all the leakages on the left side of the equal sign, and putting all of the injections on the right side, yields our alternative but equivalent formulation of the equilibrium condition, or

$$\_\_\_\_ + \_\_\_\_ + \_\_\_\_ = \_\_\_\_ + \_\_\_\_ + \_\_\_\_$$

Appendix B: The Simple Algebra of Income Determination

BASIC EXERCISE

This exercise is meant to illustrate the material in Appendix B to Chapter 8. If we are willing to use algebra we can use equations rather than graphs or tables to determine the equilibrium level of output. If we have done all our work accurately, we should get the same answer regardless of whether we use graphs, tables, or algebra.

The following equations are consistent with the numbers in Table 8-1

1) $C = 1850 + .5\, DI$
2) $DI = Y - T$
3) $T = 700$
4) $I = 900$
5) $G = 800$
6) $X = 500$
7) $IM = 600$
8) $Y = C + I + G + (X - IM)$

1. Equation 1 is the consumption function. It shows how consumption spending changes with changes in disposable income. To derive the expenditure schedule we need to figure out how spending changes with changes in national income. Start by substituting equations 2 and 3 for disposable income and taxes into equation 1 to see how C varies with Y.

$1850 + .5(Y-700)$

9) $C = \underline{\qquad 1475 \qquad} + \underline{\qquad .5 \qquad} Y.$

2. Now use equation 9, along with equations, 4, 5, 6 and 7 to show how total spending varies with Y.

10) $C + I + G + (X - IM) = \underline{\qquad\qquad} + \underline{\qquad} Y.$

3. To find the one level of income where spending equals output (and income) substitute the right-hand side of equation 10 for the right-hand side of equation 8 and solve for the equilibrium level of Y.

$Y = \underline{\qquad\qquad\qquad}$

Equation 10 is the expenditure schedule. Equation 8 is the 45–degree line. Substituting the right-hand side of equation 10 for the right hand side of equation is the algebraic way of finding the intersection of these two lines.

ECONOMICS IN ACTIONS

Military Spending and Aggregate Demand

Some critics on the left argue that America's economic strength is dependent upon large military outlays. These critics point out that the periods of lowest unemployment over the past 50 years were also periods of war—World War II, Korea, and Vietnam. Many also argue that the years of economic expansion under Presidents Reagan and Bush were associated with a substantial increase in defense spending and that unemployment in the early 1990s has been aggravated by defense-related layoffs.

Others are not so sure, arguing that employment will be determined by the level of aggregate demand relative to full employment. Defense spending increases aggregate demand and employment, but so does any other type of spending. While increased military spending has been associated with periods of full employment, this does not mean that only military spending can result in low rates of unemployment. Increases in other types of spending, public or private, also increase employment and lower unemployment. On this view, the historical correlation between defense spending and full employment may really reflect politics not economics. That is, it may be easier to organize the political commitment for high levels of defense spending than for high levels of non-defense spending.

When evaluating these arguments, it is also instructive to look at data. World War II saw the most dramatic increase in defense spending when measured as a proportion of GDP. From about 3 percent in 1940, defense spending climbed to over 40 percent of GDP by 1943. The Korean conflict saw an increase in defense spending from less than 5 percent of GDP to just over 13 percent in two years. The Vietnam increase was substantially smaller, less than 2 percent of GDP. It began after a four year period when both the unemployment rate and defense as a proportion of GDP had been falling. The increase in defense spending under President Reagan actually started in 1979 and was a bit smaller than the Vietnam increase. Furthermore, as in the immediate pre-Vietnam period, the unemployment rate continued to decline even after the growth in defense budgets stopped. From 1987 to 1989, the unemployment rate declined from 6.1 percent to 5.2 percent as real defense spending declined by 4 percent.

To argue that full employment is not dependent upon high levels of defense spending does not imply that changes in defense spending will not affect aggregate demand and employment. In the absence of offsetting changes increases in defense spending would add to aggregate demand while decreases would subtract. The closing of a military base and the termination of defense contracts will typically have an immediate and significant impact on particular communities and states. A number of observers have argued that planned reductions in military spending should be accompanied by special government financed adjustment assistant for the individuals and communities suddenly without jobs. Others would argue that jobs losses from defense cutbacks should be treated no differently than job losses from any other cause. That is, individuals and communities should be eligible for the same assistance they would receive for any job loss but should not receive special treatment.

1. Are concerns about full employment an appropriate argument in support of high levels of defense spending?
2. Reductions in defense spending are sometimes referred to as a "peace dividend." Assuming that planned reductions in defense are realized, what should the federal government do with the peace dividend?
3. Should there be special assistance for individuals and communities who are affected by base closings and the cancellation of military contracts?

You might want to look at the following recent articles about defense conversion:

Jurgen Brauer and John T. Marlin, "Converting Resources from Military to Non-Military Uses," *The Journal of Economic Perspectives*, (Vol. 6, Number 4), Fall 1992, pp. 145-164.

Michelle R. Garfinkel, "The Economic Consequences of Reducing Military Spending," *Review*, Federal Reserve Bank of St. Louis, (Nov./Dec. 1990) pp. 47-58.

STUDY QUESTIONS

1. Why is investment spending so volatile?
2. If one says that investment is a flighty bird does that mean that policy changes by the government will have no impact on investment?
3. "Exports will change with changes in foreign but not domestic income. They will also change if foreign or domestic prices change." How can it be that exports respond to domestic prices but not domestic income?
4. How do imports respond to changes in domestic income, foreign income, domestic prices and foreign prices?
5. The expenditure schedule shows how total spending changes with domestic income. What categories of spending does the expenditure schedule need to include?
6. What would happen to the expenditure schedule if the marginal propensity to consume were larger or smaller? Why?
7. What would happen to the expenditure schedule if there were a change in any of the following: investment spending, government purchases of goods and services, exports or imports?
8. According to the text, equilibrium occurs at the intersection of the expenditure schedule and the 45–degree line. Why there? What prevents points to the left or right of the intersection from also being points of equilibrium?

9. Why do we say the expenditure schedule is drawn for a given level of prices?

10. What happens to the expenditure schedule if prices increase or if they decrease?

11. Plotting different price levels and the corresponding equilibrium level of income from the income–expenditure diagram results in what curve?

C h a p t e r **9**

Changes on the Demand Side: Multiplier Analysis

LEARNING OBJECTIVES

After completing this chapter you should be able to:

- explain why any autonomous increases in expenditures will have a multiplier effect on GDP.

- calculate the value of the multiplier in specific examples.

- explain how and why the value of the multiplier would change if MPC changed.

- explain why the multiplier expression, $1/(1 - MPC)$, is oversimplified.

- explain the difference between an autonomous and an induced increase in consumption expenditures.

- explain how and why economic booms and recessions tend to be transmitted across national boundaries.

- explain why an increase in savings may be good for an individual but bad for the economy as a whole.

- describe how any change in autonomous spending leads to a shift in the aggregate demand curve.

IMPORTANT TERMS AND CONCEPTS

The multiplier
Induced increase in consumption
Autonomous increase in consumption
Paradox of thrift

CHAPTER REVIEW

The main topic of this chapter is the *multiplier*. It is a fundamental concept in economics, which is why a whole chapter is devoted to explaining how it works. The multiplier has already played an important but unheralded role in Chapter 8, so those of you who paid close attention then should have an easier time grasping the concept of multiplier analysis presented here.

(1) The idea of the multiplier is that a change in autonomous spending by one sector of the economy will change the equilibrium level of income by (more than/the same as/less than) the change in autonomous spending. We have been studying the determination of the equilibrium level of income in the income–expenditure diagram. Multiplier analysis investigates changes in the equilibrium level of income when the expenditure schedule shifts. In this chapter we will be concerned with parallel shifts in the expenditure schedule which are represented graphically as a change in the vertical axis intercept of the expenditure schedule. A parallel shift in the expenditure schedule shows the same change in spending at all levels of income and is thus a change in (autonomous/induced) spending. Spending that changes when income changes, such as the response of consumption spending to a change in income, is called an _____ change.

Multiplier analysis shows that the equilibrium level of GDP changes by a multiple of the change in autonomous spending, which is where the term "multiplier" comes from. The basic reason for this multiplier result is relatively simple: Increased spending by one sector of the economy means increased sales receipts for other sectors of the economy. Higher sales receipts will show up in bigger paychecks, or profits, or both; in short, higher income for some people. These higher incomes will then induce more consumer spending, which in turn will result in still higher incomes and more consumption spending by others, and so on and so on.

You may be wondering at this point whether the multiplier is finite or whether income will increase without limit. Another way of looking at this question is to ask what determines the value of the multiplier. There are several alternative, but equally good, ways of answering this question. In the text the value is determined by summing the increments to spending and income that follow from the original autonomous change in spending. When

consumption is the only induced spending, the oversimplified multiplier expression turns
(2) out to be $1/(1 -$ _____$)$.

Here is an alternative derivation of the same result. We know that in equilibrium
national output, or income, will equal total spending:

$$Y = C + I + G + (X - IM).$$

Now assume that there is an autonomous increase in investment spending which induces subsequent increases in consumption spending. At the new equilibrium, we know
that the change in the equilibrium level of national output must equal the change in total
spending. If net exports and government purchases are the same at all levels of income, the
change in total spending will have two parts. One is the autonomous change in investment
spending and the other is the induced change in consumption spending. We know that

(3)

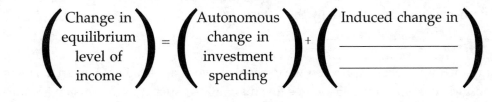

It is possible to represent this symbolically. Let ΔY represent the change in the equilibrium level of income and ΔI represent the autonomous change in investment spending.
What about the induced change in consumption spending? The discussion in Chapter 7 told
(4) us that consumption spending will change as disposable _____ changes.
Further, with the use of the concept of the marginal propensity to consume, we can represent the change in consumption spending as the product of the change in disposable income
multiplied by the _____. When taxes are constant, disposable income
changes dollar for dollar whenever GDP or Y changes. We could represent the induced
change in consumption spending as $\Delta DI \times MPC$. As $\Delta DI = \Delta Y$, the change in consumption
can also be represented as $\Delta Y \times MPC$. If we substitute all these symbols for the words above,
we see that

$$\Delta Y = \Delta I + (\Delta Y \times MPC).$$

We can now solve this equation for the change in income by moving all terms in ΔY to
the left-hand side of the equation:

$$\Delta Y - (\Delta Y \times MPC) = \Delta I.$$

If we factor out the ΔY we can rewrite the expression as

$$\Delta Y (1 - MPC) = \Delta I.$$

We can now solve for ΔY by dividing both sides of the equation by $(1 - MPC)$.

$$\Delta Y = \left(\frac{1}{1 - MPC} \right) \Delta I.$$

Therefore we find that

$$
\begin{pmatrix}
\text{Change in} \\
\text{equilibrium} \\
\text{level of} \\
\text{income}
\end{pmatrix}
= \quad \text{Multiplier} \quad \times \quad
\begin{pmatrix}
\text{Autonomous} \\
\text{change in} \\
\text{investment} \\
\text{spending}
\end{pmatrix}
$$

Would our calculation of the multiplier be any different if we considered a change in net exports or an autonomous change in consumption spending? The Basic Exercises to this chapter are designed to help answer this question.

(5) The multiplier expression we just derived, $1/(1{-}\text{MPC})$, is the same as the one in Chapter 9 the text and is subject to the same limitations[1]. That is, this expression is oversimplified. There are four important reasons why real world multipliers will be (<u>smaller/larger</u>) than our formula. These reasons are related to the effects of _____ _____, _____, _____ taxes, and the _____ system.

(6) The simplified multiplier expression we derived above is applicable when analyzing a shift in the expenditure schedule in the 45–degree line diagram. As such, this expression assumes that prices (<u>do/do not</u>) change. In Chapter 8 we saw that the income–expenditure diagram is only a building-block on the way to the aggregate demand curve. (Remember from Chapter 5 that even the aggregate demand curve is only part of the story. For a complete analysis we need to consider both the aggregate demand and the aggregate _____ curves.) To complete our analysis on the demand side, we need to see how our multiplier analysis affects the aggregate demand curve. The multiplier analysis we have done by using the income–expenditure diagram shows us that if prices are constant, the equilibrium level of income will change following any change in (<u>autonomous/induced</u>) spending. This result is true at all price levels and implies that a shift in the expenditure schedule following a change in autonomous spending leads to a (<u>movement along/shift in</u>) demand curve. In fact, it leads to a (<u>horizontal/vertical</u>) shift in the aggregate demand curve. The magnitude of the shift can be computed with the help of the multiplier, as shown in Figure 9-4 of the text and Figure 10-4 of the study guide.

---

[1]A somewhat more general expression for the multiplier is $1/(1 - \text{slope of the expenditure schedule})$. The multiplier is based on summing the rounds of spending induced by an autonomous increase in spending. In the model of this chapter only consumption spending change as income change. As taxes do not vary with changes in income, every dollar change in national income is also a dollar change in disposable income which induces a change in consumption spending determined by the MPC. In this case consumption spending goes up by MPC for every dollar increase in national income and the slope of the expenditure schedule is equal to the MPC.

IMPORTANT TERMS AND CONCEPTS QUIZ

Choose the best definition for the following terms.

1. _____ Multiplier
2. _____ Induced increase in consumption
3. _____ Autonomous increase in consumption
4. _____ Paradox of thrift

a. Increase in consumer spending due to an increase in disposable income.
b. Attempts to increase savings that cause national income to fall with little net impact on savings.
c. Ratio of change in spending to change in equilibrium GDP.
d. Ratio of change in equilibrium GDP to change in autonomous spending that cause GDP to change.
e. Increase in consumer spending not due to increased incomes.

BASIC EXERCISES

These exercises are designed to illustrate the concepts of the multiplier and the paradox of thrift.

1. **The Multiplier**
   a. Using the data in Table 9-1, fill in the values for total spending and then find the equilibrium level of income.

TABLE 9-1
(CONSTANT PRICES)

Income (Output) Y	Taxes T	Disposable Income DI	Consumption Spending C	Investment Spending I	Government Purchases G	Exports X	Imports IM	Total Spending C + I + G + (X − IM)
5,500	800	4,700	4,100	800	850	500	650	
5,750	800	4,950	4,300	800	850	500	650	
6,000	800	5,200	4,500	800	850	500	650	
6,250	800	5,450	4,700	800	850	500	650	
6,500	800	5,700	4,900	800	850	500	650	
6,750	800	5,950	5,100	800	850	500	650	
7,000	800	6,200	5,300	800	850	500	650	

b. Table 9-2 has a similar set of data except that investment spending has risen by $100 billion. Find the equilibrium level of income after the rise in investment spending.

c. What is the change in the equilibrium level of income following the increase in investment spending? _____

d. What is the value of the multiplier for this increase in autonomous investment spending? _____

(Remember that the multiplier is defined as the ratio of the change in the _____ of _____ divided by the change in _____ that produced the change in income.)

e. Now let us verify that the value of the multiplier that you found in question d is the same as the simplified formula 1/(1 – MPC). To do this we will first need to calculate the MPC for the economy in Table 9-1. Write the value of the MPC here: _____ (If you do not remember how to calculate the MPC, review the material in Chapter 7 of the textbook and in this study guide.)

f. Now calculate the value of the multiplier from the oversimplified formula 1/(1 – MPC). Write your answer here: _____.

g. (Optional) The multiplier can also be calculated as

$$\frac{1}{(1 - \text{slope of the expenditure schedule})}$$

The slope of the expenditure schedule tells us how total spending changes when income changes. Calculate the slope of the expenditure schedule by dividing any of the changes in the last column of Table 9-1 by the corresponding change in income in the first column. What is the slope of the expenditure schedule and how is it related to the multiplier?

TABLE 9-2
(CONSTANT PRICES)

Income (Output) Y	Taxes T	Disposable Income DI	Consumption Spending C	Investment Spending I	Government Purchases G	Exports X	Imports IM	Total Spending C + I + G + (X – IM)
5,500	800	4,700	4,100	900	850	500	650	_____
5,750	800	4,950	4,300	900	850	500	650	_____
6,000	800	5,200	4,500	900	850	500	650	_____
6,250	800	5,450	4,700	900	850	500	650	_____
6,500	800	5,700	4,900	900	850	500	650	_____
6,750	800	5,950	5,100	900	850	500	650	_____
7,000	800	6,200	5,300	900	850	500	650	_____

TABLE 9-3
(CONSTANT PRICES)

Income (Output) Y	Taxes T	Disposable Income DI	Consumption Spending C	Investment Spending I	Government Purchases G	Exports X	Imports IM	Total Spending C + I + G + (X − IM)
5,500	800	4,700	4,100	900	850	600	650	_____
5,750	800	4,950	4,300	900	850	600	650	_____
6,000	800	5,200	4,500	900	850	600	650	_____
6,250	800	5,450	4,700	900	850	600	650	_____
6,500	800	5,700	4,900	900	850	600	650	_____
6,750	800	5,950	5,100	900	850	600	650	_____
7,000	800	6,200	5,300	900	850	600	650	_____

2. International Trade

Assume that an increase in income abroad has increased the demand for exports by $100 billion. Table 9-3 shows consumption spending, investment spending, and net exports following this increase in foreign demand.

a. What is the new equilibrium level of domestic income following the increase in net exports?

_____

b. What is the change in the equilibrium level of income from its equilibrium in Table 9-2?

_____

c. What is the multiplier for the change in the equilibrium level of income following the $100 billion increase in net exports, and how does it compare to the multiplier computed above for a change in investment spending?

_____

3. The Paradox of Thrift

Assume that in the aggregate all consumers suddenly decided to save $50 billion more than they have been saving at every level of income. If people want to save more it means they must consume _____.

This change is an (<u>autonomous/induced</u>) change in savings and consumption. Table 9-4 shows the new values for consumption spending following the increased desire to save. Notice that the numbers for consumption spending in Table 9-4 are all $50 billion less than the numbers in the earlier tables, while investment spending and net exports are unchanged from Table 9-3.

TABLE 9-4
(CONSTANT PRICES)

Income (Output) Y	Taxes T	Disposable Income DI	Consumption Spending C	Investment Spending I	Government Purchases G	Exports X	Imports IM	Total Spending C + I + G + (X − IM)
5,500	800	4,700	4,050	900	850	600	650	_____
5,750	800	4,950	4,250	900	850	600	650	_____
6,000	800	5,200	4,450	900	850	600	650	_____
6,250	800	5,450	4,650	900	850	600	650	_____
6,500	800	5,700	4,850	900	850	600	650	_____
6,750	800	5,950	5,050	900	850	600	650	_____
7,000	800	6,200	5,250	900	850	600	650	_____

a. Using the data in Table 9-4, find the new equilibrium level of income.
b. What is the change in the equilibrium level of income compared with Table 9-3?
_____

c. At this point we can conclude that if consumer saving shows an autonomous increase while investment spending and net exports are unchanged, then the equilibrium level of income will (rise/fall).
d. The multiplier for this change is _____.
e. How does this multiplier compare with the multiplier you computed for the increase in investment spending?
f. Why is the specific numerical value you have calculated likely to be an overstatement of the multiplier response of a real economy to a change in investment spending, net exports, or saving?

SELF-TESTS FOR UNDERSTANDING

Test A

Circle the most appropriate answer.

1. The multiplier is defined as the ratio of the change in
   a. autonomous spending divided by the change in consumption expenditures.
   b. the equilibrium level of income divided by the increase in consumption spending.
   c. the equilibrium level of income divided by the change in autonomous spending that produced the change in income.
   d. consumption spending divided by the change in autonomous spending.

2. The multiplier shows that
   a. any increase in induced spending will be a multiple of the increase in income.
   b. an autonomous increase in spending will increase income by more than the increase in autonomous spending.
   c. to influence income, any change in autonomous spending must be a multiple of the induced changes in spending.
   d. an induced change in spending will lead to a multiple increase in income.

3. The oversimplified multiplier formula is
   a. 1/MPC.
   b. 1/(MPC–1)
   c. MPC × (1–MPC)
   d. 1/(1–MPC)

4. The secret behind the multiplier is
   a. the government's printing press.
   b. understanding that an autonomous increase in investment spending leads to an autonomous increase in consumption spending.
   c. understanding that an autonomous increase in investment spending induces additional increases in spending as income increases.
   d. the gnomes of Zurich.

5. Actual multipliers will be less than theoretical multipliers because of which of the following? (There may be more than one correct answer.)
   a. Inflation.
   b. Accounting practices.
   c. International trade.
   d. The government deficit.
   e. Income taxes.
   f. Price controls.
   g. The financial system.

6. An autonomous change in spending can be modeled as
   a. a horizontal shift in the expenditure schedule.
   b. a tilt in the slope of the expenditure schedule.
   c. a vertical shift in the expenditure schedule.
   d. an increase in MPC.

7. Which one of the following is not the beginning of a multiplier process?
   a. An autonomous increase in net exports.
   b. An induced increase in consumption spending.
   c. An autonomous increase in investment spending.
   d. An autonomous increase in savings.

8. The multiplier will be largest for which type of change
    a. An increase in investment spending.
    b. An autonomous decrease in consumption spending.
    c. A decrease in exports.
    d. An increase in government purchases.
    e. The multiplier should be similar for all changes.

9. If MPC were 0.6 and prices did not change, the multiplier would be
    a. $\dfrac{1}{0.6} = 1.67$.
    b. 0.6.
    c. $\dfrac{1}{1-0.6} = 2.5$.
    d. $\dfrac{1}{1+0.6} = 0.63$.

10. If MPC were 0.7 instead of 0.6, the textbook multiplier would be
    a. larger than in question 9.
    b. smaller than in question 9.
    c. the same as in question 9.

11. The textbook multiplier would be largest if MPC were
    a. 0.73.
    b. 0.45.
    c. 0.89.
    d. 0.67.

12. When compared with changes in investment spending, the multiplier associated with autonomous changes in consumption spending will be
    a. larger.
    b. smaller.
    c. about the same.

13. A boom in Japan would likely lead to an increased demand for
    (There may be more than one correct answer.)
    a. Japanese exports.
    b. American exports.
    c. American imports.
    d. Japanese imports

14. If a $100 billion increase in exports led to $300 billion increase in GDP, we could conclude that the multiplier is
    a. 1.
    b. 2.
    c. 3.
    d. 4.

15. An increase in which of the following will not lead to an increase in GDP?
    a. Investment spending.
    b. Government purchases of goods and services.
    c. Exports.
    d. Imports.

16. The multiplier is useful in calculating
    a. the slope of the consumption function.
    b. the horizontal shift in the aggregate demand curve following an increase in autonomous spending.
    c. the vertical shift of the expenditure schedule following a change in autonomous spending.
    d. the shift of the consumption function following an increase in autonomous spending.

17. The multiplier response following an increase in exports would have what impact on the aggregate demand curve?
    a. Horizontal shift to the left.
    b. No impact.
    c. Horizontal shift to the right.

18. The multiplier response following a decrease in investment spending would have what impact on the aggregate demand curve?
    a. Horizontal shift to the left.
    b. No impact.
    c. Horizontal shift to the right.

19. An autonomous increase in savings
    a. is necessarily accompanied by an increase in consumption spending.
    b. will shift the expenditure schedule down.
    c. will not affect the level of income as neither the aggregate demand nor the aggregate supply curve will shift.
    d. shifts the aggregate demand curve to the right.

20. When compared with increases in autonomous spending, multiplier responses to decreases in autonomous spending are likely to be
    a. smaller.
    b. larger.
    c. about the same.
    d. zero.

Test B

Circle T or F for true or false.

T F 1. The multiplier is defined as the ratio of a change in autonomous spending divided by the resulting change in the equilibrium level of income.

T F 2. Multiplier responses mean that the equilibrium level of national income is likely to change by less than any change in autonomous spending.

T F 3. Multiplier increases illustrated on the income–expenditure diagram are based on the assumption that prices do not change.

T F 4. Actual multiplier responses to changes in autonomous spending are likely to be less than that suggested by the theoretical formula $1/(1 - \text{MPC})$.

T F 5. If income increases because of an autonomous increase in investment spending, the resulting increase in consumption spending is called an induced increase.

T F 6. An autonomous increase in savings by all consumers will immediately lead to a higher level of real GDP, as resources are freed for higher levels of investment.

T F 7. The multiplier for autonomous increases in investment spending is always greater than the multiplier for autonomous increases in consumption spending.

T F 8. An increase in European income that resulted in an increased demand for American exports would have no effect on the equilibrium level of American income.

T F 9. The multiplier works for increases in autonomous spending, but because of price and wage rigidities the multiplier is irrelevant when we examine decreases in autonomous spending.

T F 10. The impact of a shift in the aggregate demand curve on prices and real output will depend upon the slope of the aggregate supply curve.

Appendix A
Basic Exercises: Appendix A

The following exercise is meant to give you practice working with the algebraic representation of the multiplier found in Appendix A.

1. The consumption function can be represented as $C = a + b\, DI$. In this economy $DI = Y - T$. Substitute the expression for disposable income into the consumption function and then substitute the consumption function into the following in order to solve for national income: $Y = C + I + G + (X{-}IM)$.

   What is the resulting expression for national income? Identify the multiplier in your expression.

2. An autonomous change in spending would be a change in a, I, G, X or IM. What does your equation for national income (Y) indicate will happen if a or any of the other components of autonomous spending change?

Appendix B
Basic Exercises: Appendix B

The following exercise is meant to illustrate the major point of Appendix B: When the demand for imports increases with domestic GDP, the multiplier will be smaller.

1. Table 9-5 is similar to 9-1 except that imports increase with income. Compute total spending to verify that the equilibrium level of income in Table 9-5 is the same as in Table 9-1.

2. Table 9-6 is based on the assumption that investment spending has increased by $125. The new equilibrium level of income is _____.

3. We calculate the multiplier as before: the change in the equilibrium level of income divided by the change that changed income. Now the multiplier is _____.

4. Explain any difference between this multiplier and the one you calculated for Table 9-2.

TABLE 9-5
(CONSTANT PRICES)

Income (Output) Y	Taxes T	Disposable Income DI	Consumption Spending C	Investment Spending I	Government Purchases G	Exports X	Imports IM	Total Spending C + I + G + (X − IM)
5,500	800	4,700	4,100	800	850	500	625	_____
5,750	800	4,950	4,300	800	850	500	637.5	_____
6,000	800	5,200	4,500	800	850	500	650	_____
6,250	800	5,450	4,700	800	850	500	662.5	_____
6,500	800	5,700	4,900	800	850	500	675	_____
6,750	800	5,950	5,100	800	850	500	687.5	_____
7,000	800	6,200	5,300	800	850	500	700	_____

TABLE 9-6
(CONSTANT PRICES)

Income (Output) Y	Taxes T	Disposable Income DI	Consumption Spending C	Investment Spending I	Government Purchases G	Exports X	Imports IM	Total Spending C + I + G + (X − IM)
5,500	800	4,700	4,100	925	850	500	625	_____
5,750	800	4,950	4,300	925	850	500	637.5	_____
6,000	800	5,200	4,500	925	850	500	650	_____
6,250	800	5,450	4,700	925	850	500	662.5	_____
6,500	800	5,700	4,900	925	850	500	675	_____
6,750	800	5,950	5,100	925	850	500	687.5	_____
7,000	800	6,200	5,300	925	850	500	700	_____

SUPPLEMENTARY EXERCISES

1. In 1963 the President's Council of Economic Advisers was considering how large a tax cut would be necessary to return the economy to full employment. These economists estimated that actual output was about $30 to $35 billion less than potential, or full-employment, output. That is, they wanted a tax cut that would increase output by $30 to $35 billion, yet they recommended a tax cut of only $13 billion, to be divided between consumers ($10 billion) and businesses ($3 billion). How could these economists expect that total spending could rise by $30 to $35 billion when taxes were only reduced by $13 billion? Even if consumers and businesses spent the whole reduction in taxes, spending would only rise by $13 billion, not nearly enough to return the economy to full employment. What is wrong with this line of reasoning?

2. Use the data in Table 9-1 and a piece of graph paper to draw the income-expenditure diagram.
   a. Show how the expenditure schedule shifts as a result of the increase in investment spending in Basic Exercise 1b. Does your graph give you the same result as Basic Exercise 1c?
   b. Show how the expenditure schedule shifts following the increase in net exports in Basic Exercise 2. How does the new equilibrium level of income, and hence the multiplier, on your graph, compare to your answers in the Basic Exercise?
   c. Show how the expenditure schedule shifts after the increase in savings described in Basic Exercise 3. How does your graph compare with your answer to 3c?

3. If you have access to a micro computer try programming or using a spread sheet to simulate the following model to investigate the dynamics of the multiplier.

   Assume that consumption spending responds to income with a one-period lag as follows

   $$C = 340 + .8DI\ (-1)$$

   where C is consumption and DI is disposable income. Other important elements of the model are:

   $$
   \begin{aligned}
   DI &= Y-T \\
   T &= 800 \\
   I &= 900 \\
   G &= 850 \\
   X &= 500 \\
   IM &= 650
   \end{aligned}
   $$

   a. If confirm that the equilibrium level of income is 6,000. That is, if income last period was 6,000, then $C + I + G + (X - IM)$ will equal 6,000 this period.
   b. Now assume that investment spending increases by 100. Assuming that consumption responds with the one-period lag, simulate your model to investigate how the change in investment spending affects income over time. Does the level of income appear to

converge to a new equilibrium value? What is that value? What is the multiplier for the change in investment spending? How does the multiplier from your simulation compare to the oversimplified formula of 1/(1–MPC)?

c. Investigate the impact of increases and decreases in net exports. Investigate the impact of a change in government purchases. Investigate the impact of autonomous changes in consumption spending, that is a change in the constant term of the consumption function. How would you model an autonomous change in savings?

d. What happens if the MPC changes? You will need first to determine the initial equilibrium level of income for given levels of investment spending, net exports, and autonomous consumption spending. Then simulate your model to see how the change in the MPC affects the multiplier.

ECONOMICS IN ACTION
Autonomous and Induced Changes in Consumption Spending

As Chapter 9 discusses, the multiplier shows how an autonomous increase in spending, through its impact on income, induces additional spending. The final result is that the equilibrium level of income increases by more than, or by a multiple of, the original autonomous change. Chapter 7 discussed the close link between disposable income and consumption spending. As seen in Chapter 9, the induced changes in consumption spending are an important part of the multiplier process.

Can changes in consumption spending ever initiate multiplier changes or are they only a part of a process that must be initiated by some other element of spending? To answer this question one must distinguish between factors that shift the consumption function and factors that lead to a movement along the consumption function. As a particular example, consider material from the 1991 Report of the Council of Economic Advisers.

Each January, the President's Council of Economic Advisers issues its annual report. The Council's report is published along with the Economic Report of the President. The volume's statistical appendix reports numerous data series that measure the macroeconomic performance of the economy. The report itself includes commentary on recent developments, a forecast for the upcoming year, and a detailed study of two or three topics of interest. The report is a mixture of politics and economic analysis as it is, in part, a brief for the policies of the President.

The January 1992 report was issued at the beginning of an election year and after the sluggish economic performance of 1991. When discussing factors influencing consumer spending, the report noted the large accumulation of consumer debt, both installment and mortgage debt, that had occurred during the economic expansion of the 1980s.

By the end of the expansion, many consumers had accumulated relatively high levels of debt. At the same time, the value of their largest asset, their homes—was flat or declining. Householders' expectations of continued increases in the equity of their homes were not being realized. After rising at an average annual rate of 7.5 percent—

about twice the rate of inflation—from the end of 1984 through 1989, the value of owner-occupied housing and land fell 1.6 percent in 1990. In addition, the value of other household assets, such as durable goods, stocks, bonds, pensions and other financial assets, grew only slowly in 1990. Total household net worth—the difference between the household sector's assets and liabilities—fell 2 percent in 1990 (page 43).

The report went on to note:

During 1991, real consumer spending rose 0.3 percent. Real disposable personal income, a key determinant of consumer spending rose 0.4 percent during 1991. . . Consumer confidence was on a roller coaster, falling in the second half after a strong post-Operation Desert Storm rebound. In fact, consumer confidence by year-end was very low, which suggests that consumer spending in early 1992 will be sluggish. (page 57)

1. What factors does the report cite to explain the slow growth in consumer spending?
2. Which of these factors reflect a movement along an unchanged consumption function and which reflect a shift in the consumption function? Which would initiate a multiplier process and which would be part of the multiplier response to an autonomous change in spending?

SOURCE: *Economic Report of the President*, Transmitted to Congress, January 1992, (United States Government Printing Office: Washington, D.C.)

STUDY QUESTIONS

1. Looking just at the expenditure schedule, how can you represent a change in autonomous spending? A change in induced spending?
2. How can it be that a change in autonomous spending results in an even larger change in the equilibrium level of income?
3. What happens to the value of the multiplier if the MPC is larger? Smaller? Why?
4. What are the four shortcomings of the multiplier formula 1/(1–MPC)?
5. Do these shortcomings mean that the formula overstates or understates the likely value of the multiplier?
6. What is the mechanism by which a recession in Europe may lead to a decline in output in the United States?
7. If an increase in savings is good for an individual, how can it be bad for a nation as a whole? (Explain the reasoning behind the paradox of thrift.)
8. How would results differ if an autonomous increase in savings were matched by an increase in investment spending, as contrasted with the situation where savings increase without any increase in investment spending?
9. What is the relation between the multiplier analysis on the income-expenditure diagram following an autonomous change in spending and the resulting shift of the aggregate demand curve?

Chapter **10**

Supply-Side Equilibrium: Unemployment *and* Inflation?

LEARNING OBJECTIVES

After completing this chapter you should be able to:

- describe how the aggregate supply curve is derived from an analysis of business costs and why it slopes upward.
- distinguish between factors that will lead to a movement along or a shift in the aggregate supply curve.
- explain why the aggregate supply curve normally gets steeper as output increases.
- use a graph depicting both the aggregate demand curve and the aggregate supply curve to determine the price level and the final equilibrium level of real GDP.
- use the same graph as above to analyze how factors that shift either the aggregate demand curve or the aggregate supply curve will affect the equilibrium level of prices and output.
- use the same graph to explain what kinds of shifts in the aggregate demand curve and the aggregate supply curve can give rise to a period of stagflation.
- explain why an inflationary gap is apt to self-destruct.
- explain why a recessionary gap is not apt to self-destruct.
- use the aggregate demand/aggregate supply diagram to show how increases in prices reduce the value of the multiplier.

IMPORTANT TERMS AND CONCEPTS

Aggregate supply curve
Productivity
Equilibrium of real GDP and the price level
Inflationary gap
Self-correcting mechanism
Stagflation
Recessionary gap
Inflation and the multiplier

CHAPTER REVIEW

In Chapter 4 we first learned that for individual commodities equilibrium price and quantity are determined by the intersection of the relevant demand and supply curves. The same logic holds when analyzing the economy as a whole. The level of prices and aggregate output is determined by the intersection of the aggregate demand and aggregate supply curves. In Chapter 8 we saw how the aggregate demand curve could be derived from analyzing how changes in the price level affect the spending decisions that underlie the expenditure schedule. In this chapter we will derive the aggregate supply curve and use both curves to show how the price level and a aggregate output are determined.

The aggregate supply curve is a schedule, showing for each possible price level, the total quantity of goods and services that all businesses are willing to supply during a specified period of time, holding all other factors influencing aggregate supply constant. You should note that the same logic applies here as to discussions of the supply decisions of individual firms. Businesses will adjust supply in pursuit of profits.

If prices rise while production costs per unit of output remain unchanged, we expect firms

(1) to (<u>increase/decrease</u>) output. In fact, if prices stayed higher and production costs did not increase at all, there would be no limit to the increase in profits firms could derive from increases in output. However, even if the prices of inputs do not increase, production costs will eventually rise as firms try to expand output, putting a limit on the profitable increase in output. (Remember that in the short run the supply curve for an individual firm is the upward sloping portion of the firm's marginal cost curve.) The increase in output induced by an increase in the price level is a (<u>movement along/shift in</u>) the aggregate supply curve. Any change in production costs in the face of an otherwise unchanged price level-for example, an increase in energy prices imposed by a foreign supplier or an increase in money wages–will also affect profits and will lead to an adjustment in the quantity of goods and services that businesses are willing to supply. This time, however, the change in supply is a _____ _____ the aggregate supply curve. The aggregate supply curve would also shift following a change in productivity or in the available supplies of labor or capital. For example, as investment increases the stock of capital, the aggregate supply curve will shift to the (<u>left/right</u>).

The increase in production costs associated with higher levels of output, the very increase that put a limit on the profitable increase in supply and helped to define the aggregate supply curve, is likely to be especially severe near full-employment levels of output and is an important reason why the slope of the aggregate supply curve depends upon the level

(2) of resource utilization. Near full employment, the aggregate supply curve is (<u>steeper/flatter</u>).

Now, having derived both the aggregate demand curve and the aggregate supply curve, we are in a position to use both to determine the final equilibrium level of prices and aggregate output, or GDP. See, for example, Figure 10-1, where the equilibrium price level of

(3) 100 and the equilibrium level of GDP of $6000 billion are given by the (<u>intersection/slope</u>) of the aggregate demand and supply curves. A higher price level, say, 110, implies (1) a lower quantity of aggregate demand as consumers respond to the loss of purchasing power of their money assets and net exports (<u>increase/decrease</u>) following the increase in domestic prices, and (2) a larger quantity of aggregate supply as firms respond to higher prices. Clearly, more supply and less demand cannot be a point of equilibrium, since firms would experience continual (<u>increases/decreases</u>) in inventories. The result is likely to be reduced output and price reductions that move the economy toward equilibrium. Similarly, a lower price level, such as 90, would induce analogous, although opposite, reactions.

Nothing in the analysis so far guarantees that the intersection of the aggregate demand and aggregate supply curves will be at the level of output corresponding to full employment. If the final equilibrium level of output is different from the full-employment level of output, the result is either a recessionary gap or an inflationary gap. Consider Figure 10-2,

(4) which shows a(n) _____ gap. The gap (<u>is/is not</u>) likely to self-destruct as continuing increases in the price of inputs lead to shifts in the aggregate supply

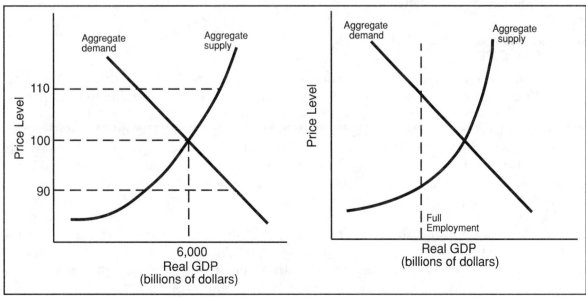

FIGURE 10-1   **FIGURE 10-2**

curve. As unemployment falls below frictional levels and material inputs become scarce, higher input prices will shift the aggregate supply curve (<u>inward/outward</u>) leading to a (<u>movement along/shift in</u>) the aggregate demand curve, (<u>higher/lower</u>) prices, (<u>higher/lower</u>) output, and the elimination of the inflationary gap. Note that the simultaneous increase in prices and wages does not prove that increasing wages cause inflation. Both are best seen as a symptom of the original inflationary gap.

By contrast, the rigidity of wages and other input prices in the face of unemployment
(5) means that a recessionary gap is (<u>more/less</u>) likely to self-destruct than an inflationary gap.

Stagflation refers to the simultaneous occurrence of increasing prices and increasing employment. The previous analysis suggests that stagflation is a natural result of the self-
(6) destruction of a(n) (<u>inflationary/recessionary</u>) gap. Stagflation can also occur as a result of adverse shifts in the aggregate _____ curve.

IMPORTANT TERMS AND CONCEPTS QUIZ

Choose the best definition for the following terms.

1. _____ Aggregate supply curve
2. _____ Productivity
3. _____ Self-correcting mechanism
4. _____ Stagflation

a. Economy's way of restoring equilibrium through inflation or deflation.

b. Amount of a given input required to produce a unit of output.

c. Graph of total quantity of goods and services produced at each possible price level.

d. Inflation that occurs while the economy is growing slowly or in recession.

e. Amount of output produced per unit of input.

BASIC EXERCISES

1. This first exercise reviews the derivation of the aggregate demand curve and then uses both the aggregate demand and aggregate supply curves to determine the equilibrium level of income. Figure 10-3 shows an income–expenditure diagram in the top half and a price level–aggregate output diagram in the bottom half. The middle expenditure schedule in the top half duplicates the original situation described in Basic Exercise 1 of Chapter 9 and assumes that the price level with this expenditure schedule is 100. The dashed line extending into the bottom figure shows how this output level, together with its associated price level, can be plotted in the lower diagram. It is one point on the aggregate demand curve.
   a. A decrease in the price level to 90 would increase consumption spending because a reduction in prices (<u>decreases/increases</u>) the purchasing power of consumer money assets and increases net exports. The (<u>movement along/shift in</u>) the consumption function and the change in net exports shifts the expenditure schedule up. The

new expenditure schedule, for a price level of 90, is shown in the top half of Figure 10-3. What is the equilibrium level of income in the income-expenditure diagram for a price level of 90?

b. Plot the combination of prices and output from a in the lower diagram. This is a second point on the aggregate demand curve.

c. A price level of 110 would depress consumer spending and net exports, shifting both the consumption function and the expenditure schedule. Use the expenditure schedule for a price level of 110 to plot a third point on the aggregate demand curve.

d. Draw the aggregate demand curve by connecting the three points now plotted in the lower diagram.

e. Using the aggregate demand curve you have just derived and the aggregate supply curve that is already drawn, what is the equilibrium level of prices and real GDP?

f. If the level of full-employment output were $6 trillion, would there be an inflationary gap or recessionary gap? How, if at all, might such a gap self-destruct and where would the price level and real GDP end up?

g. If the level of full-employment output were $6.125 trillion, would there be an inflationary gap or recessionary gap? How, if at all, might such a gap self-destruct and where would the price level and real GDP end up?

h. If the level of full-employment output were $6.25 trillion, would there be an inflationary or recessionary gap? How, if at all, might such a gap self-destruct and where would the price level and real GDP end up?

FIGURE 10-3

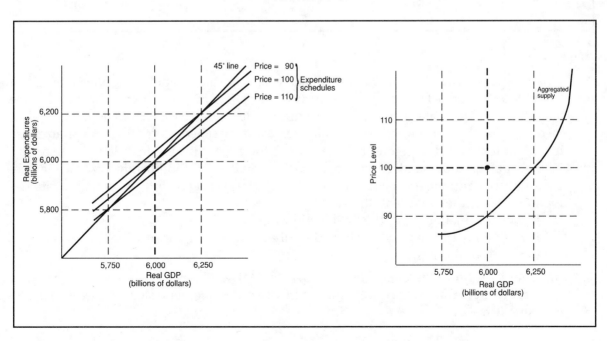

FIGURE 10-4

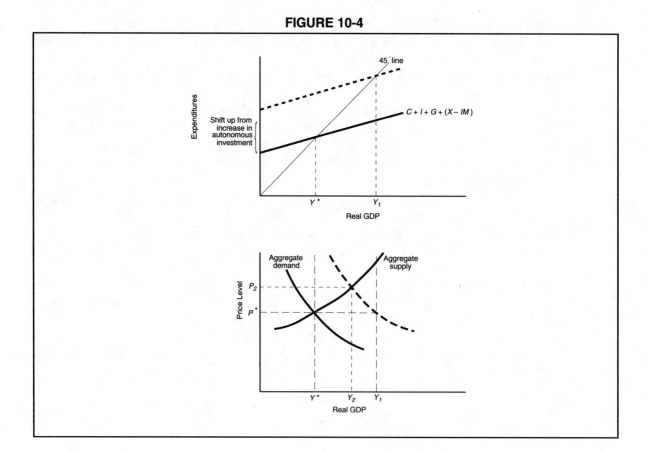

2. This exercise reviews the impact of higher prices on the simple multiplier derived in Chapter 9. Consider Figure 10-4. The heavy lines show an initial expenditure schedule and the associated aggregate demand curve. The initial equilibrium is at a level of income Y^*, and price level P^*. The dashed expenditure schedule comes from an increase in investment spending. Note that the shift in the expenditure schedule leads to a shift in the aggregate demand curve. In fact, the initial new equilibrium on the income-expenditure diagram, Y, is equal to the (<u>horizontal/vertical</u>) shift of the aggregate demand curve in the lower half of the diagram.
   a. Is the combination Y_1, P^* the final equilibrium?
   b. If Y_1, P^* is not the final equilibrium, describe what will happen during the transition to the final equilibrium

3. In Table 10-1, fill in the blanks as indicated to analyze the response to each change. In the first two columns use S or M for "shift in" or "movement along." In the last two columns use + or −.

TABLE 10-1

	Aggregate demand curve	Aggregate supply curve	Equilibrium real GDP	Price level
A reduction in business investment spending				
An increase in the price of many basic commodities used as inputs in the production of final goods and services				
An increase in the demand for exports caused by an economic boom abroad				
An increase in the labor productivity due to a technological breakthrough				
An upward shift in the consumption function due to a stock market boom				
A large increase in energy prices				

SELF-TESTS FOR UNDERSTANDING

Test A

Circle the most appropriate answer.

1. The aggregate supply curve
    a. slopes down to the right.
    b. has a positive slope.
    c. slopes up to the left.
    d. has a negative slope.

2. The slope of the aggregate supply curve reflects the fact that
    a. inflation reduces the value of the oversimplified multiplier.
    b. the costs of important inputs, such as labor, are relatively fixed in the short run.
    c. the marginal propensity to consume is less than 1.0.
    d. recessionary gaps take a long time to self-destruct.

3. The aggregate supply curve will shift following changes in all but which of the following?
   a. The price level.
   b. Wage rates.
   c. Technology and productivity.
   d. Available supplies of factories and machines.

4. The equilibrium price level and the equilibrium level of real GDP.
   a. are determined by the intersection of the aggregate demand, and aggregate supply curves.
   b. will always occur at full employment.
   c. can be found in the income-expenditure diagram.
   d. do not change unless the aggregate demand curve shifts.

5. A change in the equilibrium price level
   a. will lead to a shift in the aggregate supply curve.
   b. will lead to a shift in the aggregate demand curve.
   c. reflects a shift in the aggregate demand curve and/or aggregate supply curve.
   d. will always lead to stagflation.

6. A higher price level will lead to which of the following? (There may be more than one correct answer.)
   a. A reduction in the purchasing power of consumers' money fixed assets.
   b. A downward shift in the consumption function.
   c. An increase in imports.
   d. A decrease in exports.
   e. A downward shift in the expenditure schedule.

7. Near full employment, the slope of the aggregate supply curve is likely to
   a. become negative.
   b. drop to zero.
   c. decrease, but still remain positive.
   d. increase.

8. An inflationary gap occurs
   a. when the equilibrium level of GDP exceeds potential GDP.
   b. whenever there is an upward shift in the expenditure schedule.
   c. whenever aggregate supply exceeds aggregate demand.
   d. during periods of high unemployment.

9. From an initial position of full employment, which one of the following will not lead to a recessionary gap?
   a. A shift in the aggregate supply curve in response to an increase in energy prices.
   b. A reduction in investment spending due to an increase in business taxes.
   c. A reduction in consumer spending due to an adverse shift in consumer expectations.
   d. An increase in exports the follows a business expansion in Europe.

10. Which of the following is not associated with the elimination of an inflationary gap?
    a. Rising prices.
    b. Falling output.
    c. Increased employment.
    d. Increased unemployment.

11. Which of the following is most likely to lead to an inflationary gap?
    a. An increase in government purchases of goods and services to fight a recession.
    b. An increase in exports that occurs when unemployment rates are high.
    c. A significant increase in energy prices.
    d. Any increase in spending that shifts the aggregate demand curve to the right when GDP is at or beyond potential GDP.

12. The economy's self-correcting mechanisms are likely to work better when
    a. there is an inflationary gap.
    b. there is a recessionary gap.
    c. there is a federal government deficit.
    d. the multiplier is working.

13. Which of the following is most likely to lead to stagflation?
    a. An increase in aggregate demand that comes from an increase in government purchases of goods and services.
    b. An increase in exports that occurs when unemployment rates are high.
    c. A significant increase in energy prices.
    d. Any increase in spending that shifts the aggregate demand curve to the right when GDP is at or beyond potential GDP.

14. Which of the following lead to an increase in net exports? (There may be more than one correct answer.)
    a. Decrease in exports.
    b. Decrease in imports.
    c. Increase in imports.
    d. Increase in exports.

15. From an initial position of equilibrium, exports increase by $100 billion as both Japan and Europe experience business booms. This change will lead to which of the following? (There may be more than one correct answer.)
    a. An upward shift of the expenditure schedule.
    b. A shift to the right in the aggregate supply curve.
    c. A shift to the right in the aggregate demand curve.
    d. An increase in net exports.

16. At the new equilibrium following the increase in exports, American GDP will be _____ and the American price level will be _____.
    a. higher, lower
    b. lower, lower
    c. higher, higher
    d. lower, higher

17. There is likely to be a greater change in prices and a smaller change in output following the increase in exports if
    a. the initial position of equilibrium for the American economy is below potential GDP.
    b. the aggregate supply curve does not shift.
    c. there is an autonomous increase in savings.
    d. initial unemployment rates in the United States are low.

18. Year-to-year changes in GDP and prices are probably best seen as the result of
    a. shifts in the aggregate demand curve that move the economy along an unchanged aggregate supply curve.
    b. shifts in the aggregate supply curve that move the economy along an unchanged aggregate demand curve.
    c. shifts in the both the aggregate demand and aggregate supply curves.

19. Prices rise following an increase in autonomous spending whenever the
    a. aggregate demand curve shifts.
    b. multiplier is greater than 1.0.
    c. aggregate demand curve has a negative slope.
    d. aggregate supply curve is not horizontal.

20. The aggregate demand curve-aggregate supply curve diagram shows that the multiplier will be smaller on the income–expenditure diagram whenever
    a. the aggregate demand curve slopes down and to the right.
    b. the aggregate demand curve slopes up and to the right.
    c. the aggregate supply curve slopes up and to the right.
    d. the MPC is less than 1.0.

Test B

Circle T or F for true or false.

T F 1. The aggregate supply curve shows for each possible price the total quantity of goods and services that the nation's businesses are willing to supply.

T F 2. The aggregate supply curve slopes upward because businesses will expand output as long as higher prices make expansion profitable.

T F 3. The aggregate supply curve is likely to be steeper at low levels of unemployment.

T F 4. The impact of unemployment on wages and prices means that recessionary gaps are likely to quickly self-destruct.

T F 5. If the aggregate supply curve shifts inward, the result will be stagflation.

T F   6. The economy's self-correcting mechanisms insure that the aggregate demand and aggregate supply curves will always intersect at potential output.

T F   7. The final equilibrium level of prices and aggregate output is determined by the slope of the aggregate supply curve.

T F   8. A period of excessive aggregate demand is likely to be followed by a period of stagflation as the inflationary gap self-destructs.

T F   9. During the elimination of an inflationary gap, the real cause of inflation is excessive wage demands on the part of labor.

T F 10. Analysis of the aggregate supply curve shows that the multiplier derived from the income–expenditure diagram typically understates the final change in output.

SUPPLEMENTARY EXERCISE

The following equations are consistent with Basic Exercise 1.

$$T = 800 \qquad\qquad T = \text{taxes}$$
$$DI = Y - T \qquad\qquad DI = \text{disposable income}$$
$$C = 740 + .8DI - 3.5P \qquad\qquad C = \text{consumption expenditures}$$
$$I = 800 \qquad\qquad I = \text{investment expenditures}$$
$$G = 850 \qquad\qquad G = \text{government purchases}$$
$$X - IM = -50 - 0.5P \qquad\qquad X = \text{exports}$$
$$C + I + G + (X - IM) = Y \text{ (45–degree line)} \qquad\qquad IM = \text{imports}$$
$$\text{Aggregate supply curve} \qquad\qquad Y = \text{GDP}$$
$$Y = 3750 + 25P \qquad\qquad P = \text{price level}$$

1. Use the consumption function along with the level of investment spending, government purchases, and net exports to determine an expression for the expenditure schedule. (Don't forget to substitute for disposable income and note that this expression will involve the variable P.)

2. Use the expenditure schedule and the equation for the 45–degree line to determine an expression for the aggregate demand curve.

3. Now use both the aggregate demand curve and the aggregate supply curve to determine the equilibrium level of prices and GDP.

4. Resolve the system on the assumption that investment expenditures decrease to $750.

ECONOMICS IN ACTION
How Variable is the Aggregate Supply Curve?

What explains fluctuations in GDP—shifts in the aggregate demand curve or shifts in the aggregate supply curve? Keynesian analysis focuses on shifts in aggregate demand as the major source of fluctuations in output. On this view, the aggregate supply curve shifts out year by year more or less regularly and deviations from potential or full-employment output are the result of shifts in the aggregate demand curve that are greater or less than the shift in the aggregate supply curve. In recent years an alternative view has argued that the growth of potential output and the associated shifts in the aggregate supply curve may be less regular and more variable than had been suspected.

What difference does it make whether potential output grows smoothly or fluctuates from year to year? Estimates of potential output and the difference of actual output from potential are an important determinant of changes in fiscal and monetary policy. For example, when the economy is operating below potential, expansionary policies that increase aggregate demand can increase output and employment. If the aggregate supply curve is relatively flat to the left of full employment, the increase in output may have little impact on prices. The magnitude of changes in fiscal and monetary policy to increase aggregate demand will be influenced by estimates of the shortfall from potential output.

But if GDP is low in part because of an adverse shift in the aggregate supply curve, then expansionary policy that ignores the decrease in potential output could turn out to be too expansionary, push the economy above potential, and create unwanted inflationary pressures. On the other hand, if GDP increased above traditional estimates of potential output because of a favorable shift in the aggregate supply curve, stabilization policy that tried to reduce aggregate demand because of a concern about possible inflationary pressures would unnecessarily increase unemployment.

Why is it so difficult to figure out how the aggregate supply curve is shifting? As economists John Boschen and Leonard Mills point out, potential GDP is not directly observable. Neither is the aggregate demand curve or the aggregate supply curve. The level of output and prices that we observe give us information about where these curves intersect, but by themselves do not identify one curve or the other. In order to identify the aggregate supply curve one needs to use economic theory and make appropriate assumptions about factors that affect aggregate supply, just as we have done with regard to factors that affect aggregate demand. These theories of the aggregate supply curve are then tested by comparing implications of the models with data from the real world. Models of the aggregate supply curve are still in their infancy and estimates of the importance of supply-side factors in explaining fluctuations in output cover a wide range. Boschen and Mills surveyed recent attempts to model shifts in the aggregate supply curve. A number of these estimates suggest that a third of the variation in output might be attributed to variability in the growth of potential GDP while others range as high as 50 to 70 percent.

1. What are the implications for stabilization policy if fluctuations in the aggregate supply curve account for 10 percent or 50 percent of the fluctuations in output?

SOURCE: John Boschen and Leonard Mills, "Monetary Policy with a New View of Potential GNP," *Business Review*, Federal Reserve Bank of Philadelphia, (July/August 1990), pp. 3-10.

STUDY QUESTIONS

1. Why is the aggregate supply curve drawn sloping upward to the right?
2. Why is the slope of the aggregate supply curve likely to get steeper as output increases?
3. What factors influence the position of the aggregate supply curve?
4. What market forces move the economy to the equilibrium level of output and prices given by the intersection of the aggregate demand curve and aggregate supply curve?
5. Evaluate the following statement: "All periods of inflation are caused by excessive demands for high wages on the part of labor."
6. What is the process by which an inflationary gap self-destructs?
7. Is an adverse supply shock likely to give rise to an inflationary gap or a recessionary gap? Why?
8. What are some of the reasons the economy's self-correcting mechanisms might not work as quickly in the face of a recessionary gap?
9. What is meant by stagflation and when is it likely to occur?
10. How do considerations of aggregate supply reduce the value of the multiplier calculated in Chapter 9?
11. Consider a shift in the expenditure schedule, say due to a $100 billion increase in exports. Which increase in net exports would have the largest multiplier impact on the economy, one that occurs when unemployment rates are high and GDP is less than potential GDP or the same increase in exports that occurs at a time when GDP is close to potential? Why?

Managing the Economy with Fiscal Policy

LEARNING OBJECTIVES

After completing this chapter you should be able to:

♦ describe the process by which a change in government purchases of goods and services will lead to a shift in the aggregate demand curve.

♦ describe the process by which a change in taxes will lead to a shift in the aggregate demand curve.

♦ explain why taxes that depend upon income reduce the value of the multiplier below the oversimplified expression in Chapter 9.

♦ show on an income-expenditure diagram how a change from fixed to variable taxes affects the slope of the expenditure schedule.

♦ explain why the multiplier for a change in income taxes will be less than the multiplier for a change in government purchases of goods and services.

♦ explain why economists treat government transfer payments like taxes, not like government purchases of goods and services.

♦ describe the process by which a change in government transfer payments will lead to a shift in the aggregate demand curve.

♦ explain why active stabilization policy need not imply that government must get bigger and bigger.

♦ use the aggregate demand and supply diagram to show how supply-side tax cuts hope to reduce the impact on prices associated with the elimination of a recessionary gap.

♦ describe the kernel of truth in supply-side economics.

♦ discuss the reservations that most economists have in regard to supply-side economics.

IMPORTANT TERMS AND CONCEPTS

Fiscal policy
Fixed taxes
Variable taxes
Government transfer payments
Effect of income taxes on the multiplier
Supply-side tax cuts

CHAPTER REVIEW

The models of income determination in earlier chapters included a rather passive government. This chapter uses a more realistic model of taxes and provides a framework for considering how and when the government should vary spending and taxes. The
(1) government's plans for spending and taxes are called (<u>fiscal/monetary</u>) policy. The only trick is to understand how government spending and taxes affect the curves we have already derived, that is, how government spending and taxes affect the expenditure schedule, the aggregate demand curve, and the aggregate supply curve. After this, the analysis proceeds exactly as before: For a given price level, the equilibrium level of income on the income-expenditure diagram is determined by the intersection of the (<u>consumption/expenditure</u>) schedule and the 45-degree line. A change in prices will affect consumption spending and net exports. The different price levels and the associated equilibrium levels of income on the income-expenditure diagram can be combined to form the aggregate _____ curve. This curve together with the aggregate _____ curve will determine the final equilibrium for income and prices, just as before. A change in the government's fiscal policy will shift one or more of the curves and lead to new equilibrium values for income and prices.

There are three important ways government fiscal policy influences total spending in the economy:

1. The government *purchases goods* and *services*.

2. The government *collects taxes*, reducing the spending power of households and firms. Particular taxes may affect incentives for working, saving, investing or spending.

3. The government gives *transfer payments* to some individuals, thereby increasing their purchasing power.

Government purchases of goods and services are a direct addition to total spending in
(2) the economy; that is, they shift the expenditure schedule (<u>up/down</u>) by the full amount of the purchases. Thus, if government spending increased by $1, the expenditure schedule would shift up by $_____. (An increase in autonomous investment spending or exports of $1 would also shift the expenditure schedule up by $_____.) Thus, changes in

government spending shift the expenditure schedule in exactly the same way as other changes in autonomous spending and should have similar multiplier effects.

(3)   Government taxes (<u>are/are not</u>) a direct component of spending on currently produced goods and services. Personal income taxes affect consumption spending through their impact on disposable income. Following a decrease in personal income taxes, consumers' disposable income will be (<u>higher/lower</u>). The initial effect on consumption spending will depend in part on whether consumers view the tax change as permanent or temporary. The largest impact will come from a (<u>permanent/temporary</u>) tax cut. The change in consumption spending will be determined by the marginal _____ to consume which is (<u>less than/equal to/greater than</u>) 1.0. Thus, changes in personal income taxes affect spending, but indirectly through their effect on consumption expenditures. A change in corporate income taxes will change corporate profits after taxes, and is likely to affect _____ expenditures.

The third important function of the government regarding total spending in the economy is the magnitude of government transfer payments. These payments, like taxes, are not a direct element of total spending on goods and services. Also, like personal taxes, they affect

(4) total spending because they affect people's disposable _____ and thus their _____ expenditures. Remember that taxes are earned but not received while transfers are received but not earned. Thus in the models we will be working with, disposable income is equal to GDP (<u>−/+</u>) taxes (<u>−/+</u>) transfers and transfers can be thought of as negative taxes.

An important feature of income taxes (and some transfer payments) is that they vary

(5) with GDP. Typically taxes go (<u>down/up</u>) as GDP goes up. If taxes change whenever income changes they are called _____ taxes. Taxes that do not change when GDP changes are called _____ taxes. Understanding the difference between fixed and variable taxes is important for understanding how to model changes in taxes on the income-expenditure diagram and for understanding how income taxes affect the value of the multiplier.

In Chapter 9 we saw that the multiplier process arises because any autonomous increase in spending means higher income for those who supply the newly demanded goods. These higher incomes will lead to more consumption spending, and so on, and so on. This process continues to take place, but now we see that each round of spending results in an increase in income *before* taxes. Because some of the increase in before-tax income goes to pay

(6) higher taxes, after-tax income (or disposable income) will increase by (<u>more/less</u>). Thus, each induced round of consumption spending, responding to the increase in disposable income, will be (<u>smaller/larger</u>) than before.

To summarize, in an economy with income taxes (and transfer payments) that vary with income, each round in the multiplier process will be smaller than before, and thus the

(7) multiplier effect on income, from any increase in automatic spending, will be (<u>smaller/larger</u>) than before. The impact of income taxes on the multiplier is another important reason why the formula for the multiplier in Chapter 9 was oversimplified.

We can see these same results graphically on the income-expenditure diagram. In Chapter 9 we assumed that taxes did not vary with income, that is the model of Chapter 9 considered only fixed taxes. A $1 change in GDP meant a $1 increase in disposable income and led to an increase in consumption spending given by the MPC. Since in the model of Chapter 9 consumption spending was the only type of spending that changed when GDP

(8) changed, the slope of the expenditure schedule was equal to the _____. Now when we consider the impact of variable taxes, we see that a $1 increase in GDP leads to a(n) (smaller/equal/larger) increase in disposable income and a(n) _____ increase in consumption spending as compared with the case of fixed taxes. The result is that increases in GDP are associated with smaller increases in total spending and a (flatter/steeper) expenditure schedule. As we saw in Chapter 9, the multiplier can be derived from the slope of the expenditure schedule. A flatter expenditure schedule means a smaller multiplier.

Modeling the impact of a change in taxes will depend upon whether the change is in the fixed or variable component of taxes. A reduction in fixed taxes would increase disposable income, and thus consumption, by the same amount at every level of GDP. Thus, it can be modeled as a parallel shift in the expenditure schedule. A change in variable taxes would be a change in the tax rate. A reduction in variable taxes means less of any increase in income

(9) goes for taxes and more ends up in disposable income. The larger change in disposable income means that a given change in GDP will be associated with a larger change in consumption spending. The result is that a change in variable taxes leads to a change in the slope of the expenditure schedule. Following a reduction in tax rates the expenditure schedule would become (flatter/steeper).

Let us be more specific about how we can model a change in the fixed component of taxes. (Changes in transfer payments will have similar but opposite effects since transfer payments can be viewed as negative taxes.) We saw earlier that a $1 change in government purchases will shift the expenditure schedule by $1. Consider a permanent $1 reduction in the fixed component of income taxes. What is the magnitude of the initial shift of the expenditure schedule that initiates the multiplier process? At the initial equilibrium level of income, the reduction in income taxes will increase disposable income and increase

(10) _____ spending. It is this initial impact on spending that determines the magnitude of the shift in the expenditure schedule. Our discussion of the consumption function in Chapter 7 showed that a $1 increase in disposable income will increase consumption spending by less than $1 because the _____ is (less than/equal to/greater than) 1.0. The result is that a $1 change in the fixed component of taxes shifts the expenditure schedule by (less/more) than a $1 change in government purchases. As a result, the multiplier associated with changes in income taxes will be (larger/smaller) than the multiplier associated with changes in government purchases.

We have added government purchases of goods and services, taxes, and transfers to our model of income determination. Taken together, these variables are an important determinant of the equilibrium level of income. Changes in these variables, just like the autonomous changes we considered in earlier chapters, will have multiplier effects on the equilibrium level of

GDP. Thus deliberate manipulation of these variables may help the government achieve its desired objectives for GDP and prices. Manipulation of government fiscal policy variables for GDP objectives is an example of stabilization policy. For example, if the government wants

(11) to increase GDP, it can decide to (<u>increase/decrease</u>) government purchases of goods and services, _____ personal taxes, _____ corporate taxes, or _____ transfer payments to individuals.

One of the reasons it is so difficult to agree on fiscal policy is that there are so many choices, all of which could have the same impact on national income, but very different impacts on other issues, such as the size of the public versus private sector, the burden of taxes between individuals and corporations, the composition of output between consumption and investment spending, and the amount of income redistribution through transfers to low-income families.

One might believe that if we could decide upon the amounts of government purchases, taxes, and transfers, effective fiscal policy would be simply a technical matter of choosing the right numbers so that the expenditure schedule would intersect the 45–degree line, and the aggregate demand curve would intersect the aggregate supply curve at full-employment. In actuality, uncertainties about (1) private components of aggregate demand, (2) the precise size of the multiplier, (3) exactly what level of GDP is associated with full employment, and (4) the slope of the aggregate supply curve all mean that fiscal policy will continue to be subject to much political give and take. One hopes that appropriate economic analysis will contribute to a more informed level of debate.

Changes in government spending or tax rates shift the aggregate demand curve directly, in the case of government purchases, and indirectly through impacts on private spending, in the case of taxes and transfer payments. Any shift in the aggregate demand curve, including government shifts, affects both prices and output as we move along the

(12) aggregate _____ curve. Thus, expansionary fiscal policy, designed to increase GDP, is also likely to (<u>increase/decrease</u>) prices. Supply-side policies attempt to minimize the impact on prices through changes in fiscal policy that shift the aggregate supply curve at the same time that they shift the aggregate demand curve. Recently there has been much attention given to supply-side tax cuts, including such measures as speeding up depreciation allowances, reducing taxes for increased research and development expenditures, reducing the corporate income tax, reducing taxes on income from savings, reducing taxes on capital gains, and reducing income taxes to encourage more work effort.

Most economists have a number of reservations about the exaggerated claims of ardent supporters of supply-side tax cuts: Specific effects will depend on exactly which taxes are reduced; increases in aggregate supply are likely to take some time, while effects on aggregate demand will be much quicker. A realistic assessment suggests that by themselves supply-side tax cuts are likely to lead to increased income inequality and to bigger, not smaller, government budget deficits. Do not let these serious objections to exaggerated claims blind you to the kernel of truth in supply-side economics: Marginal tax rates are important for decisions by individuals and firms. Reductions in marginal tax rates can improve economic incentives.

IMPORTANT TERMS AND CONCEPTS QUIZ

Choose the best definition for the following terms.

1. _____ Fiscal policy
2. _____ Fixed taxes
3. _____ Variable taxes
4. _____ Government transfer payments
5. _____ Supply-side tax cuts

a. Tax deductions that businesses may claim when they invest.
b. Money the government gives to individuals in the form of outright grants.
c. Taxes that do not change when GDP changes
d. The government's plan for spending and taxes.
e. Tax policy designed to shift the aggregate supply curve to the right.
f. Taxes that change when GDP changes.

BASIC EXERCISE

This exercise is designed to show how changes in government purchases and taxes will have multiplier effects on the equilibrium level of income and how these multipliers can be used to help determine appropriate fiscal policy. To simplify the numerical calculations, the exercise focuses on the shift in the expenditure schedule, holding prices constant. That is, we will consider how changes in fiscal policy shift the aggregate demand curve. Table 11-1 has data on GDP, taxes, disposable income, consumption investment, government spending, exports and imports. This table is the same as Table 9-1 except that here taxes vary with income while in Table 9-1 they did not. Alternatively one could say that Table 11-1 considers an economy with variable taxes while Table 9-1 assumed that taxes were fixed taxes.

1. Complete the column for total spending to verify that the initial equilibrium level of income is the same as you found in Table 9-1.

   Equilibrium level of GDP _____

2. Assume now that government purchases decrease by $200 to $650 as shown in Table 11-2. Following the decrease in government purchases, the new equilibrium level of income is _____.

3. The multiplier for this decrease in government purchases is _____ (This multiplier can be computed by dividing the change in the equilibrium level of income by the change in government purchases.)

4. Now consider a subsequent across-the-board reduction in income taxes of $250. Table 11-3 shows the new relevant data for national income, taxes, disposable income, and consumption. The new equilibrium level of income after the reduction in taxes is

   _____.

TABLE 11-1
(CONSTANT PRICES)

Income (Output) Y	Taxes T	Disposable Income DI	Consumption Spending C	Investment Spending I	Government Purchases G	Exports X	Imports IM	Total Spending C + I + G + (X − IM)
5,500	675.0	4,825.0	4,200	800	850	500	650	_____
5,750	737.5	5,012.5	4,350	800	850	500	650	_____
6,000	800.0	5,200.0	4,500	800	850	500	650	_____
6,250	862.5	5,387.5	4,650	800	850	500	650	_____
6,500	925.0	5,575.0	4,800	800	850	500	650	_____
6,750	987.5	5,762.5	4,950	800	850	500	650	_____
7,000	1,050.0	5,950.0	5,100	800	850	500	650	_____

TABLE 11-2
(CONSTANT PRICES)

Income (Output) Y	Taxes T	Disposable Income DI	Consumption Spending C	Investment Spending I	Government Purchases G	Exports X	Imports IM	Total Spending C + I + G + (X − IM)
5,500	675.0	4,825.0	4,200	800	650	500	650	_____
5,750	737.5	5,012.5	4,350	800	650	500	650	_____
6,000	800.0	5,200.0	4,500	800	650	500	650	_____
6,250	862.5	5,387.5	4,650	800	650	500	650	_____
6,500	925.0	5,575.0	4,800	800	650	500	650	_____
6,750	987.5	5,762.5	4,950	800	650	500	650	_____
7,000	1,050.0	5,950.0	5,100	800	650	500	650	_____

TABLE 11-3
(CONSTANT PRICES)

Income (Output) Y	Taxes T	Disposable Income DI	Consumption Spending C	Investment Spending I	Government Purchases G	Exports X	Imports IM	Total Spending C + I + G + (X − IM)
5,500	425.0	5,075.0	4,400	800	650	500	650	_____
5,750	487.5	5,262.5	4,550	800	650	500	650	_____
6,000	550.0	5,450.0	4,700	800	650	500	650	_____
6,250	612.5	5,637.5	4,850	800	650	500	650	_____
6,500	675.0	5,825.0	5,000	800	650	500	650	_____
6,750	737.5	6,012.5	5,150	800	650	500	650	_____
7,000	800.0	6,200.0	5,300	800	650	500	650	_____

5. The multiplier for the across-the-board change in taxes is _____.

6. Why did it take a larger reduction in taxes to restore GDP to its initial level following the reduction in government purchases?

7. Question 4 asked you to analyze the impact of a reduction in income taxes. Was this reduction in taxes self-financing? That is, was the increase in GDP stimulated by the reduction in taxes large enough so that on balance there was no decrease in government tax revenues? (Be sure to compare tax receipts at the equilibrium level of income in Table 11-2 with those at the equilibrium in Table 11-3.)

8. Now let us use the multipliers computed in questions 3 and 5 to figure out what changes in government purchases or taxes would be necessary to raise the equilibrium level of income from its initial value given in question 1 to its full-employment level of $6,250. Assuming no change in tax rates, the necessary increase in government purchases is $_____ billion. Assuming no change in government purchases, the necessary reduction in taxes is $_____. (You can answer these questions by figuring out what appropriate change in government purchases or taxes, when multiplied by the relevant multiplier, will equal the desired change in income.) How would you choose between using changes in government purchases of goods and services on the one hand and reductions in taxes on the other?

9. What is the new equilibrium level of income if, from the initial equilibrium given in question 1, investment expenditures rather than government purchases fall by $200? (Now investment spending will be $600 while government purchases stay at $650. Create a new version of Table 11-1 if necessary.) What can one say about multipliers for autonomous changes in public versus private purchases of goods and services?

SELF-TESTS FOR UNDERSTANDING

Test A

Circle the most appropriate answer.

1. Fiscal policy involves decisions about all but which one of the following?
   a. Income tax rates.
   b. Eligibility rules for transfer payments.
   c. The money supply.
   d. Government purchases of goods and services.

2. The impact of transfer payments on disposable income suggests that an increase in transfer payments will have the same effect as
   a. an increase in taxes.
   b. an increase in government purchases of goods and services.
   c. a decrease in government purchases of goods and services.
   d. a decrease in taxes.

3. A simultaneous reduction in income taxes and transfer payments of $15 billion will leave aggregate disposable income
   a. lower than before the change.
   b. unchanged.
   c. higher than before the change.

4. Fixed taxes
   a. do not vary with GDP.
   b. increase whenever GDP increases.
   c. are the best way to model income taxes in the American economy.
   d. will be a constant proportion of GDP.

5. Variable taxes mean that the difference between GDP and disposable income will _____ as GDP increases.
   a. decrease
   b. stay the same
   c. increase

6. With fixed taxes, when other categories of aggregate demand—investment spending, net exports, government purchases—do not vary with GDP, the slope of the expenditure schedule will be
   a. less than the MPC.
   b. equal to the MPC.
   c. greater than the MPC.

7. With variable taxes, when other categories of aggregate demand—investment spending, net exports, government purchases—do not vary with GDP, the slope of the expenditure schedule will be
   a. less than the marginal propensity to consume.
   b. equal to the marginal propensity to consume.
   c. greater than the marginal propensity to consume.

8. The initial impact of a change in income taxes is on _____ and

   _____.
   a. imports, exports
   b. disposable income, investment
   c. GDP, consumption
   d. disposable income, consumption

9. A change in fixed taxes can be modeled as
   a. a shift in the consumption function.
   b. a twist of the expenditure schedule.
   c. a parallel shift in the expenditure schedule.
   d. a change in the MPC.

10. Equal reductions in government purchases and taxes are likely to
    a. shift the expenditure schedule down.
    b. leave the expenditure schedule unchanged.
    c. shift the expenditure schedule up.

11. Equal increases in transfer payments and taxes are likely to
    a. reduce aggregate demand at all levels of GDP.
    b. have equal and offsetting impacts on aggregate demand for no net impact.
    c. increase aggregate demand at all levels of GDP.

12. If the basic expenditure multiplier is 2.0 and if the government wishes to decrease the level of GDP by $80 billion, what decrease in government purchases of goods and services would do the job?
    a. $20 billion.
    b. $40 billion.
    c. $80 billion.
    d. $160 billion.

13. Instead of decreasing government expenditures, the same objectives, in terms of reducing GDP, could also be achieved by
    a. reducing government transfer payments.
    b. reducing taxes.
    c. increasing both taxes and government transfer payments by equal amounts.
    d. reducing both taxes and government transfer payments by equal amounts.

14. If the basic expenditure multiplier is 2.0, a reduction in personal income taxes of $25 billion is likely to
    a. increase GDP by $50 billion.
    b. increase GDP by more than $50 billion.
    c. increase GDP by less than $50 billion.

15. A 10 percent reduction in income tax rates would
    a. lower the value of the basic expenditure multiplier.
    b. raise the value of the basic expenditure multiplier.
    c. not affect the value of the basic expenditure multiplier.

16. An increase in tax rates will lead to all but which one of the following?
    a. A decrease in the multiplier.
    b. A movement along the aggregate demand curve.
    c. A reduction in the equilibrium level of GDP.
    d. A shift of the expenditure schedule.

17. Assume that from a position of full employment the government wants to reduce defense spending by $50 billion in response to an easing of international tensions. To avoid a possible recession, the government simultaneously decides to reduce income taxes. The necessary change in taxes to keep the equilibrium level of income unchanged is
    a. less than $50 billion.
    b. $50 billion.
    c. more than $50 billion.

18. Political conservatives could still argue for active stabilization policy as long as the government agreed to _____ during periods of boom and _____ during recessions.
    a. increase taxes; increase government spending
    b. increase government spending; lower taxes
    c. lower government spending; lower taxes
    d. lower taxes; increase government spending

19. Which one of the following is *not* an example of supply-side policies?
    a. Lowering the corporate income tax rate.
    b. Establishing tax-free retirement savings accounts.
    c. Reducing tax rates on capital gains.
    d. Requiring firms to depreciate assets over a longer rather than a shorter period of time.

20. Critics of supply-side tax cuts would agree with all but which one of the following?
    a. Supply-side tax cuts are likely to increase inequality in the distribution of income.
    b. Supply-side tax cuts will substantially reduce the rate of inflation.
    c. Supply-side tax cuts are likely to mean bigger deficits for the federal government.
    d. Supply-side tax cuts will have a larger initial impact on aggregate demand than on aggregate supply.

Test B

Circle T or F for true or false.

T F 1. An increase in income tax rates will increase the multiplier.

T F 2. With income taxes, a $1 change in GDP will lead to a smaller change in consumption than would a $1 change in disposable income.

T F 3. Income taxation reduces the value of the multiplier for changes in government purchases but does not affect the multiplier for changes in investment.

T F 4. Since taxes are not a direct component of aggregate demand, changes in taxes do not have multiplier effects of income.

T F 5. Changes in government purchases of goods and services and in government transfer payments to individuals are both changes in government spending and thus have the same multiplier effects on the equilibrium level of income.

T F 6. A reduction in taxes matched by an equal reduction in government purchases of goods and services is likely to leave the expenditure schedule unchanged.

T F   7. Active stabilization policy implies that the government must get bigger and bigger.

T F   8. Since income taxes and transfer payments to individuals have their first impact on the disposable income of consumers, they should have similar multipliers.

T F   9. Only the aggregate supply curve will shift following a supply-side tax cut that increases investment spending by firms.

T F 10. There is general agreement among economists that supply-side tax cuts will increase output with little impact on prices.

SUPPLEMENTARY EXERCISES

1. In his analysis of the impact of the 1964 tax cut, which reduced taxes on a permanent basis, Arthur Okun estimated that the MPC was 0.95.[1] At the same time, Okun estimated that the basic expenditure multiplier, applicable for any increase in autonomous spending, was only 2.73, not 20, which comes from the oversimplified formula of Chapter 9. (1/(1 – MPC). How can such a large MPC be consistent with such a small multiplier?

2. The 1964 reduction in personal taxes was about $10 billion. Okun estimated that this tax reduction raised GDP by $25.9 billion. The ratio of the change in GDP to the change in taxes was only 2.59, not 2.73, the value of the basic expenditure multiplier. How can you account for this discrepancy? (*Hint:* In his analysis, Okun assumed prices did not change, so price effects on consumption expenditures are not part of the answer. You should think about whether the basic expenditure multiplier—the multiplier for a shift in the expenditure schedule—is the appropriate multiplier to apply directly to the change in taxes.)

3. What is it like to advise the President of the United States about economic policy? Martin S. Feldstein was Chairman of the Council of Economic Advisers during the Reagan administration. You might enjoy reading his observations on the workings of the Council and the Chair of the Council, "The Council of Economic Advisers and Economic Advising in the United States," *The Economic Journal*, September 1992, pages 1223-1234.

---

[1]Arthur M. Okun, :Measuring the Impact of the 1964 Tax Cut." in W.W. Heller, ed., *Perspectives on Economic Growth* (New York: Vintage Books, 1968), pages 25-49.

Appendix: Algebraic Treatment of Fiscal Policy and Aggregate Demand

BASIC EXERCISE

This exercise is meant to illustrate the material in the Appendix to Chapter 11. Just as in the Appendix to Chapter 8, we can use equations rather than graphs or tables to determine the equilibrium level of output and relevant multipliers. If we have done our work accurately, we should get the same answer regardless of whether we use graphs, tables, or algebra.

The following equations underlie the numerical example in the Basic Exercise.

$$C = 340 + 0.8DI$$
$$T = -700 + 0.25Y$$
$$DI = Y - T$$
$$Y = C + I + G + (X - IM)$$

1. What is the equilibrium level of income if investment spending is $800 billion, net exports are $150 billion, and government purchases are $650 billion? Be sure that $C + I + G + (X–IM) = Y$

2. Assume that both across-the-board taxes and government purchases decline by $50 billion so that government purchases are $600 billion and the tax equation is

$$T = -750 + 0.25Y$$

Is the equilibrium level of income unchanged following the balanced reduction in the size of the government? Why? What about the government deficit $(G - T)$?

3. What is the multiplier for the following:
   • change in investment spending
   • change in net exports
   • change in government purchases
   • change in taxes (that is, change in intercept of tax equation)

STUDY QUESTIONS

1. How does the multiplier for a change in government spending compare to the multipliers in earlier chapters for changes in investment spending, net exports, and the autonomous component of consumption spending?

2. Consider a change from fixed to variable taxes. Does this change make the multiplier larger or smaller? Why?

3. How does one show the impact on the expenditure schedule of a change from fixed taxes to variable taxes?

4. Consider a change in taxes. How does one show the change in the expenditure schedule when the change in taxes is a change in fixed taxes? When it is a change in the tax rate underlying variable taxes?

5. Why wouldn't an equal increase in government purchases and taxes leave aggregate demand unchanged?

6. If you were charged with recommending changes in government purchases, taxes and transfers to shift the aggregate demand curve to the right, what sorts of changes in each of these elements of fiscal policy would do the job?

7. How would you choose between the alternatives you proposed when answering question 6?

8. Why is designing fiscal policy to achieve full-employment subject to such intense political debate rather than being a technical exercise best left to economists?

9. "Active stabilization policy—the deliberate use of fiscal policy to avoid recessions and inflation—must inevitably lead to bigger and bigger government." Do you agree or disagree? Why?

10. What are some examples of supply-sides tax cuts? Explain how and why each of your examples is expected to affect the aggregate supply curve.

11. If supply-side tax cuts could increase the equilibrium level of output without increasing prices they would be a superior instrument for short-run stabilization policy. Are supply-side tax cuts likely to work in this way? Why or why not? If not, what are supply-side tax cuts good for?

ECONOMICS IN ACTION
Tax Rates and Tax Revenue

In the spring and summer of 1993, as Congress considered President Clinton's deficit reduction proposals, a spirited debate took place about the link between tax rates and tax revenues. In the early 1980s supply-siders had argued that a reduction in tax rates would actually increase tax revenues. In 1993 the question was whether an increase in tax rates on the wealthiest taxpayers would increase tax revenues.

Kurt Hauser, an investment counselor in San Francisco, writing in the *Wall Street Journal*, argued that changes in tax rates have made no difference in federal revenues. Mr. Hauser argued that, despite numerous changes in the federal tax code and reductions in the top marginal tax rate for personal income from 92 percent to 28 percent, total federal government revenues—personal, corporate, social security, and other federal taxes—had varied only slightly from the historical average of 19.5 percent of GDP. He found no correlation between changes in tax rates and changes in federal revenue as a proportion of GDP. As for President Clinton's proposals, Mr. Hauser offered the prediction that within a couple of quarters, federal revenues would adjust to the historic 19.5 percent level.

Laura Tyson, Professor of Economics at Berkeley and chair of the President's Council of Economic Advisers, took exception to Mr. Hauser's argument. Focusing on revenues from personal income taxes, Tyson argued that tax revenues were responsive to changes in tax rates. Looking just at personal income tax receipts as a proportion of GDP, Tyson argued that its ups and downs were correlated with changes in tax rates. Specifically she argued that although other factors influence tax revenues, a strong and statistically significant relationship exists between the marginal tax rate for a hypothetical family of four that earns twice the median income and personal income tax revenues as a proportion of GDP.

It should be noted that the changes in taxes finally adopted in the summer of 1993 included increased income tax rates for a limited number of taxpayers: the proportion of social security income subject to tax was increased for social security recipients with significant other income, and the marginal tax rate was increased for the wealthiest taxpayers. A number of economists argued that the Clinton administration had overestimated the likely increase in revenue from these changes. In their opinion, tax-free municipal bonds, stock options instead of salary, deferred compensation along with adjustments in work effort, and tax reducing deductions can all be manipulated to minimize taxes. For most taxpayers the return to such tax avoidance strategies is quite small. When marginal tax rates become high enough and when there is a significant difference between the tax rate on regular income and capital gains, there can be a significant incentive for the wealthiest taxpayers to consider these strategies. Economist Robert Barro saw confirmation of such behavior when he noted that from 1981 to 1990 the proportion of taxes paid by the top one-half of one percent of the income distribution (about $220,000 in 1991) increased as marginal tax rates for the wealthiest taxpayers declined, tax loopholes were closed, and the difference between tax rates on regular income and capital gains was eliminated.

1. What has happened to total tax revenues and the proportion of taxes paid by the wealthiest taxpayers?

SOURCES: "The Tax and Revenue Equation," W. Kurt Hauser, *Wall Street Journal*, May 7, 1993.
    "Higher Taxes, Lower Revenues," Robert J. Barro, *Wall Street Journal*, July 9, 1993.
    "Higher Taxes Do So Raise Money," Laura Tyson, *Wall Street Journal*, August 3, 1993.

Chapter **12**

Money and the Banking System

LEARNING OBJECTIVES

After completing this chapter you should be able to:

- ♦ distinguish between various functions of money. Which are unique to money? Which are shared with other assets?
- ♦ distinguish between commodity money and fiat money.
- ♦ explain the differences between M1 and M2 as measures of money.
- ♦ describe the historical origins of fractional reserve banking and explain why the industry is so heavily regulated today.
- ♦ explain how the banking system as a whole can create deposits, given an initial injection of bank reserves.
- ♦ use the required reserve fraction to derive the oversimplified deposit creation multiplier.
- ♦ explain why the deposit creation multiplier, based on the required reserve fraction, is oversimplified.

IMPORTANT TERMS AND CONCEPTS

Run on a bank
Barter
Unit of account
Money
Medium of exchange
Store of value
Fiat money
Commodity money
Ml versus M2
Near moneys
Liquidity

Fractional reserve banking
Deposit insurance
Federal Deposit Insurance Corporation (FDIC)
Required reserves
Asset
Liability
Balance sheet
Net worth
Deposit creation
Excess reserves

CHAPTER REVIEW

Whether it is the root of all evil or not, there is no argument that money has an important influence on the way our economy operates. The right amount of money can help to keep employment up and prices stable. Too much money may lead to excessive inflation; too little money may lead to excessive unemployment. This chapter is an introduction to money. What is it? Where did it come from? What role do banks play in the creation of money? Chapter 13 discusses how the government now regulates the amount of money in the economy, and Chapter 14 discusses the influence of money on economic activity.

It is possible that a society could be organized without money. If everyone were self-sufficient there would, by definition, be no trading between individuals and no need for money. Even if people concentrated their productive activities on what they did best and traded with each other to get goods they did not produce themselves, they might still be able to get along without money. Direct trading of goods for goods, or goods for services, is

(1) called _____. For it to be successful there must be a double coincidence of wants. As societies become more complicated and people become ever more specialized, it is clear that barter becomes (<u>less difficult/more difficult</u>).

When a society uses a standard object for exchanging goods and services, a seller will provide goods or services to a buyer and receive the standard object as payment. The efficiency of such a system should be obvious. You no longer have to find someone who not only has what you want but also wants what you have. Anyone who has what you want

(2) will now do. Economists would call the standard object _____. If the object serving as money has intrinsic value, such as gold or jewelry, it is called _____ money. When objects serve as money it is useful that they are divisible, of uniform quality, durable, storable at little or no cost, and compact. Many commodity monies fail on one or more of these criteria. Today money has little intrinsic value and is called _____

money. Such money has value because everyone believes that everyone else will exchange goods and services for it. The bedrock for this foundation of faith is that the government will stand behind the money and limit its production.

When it comes to measuring the quantity of money, exactly where one draws the line is a bit unclear. We have defined money as a standard object used for exchanging goods and services. On this count, the sum of all coins and currency outside of banks plus the wide variety of checking accounts at banks and credit unions surely belongs in any measure of

(3) money. The measure that includes only these items is known as _____. If one also includes savings accounts (because they can easily be transferred into checking accounts), money market deposit accounts, and money market mutual funds, one is measuring _____.

Below are some data for December 1992.

Currency	$292.3 billion
Travelers checks	8.1 billion
Checkable deposits	726.1 billion
Savings deposits including money market deposit accounts	2,056.2 billion
Money market mutual funds plus other deposit type securities	414.3 billion

SOURCE: H.6 Statistical Release, Board of Governors of the Federal Reserve System, June 3, 1993.

How big is

(4) M1? $_____ billion.

M2? $_____ billion.

Given the importance of bank deposits in all measures of money, it is important to understand *how the banking system can create money*. Banks subject to deposit reserve requirements must hold reserves that are at least as great as some stated percentage of their deposits. Reserves can be either cash in a bank's vaults or money that the bank has on deposit at its local Federal Reserve Bank. We will learn more about the Federal Reserve System in Chapter 13. The stated percentage is the required reserve ratio. Thus, only some of the money used to open or to add to a bank deposit must be kept by the bank to meet reserve requirements. The rest can be used to make loans in the search for more profits. This system is known as fractional reserve banking.

(5)   The multiple creation of deposits is the counterpart to bank (lending/borrowing). Consider an individual bank that is subject to a 10 percent reserve requirement. Following a new

deposit of $1,000, the maximum amount of the new deposit that this bank could lend out and still meet the reserve requirement is $_____. As the proceeds of the loan are deposited in other banks, new deposits will be created. For the banking system as a whole, the maximum amount of loans that can be made, and thus the maximum amount of deposits that can be created following an increase in bank reserves, is limited by the _____ _____. The precise sequence of the multiple deposit creation is illustrated in the Basic Exercise for this chapter.

Mathematical formulas have been devised to determine the maximum increase in deposits that can be created by the banking system following an increase in bank reserves:

(6)

$$\left(\begin{array}{c}\text{Maximum}\\\text{increase}\\\text{in}\\\text{deposits}\end{array}\right) = \left(\begin{array}{c}\text{Initial}\\\text{increase}\\\text{in bank}\\\text{reserves}\end{array}\right) \times \left(\underline{}\right)$$

The increase in bank reserves may come from a deposit of cash. In this case, while deposits are up, cash outside banks is down, as some was deposited to start the process of multiple deposit creation. Thus, following a cash deposit, the maximum increase in the money supply will be (more/less) than the maximum increase in deposits.

The deposit creation formula is oversimplified for two reasons:

1. The formula assumes that the proceeds of each loan will eventually be redeposited in the banking system. If some of the proceeds of a loan do not get redeposited, then the

(7)   deposit creation multiplier will be (larger/smaller).

2. The formula also assumes that every bank makes as large a loan as possible; that is, each bank is assumed to hold no _____ reserves. If banks do choose to hold such reserves, then the money creation formula would be (larger/smaller).

The discussion of the deposit creation multiplier showed how deposits can be created following an increase in bank reserves. The emphasis was on how a change in reserves leads to a change in deposits. One should not be surprised to learn that *total* deposits in all banks are similarly limited by *total* reserves. The cash deposit discussed in the text results in an increase in total reserves of the banking system. Most increases in reserves at one bank are offset by a decrease in reserves at some other bank, with no increase in total reserves. Consider Derek, who takes money out of his account at Bank A. Derek uses the money to buy a home computer, and the dealer deposits this money in his bank, Bank B. At the same time reserves increase at Bank B, they decrease at Bank A. The process of multiple deposit creation initiated at Bank B is offset by

(8) a process of multiple deposit _____ starting with Bank A, and the net effect is (some/no) increase in deposits. The important factor for expanding deposits is new reserves available to the banking system. We will learn in Chapter 13 how the Federal Reserve is able to influence the volume of reserves available to the banking system.

IMPORTANT TERMS AND CONCEPTS QUIZ

Choose the best definition for the following terms.

1. _____ Run on a bank
2. _____ Barter
3. _____ Unit of account
4. _____ Money
5. _____ Medium of exchange
6. _____ Store of value
7. _____ Commodity money
8. _____ Fiat money
9. _____ M1
10. _____ M2
11. _____ Near moneys
12. _____ Liquidity
13. _____ Fractional reserve banking
14. _____ Deposit insurance
15. _____ FDIC
16. _____ Required reserves
17. _____ Asset
18. _____ Liability
19. _____ Balance sheet
20. _____ Net worth
21. _____ Deposit creation
22. _____ Excess reserves

a. Reserves in excess of the legal minimum.
b. Item an individual or firm owns.
c. Many depositors concurrently withdrawing cash from their accounts.
d. Item used to hold wealth from one point in time to another.
e. Ease with which an asset can be converted into cash.
f. System where bankers keep reserves equal to only a portion of total deposits.

g. Standard unit for quoting prices.
h. Value of all assets minus the value of all liabilities.
i. Amount of money balances the public will hold at a given price level.
j. System of exchange where people trade one good for another without using money.
k. Sum of coins, paper money, checkable deposits, money market mutual funds, and most savings account balances.
l. Accounting statement listing values of assets on the left-hand side and those of liabilities and net worth on the right-hand side.
m. Standard object used in exchanging goods and services.
n. Object, without value as commodity, which serves as money by government decree.
o. Liquid assets which are close substitutes for money.
p. System which guarantees depositors against loss if bank goes bankrupt.
q. Process by which banking system turns one dollar of reserves into several dollars of deposits.
r. Item an individual or firm owes.
s. Sum of coins, paper money, and checkable deposits.
t. Object used as a medium of exchange that also has substantial nonmonetary uses.
u. Minimum amount of reserves a bank must hold.
v. Government agency that insures depositors' checking and savings accounts.

BASIC EXERCISE

This exercise is designed to help you understand the multiple creation of bank deposits by working through a specific simplified example.

1. Column 1 of Table 12-1 is partly filled in for you to show the changes in the balance sheet of Bank A immediately following Janet's cash deposit of $10,000. At this point, bank deposits have increased by $_____ and the stock of money in the economy—that is, bank deposits plus currency outside banks—is (higher/lower/unchanged). Assuming the required reserve fraction is 10 percent, fill in the last two rows of column 1, showing the initial changes in required and excess reserves.

2. Assume that Bank A responds to Janet's deposit by making as large a loan as it can to Earl, given the required reserve ratio. Now fill in column 2 to represent the changes in Bank A's balance sheet after the loan has been made and Earl has taken the proceeds of the loan in cash.

3. Earl uses the money from the loan to buy a car and the car dealer deposits this cash in Bank B. Fill in column 3 to represent the changes in Bank B's balance sheet following this cash deposit. At this point, total bank deposits have increased by $_____ and the stock of money in the economy has increased by $_____.

4. Assume now that Bank B also makes as large a loan as possible. Fill in column 4 to represent changes in Bank B's balance sheet after it makes the loan and this latest borrower takes the proceeds in cash.

TABLE 12-1
BALANCE SHEET CHANGES

	(1) Bank A	(2) Bank A	(3) Bank B	(4) Bank B	(5) Bank C
Assets					
Reserves	$10,000	_____	_____	_____	_____
Loans	0	_____	_____	_____	_____
Liabilities					
Deposits	$10,000	_____	_____	_____	_____
Addendum					
Required reserves	_____	_____	_____	_____	_____
Excess reserves	_____	_____	_____	_____	_____

Note: Required reserve ratio is 10 percent.

5. Assume that the proceeds of this loan eventually get deposited in Bank C. Fill in column 5 to represent the changes in the balance sheet of Bank C following the increase in deposits. At this point total bank deposits have increased by $_____ and the stock of money has increased by $_____.

6. Fill in the following sequence of increased deposits following the initial increase at Bank A, assuming that each bank makes the largest possible loan.

   Increased deposits at Bank A ___$10,000___

   Increased deposits at Bank B _____

   Increased deposits at Bank C _____

   Increased deposits at Bank D _____

   Increased deposits at Bank E _____

   If you have not made any mistakes you will notice that each increase in deposit is less than the previous increase and can be expressed as

   $(1.0 - 0.1) \times$ (the previous increase in deposits).

   Mathematically this is an infinite geometric progression with decreasing increments. If we carried the sum out far enough it would approach a limit given by $10,000 ÷ _____, or $_____ . (If you have a suitable electronic calculator or microcomputer you might try testing this result by actually calculating the sum for a very large number of terms.) This specific numerical example illustrates the more general principle that the multiplier for the maximum increase in deposits following an increase in bank reserves is 1 ÷ _____ _____ _____.

SELF-TESTS FOR UNDERSTANDING

Test A

Circle the most appropriate answer.

1. Money serves all but which one of the following functions?
   a. Medium of exchange.
   b. Hedge against inflation.
   c. Unit of account.
   d. Store of value.

2. Which of the following is *not* an example of commodity money?
   a. Gold coins.
   b. Wampum.
   c. A $10 bill.
   d. Diamonds.

3. Where was paper money first used?
   a. China.
   b. Egypt.
   c. India.
   d. Italy.

4. Which of the following does not belong in M1?
   a. The coins in your pocket.
   b. Jodi's checking account.
   c. The cash in the vault at the bank downtown.
   d. The traveler's check that Heather has left over from last summer.

5. The difference between M2 and M1 includes which of the following? (There may be more one correct answer.)
   a. Traveler's checks.
   b. Money market mutual fund balances.
   c. Marketable U.S. government debt.
   d. Savings deposits.

6. Liquidity is defined as the
   a. viscosity of financial assets.
   b. ease with which assets can be converted to money.
   c. net worth of a financial institution.
   d. ratio of liabilities to assets.

7. A bank's (or your) net worth is found by
   a. summing up all assets.
   b. adding total assets to total liabilities.
   c. subtracting total liabilities from total assets.
   d. dividing total assets by total liabilities.

8. Which of the following is not an asset for a bank?
   a. Excess reserves.
   b. Holdings of U.S. government securities.
   c. Checking account balances.
   d. Mortgage loans made by the bank.

9. The key item that makes balance sheets balance is a bank's
   a. holdings of excess reserves.
   b. assets.
   c. required reserves.
   d. net worth.

10. If a bank holds more reserves than required, the difference is
    a. the bank's net worth.
    b. liquidity.
    c. solvency.
    d. excess reserves.

11. Banks could increase profits by
    a. holding more commodity money and less fiat money.
    b. reducing their liabilities.
    c. holding fewer excess reserves in order to make more loans.
    d. substituting M2 for M1.

12. If Damien deposits cash that he used to keep under his mattress in his checking account, the initial deposit will result in
    a. an increase M1.
    b. a decrease in M2.
    c. an increase in the net worth of the banking system.
    d. no change in M1.

13. The most important government regulation of banks in terms of limiting the multiple creation of deposits is
    a. bank examinations and audits.
    b. limits on the kinds of assets that banks can buy.
    c. the required reserve ratio.
    d. requirements to disclose the volume of loans to bank officials.

14. If the minimum reserve requirement for all bank deposits is 10 percent, then the maximum multiple creation of deposits by the banking system as a whole following a cash deposit of $2,000 would be
    a. $(0.1) \times (\$2,000) = \$200$.
    b. $(1 + 0.1) \times (\$2,000) = \$2,200$.
    c. $(\$2,000) \div (1 - 0.1) = \$2,222$.
    d. $(\$2,000) \div (0.1) = \$20,000$.

15. The maximum increase in the money supply would be
    a. smaller than in question 14.
    b. larger than in question 14.
    c. the same as in question 14.

    (In fact, it would be $_____.)

16. If the reserve requirement is 15 percent instead of 10 percent, then the maximum multiple creation of deposits would be
    a. smaller than in question 14.
    b. larger than in question 14.
    c. the same as in question 14.

17. If banks hold some of every increase in deposits in the form of excess reserves, then the amount of deposits actually created following a cash deposit would be
    a. less than that indicated in question 14.
    b. the same as that indicated in question 14.
    c. more than that indicated in question 14.

18. If the required reserve ratio is 20 percent and Rachel deposits $100 in cash in the First National Bank, the maximum increase in deposits by the banking system as a whole is
    a. 0.
    b. $20.
    c. $100.
    d. $500.

19. If the required reserve ratio is 20 percent and Rachel deposits $100 in the First National Bank by depositing a check from her mother written on the Second National Bank, the maximum increase in deposits by the banking system as a whole is
    a. 0.
    b. $20.
    c. $100.
    d. $500.

20. If a bank's total reserve holdings are $35 million and it has $12 million of excess reserves, then its required reserves are
    a. $12 million.
    b. $23 million.
    c. $35 million.
    d. $47 million.

Test B

Circle T or F for true or false.

T F 1. A major advantage of the use of money rather than barter is that money avoids the problems of finding a "double coincidence of wants."

T F 2. Fiat money in the United States may be redeemed for gold from the U.S. Treasury.

T F 3. Many assets serve as a store of value but only money is also a medium of exchange.

T F 4. In periods with high rates of inflation, money is a good store of value.

T F 5. Banks could increase their profitability by holding higher levels of excess reserves.

T F 6. The existence of deposit insurance is an important reason for the dramatic decline in the number of bank failures.

T F 7. The oversimplified deposit creation multiplier of 1 divided by the required reserve ratio is an underestimate of the more appropriate, but more complicated, deposit multiplier.

T F   8.   Multiple deposit creation applies to increases in the money supply but reductions in the money supply can come about only through government taxation.

T F   9.   Required reserves are part of a bank's liabilities, whereas excess reserves are part of a bank's assets.

T F 10.   If a bank's liabilities exceed its assets, the bank is said to have negative net worth.

SUPPLEMENTARY EXERCISES

1. If the required reserve ratio is 20 percent and banks want to hold 10 percent of any increase in deposits in the form of excess reserves and people want to hold $1 more in currency for every $10 increase in deposits, what is the eventual increase in deposits following a $1,000 cash deposit in the First National Bank? What is the eventual increase in the money supply?

2. If M is the required reserve fraction, E is the ratio of excess reserves to deposits, and C is the ratio of currency to deposits, what is the formula that relates the change in deposits to a change in reserves?

ECONOMICS IN ACTION

The Reform of Deposit Insurance

As described in the text, the establishment of federal deposit insurance had a dramatic effect on the number of bank failures. Some critics argue that experience since the late 1970s suggests that we may have had too much of a good thing. Economist Edward J. Kane has been especially critical of the actions of federal government officials, both elected and appointed, concerning deposit insurance. He was one of the first to describe the collapse of the Federal Savings and Loan Insurance Corporation (FSLIC), the deposit insurance agency for S&Ls, as resulting from a combination a moral hazard and a principal-agent problem.[1]

Moral hazard arose because deposit insurance provided an incentive for some S&Ls to engage in risky behavior. The period of high interest rates in the late 1970s and early 1980s had left these institutions with little or negative net worth. Owners of these institutions saw high-risk but potentially high-return loans as their only salvation. Insurance protected their depositors. Negative net worth meant that their own investment in the S&L had already been wiped out. They literally had nothing to lose by engaging in risky behavior.

---

[1]Moral hazard refers to the tendency of insurance to make people less concerned with the risks associated with their behavior, after all its covered by insurance. Principal-agent relationships occur whenever one party, the principal, has to hire others, the agents, to act on their behalf. An example would be stockholders who hire executives to manage corporations. It is often difficult for the principals to monitor the behavior of their agents to insure that the agents act to promote the principal's interests and not their (the agent's) own.

Kane also charges that Congress and bank regulators (the agents) failed to act in the best interest of U.S. taxpayers (the principals). Kane charges that at critical points, and with the support and encouragement of key members of Congress, the FSLIC allowed bankrupt institutions to continue in business. Succumbing to lobbying pressures to focus on the original book value of assets rather than current market value allowed officials to pretend that bankrupt institutions were still solvent. The result was that problems were deferred as the cost of appropriate action increased. Opposition to increased federal spending and the impact on the deficit that would accompany the official closing of failed institutions further contributed to delay.

What is an appropriate stance for deposit insurance? There have been a large number of proposals. They include the mandatory use of market prices to value assets; mandatory and higher net worth requirements for financial institutions; automatic rules for closing insolvent institutions that remove the element of discretion on the part of regulators; deposit insurance premiums that vary with the riskiness of a bank's portfolio; and public notice of the results of bank examinations.

A number of observers have also argued that the present deposit insurance limit is so high that depositors have little incentive to concern themselves with the riskiness of a bank's portfolio. If a smaller amount, perhaps the first $40,000 or $50,000 of deposits, were insured and it was clear that deposits above this level had no insurance protection, depositors with large balances, including businesses, would have a real incentive to pay attention to the riskiness of their bank's assets. According to this view, a bank that was imprudent would (and should) suffer a run on its deposits with little reason to expect that the run would spill over and harm sound banks.

1. What changes, if any, do you think there should be to the system of deposit insurance? Why? How far should the government go to protect depositors? How does one design a system of deposit insurance that addresses the problem of moral hazard?

You might want to consult the following:

Reforming Federal Deposit Insurance, Congressional Budget Office, (GPO: Washington, D.C.) September 1990.

The S&L Insurance Mess: How Did It Happen, Edward J. Kane, (The Urban Institute Press: Washington, D.C.) 1991.

The S&L Debacle, Lawrence J. White, (Oxford University Press: New York) 1991.

STUDY QUESTIONS

1. What functions does money share with other assets and what functions are unique to money?

2. How does fiat money differ from commodity money? In particular, how do they compare with regard to the list of desirable characteristics discussed in the text?

3. Where would you draw the line if asked to come up with a measure of money for the American economy?

4. Rank the following in terms of their liquidity and justify your ranking: a 12 month savings certificate, the balance in your checking account, a corporate bond issued by Microsoft, some left-over traveler's checks from your most recent trip, a share of stock in Dupont, a $20 bill, a piece of lakeside vacation property.

5. What is full-bodied money? Is money in the United States today full-bodied? If not, where does its value come from?

6. If the government is going to insure deposits, it seems natural that it be allowed to examine a bank's books and put limits on some types of loans to control its risk. Alternatively, the need for deposit insurance could be eliminated if reserve requirements were set at 100 percent. What do you think would happen to bank service charges if reserve requirements were 100 percent? What other changes might you expect? In particular think about the incentive to create alternatives to bank deposits.

7. How can you tell when something is an asset or a liability?

8. As a bank is worth more if its assets exceed its liabilities, in what sense does its balance sheet balance?

9. As the government controls the printing press, how can banks create money?

10. In what ways is the deposit creation multiplier, $1/m$, oversimplified? Does adjusting for these complications make the deposit creation multiplier larger or smaller?

Chapter **13**

Monetary Policy and the National Economy

LEARNING OBJECTIVES

After completing this chapter you should be able to:

♦ distinguish between the concepts "money" and "income."

♦ analyze arguments in favor of and opposed to the independence of the Federal Reserve System.

♦ draw and explain the logic behind both the supply-of-money schedule and the demand-for-money schedule.

♦ analyze the impact of changes in the three major monetary policy instruments both in words and by using the demand-for- and supply-of-money schedules.

♦ explain how bond prices and interest rates are related.

♦ describe the impact of open market operations on bond prices and interest rates.

♦ explain why the Fed's control of the stock of money is not exact.

♦ explain how some suggested reforms might change the degree of control that the Fed has over the stock of money.

♦ describe how changes in monetary policy affect the expenditure schedule and the aggregate demand curve.

♦ use the expenditure schedule and aggregate demand curve to describe how changes in monetary policy affect the economy's macroeconomic equilibrium, that is, interest rates, investment spending, GDP, and prices.

♦ explain how the impact of higher prices on the demand for money helps to explain why the aggregate demand curve has a negative slope.

IMPORTANT TERMS AND CONCEPTS

Central bank
Federal Reserve System
Federal Open Market Committee (FOMC)
Independence of the Fed
Reserve requirements
Open market operations
Bond prices and interest rates
Contraction and expansion of the money
    supply

Federal Reserve lending to banks
Moral suasion
Supply of money
Demand for money
Opportunity cost
Equilibrium in the money market
Monetary policy
Why the aggregate demand curve slopes down

CHAPTER REVIEW

In Chapter 12 we learned how deposits are created by the actions of banks. In this chapter we will see how actions taken by the Federal Reserve System can influence the stock of money. Reserve requirements and the total amount of bank reserves are important keys to the Federal Reserve's control of bank deposits and the stock of money. We will also see how the equilibrium in the money market influences the economy's overall macroeconomic equilibrium. The emphasis in this chapter is on building models. In subsequent chapters we will use these models to understand policy issues.

(1)   The Federal Reserve System was established in _____ and is the nation's _____ bank. There are _____ district banks throughout the country, with headquarters in Washington, D.C. The people in charge in Washington are the seven members of the _____ of _____ of the Federal Reserve System. Major decisions about the stock of money are made by the FOMC, or the _____ _____ _____ Committee. Government spending and taxes are the nation's (<u>fiscal/monetary</u>) policy. Policy actions by the Federal Reserve constitute the nation's _____ policy.

   We saw in Chapter 12 that the multiple creation of bank deposits is limited by the required reserve ratio and by the volume of bank reserves. Reserve requirements help to determine the deposit creation multiplier. The other two major policy instruments—open market operations and lending to banks—directly affect total bank reserves. We also saw in Chapter 12 that controlling reserve requirements and the volume of bank reserves does not allow for the

(2) precise control of the stock of money because of possible changes in (<u>excess/required</u>) reserve holdings by banks and in currency holdings by the public. These slippages in the deposit creation formula are an important reason why the Federal Reserve's control over the stock of money, while strong and important, is not complete.

(3) A reduction in reserve requirements does not change total bank reserves, but it will initially result in a(n) (increase/decrease) in noninterest-earning excess reserves. Multiple deposit creation will take place as banks try to put these nonearning excess reserves to work. Thus, a reduction in minimum reserve requirements should be associated with a (larger/smaller) volume of deposits and is an example of a(n) (expansionary/contractionary) change in monetary policy. An increase in reserve requirements will typically force banks to curtail lending in order to meet new, higher holdings of (excess/required) reserves. Such an increase would be an example of a _____ change in monetary policy.

(4) Open market operations—the purchase and sale of government _____ represent the most important and most commonly used instrument of monetary policy. Open market operations affect bank behavior by adding to or subtracting from the amount of bank reserves. The essence of an open market purchase is that the Fed creates bank reserves when it (buys/sells) a government security. The result is a(n) (increase/decrease) in noninterest-earning excess reserves, and the usual multiple deposit creation process is set in motion. An open market sale has exactly opposite effects. Payment to the Fed for government securities means a(n) (reduction/increase) in bank reserves and initiates a process of multiple deposit (creation/destruction).

Banks can add to their reserve holdings by borrowing directly from the Fed. Such borrowings might facilitate a multiple expansion of deposits or, more frequently, might forestall a multiple destruction of deposits. The Fed influences the volume of borrowing by

(5) changing the interest rate it charges banks and by _____ _____, which is the Fed's way of letting banks know that they are misusing their borrowing privileges. More bank borrowing would mean a (higher/lower) amount of bank reserves than otherwise, and eventually a (higher/lower) volume of bank deposits. When banks borrow reserves from the Fed they must pay interest on these borrowings. In the United States the interest rate for these borrowings is called the _____ _____.

Monetary policy decisions, affecting reserve requirements and the total volume of bank reserves, can be seen as putting an upper limit on the possible creation of bank deposits and hence on the stock of money. How much banks will want to exploit the potential to create deposits will be determined by the profitability of increased bank operations—more loans and

(6) more deposits. Higher interest rates on loans will induce banks to make (more/fewer) loans, hold (more/fewer) nonearning excess reserves, and borrow (more/less) from the Fed (if they can). All of these actions will expand the volume of deposits and hence the stock of money. In brief, considering just banks, higher interest rates should be associated with a (larger/smaller) stock of money.

This behavior by banks is summarized in Figure 13-1, which shows an upward-sloping supply of money schedule. Movements along the schedule are related to the decisions of commercial banks. Shifts in the schedule come from changes in monetary policy. For example, an

open market purchase increases the amount of bank reserves and shifts the money supply
(7) schedule to the (left/right). Changes in other monetary policy variables will also shift the money supply schedule. To repeat, monetary policy decisions determine the position of the money supply schedule; they do not, by themselves, determine either the stock of money or the interest rate. The actual stock of money and the interest rate will be determined by the intersection of the supply-of-money schedule and the _____ for-money schedule.

Figure 13-2 shows a demand schedule for money. The schedule has a negative slope
(8) because, as the interest rate rises, the demand for money (increases/decreases). The increase in interest rates means that the opportunity cost of holding money has (increased/decreased). If nominal GDP increases, that is, if real GDP or prices increase, the demand schedule will shift to the (right/left) as more transactions associated with a higher GDP will lead to a(n) (increased/decreased) demand for money at every interest rate. If nominal GDP decreases, the demand schedule will shift to the _____.

Equilibrium values for the stock of money and the rate of interest will be determined by the forces of both supply and demand consistent with the process described in Chapter 4.
(9) Graphically, the equilibrium can be represented by the _____ of the demand and supply curves, as in Figure 13-3. Changes in monetary policy will change the equilibrium values for both the stock of money and the rate of interest. An expansionary change in monetary policy would be represented by a shift of the (demand/supply) schedule to the (left/right), a(n) (increase/decrease) in the stock of money, and a(n) (increase/decrease) in the interest rate. A contractionary change in monetary policy would be represented by a shift of the supply schedule to the _____, a(n) _____ in the stock of money, and a(n) _____ in the interest rate.

With an understanding of how the demand and supply for money work together to determine interest rates, we are in a position to see how changes in monetary policy affect
(10) aggregate demand. Policy shifts in the (supply/demand) of money schedule will change interest rates as we move along the _____ for money schedule. The change in interest rates will affect interest sensitive categories of demand, especially investment spending. Changes in investment spending lead to a (shift in/movement along) the expenditure schedule. The (shift in/movement along) the expenditure schedule will shift the aggregate (demand/supply) curve through the multiplier process described in Chapter 9. Overall macroeconomic equilibrium is reestablished at the new intersection of the aggregate demand curve and the aggregate supply curve. The division of effects, as between real output and prices, is determined by the slope of the aggregate _____ curve. This sequence of events is diagrammed at the end of Chapter 13 of the text.

FIGURE 13-1   **FIGURE 13-2**   **FIGURE 13-3**

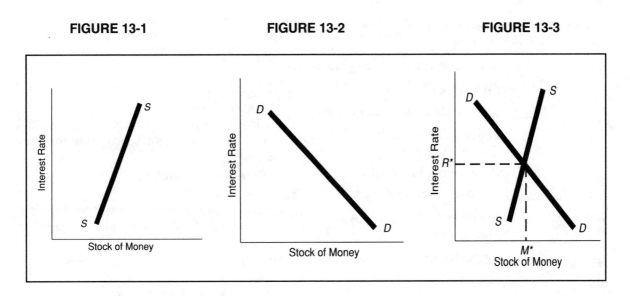

The same reasoning helps us to understand two other important points:

Why the aggregate demand curve has a negative slope

Higher prices not only reduce the purchasing power of money fixed assets, they also increase the transactions demand for money. With an unchanged supply-of-money schedule, the increase in the demand for money that comes with a higher price level will shift the demand-for-money schedule to the right, leading to an increase in interest rates and lower investment spending. Thus higher prices affect aggregate demand through their impact on investment as well as consumption and net exports.

Why the multiplier formula 1/(1 – MPC) is oversimplified

Increases in nominal GDP from the multiplier process increase the transactions demand for money. Interest rates rise as the demand-for-money schedule moves along an unchanged supply-of-money schedule. The reduction in investment spending induced by the rise in interest rates is the third important reason why the multiplier process of Chapter 9 was oversimplified.

IMPORTANT TERMS AND CONCEPTS QUIZ

Choose the best definition for the following terms.

1. _____ Central bank
2. _____ Federal Reserve System
3. _____ Federal Open Market Committee
4. _____ Reserve requirement
5. _____ Open-market operations
6. _____ Moral suasion
7. _____ Discount rate
8. _____ Opportunity cost
9. _____ Equilibrium in the money market
10. _____ Monetary policy

a. Foregone value of next best alternative that is not chosen.
b. A bank for banks responsible for the conduct of monetary policy.
c. Branch of Treasury responsible for minting coins.
d. Quantity of money and level of interest rate where money demand equals money supply.
e. Minimum amount of reserves a bank must hold.
f. Fed's informal requests and warnings to persuade banks to limit their borrowings.
g. Actions Fed takes to affect money supply, interest rates, or both.
h. Central bank of the United States.
i. Interest rate Fed charges on loans to banks.
j. Fed's purchase or sale of government securities.
k. Chief policymaking committee of the Federal Reserve System.

BASIC EXERCISES

1. Instruments of Monetary Policy

This exercise is designed to review the impact of various changes in monetary policy instruments.

a. Use Figure 13-4 to analyze the impact of an open market sale. The sale of a government security by the Fed results in a(n) (increase/decrease) in total bank reserves. This change in bank reserves can be represented as a shift of the supply-of-money schedule to the _____. (Be sure you can explain in words why the schedule shifts.) Draw a new supply-of-money schedule that represents the result of the open market sale. As a result of this (expansionary/contractionary) change in monetary policy, the equilibrium stock of money will (fall/rise) and interest rates will _____.

b. Use Figure 13-5 to analyze the impact of a reduction in minimum reserve requirements. The initial result of a reduction in minimum reserve requirements will be a(n) (increase/decrease) in excess reserves. The likely response by banks to this change in excess reserves will result in a process of multiple deposit (creation/destruction). In

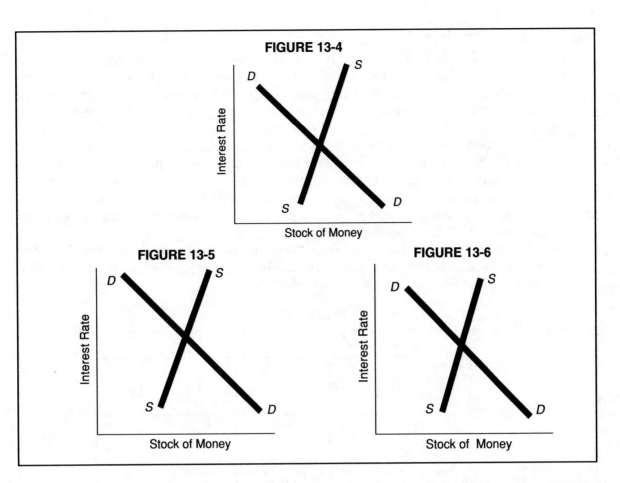

FIGURE 13-4

FIGURE 13-5

FIGURE 13-6

Figure 13-5 such a development can be represented as a shift of the supply-of-money schedule to the _____. Draw the new supply-of-money schedule. As a result of this _____ change in monetary policy, the equilibrium stock of money will _____ and interest rates will _____.

c. Use Figure 13-6 to analyze the impact of an increase in the discount rate. An increase in this rate will make banks (<u>more/less</u>) willing to borrow from the Fed. One expects that the volume of member bank borrowing will _____. The change in member bank borrowing is a direct change in bank reserves; so, as a result of the increase in the discount rate, total bank reserves will _____ and the supply-of-money schedule will shift to the _____. Draw the new supply-of-money schedule in Figure 13-6. As a result of this _____ change in monetary policy, the equilibrium stock of money will _____ and interest rates will _____.

d. You should also be able to analyze the impact of each opposite change in monetary policy; that is, an open market purchase, an increase in minimum reserve requirements, and a decrease in the discount rate.

2. Borrowing from the Fed

Consider the data in Table 13-1 on interest rates and borrowings by depository institutions from the Federal Reserve. The federal funds rate is a market interest rate: it is the interest rate on most short term lending and borrowing between depository institutions. Follow the instructions below to explore the influence of market interest rates on bank borrowings from the Fed.

a. The financial incentive to borrow from the Fed can be represented by the difference between the discount rate and market interest rates, represented here by the federal funds rate. Plot the data from the last two columns of Table 13-1, one point for each month, in the two-variable diagram in Figure 13-7. What does this data suggest is likely to happen to bank borrowings from the Fed if market interest rates increase while the discount rate remains unchanged?

b. Whenever the federal funds rate exceeds the discount rate, banks can make money by borrowing cheaply from the Fed and by lending at the higher federal funds rate. Why then wasn't there more borrowing in 1989?

FIGURE 13-7

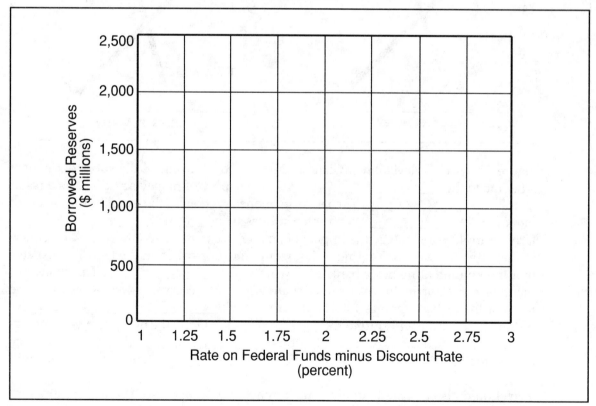

TABLE 13-1

		Discount Rate (percent)	Federal Funds Rate (percent)	Fed Funds Rate minus Discount Rate (percent)	Borrowings from the Federal Reserve ($ millions)
Jan	1989	6.50	9.12	2.62	1,662
Feb	1989	6.59	9.36	2.77	1,487
Mar	1989	7.00	9.85	2.85	1,813
Apr	1989	7.00	9.84	2.84	2,289
May	1989	7.00	9.81	2.81	1,720
Jun	1989	7.00	9.53	2.53	1,490
Jul	1989	7.00	9.24	2.24	694
Aug	1989	7.00	8.99	1.99	675
Sep	1989	7.00	9.02	2.02	693
Oct	1989	7.00	8.84	1.84	555
Nov	1989	7.00	8.55	1.55	349
Dec	1989	7.00	8.45	1.45	265

Source: *Economic Report of the President, 1990*, Tables C–69 and C–71.

SELF-TESTS FOR UNDERSTANDING

Test A

Circle the most appropriate answer.

1. The Federal Reserve is responsible for the conduct of
    a. domestic economic policy.
    b. fiscal policy.
    c. international economic policy.
    d. monetary policy.

2. The Federal Reserve is a bank for
    a. the Treasury.
    b. households.
    c. businesses.
    d. banks.

3. Which of the following is *not* an instrument of monetary policy?
    a. Open market operations.
    b. Lending to banks.
    c. Antitrust actions to promote competition in banking.
    d. Required reserve ratios.

4. Who has direct responsibility for open market operations?
   a. The Board of Governors.
   b. The Federal Open Market Committee.
   c. The President of the United States.
   d. The Banking Committee of the U.S. Senate.

5. Open market operations involve the Fed buying and selling
   a. stocks in American companies.
   b. U.S. government securities.
   c. gold.
   d. corporate bonds.

6. When making an open market purchase, the Fed gets the money to make the purchase from
   a. the Treasury.
   b. the Bureau of Printing and Engraving.
   c. cash in its vault.
   d. making a computer entry on its own books to credit the reserve account of the bank from which it purchases the security.

7. An open market purchase will lead to all but which one of the following?
   a. Supply-of-money schedule shifts to the right.
   b. Expenditure schedule shifts up.
   c. Multiplier increases.
   d. Aggregate demand curve shifts to the right.

8. An open market sale will result in all but which one of the following?
   a. decrease in the stock of money.
   b. increase in interest rates.
   c. lower investment spending.
   d. higher prices.

9. The immediate impact of a change in reserve requirements will be on the
   a. total volume of bank reserves.
   b. division of reserves (between required reserves and excess reserves).
   c. demand for money.
   d. discount rate.

10. An increase in reserve requirements will lead to all but which one of the following?
    a. An initial increase in required reserves.
    b. A reduction in the stock of money.
    c. An increase in interest rates.
    d. Higher investment spending.

11. A reduction in the discount rate will lead to all but which one of the following?
    a. An increased incentive for banks to borrow from the Fed.
    b. An expansion of bank reserves as banks borrow more.
    c. The money supply schedule shifts to the left.
    d. A reduction in interest rates.

12. Which of the following is *not* an example of expansionary monetary policy?
    a. An open market purchase.
    b. A reduction in reserve requirements.
    c. An increase in the interest rates charged on loans by the Fed to commercial banks.
    d. A reduction in the discount rate.

13. If the Fed wants to reduce the stock of money, which of the following policy actions would be inappropriate?
    a. An increase in minimum reserve requirements.
    b. The sale of a government bond from the Fed's portfolio.
    c. An increase in the discount rate.
    d. An open market purchase.

14. Which of the following help to explain why the Fed does not have precise control of the money supply? (There may be more than one correct answer.)
    a. Banks may vary the amount of excess reserves they desire to hold.
    b. Open market operations can change the volume of bank reserves.
    c. Changes in the amount of currency as opposed to bank deposits that individuals and businesses want to hold.
    d. Changes in reserve requirements will affect the deposit creation multiplier.

15. Important determinants of the demand for money include all but which one of the following?
    a. The discount rate.
    b. The level of real output.
    c. Market interest rates.
    d. The price level.

16. A change in which of the following would lead to a shift in the demand-for-money schedule?
    a. Market interest rates.
    b. Reserve requirements.
    c. GDP.
    d. The discount rate.

17. The positive slope of the supply-of-money schedule indicates that
    a. at higher interest rates people will demand more money.
    b. banks are likely to respond to higher interest rates by holding fewer excess reserves.
    c. minimum reserve requirements increase directly with interest rates.
    d. the Fed is likely to engage in expansionary monetary policy actions as interest rates increase.

18. An increase in interest rates from 8 percent to 9 percent would be associated with
    _____ in the price of existing bonds.
    a. a decline
    b. no change
    c. an increase

19. Changes in interest rates resulting from changes in monetary policy are likely to affect investment spending and initially lead to a shift in the
    (There may be more than one correct answer.)
    a. Expenditure schedule
    b. Aggregate supply curve
    c. Consumption function
    d. Aggregate demand curve

20. Knowing that an increase in the level of prices will increase the demand for money for transactions purposes helps to explain why
    a. the aggregate supply curve has a positive slope.
    b. the aggregate demand curve has a negative slope.
    c. equilibrium occurs at the intersection of the aggregate demand and aggregate supply curves.
    d. the multiplier response to a change in autonomous spending may be greater than 1.0.

Test B

Circle T or F for true or false.

T F 1. The independence of the Federal Reserve System is now so well established that it is beyond debate.

T F 2. Most power in the Federal Reserve System is held by the 12 district Federal Reserve banks.

T F 3. Monetary policy decisions by the Federal Reserve are subject to review by the President of the United States before being implemented.

T F 4. An open market purchase by the Fed lowers interest rates without changing the stock of money.

T F 5. A reduction in minimum reserve requirements is likely to lead to an increase in both the stock of money and the interest rate.

T F 6. Changing the discount rate is the most frequently used instrument of monetary policy today.

T F 7. Since many forms of money do not earn interest, people's demand for money is unaffected by changes in interest rates.

T F 8. Higher interest rates would normally lead banks to reduce their holdings of excess reserves.

T F 9. The impact of changes in monetary policy on interest-sensitive categories of demand affects GDP and prices as the economy moves along a given aggregate demand curve.

T F 10. The impact of the price level on the demand for money, and hence interest rates, helps to explain why the aggregate demand curve has a negative slope.

SUPPLEMENTARY EXERCISES

1. Consider an economy where consumption and investment spending are given by

$$C = 650 + .6 \, DI$$
$$I = 1710 - 30r$$

where r is the interest rate. In this economy, taxes are one-sixth of income and net exports are 100.
   a. If government purchases are 900 and r is 12 (that is, 12 percent), what is the equilibrium level of income?
   b. If the Fed lowers the interest rate to 8, what happens to the equilibrium level of income?
   c. The Fed can lower the interest rate by an appropriate increase in bank reserves; that is, an appropriate shift in the money supply schedule. But what is appropriate? Assume the demand for money is

$$M^D = .25Y - 10r$$

   and the supply of money is

$$M^S = 5BR + 2.5r$$

   where BR is the amount of bank reserves. If $BR = 270$, what is the equilibrium level of income? r? and M?
   d. What increase in BR will reduce the interest rate to 8 and produce the increase in Y you found in question 2? What happens to M? (You might start by trying an increase in BR of 10 and figuring out what happens to Y and r. Then use these results to figure out how to get r to drop to 8.)

2. **Bond Prices and Interest Rates**
   a. Consider a bond that pays $90 a year forever. If interest rates are 9 percent, such a bond should sell for $1,000 as ($90 ÷ $1,000) = .09. Assume now that interest rates fall to 6 percent. With bond payments of $90, what bond price offers investors a return of 6 percent? If interest rates rise to 15 percent, what must be the price of the bond paying $90 to offer investors a return of 15 percent?
   b. Bonds that pay only interest and never repay principal are called consols. Most bonds pay interest for a certain number of years and then repay the original borrowing or principal. Bond prices reflect the present value of those interest and principal payments as follows:

$$\text{Price} = \sum_{t=1}^{N} \frac{\text{INT}}{(1+r)^t} + \frac{\text{PRIN}}{(1+r)^N}$$

where INT = interest payments
      r = interest rate
   PRIN = principal
     N = number of years of interest payments (also number of years to principal payment)

It may be easier to answer the following questions if you have access to a microcomputer or sophisticated hand calculator.

Verify that if INT = $90, PRIN = $1,000, N = 10, and r = .09, the price of the bond = $1,000.

Calculate the price of the bond when r = .06 and when r = .15 while INT, PRIN, and N remain unchanged. These calculations show what would happen to the price of an existing bond if interest rates change. Do your results confirm the negative correlation between bond prices and interest rates discussed in the text?

ECONOMICS IN ACTION

Independence of the Federal Reserve

In the October 1993, Congressman Henry Gonzales (D-Texas), Chairman of the House Banking Committee, convened a series of committee hearings to consider issues related to the degree of independence of the Federal Reserve. The secrecy surrounding meetings of the Federal Open Market Committee (FOMC) and appointment procedures for presidents of the twelve district Federal Reserve Banks were among the items of special concern to Congressman Gonzales.

With regard to the meetings of the FOMC, Congressman Gonzales proposed that decisions be disclosed within a week and that detailed transcripts and videotapes of each meeting be released within 60 days. He argued that his proposals would promote individual accountability and that "Accurate information does not undermine markets. Partial information and leaked information undermines market efficiency."[1] Alan Greenspan, Chairman of the Board of Governors, and the other Federal representatives who appeared before the Committee argued that videotaping would hinder free debate as individuals concerned that their remarks might be misinterpreted and "cause unnecessary volatility in financial markets," would self-censor what they said. "Unconventional policy prescriptions and ruminations about the longer-term outlook for economic and financial market developments might

---

[1]"Greenspan Warns Against Easing Fed's Secrecy," *The New York Times*, October 20, 1992.

never be surfaced . . . for fear of igniting a speculative reaction when the discussion was disclosed." Chairman Greenspan went on to argue that premature disclosure "could inhibit or even thwart" the ability of the FOMC to implement decisions. He was especially concerned that immediate disclosure would compromise the ability of the FOMC to implement "contingent plans—that is, if a given economic or financial event occurs, a particular policy action would ensue."[2]

Currently the president of each district bank is appointed by the district bank's Board of Directors, subject to the approval of the Board of Governors in Washington, D.C. District bank presidents serve as voting members of the FOMC on a rotating basis. Critics of the Federal Reserve argue that, in view of their membership on the FOMC and the importance of monetary policy, district bank presidents should be selected or reviewed by elected officials rather than appointed bodies. Options might include appointment by the President and/or confirmation by the Senate. Again Chairman Greenspan spoke against these changes, arguing that the current system represents a deliberate choice by the Congress to isolate decisions about monetary policy from political pressures. He argued that the Federal Reserve is accountable to the Congress and the public through reporting requirements and the daily scrutiny of the business and financial press. However he warned that "if accountability is achieved by putting the conduct of monetary policy under the close influence of politicians subject to short-term election-cycle pressures, the resulting policy would likely prove disappointing over time. . . . The public–private and regional makeup of the Federal Reserve was chosen by Congress, in preference to a unitary public central bank, only after long and careful debate. The system was designed to avoid an excessive concentration of authority in federal hands and to ensure responsiveness to local needs."[3]

1. When and in how much detail should decisions and minutes of the FOMC be released? Is Greenspan right when he argues that the advance announcement of contingent plans limits their effectiveness?
2. Who should select district bank presidents? Should voting membership on the FOMC be restricted to members of the Board of Governors and exclude district bank presidents?

---

[2]Testimony by Alan Greenspan, Chairman, Board of Governors of the Federal Reserve System, before the Committee on Banking, Finance and Urban Affairs, U.S. House of Representatives, October 13, 1993. A complete transcript of the Committee Hearing should be available by the Spring of 1994.
[3]*Ibid.*

STUDY QUESTIONS

1. What is the difference between money and income?
2. How much independence do you think is desirable for the Fed? Why?
3. What are the major instruments of monetary policy? Use a demand and supply diagram to show how changes in each instrument affects the stock of money and interest rates.

4. Open market operations are the most used instrument of monetary policy. Reserve requirements are changed only infrequently and the changes in the discount rate tend to be passive rather than active. What do you think explains the heavy reliance on open market operations rather than other instruments of monetary policy?

5. Why do interest rates and bond prices move inversely to each other?

6. Why can't the Fed control the stock of money to the penny? Would you favor reforms that increase the ability of the Fed to control the stock of money? If so, which reforms and why? If not, why not?

7. Why does the supply-of-money schedule have a positive slope while the demand-for-money schedule has a negative slope?

8. What are the links by which changes in monetary policy affect spending and thus output, employment, and prices? Use an expenditure diagram and an aggregate demand-aggregate supply diagram to illustrate your answer.

9. "Recognizing that an increase in prices increases the demand for money for transactions purposes helps to explain why the aggregate demand curve has a negative slope." What is the logic behind this statement?

14

The Debate over Monetary Policy

LEARNING OBJECTIVES

After completing this chapter you should be able to:

- compute velocity given data on nominal income and the stock of money.

- describe the determinants of velocity.

- explain the difference between the quantity theory and the equation of exchange.

- describe why the equation of exchange is not a theory of income determination and why monetarists' use of the same equation turns it into a theory of income determination.

- explain how investment spending and interest rates interact to help determine how monetary policy works in a Keynesian model of income determination.

- explain how expansionary fiscal policy and related increases in the demand for money, interest rates, and velocity interact to determine how fiscal policy works in a monetarist model.

- distinguish between lags affecting fiscal policy and those affecting monetary policy.

- explain why the Fed cannot control M and r.

- explain how and why the slope of the aggregate supply curve helps to determine the effectiveness of stabilization policy.

- explain how long lags might mean that efforts to stabilize the economy could end up destabilizing it.

- explain how automatic stabilizers help to reduce fluctuations in GDP.

- summarize the views of advocates and opponents of activist stabilization policy by the government.

- describe and distinguish between different types of economic forecasting: econometric models, leading indicators, survey data, and judgmental forecasts.

IMPORTANT TERMS AND CONCEPTS

Quantity theory of money
Velocity
Equation of exchange
Effect of interest rate on velocity
Monetarism
Effect of fiscal policy on interest rates
Lags in stabilization policy
Shape of the aggregate supply curve
Controlling M versus controlling r
Automatic stabilizers
Econometric models
Leading indicators
Judgmental forecasts
Rules versus discretionary policy

CHAPTER REVIEW

This is one of the most important and most difficult of the macroeconomic chapters. While not much new material is introduced, the chapter summarizes and synthesizes many of the concepts presented in preceding chapters concerning the theory of income determination as it discusses a number of issues that confront policymakers.

Earlier chapters presented an essentially Keynesian model of income determination. The monetarist viewpoint is a modern manifestation of an even older tradition known as the quantity theory of money. The concept of *velocity* is perhaps the most important tool associated with this theory. Velocity is the average number of times per year that a dollar changes hands to accomplish transactions associated with GDP. Velocity is measured as nominal

(1) _____ divided by the stock of _____. Alternative measures of money, for example, M_1 and M_2, give rise to alternative measures of velocity, V_1 and V_2.

Related to the concept of velocity is something called the equation of exchange, which is simply another way of defining velocity. The equation of exchange says:

(2)   Money supply × velocity = _____ _____.

In symbols, it is: _____ × _____ = _____ × _____. Statisticians and national income accountants measure the stock of money and nominal GDP. Economists then calculate velocity by division. Different values of the stock of money could be consistent with the same level of nominal GDP if _____ changes appropriately.

The quantity theory asserts that there is a close link between changes in nominal GDP

(3) and changes in the stock of _____. This link comes about because the quantity

theory assumes that velocity (<u>does/does not</u>) change very much. If velocity is constant, then a change in the money stock translates directly into a change in _____ _____. If velocity is 5 and the money stock increases by $20 billion, then nominal GDP will rise by $_____ billion.

(4)   Historical data, as well as an analysis of the determinants of velocity, suggest that one (<u>should/should not</u>) expect velocity to be constant. Velocity reflects how much money people hold to make transactions, which in turn reflects such institutional factors as the frequency of paychecks and the efficiency of moving money between checking accounts and other assets, such as savings accounts. In Chapter 13 we saw that the amount of money people want to hold, and hence velocity, is also affected by the interest rate as a measure of the _____ _____ of holding money.

Monetarism, like the quantity theory, starts with the equation of exchange. But rather than assuming that velocity does not change, monetarists try to predict *how* velocity will change. From a monetarist perspective, determinants of nominal GDP are broken down into

(5) implications for the stock of money and implications for _____. After accounting for appropriate changes, simple multiplication can be used to predict nominal GDP.

At first glance it may appear that a Keynesian approach to income determination cannot analyze changes in monetary policy whereas a monetarist approach ignores fiscal policy. Such a conclusion would be oversimplified and misleading. In formal theory the two viewpoints are closer than is commonly recognized. Keynesian theory implies that monetary policy can have important impacts on aggregate demand through its impact on interest rates and investment spending. In Chapter 13 we saw that expansionary monetary policy will

(6) lead to a(n) (<u>decline/increase</u>) in interest rates. In Chapter 8 we saw that as a result of lower interest rates investment spending will (<u>increase/decrease</u>). In Chapter 8 we also saw that an increase in investment spending shifts both the expenditure schedule and the aggregate demand curve. Putting all the pieces together we can see that expansionary monetary policy will tend to (<u>increase/decrease</u>) GDP. Restrictive monetary policy would work in exactly the opposite way.

Monetarists are able to analyze the impact of changes in fiscal policy as follows: Expan-

(7) sionary fiscal policy will be associated with (<u>higher/lower</u>) interest rates. As a result, velocity will (<u>increase/decrease</u>) and a monetarist would forecast a (<u>higher/lower</u>) value for nominal GDP. Neither alone nor together are Keynesian and monetarist theories sufficient to determine output and prices as both are theories of the (<u>demand/supply</u>) side of the economy and ignore the other side.

The impact of changes in fiscal policy on interest rates is not only important to a monetarist analysis of changes in fiscal policy, it is also one of the reasons why the multiplier formula for Chapter 9 is oversimplified; increases in autonomous spending will tend to increase interest rates which in turn induce partially offsetting changes in investment spending.

FIGURE 14-1

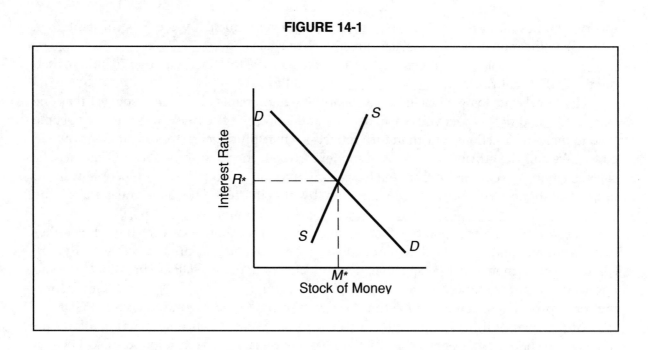

The choice between monetary and fiscal policy is often influenced by how quickly changes in policy can occur and how long it takes for changes, once made, to affect the behavior of firms and consumers. In general, lags in formulating policy are shorter for **(8)** (fiscal/monetary) policy, whereas spending responses of firms and households are typically shorter for _____ policy.

A major controversy in monetary policy is whether, when formulating monetary-policy decisions, the Federal Reserve should pay greater attention to the money supply or to the interest rates. Imagine, for instance, that the Fed is happy with the stock of money and the interest rate given in Figure 14-1. Suddenly the demand-for-money schedule shifts to the right because of an increase in the demand for money from some factor other than interest rates. Draw in the new schedule. If the Fed did nothing, then, as a result of this shift in the **(9)** demand for money, the stock of money would be (higher/lower) and the interest rate would _____. To maintain the original money supply, M^*, the Fed should shift the supply-of-money schedule to the _____; while to maintain the same rate of interest, the Fed should shift the supply curve to the _____. It should be obvious that the Fed cannot do both at the same time.

Decisions to stick to original monetary targets are likely to mean greater changes in interest rates, while decisions to stabilize interest rates will mean greater changes in the stock of money. The appropriate choice will depend upon the state of the economy and the source of the original unexpected changes in interest rates and the stock of money.

Stabilization policy affects the economy primarily by shifting the aggregate demand curve. The final result, however, in terms of changes in output and prices, also depends upon the slope of the aggregate supply curve. A flat aggregate supply curve means that shifts in the aggregate

(10) demand curve will have large effects on (output/prices) with only a small change in _____. On the other hand, shifts of the aggregate demand curve will have big effects on prices without much change in output if the aggregate supply curve is (steep/flat). While some argue that the aggregate supply curve is flat and others that it is steep, an emerging consensus sees the slope of the aggregate supply curve as dependent upon the degree of resource utilization. When the economy is operating close to full-employment, the aggregate supply curve is likely to be (flat/steep), while during periods of significant slack in the economy, the aggregate supply curve is likely to be _____.

Some economists favor an activist-oriented approach to stabilization policy. Others fa-

(11) vor less activism and rely on _____ stabilizers to keep the economy on an even keel. Beyond views about the slope of the aggregate supply curve, these differences reflect differing political philosophies and judgments concerning the importance of such factors as the economy's self-correcting mechanisms, the length of various policy lags, the stability of the multiplier and velocity, and the accuracy of economic forecasting.

It takes time before someone notices that the economy is not operating as hoped for and before the appropriate part of the government can decide what policy measures should be adopted. Once a particular policy is decided upon, there may not be much effect on output and prices until the buying habits of households and firms adjust to the new policy. Because of lags, it is not enough to design policies just for today's problems. Economists must also try to predict the future. One way they attempt to do this is through the use of mathematical formulas called econometric models. Another method concentrates on historical timing relationships of some economic variables, called leading indicators.

In addition, the U.S. government and several private organizations periodically ask people and firms about their spending plans for the future. This survey data can also be a useful tool in forecasting. Forecasters who look at the results of all these techniques, as well as such things as sun spots, the length of women's skirts, and so forth, make what are called

(12) _____ forecasts. The more accurate the economic forecasts, the more demanding the standards we can set for stabilization policy. At the present time economic forecasts (are/are not) good enough for fine-tuning the economy.

Active use of fiscal policy to correct persistent and sustained deviations from potential output calls for changes in government spending or taxes. The fact that spending, taxes, and

(13) monetary policy can be changed means that government spending (must/need not) take an ever larger proportion of the economic pie.

IMPORTANT TERMS AND CONCEPTS QUIZ

Choose the best definition for the following terms.

1. _____ Quantity theory of money
2. _____ Velocity
3. _____ Equation of exchange
4. _____ Monetarism
5. _____ Automatic stabilizers
6. _____ Econometric models
7. _____ Leading indicators

a. Features of the economy that reduce its sensitivity to shifts in demand.
b. Mode of analysis that uses the equation of exchange to organize and analyze macroeconomic data.
c. Average number of times a dollar is spent in a year.
d. Variables that normally turn down prior to recessions and turn up prior to expansions.
e. Theory of aggregate demand stating that nominal GDP is proportional to the money stock.
f. Sets of mathematical equations that form a model of the economy.
g. Features of the economy that move opposite the business cycle.
h. Formula that states that nominal GDP equals the product of money stock and velocity.

BASIC EXERCISE

1. This exercise is designed to give you practice computing and using velocity.

   Table 14-1 contains historical data for nominal GDP, M_1 and M_2

   a. Use this data to compute V_1, velocity based on M_1; and V_2, velocity based on M_2.
   b. Assume you are a monetarist working for the Federal Reserve and are asked to predict nominal GDP one year in advance. Even if you knew the money supply, M, you would still need an estimate of V. One way to estimate velocity is to use data from the previous year. The idea is that, since you can't know velocity for, say, 1982 until you know nominal GDP and M_1 or M_2 for 1982, you might use velocity for 1981 to predict GDP for 1982. Table 14-2 assumes that the Federal Reserve can control the money supply exactly. Use your numbers for veloci to fill in the blank columns in Table 14-2 to predict income.
   c. Which years show the largest prediction errors? Why?

TABLE 14-1

	Nominal GDP ($billions)	M₁ ($billions)	M₂ ($billions)	V₁	V₂
1980	2,708.0	395.8	1,563.1	_____	_____
1981	3,030.6	422.7	1,711.2	_____	_____
1982	3,149.6	455.6	1,872.4	_____	_____
1983	3,405.0	497.9	2,069.2	_____	_____
1984	3,777.2	536.8	2,281.3	_____	_____
1985	4,038.7	586.3	2,474.2	_____	_____
1986	4,268.6	672.3	2,694.2	_____	_____
1987	4,539.9	737.3	2,866.6	_____	_____
1988	4,900.4	768.6	2,997.8	_____	_____
1989	5,250.8	790.9	3,155.8	_____	_____
1990	5,522.2	810.9	3,289.4	_____	_____
1991	5,677.5	863.3	3,395.7	_____	_____
1992	5,950.7	963.0	3,471.4	_____	_____

Source: Economic Report of the President , 1993, Tables B-1 and B-65;
Economic Indicators, May 1993

TABLE 14-2

	Actual M₁ (billions)	V₁ from Previous Year	Estimated Income ($billions)	Actual Income ($billions)	Estimated Income ($billions)	V₂ from Previous Year	Actual M₂ (billions)
1981	422.7	____	____	3,030.6	____	____	1,711.2
1982	455.6	____	____	3,149.6	____	____	1,872.4
1983	497.9	____	____	3,405.0	____	____	2,069.2
1984	536.8	____	____	3,777.2	____	____	2,281.3
1985	586.3	____	____	4,038.7	____	____	2,474.2
1986	672.3	____	____	4,268.6	____	____	2,694.2
1987	737.3	____	____	4,539.9	____	____	2,866.6
1988	768.6	____	____	4,900.4	____	____	2,997.8
1989	790.9	____	____	5,250.8	____	____	3,155.8
1990	810.9	____	____	5,522.2	____	____	3,289.4
1991	863.3	____	____	5,677.5	____	____	3,395.7
1992	963.0	____	____	5,950.7	____	____	3,471.4

2. For this exercise you are asked to assume the role of adviser to the Federal Reserve's Open Market Committee. Figure 14-2 uses the demand and supply for money to show the actual stock of money and the rate of interest. Assume that initially the economy is at full-employment with price stability. The next meeting of the Open Market Committee begins with a report detailing the increase in the stock of money and interest rates since the last meeting. What to do is not so obvious, however, as suggested by the following arguments offered by two different members of the Committee:

A: This report confirms my fear that aggregate demand is expanding too rapidly. We risk unnecessary inflation and should move to reduce aggregate demand by an appropriate change in monetary policy.

B: This report confirms my concern that there has been an increase in the demand for money that is unrelated to GDP. Businesses and individuals have been harmed buying esoteric and risky financial securities. As a result of these losses there has been a general increase in the demand for money. If we do not take appropriate action the increase in interest rates since our last meeting will reduce aggregate demand and threatens recession.

You are asked to use Figure 14-2 to illustrate what each speaker is arguing and what actions they are suggesting. For each speaker try to determine what curve has shifted and how. Each is arguing for a particular policy to shift the supply-of-money schedule. What is that shift and how is it consistent with the speaker's analysis?

FIGURE 14-2

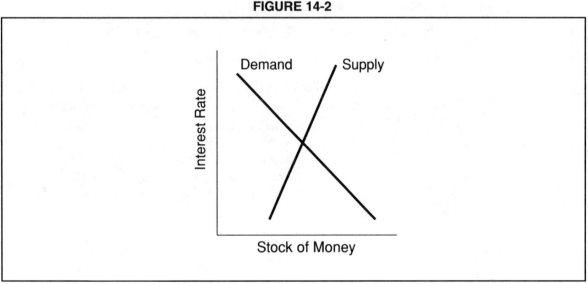

SELF-TESTS FOR UNDERSTANDING

Test A

Circle the most appropriate answer.

1. Velocity is measured by
    a. dividing the money stock by nominal GDP.
    b. computing the percentage change in nominal GDP from year to year.
    c. dividing nominal GDP by the stock of money.
    d. subtracting the rate of inflation from nominal interest rates.

2. The equation of exchange says that
    a. for every buyer there is a seller.
    b. $M \times V =$ Nominal GDP.
    c. demand equals supply.
    d. P.T. Barnum was right when he said, "There is a sucker born every minute."

3. According to the equation of exchange an increase in M may lead to
    a. an increase in Y (real GDP).
    b. an increase in P.
    c. a reduction in V.
    d. an increase in nominal GDP.
    e. any of the above.

4. According to the quantity theory an increase in M will lead to
    (There may be more than one correct answer.)
    a. an increase in Y (real GDP).
    b. an increase in P.
    c. a reduction in V.
    d. an increase in nominal GDP.
    e. any of the above.

5. Between 1956 and 1957 the money supply (M_1) was essentially constant and yet nominal GDP rose by slightly over 5 percent. It must be that
    a. velocity increased.
    b. velocity decreased.
    c. velocity was unchanged.

6. From 1985 to 1986 M_1 increased by 14.7 percent. V_1 declined from 6.89 to 6.35. It must be that nominal GDP increased by _____ percent.
    a. less than 14.7.
    b. exactly 14.7.
    c. more than 14.7.

7. The historical record shows
   a. that both V_1 and V_2 have been stable since 1929.
   b. that both V_1 and V_2 have been quite variable since 1929.
   c. continual increases in V_1 since 1929.
   d. that V_2 has been more stable than V_1 since 1929.

8. Initially the stock of money is $600 billion and velocity is 5. If one can be sure that velocity will not change, what increase in M will be required to increase real GDP by $25 billion?
   a. $5 billion.
   b. $10 billion.
   c. $25 billion.
   d. Insufficient information.

9. Which of the following developments is *not* likely to lead to an increase in velocity?
   a. An increase in the expected rate of inflation.
   b. A reduction in the required reserve ratio for banks.
   c. An increase in interest rates as a result of an expansionary change in fiscal policy.
   d. A widespread trend toward more frequent pay periods.

10. If expansionary fiscal policy increases interest rates, a monetarist would expect that nominal GDP would _____ even if there is no change in the stock of money.
    a. decrease
    b. be unaffected
    c. increase

11. Which of the following is *not* likely to increase nominal GDP according to a monetarist analysis of income determination?
    a. An open market purchase that increases the stock of money.
    b. An increase in government spending.
    c. A technological change in banking practices that increases velocity.
    d. An increase in income taxes.

12. Keynesian analysis argues that the change in interest rates that accompanies an open market purchase is likely to
    a. increase velocity.
    b. have no effect on velocity.
    c. reduce velocity.

13. Which of the following make the value of the multiplier less than $1/(1-MPC)$? (There may be more than one correct answer.)
    a. The increase in interest rates that accompanies an increase in nominal GDP when the supply-of-money curve is constant.
    b. Income taxes.
    c. An increase in imports that normally accompanies an increase in GDP.
    d. Higher prices that reduce the purchasing power of money fixed assets and reduce net exports.

14. Which of the following is an example of a lag in policymaking as opposed to a lag in spending by firms and households?
    a. The construction of a new plant, induced by lower interest rates, cannot start for nine months, because it takes that long to prepare architectural drawings and contractors' bids.
    b. Congress takes five months to consider a presidential tax proposal.
    c. Through multiplier impacts, a $3 billion increase in defense spending eventually raises GDP by $5 billion.
    d. Refrigerator sales rise in the month following a $300 tax rebate.

15. Policy lags are probably shorter for _____ policy. Expenditure lags are probably shorter for _____ policy.
    a. fiscal; monetary
    b. monetary; fiscal
    c. fiscal; fiscal
    d. monetary; monetary

16. Assume that the stock of money and interest rates are both at levels desired by the Federal Reserve. Following a shift in the demand for money, the Fed can control (There may be more than one correct answer.)
    a. M but not r.
    b. r but not M.
    c. both M and r.
    d. neither M nor r.

17. Stabilization policy will be effective in combating recession if the aggregate supply curve is _____ and effective in combating inflation if the aggregate supply curve is _____.
    a. flat; steep
    b. steep; flat
    c. flat; flat
    d. steep; steep

18. If the aggregate supply curve is relatively flat, then
    a. velocity will be constant.
    b. both monetary and fiscal policy will have relatively large effects on output without much effect on prices.
    c. a change in interest rates will have little impact on investment.
    d. monetary policy will be effective while fiscal policy will not.

19. Which of the following is not an example of an automatic stabilizer?
    a. Unemployment compensation.
    b. The corporate income tax.
    c. Increased highway building enacted during a recession.
    d. Personal income taxes.

20. Forecasting by extrapolating previous timing relationships between changes in the stock of money and GDP is an example of
   a. judgmental forecasts.
   b. econometric models.
   c. leading indicators.
   d. automatic stabilizers.

Test B

Circle T or F for true or false.

T F 1. If the stock of money is $1 trillion and nominal GDP is $6 trillion, then velocity is 6.

T F 2. The quantity theory is not really a theory because velocity, by definition, is equal to the ratio of nominal GDP divided by the money stock.

T F 3. Monetarist and Keynesian theories are both incomplete in that they concentrate on demand and ignore the supply side of the economy.

T F 4. Expansionary monetary policy that increases the stock of money will only increase prices with no impact on real output.

T F 5. The lag between a change in fiscal policy and its effects on aggregate demand is probably shorter than the lag between a change in monetary policy and its effects on aggregate demand.

T F 6. The lag in adopting an appropriate policy is probably shorter for fiscal policy than for monetary policy.

T F 7. By simultaneously using open market operations and making changes in minimum reserve requirements, the Fed would be able to achieve any desired combination of the money stock and the interest rate.

T F 8. The shape of the aggregate supply curve is likely to be relatively steep when the economy is operating near full-employment and relatively flat during periods of high unemployment and low rates of capacity utilization.

T F 9. Long lags will help make for better stabilization policy because there is more time for a complete analysis of possible actions.

T F 10. Automatic stabilizers reduce the sensitivity of the economy to shifts in aggregate demand.

SUPPLEMENTARY EXERCISE

Leading Indicator

Is the stock market a good leading indicator of overall economic conditions? Figure 14-3 shows stock prices over the postwar period. Using just Figure 14-3 make an estimate of how many recessions there have been since 1950. Try to date each one approximately. Now go to the library and find a recent copy of the *Survey of Current Business*, a monthly publication of the Commerce Department that publishes data on a large number of economic series and keeps track of recessions as identified by the National Bureau of Economic Research. How many recessions does the NBER identify? How many did you identify? How many false indications of recession were there? What about the forecasting record of other leading indicators? What are the stock market and other leading indicators saying about a possible recession in the next 6 to 12 months?

In addition to the problem of false turning points, there are two other limitations to a purely mechanical use of leading indicators that you should be aware of:

a. Most large declines in a leading indicator are the result of not one large decline, but rather a series of consecutive small declines. At the same time each series has so many ups and downs that most small declines are followed by a small increase. One needs some way of separating those small declines that signal the start of a major slump from those that are quickly reversed.

b. A leading indicator that always changes direction a fixed amount of time before the economy does would be an extremely useful variable. However, the length of time between movements in most leading indicators and the economy may be quite variable.

FIGURE 14-3

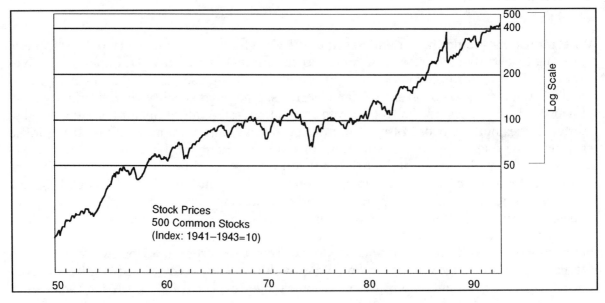

STUDY QUESTIONS

1. What is the difference between the equation of exchange, the quantity theory and monetarism?

2. What do you think explains the different historical experience of V_1 and V_2?

3. How would a monetarist explain the impact of expansionary fiscal policy on GDP and prices?

4. Why can't one use monetarism to determine nominal GDP, Keynesian analysis to determine real GDP, and then compute the price level by dividing the one by the other?

5. What is the difference between policy lags and expenditure lags? Which are likely to be more important for fiscal policy? monetary policy?

6. What's wrong with the following? "Long lags make for better policy as they provide more time for determining the best policy."

7. Why can't the Fed control both M and r?

8. Do you think monetary policy should focus on stabilizing interest rates or stabilizing the growth in the stock of money? Why?

9. Why are concerns about excessive levels of government spending not a legitimate reason to oppose active stabilization policy?

10. Do you favor a more or less activist stabilization policy? Why?

ECONOMICS IN ACTION
What to Do?

What indicators should the Federal Reserve use when formulating monetary policy? General agreement exists that monetary policy should contribute to broad macroeconomic objectives —price stability, full employment, economic growth—although some would argue that greater weight should be placed on particular objectives, e.g. price stability or full employment. However, the Fed does not control the rate of inflation or the rate of unemployment. For that matter it does not even control interest rates or any measure of money. It has strong influence over these latter variables, which in turn are important for things like GDP, employment, and prices. But strong influence is not control. A related problem is that observations on different macroeconomic variables are available at different times. Estimates of GDP come only every three months. Unemployment and inflation are measured monthly. Data on M_1 and M_2 are announced every week while interest rates are available at a moment's notice.

At times the Fed has put more emphasis on interest rates and at others on M_1, M_2, or bank reserves as indicators of monetary policy. The Humphrey–Hawkins Act requires that the Fed announce ranges it expects for the growth of money. When testifying before Congress in July of 1993, and reporting on growth ranges expected for 1994, Alan Greenspan,

Chairman of the Board of Governors of the Federal Reserve System, urged caution in interpreting the announced ranges.

> The historical relationships between money and income, and between money and the price level have largely broken down, depriving the aggregates of much of their usefulness as guides to policy. At least for the time being, M_2 has been downgraded as a reliable indicator of financial conditions in the economy, and no single variable has yet been identified to take its place. . . . In the meantime, the process of probing a variety of data to ascertain underlying economic and financial conditions has become even more essential to formulating sound monetary policy. . . . In these circumstances it is especially prudent to focus on longer-term policy guides. One important guide post is real interest rates, which have a key bearing on longer-run spending decisions and inflation prospects.

Greenspan emphasized what he called the equilibrium real rate of interest:

> . . . specifically the real rate level that, if maintained, would keep the economy at its production potential over time. . . . Real rates, of course, are not directly observable, but must be inferred from nominal interest rates and estimates of inflation expectations. The most important real rates for private spending decisions almost surely are the longer maturities. Moreover, the equilibrium rate structure responds to the ebb and flow of underlying forces affecting spending.

Greenspan concluded:

> While the guides we have for policy may have changed recently, our goals have not. As I have indicated many times to this Committee, the Federal Reserve seeks to foster maximum sustainable economic growth and rising standards of living. And in that endeavor, the most productive function the central bank can perform is to achieve and maintain price stability.

1. What indicators of monetary policy would you favor if you were a member of the Federal Open Market Committee?
2. When is it appropriate to emphasize measures of the stock of money and when it is appropriate to emphasize interest rates?
3. While one can observe nominal interest rates, how does one measure the equilibrium real rate of interest in a way that makes it operational for the conduct of monetary policy?

SOURCES: Testimony by Alan Greenspan, Chairman of the Board of Governors of the Federal Reserve System, before the Subcommittee on Economic Growth and Credit Formation of the Committee on Banking, Finance, and Urban Affairs, U.S. House of Representatives, July 20, 1993.

Chapter **15**

Budget Deficits and the National Debt: Fact and Fiction

LEARNING OBJECTIVES

After completing this chapter you should be able to:

- explain how measures to balance the budget may unbalance the economy.

- explain how appropriate fiscal policy depends on the strength of private demand and the conduct of monetary policy.

- explain the difference between the government's budget deficit and the national debt.

- discuss some facts about budget deficits and the national debt: When have budget deficits been largest? What has happened to the national debt as a proportion of GDP?

- describe how the concept of structural deficits or surpluses differs from officially reported deficits or surpluses.

- describe how traditional accounting procedures will overstate the interest component of government expenditures during a period of inflation.

- distinguish between real and fallacious arguments about the burden of the national debt.

- describe the inflationary consequences of a budget deficit and explain why deficits will be more inflationary if they are monetarized.

- evaluate arguments supporting the crowding-out and crowding-in properties of government deficit spending.

- explain how increased deficits can be associated with either higher or lower interest rates, higher or lower rates of inflation, and faster or slower growth in real output.

♦ explain how changing the mix of monetary and fiscal policy could change the budget deficit while leaving GDP and prices unchanged.

♦ explain why most economists measure the true burden of deficits by their impact on the capital stock.

IMPORTANT TERMS AND CONCEPTS

Budget deficit
National debt
Real versus nominal interest rates
Inflation accounting
Structural deficit or surplus
Monetization of deficits
Crowding-out
Crowding-in
Burden of the national debt
Mix of monetary and fiscal policy

CHAPTER REVIEW

Ever since 1980 the federal government's budget deficits have been very much like the weather: everyone has been talking about them but no one seems able to do anything about them. By itself this chapter cannot make government deficits larger or smaller, but it can help to increase your understanding of the impacts of both government deficits and the national debt.

(1)   The government runs a deficit when its (spending/revenue)exceeds its _____. There is a surplus when _____ is greater than _____. The national debt measures the government's total indebtedness. The national debt will increase if the government budget shows a (deficit/surplus). The national debt will decrease if the government budget shows a _____.

What is appropriate deficit policy? Earlier chapters discussed the use of fiscal and monetary policy to strike an appropriate balance between aggregate demand and aggregate supply in order to choose between inflation and unemployment. Considerations of balanced budgets, per se, were absent from that discussion. The conclusion that budget policy should adapt to the requirements of the economy is shared by many economists.

Some have advocated a policy of strict budget balance. There is good reason to expect that such a policy would balance the budget at the cost of unbalancing the economy. Consider an economy in an initial equilibrium at full-employment with a balanced budget. An (2) autonomous decline in private spending would shift the expenditure schedule (down/up),

resulting in a shift of the aggregate demand schedule to the (<u>right/left</u>). In the absence of any further policy action the result would be a (<u>decline/increase</u>) in GDP. The change in GDP will also mean a(n) (<u>decline/increase</u>) in tax revenues. The government's budget will move from its initial position of balance to one of (<u>deficit/surplus</u>). At this point, deliberate policy actions to reestablish budget balance would call for either a(n) (<u>decrease/increase</u>) in taxes or a(n) (<u>decrease/increase</u>) in government spending. In either case the result would be an additional shift in the expenditure schedule and aggregate demand curve that would (<u>accentuate/counteract</u>) the original shift that was due to the autonomous decline in private spending.

The fact that tax revenues depend on the state of the economy is important to understanding many complicated issues about the impact of deficits. As seen above, it helps to explain why a policy of budget balancing can unbalance the economy in the face of declines in private spending. It helps to explain why deficits can sometimes be associated with a booming economy and at other times with a sagging economy. It also helps to explain interest in alternative measures of the deficit. The concept of structural deficits, or structural surpluses is an attempt to control for the effects of the economy on the deficit. It does so by looking at spending and revenues at a specified high-employment level of income. Changes in tax revenues due to changes **(3)** in income (<u>will/will not</u>) affect the actual deficit but (<u>will/will not</u>) affect the structural deficit. For this reason, many analysts prefer to use the structural deficit as a measure of the stance of fiscal policy.

Inflation and, especially the impact of inflation on interest rates, raises complicated measurement problems. As we learned in Chapter 6, during periods of inflation, increases in nominal interest rates that reflect expectations of future inflation may not imply any change in real interest rates. To the extent that nominal interest rates include such inflationary premiums, a portion of interest payments is not payment for the use of the purchasing power embodied in the original loan; rather it is a repayment of the purchasing power of the original loan balance itself.

Are deficits inflationary? The short answer is yes and the more complete answer asks for more details. If the alternative to any deficit is more taxation or less spending, then any deficit, whether the result of deliberate policy or of a reduction in autonomous spending, will mean a higher price level, a higher level of output, and less unemployment than the alternative of a balanced budget. This is so because the deficit keeps the aggregate demand curve farther to the right than would be the case with either a decrease in spending or an increase in taxes. The exact inflationary consequences of a budget deficit depend on where along the aggregate supply curve the economy finds itself and what monetary policy is doing. A government deficit during a period of recession may find the economy operating on a relatively flat portion of the aggregate supply curve. If so, any reduction in the deficit will **(4)** likely have a (<u>large/small</u>) impact on the price level but could have a relatively large impact

on output and employment. In this situation, a deliberate increase in the deficit from expansionary fiscal policy could increase output and employment substantially (<u>with/without</u>) much impact on prices. On the other hand, substantial budget deficits at a time of full-employment will find the economy on a relatively steep portion of the aggregate supply curve. In this case, a reduction in the deficit is likely to have a (<u>large/small</u>) impact on output and a _____ impact on the price level.

A deficit that is associated with a deliberate reduction in taxes will increase output, prices, and interest rates as it shifts the aggregate demand curve to the right. Concerns about the impact of the deficit on interest rates may lead the Federal Reserve to increase the money supply. If the Federal Reserve acts to increase the stock of money by buying government **(5)** securities, one says it has _____ the deficit. As we learned in Chapter 13, expansion of the money supply will imply a further expansionary shift in the aggregate demand curve and will mean even higher prices.

Many feelings about the burden of the national debt may be as deeply ingrained and just as irrational as a Victorian's ideas about sex or a football coach's ideas about winning. Many fallacious arguments about the burden of the debt do, however, contain some elements of truth. Arguments about the burden of future interest payments or the cost of repaying the national debt are not relevant when considering debts held by domestic citizens **(6)** but are relevant when considering debts held by _____. To the extent that debt is held by domestic citizens, interest payments and debt repayments impose little burden on the nation as a whole; they are only transfers from taxpayers to bondholders, who may even be the same individuals. However, the impact on incentives by using higher taxes to accomplish these transfers should not be ignored.

A real burden of the debt would arise from a deficit in a high-employment economy **(7)** that crowded out private (<u>consumption/investment</u>) spending and left a smaller capital stock to future generations. There will continue to be arguments as to whether U.S. deficits have entailed such a burden. The federal government's deficit has shown its largest increases during periods of _____ and _____. Government deficits during periods of slack may actually result in a benefit rather than a burden if, as a result of increased demand, they lead to (<u>crowding in/crowding out</u>) rather than _____. Major concerns about deficits during the late 1980s are that they occurred during a period of (<u>high/low</u>) employment and that they are thus likely to have led to crowding _____.

IMPORTANT TERMS AND CONCEPTS QUIZ

Choose the best definition for the following terms.

1. _____ Budget deficit
2. _____ National debt
3. _____ Structural deficit
4. _____ Inflation accounting
5. _____ Monetization of deficits
6. _____ Crowding-out
7. _____ Crowding-in

a. Amount by which revenue exceeds spending.
b. Deficit under current fiscal policy if the economy was at full-employment.

c. Amount by which government spending exceeds revenue.
d. Increase in private investment spending induced by increase in government spending.
e. Adjusting standard accounting procedures for changes in purchasing power.
f. Contraction of private investment spending induced by deficit spending.
g. Federal government's total indebtedness.
h. Purchases of government bonds used to finance deficit by central bank.

BASIC EXERCISE

This exercise is designed to show how a rigid policy of balanced budgets may unbalance the economy. To simplify the calculations, the exercise assumes that prices do not change and thus focuses on the horizontal shift in the aggregate demand curve.

1. Fill in the last column of Table 15-1 to determine the initial equilibrium level of income. The equilibrium level of income is _____.

2. What is the deficit at the initial equilibrium level of income? _____

TABLE 15-1
(Constant Prices)

Income (Output) Y	Taxes T	Disposable Income DI	Consumption Spending C	Investment Spending I	Government Purchases G	Exports X	Imports IM	Total Spending C + I + G + (X − IM)
6,000	800.0	5,200.0	4,500	900	950	500	600	_____
6,250	862.5	5,387.5	4,650	900	950	500	625	_____
6,500	925.0	5,575.0	4,800	900	950	500	650	_____
6,750	987.5	5,762.5	4,950	900	950	500	675	_____
7,000	1,050.0	5,950.0	5,100	900	950	500	700	_____

TABLE 15-2
(Constant Prices)

Income (Output) Y	Taxes T	Disposable Income DI	Consumption Spending C	Investment Spending I	Government Purchases G	Exports X	Imports IM	Total Spending C + I + G + (X − IM)
6,000	800.0	5,200.0	4,500	775	950	500	600	_____
6,250	862.5	5,387.5	4,650	775	950	500	625	_____
6,500	925.0	5,575.0	4,800	775	950	500	650	_____
6,750	987.5	5,762.5	4,950	775	950	500	675	_____
7,000	1,050.0	5,950.0	5,100	775	950	500	700	_____

3. The high employment level of income is $6,750. Is the structural budget in surplus or deficit? _____

   What is the magnitude of the structural surplus or deficit? _____

4. Investment spending now declines by $125 billion. Use Table 15-2 to compute the new equilibrium level of income. What is the new equilibrium level of income?

   _____

   How has the deficit changed, if at all? _____

   How has the structural (deficit/surplus) changed, if at all?

   _____

5. If the government is committed to a balanced budget, would it raise or lower taxes to restore a balanced budget? _____ What would this change in taxes do to the equilibrium level of national income? _____

   _____

6. If the government decides to change government purchases to eliminate the deficit, would it raise or lower spending? _____ What would this change do to the equilibrium level of national income? _____

   _____

7. (Optional) How large a lump-sum change in taxes, that is, the same change at every level of income, would balance the budget? $ _____ billion. The new equilibrium level of income would be $_____ billion.

8. (Optional) How large a change in government spending would balance the budget?

   $_____ billion. The new equilibrium level of income would be $_____ billion.

SELF-TESTS FOR UNDERSTANDING

Test A

Circle the most appropriate answer.

1. The federal government deficit is
   a. the excess of tax revenues over transfer payments.
   b. another term for political gridlock.
   c. total indebtedness of the government.
   d. the difference between government spending and the government's revenue for a given year.

2. The national debt is
   a. equal to the cumulation of past federal government deficits.
   b. another term for the federal government's deficit.
   c. what the United States, government, and private businesses owe foreigners.
   d. the excess of spending over revenue for a given year.

3. The ratio of the national debt to GDP
   a. has declined continuously since World War II.
   b. has increased continuously since World War II.
   c. is about 3 to 1.
   d. has risen over the 1980s from its recent low point in the 1970s.

4. The structural deficit is
   a. equal to the deficit minus interest payments on the national debt.
   b. equal to zero, by definition.
   c. defined as the deficit the government would run if the economy were at full-employment.
   d. the excess of government investment spending over allocations for these projects.

5. At high levels of unemployment, the government's actual deficit will be _____ the structural deficit.
   a. smaller than
   b. the same as
   c. larger than

6. During the 1980s the structural deficit of the federal government
   a. decreased continuously.
   b. fluctuated but showed no trend.
   c. increased substantially.
   d. had been offset by higher tax revenues.

7. Many observers argue that the structural deficit is a better measure of the stance of fiscal policy than the actual deficit because the
   a. actual deficit can be larger or smaller than expected if GDP is smaller or larger than expected.
   b. actual deficit does not include the impact of automatic stabilizers.
   c. structural deficit is based on real rather than nominal interest rates.
   d. structural deficit represents what the President proposes rather than what is enacted by Congress.

8. Until the 1980s, large government deficits were associated with periods of (There may be more than one correct answer.)
   a. high inflation.
   b. war.
   c. recession.
   d. low unemployment.

9. A decline in private investment spending will lead to all but which one of the following?
   a. A downward shift in the expenditure schedule.
   b. A decline in the equilibrium level of GDP.
   c. An increase in the government deficit or a reduction in the surplus.
   d. A decline in the structural budget deficit or surplus.

10. Rigid adherence to budget balancing will
   a. help the economy adjust to shifts in private spending.
   b. have little impact on business cycles.
   c. accentuate swings in GDP from autonomous changes in private spending.
   d. help maintain full-employment.

11. If the Federal Reserve monetizes a budget deficit, there will be a(n)
   a. smaller inflationary impact.
   b. unchanged inflationary impact.
   c. larger inflationary impact.

12. The inflationary consequences of a budget deficit are likely to be greatest when
   a. the deficit is the result of a decline in private spending.
   b. the deficit is the result of a deliberate decision to raise taxes and monetize the resulting deficit.
   c. the economy is operating along a relatively flat portion of the aggregate supply curve.
   d. there is an increase in both the actual and structural deficit during a period of low unemployment.

13. Using real interest rates when measuring the deficit during a period of inflation would have what impact?
   a. It would make the deficit smaller.
   b. It would leave the deficit unchanged.
   c. It would make the deficit larger.

14. An increase in the deficit is likely to be correlated with which of the following? (There may be more than one correct answer.)
    a. Faster growth in GDP.
    b. Lower interest rates.
    c. A reduction in the rate of inflation.
    d. Higher interest rates.
    e. Greater inflation.
    f. A slowing of the rate of growth of GDP.

15. The macroeconomic impact of a reduction in government spending to reduce the deficit could be offset by
    a. an increase in taxes.
    b. an open market purchase.
    c. a reduction in taxes.
    d. an open market sale.

16. A deficit that follows a decline in private spending is likely to be associated with which of the following?
    a. Higher inflation.
    b. Lower interest rates.
    c. A reduction in unemployment.
    d. A reduction in the national debt.

17. Which of the following is a valid argument about the burden of the national debt for an economy whose debt is held entirely by its own citizens?
    a. Future generations will find interest payments a heavy burden.
    b. When the debt is due, future generations will be burdened with an enormous repayment.
    c. The debt will bankrupt future generations.
    d. If the deficits causing the debt reduced private investment spending, then future generations would be left with a smaller capital stock.

18. "Crowding-out" refers to
    a. increased population pressures and arguments for zero population growth.
    b. the effects of government deficits on private investment spending.
    c. what happens at the start of the New York City marathon.
    d. the impact of higher prices on the multiplier.

19. Crowding-out is likely to occur if (There may be more than one correct answer.)
    a. the amount of private savings is unchanged.
    b. the economy is operating near full-employment.
    c. the rate of unemployment is high.
    d. inflation is low.

20. Crowding-in is more likely to occur when
    a. the economy is operating near full-employment.
    b. prices are rising.
    c. the government lowers expenditures.
    d. there is substantial slack in the economy.

Test B

Circle T or F for true or false.

T F 1. A policy calling for continuous balance in the government's budget will help offset shifts in autonomous private demand.

T F 2. A balanced high-employment budget is necessary if the equilibrium level of GDP is to equal the full-employment level of GDP.

T F 3. Inflation accounting would increase the interest portion of government expenditures during periods of inflation.

T F 4. Increases in the government's deficit are always associated with increases in interest rates.

T F 5. The inflationary impact of any budget deficit depends on the conduct of monetary policy.

T F 6. Recent government deficits have meant that the ratio of national debt to GDP has never been higher than it is today.

T F 7. Interest payments on the national debt, whether to domestic citizens or foreigners, are not really a burden on future generations.

T F 8. A major limitation of the simple crowding-out argument is the assumption that the economy's total pool of savings is fixed.

T F 9. Crowding-in is likely to occur when the economy is operating with slack employment, whereas crowding-out is likely to occur at full-employment.

T F 10. Government deficits may impose a real burden on future generations if, as a result of crowding out, there is less private investment and a smaller capital stock in the future.

SUPPLEMENTARY EXERCISES

1. Government Deficits and Interest Rates

Between 1957 and 1958, the federal government's budget shifted from a surplus of $2.3 billion to a deficit of $10.3 billion. At the time this was the largest deficit since World War II and was bigger than any deficit during the Great Depression. At the same time, interest rates declined dramatically. The rate on three-month Treasury bills declined from an average of 3.267 percent in 1957 to 1.839 percent in 1958. The rate on three- to five-year securities fell from 3.62 to 2.90 percent.

Between 1974 and 1975, the federal government's budget deficit increased from $11.6 billion to $69.4 billion. At the same time, interest rates again declined. The rate on three-month Treasury bills declined from 7.886 to 5.838 percent, while the rate on three- to five-year securities declined more modestly from 7.81 to 7.55 percent.

Between 1981 and 1982 the federal government deficit increased dramatically from $58.8 billion to $135.5 billion. At the same time, interest rates declined. The rate on three-month Treasury bills declined from 14.029 percent to 10.686 percent. Interest rates on longer term government securities also declined.

Between 1991 and 1992 the federal government deficit went from $210.4 billion to $298 billion, the largest year-to-year increase to date. At the same time, interest rates on long-term government bonds declined from 7.86 percent to 7.01 percent while rates on short-term government borrowing declined almost two percentage points from 5.42 percent to 3.45 percent.

How do you explain the seemingly contradictory results that larger deficits are associated with lower, not higher, interest rates? Do these observations prove that larger deficits will always be associated with lower interest rates?

2. Repudiate the National Debt?

If the national debt is so onerous, we could solve the problem by simply repudiating the debt; that is, we would make no more interest or principal payments on the outstanding debt.

Imagine that in keeping with democratic principles such a proposition were put to American voters. Who do you think would vote pro and who would vote con? Which side would win? Would the outcome of the vote be different if the debt were held entirely by foreigners? By banks and other financial institutions? (The Treasury publishes data on who holds the national debt in the *Treasury Bulletin*. This data is also published in the annual *Economic Report of the President*. You might want to look at these data and consider what would happen to depositors, shareholders, and pensioners, both current and prospective, if the national debt held by banks, corporations, and pension funds was suddenly worthless.)

Repudiating the national debt might well limit future budget flexibility. What would be the likely consequences during periods of future recession? Inflation? War?

3. Continual Budget Deficits

What are the long-run consequences of continual budget deficits? If you have access to a programmable hand calculator or to a microcomputer, experiment with the following simulation model to discover how results depend on particular coefficients.

a. Assume that nominal GDP grows at a constant rate, λ:

$$\text{GDP}_t = (1 + \lambda)\,\text{GDP}_{t-1}$$

b. Assume that tax receipts are proportional to nominal GDP:

$$T_t = \tau \, GDP_t$$

c. Assume that government purchases of goods and services plus all transfer payments except for interest on the national debt are also some constant percentage of nominal GDP:

$$G_t = g \, GDP_t; \; g > \tau$$

(This specification means that, not counting interest payments, the government deficit is a constant proportion [g – t] of nominal GDP).

d. Assume that the government must pay interest on the national debt at a rate of interest R:

$$\text{Interest payments} = IP_t = R \, (\text{Debt}_t)$$

e. The government's total deficit is:

$$\text{Deficit}_t = G_t + IP_t - T_t$$

f. The government debt grows as follows:

$$\text{Debt}_{t+1} = \text{Debt}_t + \text{Deficit}_t$$

g. Use these relationships to simulate your model economy and investigate what happens to the ratio of debt to GDP. To start your simulations you will need values for the four parameters, λ, τ, g, and R, and initial values for GDP and the national debt. Try starting with the following:

λ	= 0.08	R	= 0.05
τ	= 0.20	GDP	= 6,000
g	= 0.22	Debt	= 2,500

What happens to the ratio of debt to GDP as your model economy evolves?

h. Try experimenting with some alternative parameters and initial values.
   (i) Change the initial value of GDP then change the initial value of the national debt. Do these changes affect what happens over time?
   (ii) Now change τ and g. What happens? Do these changes affect the eventual ratio of debt to GDP? If so, how?
   (iii) Finally, change λ and R, individually and then together. Remember that λ is the growth rate of nominal GDP and R is nominal interest rates. Higher inflation would be expected to change both λ and R, whereas a change in real growth or real interest rates would change them individually. Do these changes affect the eventual ratio of debt to GDP? If so, how?

ECONOMICS IN ACTION
Huffing and Puffing

Writing in the Summer 1989 issue of *The Brooking Review*, economist Charles Schultze asks whether the federal government deficit is best characterized as a wolf at the door, a domesticated pussycat, or termites in the basement. Schultze attributes the view of the deficit-as-wolf to Wall Street financial circles and some economists. Many who see the deficit as wolf are fearful of a sudden collapse of confidence in the U.S. economy and the dollar. In this view, the resulting sharp drop in the exchange value of the dollar would force the Federal Reserve to defend the dollar by raising interest rates, plunging the economy into a prolonged and serious recession.

Schultze identifies himself with those who hold the termite view. In Schultze's view the result of trying to muddle through, putting up with current deficits, will not be a sudden collapse but rather a steady erosion in the growth prospects of the American economy. When domestic savings decline and the government deficit increases, a country can sustain investment only through increased borrowing from abroad. [Appendix A to Chapter 8 showed that equilibrium on the income-expenditure diagram can be expressed as

$$Y = C + I + G + X - IM, \text{ or as}$$
$$I + G + X = S + T + IM.$$

This latter expression can be rewritten as $I = S - (G - T) + (IM - X)$. When S declines, and $G - T$ increases, then to avoid a drop in I, $IM - X$ must increase.] For much of the 1980s increased government deficits were, to a large extent, offset by an increased trade deficit. Schultze notes that continuation of large deficits matched by large foreign borrowing may allow the United States to sustain the level of private investment, but it does so by "increasing the future diversion of national income to overseas interest payments . . . depressing the future path of American living standards." What would happen if foreigners reduce their investments in the United States? In the absence of an increase in domestic savings or a reduction in the deficit, the result must be a decline in private investment and slower growth in American living standards.

Schultze identifies economists on both the political left and right as among those who argue that the deficit is benign, only a pussycat. The pussycat arguments Schultze identifies include: inflation adjustments advocated by Robert Eisner (discussed in Chapter 15); the debt neutrality arguments of Robert Barro (discussed in the text); the lower overall deficit when the budgets of state and local governments are combined with that of the federal government; and the lack of a capital budget on the part of the federal government. Schultze argues that if one reduces the deficit by subtracting the inflation premium in nominal interest rates, there should be a corresponding and offsetting decline in the income and savings of bond holders. While the deficit may be smaller, the final result is no change in net national savings or investment. Like many other economists, Schultze is skeptical of the applicability of arguments about debt neutrality. When discussing the surpluses of state and local governments, Schultze argues that such surpluses are to a large extent accounting artifacts that reflect growing reserves by state and local governments for future pension payments. Even

if, as Schultze would prefer, one counts these reserves as private savings, one is still left with a substantial drop in private savings during the 1980s. Finally, Schultze argues that the establishment of a separate capital budget might reduce the deficit in the federal government's operating budget but, again, it would not change the fundamental imbalance between actual domestic savings and the level of private investment necessary to sustain acceptable economic growth.

1. Which view of the deficit do you think is most appropriate and why?

"Of Wolves, Termites, and Pussycats," *The Brookings Review*, Summer 1989, pp. 26 - 33.

STUDY QUESTIONS

1. What is the difference between the government's deficit and its debt? What is the link between the two?

2. What does the historical record show about when the federal government has run large deficits?

3. Why are policies to stabilize the deficit likely to destabilize the economy?

4. When is a budget deficit appropriate and why? When it is inappropriate?

5. What does the historical record show about the ratio of federal government debt to GDP?

6. What is the difference between the structural deficit and the actual deficit? Which is usually larger and why? Which is a more accurate measure of the stance of fiscal policy?

7. Does an increase in the deficit always indicate a move to expansionary fiscal policy? Why?

8. Does an increase in the deficit always lead to higher interest rates and more inflation? Why?

9. Why do economists argue that foreign-held debt imposes more of a burden than government debt held by Americans?

10. What are the real burdens of the debt?

11. Since deficits are a results of fiscal policy decisions, how does the impact of deficits depend upon monetary policy?

12. What is crowding-out and crowding-in? When is one more likely than the other and why?

Chapter **16**

The Trade-Off Between Inflation and Unemployment

LEARNING OBJECTIVES

After completing this chapter you should be able to:

- explain how prices can rise following either the rapid growth of aggregate demand or the sluggish growth of aggregate supply.
- explain what the Phillips curve is and what it is not
- explain how the slope of the Phillips curve is related to the slope of the aggregate supply curve.
- explain how the source of fluctuations in economic activity—whether predominantly from shifts of the aggregate demand curve or from shifts of the aggregate supply curve—will affect the Phillips curve.
- explain why the economy's self-correcting mechanism means that the economy's true long-run choices lie along a vertical Phillips curve.
- use the long-run Phillips curve to show how the temporary impact of aggregate demand policy on unemployment can have a permanent impact on the rate of inflation.
- explain how and why one's views on appropriate aggregate demand policy are likely to depend upon one's views on
  - the social costs of inflation vs. unemployment.
  - the slope of the short-run Phillips curve.
  - the efficiency of the economy's self-correcting mechanism.
  - how quickly inflationary expectations adjust.

- explain how the accuracy of expectations about inflation can affect the slope of both the aggregate supply curve and the Phillips curve.
- discuss the implications of and evidence for the hypotheses of rational expectations.
- discuss measures that have been advocated to reduce the natural rate of unemployment.
- calculate how indexing would be applied to wages and interest rates, given the appropriate data on prices.
- discuss the advantages and disadvantages of universal indexing.

IMPORTANT TERMS AND CONCEPTS

Demand-side inflation
Vertical (long-run) Phillips curve
Rational expectations
Supply-side inflation
Trade-off between inflation and unemployment in the short-run and in the long-run
Phillips curve
Stagflation caused by supply shocks
Self-correcting mechanism
Natural rate of unemployment
Inflationary expectations
Wage-price controls
Indexing (escalator clauses)
Real versus nominal interest rates

CHAPTER REVIEW

This chapter discusses the hard choices that policymakers must make when deciding how to respond to inflation or unemployment. Chapters 11 through 14 discussed how changes in various tools of fiscal and monetary policy can be used to influence aggregate demand. Chapter 16 uses this material to study the policy implications for fighting unemployment and inflation. Here, as in many other areas of life, one cannot have one's cake and eat it too. Actions taken to reduce unemployment will often lead to higher rates of inflation, while actions to reduce inflation will often lead to higher rates of unemployment. Economists can help to define the nature of this trade-off, examine the factors that are responsible for it, and clarify the implications of different choices, but they cannot tell anyone which choice to make. In a democratic society, this decision is left to the political process.

Any shift in the aggregate demand or aggregate supply curve, whether induced by policy or not, is likely to affect both prices and output. The nature of the association between

changes in prices and changes in output will depend upon which curve shifts. If fluctuations in economic activity are predominantly the result of shifts in the aggregate demand curve,

(1) higher prices will be associated with (<u>higher/lower</u>) levels of output. The transition to higher prices is a period of inflation. The associated higher level of output will require more employment, leading to a lower level of unemployment. Hence, shifts in the aggregate demand curve imply that inflation and unemployment are (<u>negatively/positively</u>) correlated. That is, if you plotted the rate of unemployment on the horizontal axis and the rate of inflation on the vertical axis, the resulting curve, called the _____ curve, would have a (<u>positive/negative</u>) slope.

Data for the 1950s and 1960s was consistent with the view sketched above and seemed to imply that policymakers could choose between inflation and unemployment. In particular, it used to be thought that the Phillips curve implied that policymakers could permanently increase output beyond the level of full employment or potential output at the cost of only a small increase in the rate of inflation. Subsequent experience has shown that this view

(2) is (<u>correct/incorrect</u>). We saw earlier that output beyond the level of potential output results in a(n) (<u>inflationary/recessionary</u>) gap. The economy's self-correcting mechanism will shift the aggregate supply curve to reestablish long-run equilibrium at the _____ rate of unemployment. Continual shifts of the aggregate demand curve would be necessary to maintain a lower rate of unemployment. These continual shifts of the aggregate demand curve will imply an ever-increasing rate of inflation. The only true long-run choices lie along a _____ Phillips curve.

In the short run, shifts in the aggregate demand curve will move the economy up or down the short-run Phillips curve; but the economy's self-correcting mechanism implies that this trade-off is only temporary. How long this trade-off lasts depends upon the speed of the economy's self-correcting mechanism. Differing views about the speed of the mechanism are an important part of differences in Keynesian and monetarist policy prescriptions.

Changes in money wages are an important determinant of shifts in the aggregate supply curve that lead an inflationary gap to self-destruct. It is the original increase in prices above wages that induces firms to expand output. As workers recognize that the purchasing power of their money wages has declined, the subsequent increases in wages to restore real wages will lead to shifts in the aggregate supply curve. Rather than always being a step behind, workers can try to protect their real wages by anticipating the increase in prices. On this view the expectation of higher prices will lead to higher wages and a shift in the aggregate supply curve in anticipation of inflation. Compared with cases where the aggregate supply curve did not shift, a shift in the aggregate demand curve accompanied by an

(3) expectations-induced shift in the aggregate supply curve will have a (<u>larger/smaller</u>) impact on output and a _____ impact on prices. The result will be a (<u>higher/lower</u>) rate of inflation and the slope of the short-run Phillips curve will be (<u>steeper/flatter</u>).

Economists associated with the hypothesis of rational expectations have focused attention on the formation of expectations. While much remains to be learned, these economists argue that errors in predicting inflation cannot be systematic. An implication of this view is that, except for random elements, the short-run Phillips curve is vertical. Not only is there no long-run trade-off between inflation and unemployment, but, according to this view, there is also no systematic short-run trade-off.

Others are less convinced that expectations are rational in the sense of no systematic errors. These economists believe that people tend to underpredict inflation when it is rising and overpredict it when it is falling. Long-term contracts also make it difficult to adjust to changing expectations of inflation. These economists argue that policy measures to shift the aggregate demand curve can affect output and employment in the short run. But remember that these short-run impacts are constrained by the true long-run menu of choices which lie
(4) along a _____ Phillips curve.

Most economists believe that aggregate demand policy will affect employment and inflation in the short run and will also affect the place where the economy ends up on the long-run Phillips curve. Thus, to fight a recession rather than to wait for the economy's self-correcting mechanism will mean more employment in the short run and is likely to mean more inflation in the long run as compared to a status quo policy that waits on the economy's self-correcting mechanisms. (See Figures 16-14 and 16-15 in the text.) Whether one wants to use aggregate demand policy or wait for natural processes depends on one's assessment of the costs of inflation and unemployment; the efficiency of the economy's self-correcting mechanisms; the current level of output vis-a-vis full employment, especially as it has implications for the slope of the short-run Phillips curve; and the quickness with which inflationary expectations adjust.

A number of policies have been advocated in the hope that they will improve the inflation-unemployment trade-off. These policies run the gamut from presidential exhortations to elaborate wage-price monitoring bureaucracies to proposals for new forms of labor contracts that tie a portion of wages to profits.

Voluntary wage-price guideposts call for business and labor to set wages and prices in line with standards determined, in part, by increases in labor productivity. The logic of these guidelines is that labor wage can increases in line with increases in productivity without adding to inflationary pressures from the cost side. Thus, if labor productivity is increasing at 2 percent a year and the government is aiming to hold inflation to 3 percent a year, the guidepost standard for wage increases would be 5 percent.

More drastic forms of income policies include wage-price controls or even a wage-price freeze. Neither policy is a desirable long-run option. If adhered to for a long time, either policy undermines the allocative role of prices and results in inefficient alternatives. Historically, the Nixon wage-price freeze was a tactical device in order to allow time for a program of controls. A wage-price freeze or a set of controls might work if it resulted in a significant

(5) lowering of inflationary _____. However, if there is no change in the underlying forces of aggregate demand and supply, there (is/is not) likely to be much change in expectations.

A number of individuals have argued that rather than trying to reduce the rate of inflation we should simply learn to live with it and rely on automatic adjustments of monetary payments to reflect changes in prices, a process known as indexing. The automatic adjustment of social security benefits, as well as other government transfer programs, and **(6)** escalator clauses in wage contracts are examples of _____. A number of observers also advocate this mechanism for interest rates.

Indexing does seem to offer some relief from many of the social costs of inflation discussed in Chapter 6. As workers, firms, and lenders scramble to protect them-selves against **(7)** anticipated future increases in prices, current prices and interest rates will (increase/decrease) to reflect the expectation of inflation. If actual inflation turns out to be greater or less than expected, there will be a redistribution of wealth that many feel is essentially arbitrary. Uncertainty over future prices may make individuals and businesses extremely reluctant to enter into long-term contracts. Indexing offers relief from these problems. Labor contracts and other agreements could be written in real rather than nominal terms, and arbitrary redistributions would be avoided because money payments would reflect actual, not expected, inflation. At the same time, there is concern that learning to live with inflation may make the economy (more/less) inflation prone.

IMPORTANT TERMS AND CONCEPTS QUIZ

Choose the best definition for the following terms.

1. _____ Vertical Phillips curve
2. _____ Rational expectations
3. _____ Phillips curve
4. _____ Self-correcting mechanism
5. _____ Natural rate of unemployment
6. _____ Inflationary expectations
7. _____ Wage-price controls
8. _____ Indexing

a. Graph depicting unemployment rate on horizontal axis and inflation rate on vertical axis.

b. Legal restrictions on the ability of industry and labor to raise wages and prices.
c. Unemployment rate at full employment.
d. Vertical line at natural rate of inflation.
e. Forecasts which make optimal use of available and relevant data.
f. Adjustments of monetary payments whenever a specified price index changes.
g. The economy's way of curing inflationary and recessionary gaps via changes in the price level.
h. Vertical line at the natural rate of unemployment.
i. Beliefs concerning future price level increases.

BASIC EXERCISE

This exercise is designed to illustrate the nature of the inflation-unemployment trade-off that policymakers must face when planning aggregate demand policy.

1. Figure 16-1 shows an economy with a recessionary gap. Which of the following monetary and fiscal policies could be used to help eliminate this gap?

   • open market (<u>purchase/sale</u>).

   • (<u>increase/decrease</u>) of minimum reserve requirements.

   • (<u>increase/decrease</u>) in taxes.

   • (<u>increase/decrease</u>) in government transfer payments to individuals.

   • (<u>increase/decrease</u>) in government purchases of goods and services.

2. Assume the full-employment level of income is $6,500 billion. Draw a new aggregate demand curve, representing one or more of the appropriate policies you identified in Question 1, that will restore full employment for this economy. Following a shift in the aggregate demand curve, prices will rise to _____.

FIGURE 16-1

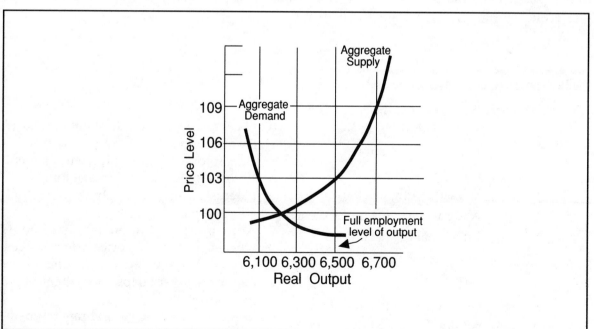

FIGURE 16-2   **FIGURE 16-3**

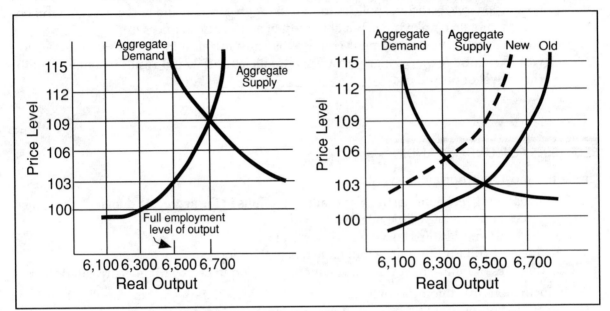

3. Consider the following statement:

"The increase in prices that resulted when we restored full employment was a small price to pay for the increased output. Why not try moving even farther along the aggregate supply curve? If we further stimulate the economy to lower unemployment we can increase output to, say, $6,700 billion and prices will only rise to 109. We can thus have a permanent increase in output of $200 billion every year in return for a one-time increase in prices of just under 6 percent. That's a pretty favorable trade-off." What is wrong with the reasoning of this argument?

Is the output-price combination of $6,700 billion and 109 a viable long-run equilibrium position? (Figure 16-2 illustrates such a combination. What is apt to happen to the aggregate supply curve? Draw in the new aggregate supply curve that restores full employment.) What would happen if government policymakers tried to keep output at $6,700 billion on a permanent basis? (That is, what would happen if every time the aggregate supply curve shifted, policymakers undertook appropriate expansionary fiscal or monetary policy to shift the aggregate demand curve in an effort to avoid any reduction in output.)

4. Figure 16-3 shows an economy following an adverse shift in the aggregate supply curve. Equilibrium used to be an output of $6,500 and a price level of 103.
   a. What is the new equilibrium immediately following the adverse shift in the supply curve?
      Output _____
      Prices _____

b. If there is to be no decline in employment, the government will need to implement (expansionary/restrictive) policies to shift the aggregate demand curve. The government could maintain employment, but at the cost of an increase in prices to _____.

c. Alternatively, the government could avoid any increase in prices. Such a decision would require (expansionary/restrictive) policies and would result in a new equilibrium level of output of _____.

SELF-TESTS FOR UNDERSTANDING

Circle the most appropriate answer.

1. If fluctuations in economic activity are caused by shifts in the aggregate demand curve, then
   a. prices and output will be negatively correlated.
   b. the short-run Phillips curve will be vertical.
   c. the long-run Phillips curve will have a negative slope.
   d. the rates of inflation and unemployment will tend to be negatively correlated.

2. If fluctuations in economic activity are the result of shifts in the aggregate supply curve, then
   a. prices and output will be positively correlated.
   b. the short-run Phillips curve will have a negative slope.
   c. the long-run Phillips curve will be horizontal.
   d. the rate of inflation and rate of unemployment will tend to be positively correlated.

3. The Phillips curve
   a. is a statistical relationship that summarizes the historical correlation between unemployment and inflation.
   b. is the set of long-term equilibrium relationships between the rate of unemployment and the rate of inflation.
   c. is the third turn at the Indianapolis 500 Speedway.
   d. shows how nominal interest rate changes when expectations of inflation change.

4. The economy's self-correcting mechanisms mean that in the long run the Phillips curve is likely to
   a. have a negative slope.
   b. have a positive slope.
   c. be horizontal.
   d. be vertical.

5. The difference between the short-run and long-run Phillips curves suggests that activist policy to eliminate a recessionary gap is likely to result in
   a. a temporary period of higher inflation and a permanently lower rate of unemployment.
   b. temporarily higher inflation and lower unemployment.
   c. a temporary period of lower unemployment and a permanently higher rate of inflation.
   d. permanently lower unemployment and inflation.

6. The positively sloped aggregate supply curve is drawn on the assumption that
   a. the cost of productive inputs remains unchanged as output changes.
   b. wages are fully indexed.
   c. the Phillips curve is never vertical.
   d. wage and price controls limit the impact of inflation.

7. An increase in wages, due either to inflation that has occurred in the past or inflation that is expected to occur in the future, can be modeled as
   a. an upward shift in the aggregate supply curve.
   b. an inward shift in the production possibilities frontier
   c. a downward shift in the aggregate demand curve.
   d. a leftward shift in the long-run Phillips curve.

8. An increased emphasis on expectations of future inflation in wage settlements will
   a. lead to a flatter Phillips curve.
   b. have no impact on the Phillips curve.
   c. lead to a steeper Phillips curve.

9. Stabilization policy faces a trade-off between inflation and unemployment in the short run because changes in monetary and fiscal policy have their most immediate impact on the _____.
   a. aggregate supply curve
   b. Phillips curve
   c. production possibilities frontier
   d. aggregate demand curve

10. Which of the following are necessary for expectations to meet the economist's definition of rational expectations? (There may be more than one correct answer.)
    a. They are based on relevant and available information.
    b. They can only be made by economists and statisticians.
    c. There are no systematic errors.
    d. They are always correct.

11. A strong believer in rational expectations would be surprised by which one of the following occurrences?
    a. An announcement by the Fed that it will increase the rate of growth of the money supply leads to expectations of higher inflation.
    b. Plans to lower taxes give rise to expectations of higher prices.
    c. Plans to fight inflation by restrictive policy succeed in reducing the rate of inflation with no increase in unemployment.
    d. An examination of the record shows that people consistently underestimate the rate of inflation during periods when it is increasing.

12. The hypothesis of rational expectations implies that increases in output beyond the level of potential output can be produced
    a. by expected increases in prices.
    b. only by unexpected increases in prices.
    c. by any increase in prices whether expected or not.
    d. by preannounced increases in the money supply or reductions in taxes.

13. Consider a shift to the right of the aggregate demand curve due to expansionary monetary and fiscal policy. Assume that the adoption of expansionary policies leads to expectations of inflation that induce a simultaneous shift in the aggregate supply curve. The resulting change in output will be _____ if there were no shift in the aggregate supply curve.
    a. smaller than
    b. the same as
    c. larger than

14. Under the same conditions as question 13, the resulting change in prices will be _____ if there were no shift in the aggregate supply curve.
    a. smaller than
    b. the same as
    c. larger than

15. Which of the following is *not* a feasible alternative for aggregate demand policy following an adverse shift of the supply curve to the left?
    a. Do nothing and initially experience both higher prices and lower output.
    b. Avoid the reduction in output at the cost of even higher prices.
    c. Avoid the increase in prices at the cost of an even greater decline in output.
    d. Avoid both the reduction in output and increase in prices by using both fiscal and monetary policy to shift the aggregate demand curve.

16. Restrictive monetary and fiscal policy adopted to reduce the rate of inflation will work quicker and have a smaller impact on unemployment when
    a. changes in inflationary expectations take a long time.
    b. the long-run Phillips curve is vertical.
    c. expectations of inflation adjust quickly to the change in macro policy.
    d. the natural rate of unemployment equals the natural rate of inflation.

17. If job retraining or other measures are successful in reducing the natural rate of unemployment,
    a. the long-run Phillips curve will shift to the left.
    b. the aggregate supply curve will become less steep.
    c. the short-run Phillips curve will become vertical.
    d. the natural rate of inflation will increase.

18. Wage-price controls
    a. may be effective if they succeed in changing expectations of inflation.
    b. were used with great success by President Nixon.
    c. have little long-run impact on economic efficiency.
    d. can be imposed on some parts of the economy without affecting the rest of the economy.

19. A general policy of indexing
    a. is an attempt to shift the aggregate supply curve downward and to the right.
    b. would help to balance the federal government's budget.
    c. is an attempt to ease the social cost of inflation, not an attempt to improve the terms of the inflation-unemployment trade-off.
    d. runs little risk of accelerating the rate of inflation.

20. Which of the following is an example of indexing?
    a. Tax penalties on firms that grant excessive wage increases.
    b. The adjustment of nominal interest rates in response to expectations of inflation.
    c. The average change in prices on the New York Stock Exchange.
    d. Increases in social security checks computed on the basis of changes in the consumer price index.

Test B

Circle T or F for true or false.

T F 1. Inflation occurs only as a result of shifts in the aggregate demand curve.

T F 2. In contrast to expansionary monetary or fiscal policy, an autonomous increase in private spending will increase output without increasing prices.

T F 3. It fluctuations in economic activity are predominantly the result of shifts in the aggregate supply curve, the rate of unemployment and the rate of inflation will tend to be positively correlated.

T F 4. The economy's self-correcting mechanism implies that the only long-run policy choices for the economy lie along a vertical Phillips curve.

T F 5. The natural rate of unemployment is given by the position of the long-run Phillips curve.

T F 6. A belief that the economy's self-correcting mechanism works quickly is an argument in favor of activist demand-management policy.

T F 7. Expectations of inflation that lead to higher wages will be somewhat self-fulfilling as the increase in wages shifts the aggregate supply curve.

T F 8. One can minimize the inflationary effects of fighting a recession by using fiscal policy rather than monetary policy.

T F 9. Following an adverse shift in the aggregate supply curve, aggregate demand policies can stop the rise in prices with no increase in unemployment.

T F 10. The economy's self-correcting mechanism means that, in the face of a recessionary gap, output and prices will eventually be the same with or without expansionary stabilization policy.

SUPPLEMENTARY EXERCISE

The following statement on wages, prices, and productivity comes from the 1962 *Annual Report of the Council of Economic Advisers*, page 186.

> If all prices remain stable, all hourly labor costs may increase as fast as economy-wide productivity without, for that reason alone, changing the relative share of labor and non-labor incomes in total output. At the same time, each kind of income increases steadily in absolute amount. If hourly labor costs increase at a slower rate than productivity, the share of non-labor incomes will grow or prices will fall, or both. Conversely, if hourly labor costs increase more rapidly than productivity, the share of labor incomes in total product will increase or prices will rise, or both. It is this relationship among long-run economy-wide productivity, wages, and prices which makes the rate of productivity change an important benchmark for noninflationary wage and price behavior.

The principles described in this quotation formed the basis of wage-price guideposts used by the Kennedy and Johnson administrations. The claim of the guideposts was that wage increases equal to the increase in labor productivity plus the target rate of inflation would, in combination with price increases equal to the target rate of inflation, allow equal percentage increases in both wages and profits. Table 16-1 is designed to check this assertion.

TABLE 16-1
ACME MANUFACTURING COMPANY

	(1)	(2)	(3)
1. Employment (people)	100	100	100
2. Labor productivity (gizmos per employee)	4,000	4,400	4,400
3. Total output [(1) × (2)]	400,000	_____	_____
4. Price per gizmo	$ 5.00	$ 5.00	$ 5.25
5. Total revenue [(4) × (3)]	$2,000,000	_____	_____
6. Hourly wage	$ 8.00	$ 8.80	$ 9.24*
7. Total wages [(6) × (2000) × (1)]	$1,600,000	$ 1,760,000	$1,848,000
8. Profits plus overhead [(5) – (7)]	$ 400,000	_____	_____

* If x is the percentage increase in labor productivity and y is the rate of inflation, the correct adjustment of wages is (1+x)(1+y) - 1 = x + y + xy. In our case, this formula works out to 15.5 percent, slightly greater than the 15 percent implied by looking just at x + y.

---

1. Column 1 of Table 16-1 illustrates the initial position of the Acme Manufacturing Company, a company that produces gizmos. According to the guideposts, if wages increased at the same rate as labor productivity, profits would also increase even if prices were held constant. In column 2, productivity and wage are both assumed to increase by 10 percent. Complete column 2 to see if profits increased when price is unchanged, while wages increase at the same rate as productivity.
2. Column 3 is meant to illustrate a situation of general inflation of 5 percent. Complete column 3 to see what happens to profits when increases in wages equal the increase in productivity plus the target rate of inflation of 5 percent.
3. If things work so simply why can't we eliminate inflation overnight by adopting an inflation target of zero?

ECONOMICS IN ACTION
How Much Inflation?

How much inflation should an economy tolerate in the long run? The concept of the natural rate of unemployment suggests that we are likely to end up with the same amount of unemployment in the long run, but it leaves open the question of how much inflation we should accept. Some argue that inflation is a necessary part of industrial economies. *The Economist* argues that inflationary experience since World War II is the exception not the rule. Bursts of inflation were typically followed by periods of stable or falling prices. By 1930, prices in Britain were not much different than in 1660 according to *The Economist*.

Those who favor low rates of inflation argue that a stable price level allows markets to function better. It is movements in relative prices that signal the need for resource reallocations. An increase in relative prices attracts resources while reductions are a signal for resources to move to other industries. Those who favor price stability argue that inflation obscures movements in relative prices and reduces the efficiency of market economies. Over time the uncertainty associated with inflation discourages risk taking, reduces long-term investment, and limits economic growth. The strong advocates of this position conclude that "These arguments suggest that the best inflation rate is the one that plays the least role in decision-making. This must be zero; anything higher will generate unnecessary uncertainty and inefficiency."*

Others argue that a little inflation need not be a bad thing. The imperfections of price indices is likely to mean that inflation at a rate of 1 or 2 percent a year is really no inflation at all. Some inflation may also facilitate real adjustments, especially in labor markets. In industries with falling demand, where wages need to decline if jobs are to be preserved, workers and unions have typically resisted cuts in nominal pay. A freeze in nominal pay while inflation continues may accomplish the necessary reduction in real pay while avoiding the labor unrest that can follow attempts to reduce nominal pay.

Even if a country were convinced of the virtues of zero inflation, the short-run costs of reducing inflation might outweigh the long-run benefit. *The Economist* argues that a major

part of short-run costs reflect the assumption of continuing inflation in many parts of the economy and the subsequent slowness of expectations to adjust. On this view, the credibility of policies and institutions committed to low rates of inflation can work to reduce the short-term costs of adjustment by keeping the lid on expectations. Advocates of this position see an independent central bank that is credibly committed to an inflation target of zero as critical to successful policy.

    1. What rate of inflation should the government strive for and why? While fiscal and monetary policy are likely to have a strong impact on prices as they affect aggregate demand, how should the government respond if an adverse shift in the aggregate supply curve suddenly raises prices?

*"Zero Inflation: How Low is Low Enough," *The Economist*, November 7, 1992, pp. 23-26.

STUDY QUESTIONS

1. Why does the slope of the Phillips curve depend upon the source of macroeconomic fluctuations?

2. Does the Phillips curve offer macroeconomic policy makers a menu of choices between the rate of unemployment and inflation? Why?

3. What is meant by the statement that the economy's self-correcting mechanisms mean that in the long run the Phillips curve is vertical?

4. What is the natural rate of unemployment?

5. How does the expectation of future inflation and the expectations-related shifts in the aggregate supply curve affect the Phillips curve?

6. How can expectations of inflation be rational if they are not always correct?

7. What sort of policies might reduce the natural rate of unemployment?

8. Should wages and interest rates be fully indexed?

9. Should stabilization policy aim to reduce inflation to zero? Why?

Chapter **17**

Productivity and Growth in the Wealth of Nations

LEARNING OBJECTIVES

After completing this chapter you should be able to:

- explain why growth in labor productivity is the major determinant of the growth in living standards.

- explain what factors are important for growth in labor productivity.

- discuss arguments and evidence about the international convergence of living standards and productivity levels.

- evaluate arguments and evidence about deindustrialization of the American economy.

- discuss and evaluate arguments about the cause of the slowdown in the growth of labor productivity since the 1960s.

- evaluate the argument that growth in labor productivity will lead only to increased unemployment.

- explain why productivity growth less than that of other countries need not imply a loss of export competitiveness, but can lower real wages relative to those in other countries.

IMPORTANT TERMS AND CONCEPTS

Labor productivity

Standard of living

GNP per capita

Gross Domestic Product (GDP)

GDP per labor hour

GDP per capita

Deindustrialization

CHAPTER REVIEW

The growth in labor productivity is the major determinant of living standards over long periods of time. Growth in labor productivity explains why, on the average, your parents are wealthier than their parents and their parents' parents. Continued growth in labor productivity will mean that your children and their children will be wealthier than you.

Discussions of productivity usually focus on labor productivity which is defined as the amount of output per unit of labor input. For a firm producing a single output, measuring labor productivity per hour is a simple matter of dividing output by total labor hours. For the American economy, output is usually measured in terms of real GDP and labor input is preferably measured in terms of total labor hours. An increase in labor productivity means

(1) that (more/less) output can be produced with the same number of labor hours. If aggregate output were unchanged, an increase in labor productivity would mean (more/less) unemployment. But remember that total output and the unemployment rate are determined by the intersection of the aggregate _____ and aggregate _____ curves. An increase in productivity means that the production possibilities frontier has shifted (out/in); that is, there has been a(n) (increase/decrease) in potential GDP. It is macroeconomic policy that helps to determine whether we take advantage of new possibilities. What makes labor more or less productive? While there are many factors, certainly the intensity of work, the quality of training, the availability of more and better equipment, and the level of technology are important factors. The nature of labor/management relations and public policy are cited by some as factors that can help or impede the growth of labor productivity.

(2) Sustained growth in labor productivity (is/is not) a relatively new phenomenon, tracing back about (2,000/200) years. As the following equation shows, growth in labor productivity is the basic determinant of living standards or output per capita:

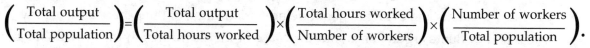

$$\left(\frac{\text{Total output}}{\text{Total population}}\right)=\left(\frac{\text{Total output}}{\text{Total hours worked}}\right)\times\left(\frac{\text{Total hours worked}}{\text{Number of workers}}\right)\times\left(\frac{\text{Number of workers}}{\text{Total population}}\right).$$

The expression on the left of the equal-sign is output per person or per capita. The first expression on the right side of the equal-sign is labor productivity. The second and third expressions measure the number of hours a typical worker works and the proportion of the population that works. (This last term is sometimes referred to as the employment ratio.) Notice that several of the numerators and denominators on the right-hand side of the equal-sign can be canceled, establishing the equality of the expression. If the number of hours per worker does not change and the proportion of the population that works is constant–that is if the second and third terms on the right-hand side do not change-then the only way that output or GDP per capita can increase is if labor productivity increases. If hours per worker decline, then increases in labor productivity will imply a smaller increase in output per capita. Much of the difference between the growth in labor productivity and the growth in output per capita over the past 100 years can be accounted for by the decline in the number of hours worked each year by a typical worker. Over the past 20 years there has been a sharp

increase in the employment ratio, a change that is related to the increased labor force participation of women along with the changing age structure of the population as baby boomers finished school and began working. These latter changes can be important for several decades but are unlikely to be sustained over a century or two. Thus in the long run, changes in GDP per capita will be dominated by changes in labor productivity.

There is much concern about the growth in labor productivity in different countries. **(3)** Long-term data for a number of industrial countries shows a (<u>convergence/divergence</u>) in levels of labor productivity. The quick dispersion of new technologies enables all industrial countries to share in the benefits of new innovations. If levels of productivity are converging, then it must be true that those countries that start with lower levels of productivity will show a (<u>faster/slower</u>) growth in labor productivity and those countries that start with higher levels of productivity will show a _____ growth in labor productivity. The concept of convergence indicates how difficult it is for any single country to sustain levels of labor productivity far in advance of other countries. It also suggests that a single industrialized country is not doomed to fall further behind the rest of the world. However, there is evidence that many developing countries (<u>are/are not</u>) participating in this process of convergence. See Chapter 21 for more discussion on prospects for these countries.

Popular discussions of changes in the growth of labor productivity and changes in the structure of employment are often based on limited data. When measured just from the end of World War II there has been a dramatic decline in the rate of growth of labor productivity in the United States and other industrialized countries in the last 20 years. (Note that a **(4)** decline in the rate of growth (<u>must/need not</u>) imply a decline in the level of labor productivity.) When viewed over a longer period of time, it is unclear which period is unusual, the 1970s and 1980s when labor productivity growth was 1 to 2 percent per year, or the period from 1950 to 1970 when labor productivity grew by over 3 percent per year.

There has been much recent concern about the declining share of manufacturing employment and the increasing share of service employment in the American economy. At least two pieces of evidence are relevant to a broader consideration of this issue. All major industrialized economies have experienced increases in the size of their service industries. **(5)** The record of productivity growth for American manufacturing shows (<u>no/a significant</u>) trend toward a declining rate of growth.

While the slowdown in productivity growth has been worldwide, the growth of labor productivity in the United States has been below that of other countries for some time. To the extent that this relative performance reflects the forces of convergence, there is less need for concern. Should this relative performance continue for a prolonged period of time, it would still be possible to sustain high levels of employment with appropriate macroeconomic policy, but there would be serious implications for American competitiveness in international markets. We could continue to export and reap the gains of international specialization that are explained in Chapter 18, but we would do so at the cost of a decline in our standard of living relative to that of the rest of the world. The experience of the British economy comes most immediately to mind.

IMPORTANT TERMS AND CONCEPTS

Choose the best definition for the following terms.

1. _____ Labor productivity
2. _____ Standard of living
3. _____ Deindustrialization

a. Total output divided by population.
b. GDP minus net exports.
c. Alleged decline in manufacturing due to a country's lagging growth in productivity.
d. Output per unit of labor input.

BASIC EXERCISES

1. Productivity growth compounds like interest on a savings account. Over long periods of time, small differences in the growth of productivity compound to quite substantial differences in the level of income. Table 17-1 reports data for GDP per capita for a number of countries for 1989. The columns for the year 2089 compound the actual data for 1989 by assumed growth rates of 1 to 2.5 percent per year for 100 years. Note how small differences in the assumed growth rates, even a difference as small as one-half of one percent, can compound to significant differences over 100 years.

   a. Pick a particular country and calculate how much output per capita increases over 100 years if it grows at 1 percent per year. In 2089 output per capita would be _____ as large as it was in 1989. (Try another country to be sure that your answer does not depend upon which country you choose. It shouldn't.)

   b. Assume now that output per capita grows at 2 percent per year for 100 years. How does the increase in output per capita compare to the situation where it increased 1 percent per year? Is it twice as large or even larger?

TABLE 17-1

	GDP per capita 1989	GDP per capita in 2089 assuming annual growth rate of			
		1.00%	1.50%	2.00%	2.50%
Canada	$18,544	$50,158	$82,188	$134,345	$219,074
France	$17,093	$46,233	$75,757	$123,833	$201,932
Germany	$16,397	$44,351	$72,672	$118,790	$193,710
Japan	$16,090	$43,520	$71,312	$116,566	$190,083
United Kingdom	$15,023	$40,634	$66,583	$108,836	$177,477
United States	$20,630	$55,800	$91,433	$149,457	$243,717

Source: Statistical Abstract of the United States, 1992, Table 1375
Note: All figures in U.S. dollars using estimates of purchasing power parities to adjust between national currencies.

c. If labor productivity in the United States grew at 1 percent per year while it grew at 2 percent per year in the rest of the world, our standard of living would not compare favorably to that of other countries after 100 years. The extrapolation of growth trends is a matter of mathematics, not economics. However, economies can offer insights as to whether mechanical trends can be realized. For example, what are the implications of the concept of convergence for the long-term maintenance of a 1 percent differential in the growth of labor productivity?

d. (Optional) Assume that output per capita in the United States grows at 1.5 percent per year while in Japan it grows at 2 percent per year. How many years will it take for output per capita in Japan to catch up with that of the United States?

2. This exercise investigates whether a decline in the growth of labor productivity results in a decline in the level of productivity. Assume that annual labor productivity is originally 23,900 of GDP per worker, and that it grows at an annual rate of 2.0 percent for 23 years, and 0.5 percent for the next 19 years.

   a. What is labor productivity at the end of the first 23 years?
   $_____

   b. What is labor productivity at the end of 42 years?
   $_____

   c. Does the decline in the rate of growth of productivity lead to a decline in the level of productivity?

   d. What happens to GDP per capita over the same 42 years if the proportion of the population that is employed increases from 39.5 percent to 46.7 percent.

SELF-TESTS FOR UNDERSTANDING

Test A

Circle the most appropriate answer.

1. Labor productivity is defined as
   a. output per capita.
   b. GDP divided by population.
   c. the growth in output per worker.
   d. output per unit of labor input.

2. A country's standard of living is usually measured as
   a. GDP per capita.
   b. output per worker.
   c. the growth in GDP.
   d. output per unit of labor input.

3. If more output can be produced with the same number of labor hours, we would say that labor productivity
   a. has decreased.
   b. is unchanged.
   c. has increased.

4. Declines in the number of hours worked per year by an average worker will mean that compared to the growth in labor productivity, the growth in GDP per capita will be
   a. smaller.
   b. about the same.
   c. larger.

5. If the proportion of a country's population that is employed increases, then the growth in GDP per capita will be _____ than the growth in labor productivity.
   a. smaller
   b. the same
   c. larger

6. Which of the following would not explain differences in labor productivity between countries?
   a. The amount of capital per worker.
   b. The level of technology.
   c. The size of the labor force.
   d. The amount of training received by workers.

7. There is some evidence that by the time of the American Civil War, average living standards were
   a. lower than at the time of the American Revolution.
   b. quite similar to living standards today.
   c. starting a decline that lasted to the end of the 19th century.
   d. about equal to those of Ancient Rome.

8. The text notes that the share of employment in agriculture in the United States has dropped from about 90 percent in 1800 to about 3 percent today. This decline is best explained by
   a. a declining demand for food.
   b. the significant increases in labor productivity in agriculture.
   c. an increasing proportion of food imported from abroad
   d. the significant increase in standards of living in the U.S. from 1800 to 1990.

9. If the growth in labor productivity declines from 3 percent per year to 1.5 percent per year, then
   a. labor will become less productive over time.
   b. standards of living will increase only if there is an expansion in average hours per worker.
   c. labor productivity will continue to increase although at a slower rate than before.
   d. the result will be a declining standard of living.

10. A comparison of labor productivity across countries shows that
(There may be more than one correct answer)
    a. labor productivity in the United States is now about the average of other industrialized counties.
    b. Japan has now emerged as the world's most productive economy.
    c. labor productivity in the United States still exceeds that of all other countries.
    d. a tendency toward convergence among the world's leading industrialized countries.

11. Lagging productivity growth in a single country is likely to lead to
    a. massive unemployment.
    b. greater exports.
    c. lower exports.
    d. a lower standard of living relative to other countries.

12. From 1967 to 1992 the share of the employment in service employment in the United States has grown
    a. less rapidly than that of other countries.
    b. about the same as in other countries.
    c. more rapidly than that of other countries.

13. The record shows that over the past two to three decades manufacturing employment in the United States (there may be more than one correct answer)
    a. has declined as a share of total employment in the U.S.
    b. has increased as a proportion of total manufacturing employment among the world's 25 leading industrial countries.
    c. has increased as labor productivity in manufacturing continued to decline.
    d. shown little change when measured as a percent of total U.S. employment.

14. Historical evidence shows that since 1800 productivity in the United States has increased at an average annual rate of
    a. less than 1 percent.
    b. slightly more than 1 percent.
    c. slightly less than 2 percent.
    d. 3.9 percent.

15. The record shows that over the past 20 years, labor productivity
    a. has increased in every industrialized country except the United States.
    b. has fallen in all industrialized countries.
    c. has grown more slowly than from 1950 to 1970 in most industrialized countries.
    d. has increased most rapidly in the United States.

16. The record of productivity growth in the United States
    a. has exceeded that of other countries ever since World War II.
    b. has been slower than that of a number of other countries for many decades.
    c. has been higher in service industries than in manufacturing industries.
    d. dooms us to a future of high unemployment and dwindling exports.

17. The convergence hypothesis suggests that the growth of labor productivity in the most advanced country
    a. will exceed that of all other countries.
    b. will be less than that of many countries.
    c. must decline.

18. A major factor leading to the convergence of growth rates across countries is probably
    a. the use of the dollar as the international currency of commerce.
    b. the increased levels of GDP devoted to military spending in many countries.
    c. the quick pace by which new technologies are spread among countries.
    d. the emergence of Japan as a major industrial country.

19. While there is evidence of a convergence of productivity and standards of living among industrialized countries, the record with regard to less-developed countries shows
    a. a similar tendency toward convergence, although at a lower level of GDP per capita.
    b. a mixed picture with some tendency toward greater differences.
    c. that most countries have had growth rates in excess of those of industrialized countries.
    d. increases in standards of living that exceed increases in productivity.

20. In the absence of increases in productivity, American goods can be made competitive in international trade if
    a. there is a reduction in the real wages of American workers relative to workers in other countries.
    b. inflation increases.
    c. the United States increases tariffs on foreign goods.
    d. foreign currency becomes less expensive in terms of dollars.

Test B

Circle T or F for true or false.

T F 1. Long-term, it makes little difference whether productivity grows at 1 percent per year or at 3 percent per year.

T F 2. Output per worker has been increasing more or less steadily for the last two millennia.

T F 3. Although productivity growth has slowed in the United States, it still remains higher than in most other industrialized countries.

T F 4. Since 1970 the growth in productivity in the United States has been about three times as high as it was right after World War II.

T F 5. There is clear evidence of a long-term decline in the productivity of American manufacturing workers.

T F 6. The historical record shows a convergence of living standards in the major industrial countries.

T F 7. Most developing countries are seeing their living standards converge with living standards in the industrial world.

T F 8. A decline in the rate of growth of American labor productivity means a decline in the productivity of American workers.

T F 9. The experience of Great Britain suggests that growth in labor productivity will only lead to massive unemployment.

T F 10. If productivity growth in the United States is lower than that of our major international competitors, we will lose export markets as foreigners can undersell us in everything.

ECONOMICS IN ACTION
Recent Productivity Growth

News of productivity growth for 1991 and 1992 seemed very much a good news/bad news situation. After almost two decades of low growth, a high rate of productivity growth was good news. At the same time, given the sluggish growth in output following the 1990-91 recession, high productivity growth held down the recovery in employment. Economist Robert Gordon argues that high productivity growth is only bad news in the shortest run. If high productivity growth results in slow growth in employment, Gordon argues that the reason must be too little stimulus to output. Over the long run, increased productivity helps to lower inflation and increase real standards of living as potential output grows more rapidly.

A number of observers argued that faster productivity growth signaled the beginning of a new era and an end to the record of subpar growth since 1973. These observers pointed to corporate downsizing and the disproportionate reduction in middle-management, white-collar employment as a sign that American business was becoming lean and mean. Economist Martin Neil Bailey was cautiously optimistic that productivity growth would remain high. He argued that the 1970s and 1980s saw significant disruptions that now appear to be behind us—gyrations in oil prices, corporate restructuring in response to new pressures for international competitiveness, the introduction of new safety and environmental regulation, and major changes in the age/sex composition of the workforce. Some argued that having made significant investments in computers, American business was now in position to reap the productivity benefits of new information technologies.

Others were not so sure. It is expensive to find and train new workers. Severance packages and the risk that good workers will be unavailable when business picks up, make it expensive to let workers go. To avoid the extra expenses associated with firing and then hiring, it can be rational during a recession for businesses to hold on to a larger workforce than necessary if it is believed that any decline in output will be short and temporary. The result of this behavior would be a sharp slowdown in productivity growth as the economy slips into recession and high rates of productivity growth as the economy recovers. The hard question is whether recent experience reflects a new higher trend for the growth of productivity

or only a normal cyclical recovery, similar to that of other business cycles. Writing in early 1993 in the *Brookings Papers on Economic Activity* Gordon concluded that available evidence was most consistent with the hypothesis of a normal cyclical recovery and not the dawning of a new era.

If experience in 1991-92 was a normal business cycle recovery, one would expect that productivity growth would then adjust downward, perhaps towards the record of the previous twenty years when productivity grew at less than 1 percent per year. Some who argued that 1992 was the dawning of a new era were predicting that productivity growth would reflect the experience of the past 70 to 80 years and average almost 2 percent per year. If the optimists are right, GDP would be about 10 percent larger after 10 years. The cumulative difference in output would be even larger, amounting to almost $3 trillion more output over 10 years. If the optimists are right a somewhat more expansionary macro policy could deliver faster growth and price stability. If they are wrong, policies for faster growth would only mean more inflation.

1. What is appropriate macro policy when there is uncertainty about the growth of potential output?
2. What has happened to the growth of productivity since 1992?

SOURCES: See Robert J. Gordon "The Jobless Recovery: Does it Signal a New Era of Productivity-Led Growth?", *Brookings Papers on Economic Activity*, 1993: 1, pp. 271-306, and "Comments" by Martin Neil Bailey, pp. 307-314.

George A. Kahn, "Sluggish Job Growth: Is Rising Productivity or an Anemic Recovery to Blame?", *Economic Review*, Federal Reserve Bank of Kansas City, (Vol. 78, No. 3), Third quarter 1993, pp. 5-25.

STUDY QUESTIONS

1. What is the difference between measures of labor productivity and output per capita?
2. Why is the growth of labor productivity so important for the growth in standards of living?
3. What factors are important for growth in labor productivity?
4. Is it possible for the growth in a country's standard of living to exceed the growth in labor productivity? If so, how, and is it likely that such a difference could be sustained over a long period of time?
5. What explains the apparent convergence of labor productivity and standards of living among the world's leading industrial countries?
6. What does the convergence hypothesis suggest about the growth of labor productivity in the United States compared to that of other industrialized countries?
7. Do you agree or disagree with the deindustrialization hypothesis? Why?
8. Why don't increases in labor productivity just lead to increased unemployment?
9. How can a country remain competitive in world markets if its growth in labor productivity lags that of other countries?

C h a p t e r **18**

International Trade and Comparative Advantage

LEARNING OBJECTIVES

After completing this chapter, you should be able to:

- list the important factors that lead countries to trade with one another.
- explain how voluntary trade, even if it does not increase total production, can be mutually beneficial to the trading partners.
- explain in what ways international and intranational trade are similar and dissimilar.
- distinguish between absolute and comparative advantage.
- explain how absolute advantage and comparative advantage are related to the location and slope of a country's production possibilities frontier.
- explain how trade means that a country's consumption possibilities can exceed its production possibilities.
- explain how world prices are relevant for determining a country's consumption possibilities.
- explain how specialization, consistent with the law of comparative advantage, can increase total world production.
- explain how world prices are determined by the interaction of demand and supply curves for trading partners.
- use a pair of demand and supply diagrams to illustrate the impact of quotas and tariffs.
- contrast the efficiency and distribution effects of tariffs and quotas.
- analyze the arguments used to advocate trade restrictions.
- explain the role of adjustment assistance in a country favoring free trade.
- explain the fallacy in the "cheap foreign labor" argument.

IMPORTANT TERMS AND CONCEPTS

Imports
Exports
Specialization
Mutual gains from trade
Absolute advantage
Comparative advantage
"Cheap foreign labor" argument
Tariff
Quota
Export subsidy
Trade adjustment assistance
Infant-industry argument
Strategic trade protection
Dumping

CHAPTER REVIEW

The material in this chapter discusses the basic economic forces that influence the international division of labor in the production of goods and the resulting pattern of international trade. The basic economic principle underlying an efficient international distribution of pro-
(1) duction is (<u>absolute/comparative</u>) advantage. It is important to remember that actual production and trade decisions are also affected by important policy interventions such as tariffs, quotas, and export subsidies.

Trade between states is, in principle, no different than trade between nations. Economists and others spend more time studying international trade rather than intranational trade for several reasons: International trade involves more than one government with a resulting host of political concerns; it usually involves more than one currency; and the mobility of labor and capital between nations is more difficult than within nations.

Exchange rates—that is, the number of units of one country's currency that are changeable into another country's currency—are an important determinant of international trade and will be discussed in the next chapter. However, the real terms of trade—how many import goods a country can get indirectly through export production rather than through direct domestic production—are the important measure of the benefits of trade, and they are considered here in some detail.

Individual countries can try to meet the consumption needs of their citizens without trade by producing everything their populations need. Alternatively, they can specialize in

the production of fewer commodities and trade for commodities they do not produce. Even if there were no differences between countries, specializing and trading would still make

(2) sense if there were important economies of _____ in production.

An important reason for trade is that differences in oil deposits, fertile soil, and other natural resources, as well as differences in labor inputs and productive capital, will affect the efficiency

(3) with which countries can produce different goods. It is the law of (<u>absolute/comparative</u>) advantage that then indicates where countries should concentrate their production to maximize the potential gains from trade.

Assume country A can produce 2,000 bushels of wheat if it produces one less car, while country B can produce only 1,200 bushels of wheat. For the same world production of cars,

(4) world production of wheat will increase if country (<u>A/B</u>) produced 10 fewer cars and country _____ produced 10 more cars. (World wheat production would increase by _____ bushels.) In this case country A has a comparative advantage in producing _____.

Looking only at its own domestic production, the opportunity cost of one more car in

(5) country A is _____ bushels of wheat. Country B can produce one more car by giving up only _____ bushels of wheat. Thus it should not be surprising if country B concentrates on the production of _____ and trades with country A, which concentrates on the production of _____.[1] It is also important to realize that comparative advantage is not a static concept. The mix of industries that maximizes a country's comparative advantage is not something that can be determined once for all time. Rather, there will need to be continuous adjustments in response to innovations and competition from foreign producers. Countries that try to isolate themselves from foreign competition have usually ended up with stagnating industries and incomes.

As countries concentrate production on those goods in which they have a comparative advantage, equilibrium world prices and trade flows—that is, exports and imports—will be

(6) determined at the point where world _____ equals world _____. This price is not at the intersection of domestic demand and supply curves; instead, it occurs at a point where the excess supply from (<u>importing/exporting</u>) countries (domestic supply minus domestic demand) equals the excess demand by _____ countries (domestic demand minus domestic supply).

Advanced courses in international trade show how prices derived under conditions of free trade will lead competitive profit-maximizing firms to exploit the comparative advantage of

---

[1]Does the law of comparative advantage imply that all countries should specialize in the production of just a few commodities? No, it does not, for several reasons. One important reason is that production possibilities frontiers are likely to be curved rather than straight lines. The implication of the curved frontier is that the opportunity cost of cars in terms of wheat for country B will rise as B produces more cars. Simultaneously, the opportunity cost of cars in terms of wheat for country A will fall as A concentrates on wheat. In equilibrium, the opportunity cost, or slope of the production possibilities frontier, in both countries will be equal. At this point neither country has an incentive for further specialization. Exactly where this point will occur will be determined by world demand and supply for cars and wheat.

(7) individual countries and help to achieve an efficient allocation of resources. Most countries do not have unrestricted free trade. Rather, imports are often restricted by the use of _____ and _____, and exports are often promoted through the use of export _____. Tariffs reduce the quantity of imports by raising their _____ while quotas raise the price of imports by restricting _____. Either a tariff or a quota could be used to achieve the same reduction in imports, but the choice between the two has other consequences.

(8) Tariff revenues accrue directly to the _____ while the benefits of higher prices under a quota are likely to accrue to private producers, both foreign and domestic. (The government might be able to capture some of these profits by auctioning import licenses, but this is not usually done.)

(9) Tariffs still require foreign suppliers to compete among themselves. This competition will favor the survival of (high/low)-cost foreign suppliers. What about domestic firms? They (do/do not) have to pay the tariff, so high-cost domestic suppliers (can/cannot) continue in business. Quotas are apt to be distributed on almost any grounds except efficiency and thus have no automatic mechanism that works in favor of low-cost foreign suppliers.

Why do countries impose tariffs and quotas? Many trade restrictions reflect the successful pleadings of high-cost domestic suppliers. Free trade and the associated reallocation of productive resources in line with the law of comparative advantage would call for the elimination of these firms in their traditional lines of business. It is not surprising that managers and workers resist these changes. If everyone is to benefit from the increased output opportuni-

(10) ties offered by free trade, then a program of trade _____ assistance will be necessary to help those most affected by the realignment of productive activities.

(11) Other traditional justifications for trade restriction include the national _____ argument and the _____ -industries argument. In both cases it is extremely difficult to separate firms with legitimate claims from those looking for a public handout. In recent years some have argued that the threat of trade restrictions should be used in a strategic manner to convince others not to impose restrictions.

Much of the free trade fuss in the United States is concerned about competing with low-cost foreign producers who pay workers lower wages. Concerns about wages need to be joined with measures of productivity. A clear understanding of comparative advantages

(12) shows that the standard of living of workers in (the exporting/the importing/both) country(ies) can rise as a result of trade and specialization. The workers with the highest standard of living, i.e., the highest wages, will be those who are most productive. While measures of absolute advantage are important when considering the standard of living workers will enjoy, even countries with high wages can benefit from trade when high wages are associated with high productivity and trade induces adjustments in the structure of world-wide production consistent with the principle of _____ advantage.

IMPORTANT TERMS AND CONCEPTS QUIZ

Choose the most appropriate definition for the following terms.

1. _____ Imports
2. _____ Exports
3. _____ Specialization
4. _____ Absolute advantage
5. _____ Comparative advantage
6. _____ Tariff
7. _____ Quota
8. _____ Export subsidy
9. _____ Trade adjustment assistance
10. _____ Infant-industry argument
11. _____ Strategic trade policy
12. _____ Dumping

a. Maximum amount of a good that can be imported per unit of time.
b. Threats to implement protectionist policies designed to promote free trade.
c. Selling goods in a foreign market at higher prices than those charged at home.
d. Domestically produced goods sold abroad.
e. Selling goods in a foreign market at lower prices than those charged at home.
f. Tax on imports.
g. Decision by a country to emphasize production of particular commodities.
h. Provision of special aid to those workers and firms harmed by foreign competition.
i. Ability of one country to produce a good less inefficiently (relative to other goods) than another country.
j. Foreign-produced goods purchased domestically.
k. Tariff protection for new industries, giving them time to mature.
l. Payment by the government that enables firms to lower prices to foreign buyers.
m. Ability of one country to produce a good using fewer resources than another country requires.

BASIC EXERCISES

1. This exercise is designed to review the law of comparative advantage.
   a. Assume that the hours of labor shown below are the only input necessary to produce hand calculators and backpacks in Canada and Japan.

	Calculators	Backpacks
Canada	6	4
Japan	2	3

   Which country has an absolute advantage in the production of hand calculators? _____. Which country has an absolute advantage in the production of backpacks? _____.
   b. If labor in Canada is reallocated from the production of calculators to the production of backpacks, how many calculators must be given up in order to produce one more backpack? _____. What about Japan? How many calculators must it give up in order to produce one more backpack? _____. Which country has

a comparative advantage in the production of backpacks? _____.
Which country has a comparative advantage in the production of calculators?
_____. According to the law of comparative advantage,
_____ should concentrate on the production of backpacks while
_____ concentrates on the production of calculators.

c. Assume each country has 12 million hours of labor input that initially is evenly
distributed in both countries between the production of backpacks and calculators: 6
million for each. Fill in the following table of outputs.

	Output of Calculators	Output of Backpacks
Canada	_____	_____
Japan	_____	_____
Total	_____	_____

d. Assume that Canada now reallocates 1.8 million labor hours away from the production of calculators and into backpacks. The change in Canadian calculator output is
−_____. The change in Canadian backpack output is + _____.

e. What reallocation of labor in Japan is necessary to be sure that world output of
calculators (Japan plus Canada) remains unchanged? _____ labor hours.
What are the changes in Japanese output from this reallocation? The change in
Japanese calculator output is + _____. The change in Japanese backpack
output is −_____.

f. By assumption, the world output of calculators has not changed, but the net change
in the world output of backpacks is a(n) (increase/decrease) of _____
backpacks.

g. Questions c through f showed how specialization according to the law of comparative advantage could increase the output of backpacks without decreasing the
output of calculators. Adjustments in line with the law of comparative advantage
could alternatively increase the output of both goods. Suppose Japan had reallocated 900,000 labor hours to the production of calculators. Fill in the following
table and compare total outputs with your answers to Question c.

	Calculators Labor Input (millions of hours)	Output
Canada	4.2	_____
Japan	6.9	_____
Total		_____

	Backpacks Labor input (millions of hours)	Output
Canada	7.8	_____
Japan	5.1	_____
Total		_____

h. Work through questions d and e again, but assume this time that the initial reallocation of 1.8 million labor hours in Canada is away from backpacks and to the production of calculators. Calculate the reallocation in Japan necessary to maintain world backpack output. What happens to the total output of calculators? Why?

i. Assume that the production of backpacks in Canada requires 9 hours rather than 4 hours. Work through the original output levels in question c and the reallocation of labor in questions d and e to see what now happens to total output of calculators and backpacks. Does your answer to question f differ from your original answer? Why?

2. This exercise is designed to give practice in analyzing the impact of quotas and tariffs. To simplify the analysis, the question assumes that the world is composed of only two countries, the United States and India.

a. Figure 18-1 shows the demand and supply for shirts in the United States and India. Prices in India are expressed in terms of American dollars. In the absence of international trade, what are the domestic price and quantity of shirts in India and the United States?

	Price	Quantity
India	_____	_____
United States	_____	_____

b. Assume now that India and the United States are free to trade without restrictions. What is the world price of shirts? _____. What happens to the production of shirts in India? _____. What happens to the production of shirts in the United States? _____. Who exports and who imports how many shirts? _____.

FIGURE 18-1

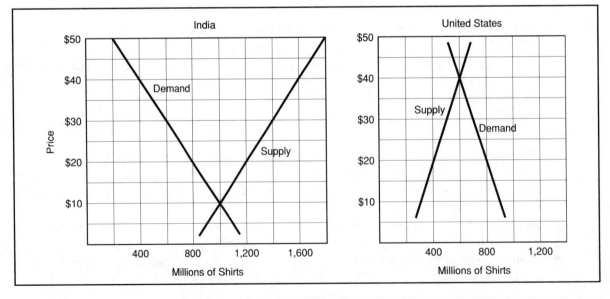

c. Assume that American producers are able to persuade the government to impose a quota limiting shirt imports to 200 million. Following imposition of the quota, what are prices and production in India and the United States?

	Price	Quantity
India	_____	_____
United States	_____	_____

Compared to the free trade equilibrium described in b, shirt prices have increased in (India/the United States) and decreased in _____. The production of shirts has increased in _____ and decreased in _____. For the world as a whole, shirt production has (increased/decreased).

d. What tariff would have yielded the same results as the quota of 200 million shirts? _____.

e. Discuss the reasons for choosing between a tariff and a quota.

SELF-TESTS FOR UNDERSTANDING

Test A

Circle the most appropriate answer.

1. Even if there were no differences in natural resources, climate, labor skills, etc., nations would still find it advantageous to specialize production and trade
   a. because of differences in absolute advantage.
   b. to take advantage of economies of scale.
   c. to take advantage of differences in national currencies.
   d. when inflation rates differ.

2. International trade is different from intranational trade because of
   a. political issues that arise from different governments.
   b. limitations of the ability of labor and capital to move between countries compared to their ability to move within countries.
   c. the use of different currencies.
   d. all of the above.

3. Economists argue that
   a. efficiency in international trade requires countries to produce those goods in which they have an absolute advantage.
   b. efficiency in international trade requires countries to produce those goods in which they have a comparative advantage.
   c. efficiency in international trade requires countries that have an absolute advantage in the production of all goods to become self-sufficient.
   d. countries with export surpluses will have a comparative advantage in the production of all goods.

4. On a per capita production possibilities frontier showing the production of clothes on the vertical axis and cars on the horizontal axis, the absolute advantage in the production of clothes would be determined
   a. by the slope of the per capita production possibilities frontier.
   b. where the per capita production possibilities frontier cuts the horizontal axis.
   c. by the area under the per capita production possibilities frontier.
   d. where the per capita production possibilities frontier cuts the vertical axis.

5. On a per capita production possibilities frontier showing the production of clothes on the vertical axis and cars on the horizontal axis, the comparative advantage in the production of clothes would be determined
   a. by the slope of the per capita production possibilities frontier.
   b. where the per capita production possibilities frontier cuts the horizontal axis.
   c. by the area under the per capita production possibilities frontier.
   d. where the per capita production possibilities frontier cuts the vertical axis.

6. Which of the following is an example of comparative advantage?
   a. Wages of textile workers are lower in India than in America.
   b. The slope of the production possibilities frontier between tomatoes and airplanes differs for Mexico and the United States.
   c. American workers must work an average of only 800 hours to purchase a car, while Russian workers must work 1,600 hours.
   d. In recent years Swedish income per capita has exceeded that of the United States.

7. Specialization and free trade consistent with the law of comparative advantage will enable
   a. increased world production of all traded goods.
   b. increases in the standard of living for workers in both exporting and importing countries.
   c. countries to consume at some point outside their production possibilities frontier.
   d. all of the above.

8. From a worldwide perspective, economic efficiency is enhanced if production and trade is organized according to the law of comparative advantage. Economic efficiency within a single country is enhanced if regional production and trade are organized according to
   a. absolute advantage.
   b. the political power of particular states or regions.
   c. which regions have the highest unemployment.
   d. comparative advantage.

9. If shoes can be produced with two hours of labor input in Italy and three hours of labor input in the United States, then it is correct to say that
   a. Italy has an absolute advantage in the production of shoes.
   b. Italy has a comparative advantage in the production of shoes.
   c. the United States has an absolute advantage in the production of shoes.
   d. the United States has a comparative advantage in the production of shoes.

10. Assuming that shoes are produced as in question 9 and shirts can be produced with four hours of labor in both countries, then it is correct to say that
    a. the United States has a comparative advantage in the production of shirts.
    b. Italy has a comparative advantage in the production of shirts.
    c. Italy has an absolute advantage in the production of shirts.
    d. the United States has an absolute advantage in the production of shirts.

11. Under free trade, world prices for exports and imports would be such that
    a. countries would specialize production along lines of absolute advantage.
    b. all countries would show a slight export surplus.
    c. the quantity supplied by exporters would just equal the quantity demanded by importers.
    d. every country would be self-sufficient in all goods.

12. All but which one of the following have been used to restrict trade?
    a. Export subsidies.
    b. Tariffs.
    c. Quotas.
    d. "Voluntary" export agreements.

13. A tariff affects trade by
    a. imposing a tax on imported goods.
    b. limiting the quantity of goods that can be imported.
    c. offering a subsidy to producers who export for foreign sales.
    d. the voluntary actions of foreign manufacturers to limit their exports.

14. A quota affects trade by
    a. imposing a tax on imported goods.
    b. limiting the quantity of goods that can be imported.
    c. offering a subsidy to producers who export for foreign sales.
    d. the voluntary action of foreign manufacturers to limit their exports.

15. Which of the following is an example of a tariff?
    a. Japanese car manufacturers agree to limit exports to the United States.
    b. U.S. law limits the imports of cotton shirts to 20 million.
    c. Television manufacturers outside Great Britain must pay a 5 percent duty on each set they ship to Great Britain.
    d. Foreign bicycle manufacturers receive a rebate of taxes from their own government for each bicycle they export.

16. One economic advantage of tariffs over quotas is that tariffs
    a. typically give preferential treatment to long-term suppliers.
    b. expose high-cost domestic producers to competition.
    c. force foreign suppliers to compete.
    d. help avoid destructive price wars.

17. The imposition of a tariff on steel will lead to all but which one of the following?
    a. A lower volume of steel imports.
    b. Higher domestic steel prices.
    c. Reduced domestic demand for steel.
    d. Reduced domestic production of steel as higher steel prices reduce demand.

18. The imposition of a quota on steel will lead to all but which one of the following?
    a. A lower volume of steel imports.
    b. Increased domestic production of steel.
    c. Lower domestic steel prices.
    d. Reduced domestic demand for steel.

19. A quota that limits the importation of foreign computer chips is likely to be in the interest of all but which of the following? (There may be more than one correct answer.)
    a. Domestic chip manufacturers.
    b. Domestic computer manufacturers.
    c. Labor employed domestically in the production of computer chips.
    d. Consumers interested in buying computers.

20. Which one of the following is not a justification for trade restrictions?
    a. Some industries would be so vital in times of war that we cannot rely on foreign suppliers.
    b. A temporary period of protection is necessary until an industry matures and is able to compete with foreign suppliers.
    c. Competition from foreign suppliers will help keep prices to consumers low.
    d. The threat of trade restrictions may prevent the adoption of restrictions by others.

Test B

Circle T or F for true or false.

T F 1. A country with an absolute advantage in producing all goods is better off being self-sufficient than engaging in trade.

T F 2. Countries gain from trade only when it allows them to adjust productive resources to take advantage of economies of scale.

T F 3. A country with an absolute advantage in the production of all goods should only export commodities.

T F 4. The unequal distribution of natural resources among countries is one important reason why countries trade.

T F 5. Which of two countries has a comparative advantage in the production of wine rather than cloth can be determined by comparing the slopes of the production possibility frontiers of both countries.

T F 6. It is possible for all countries to simultaneously expand exports and reduce imports.

T F 7. A quota on shirts would reduce the volume of imported shirts by specifying the quantity of shirts that could be imported.

T F 8. The infant-industry argument is used to justify protection for industries that are vital in times of war.

T F 9. Dumping of goods by the United States on Japanese markets would necessarily harm Japanese consumers.

T F 10. If foreign labor is paid less, foreign producers will always be able to undersell American producers.

SUPPLEMENTARY EXERCISES

1. Demand and supply for widgets in Baulmovia and Bilandia are as follows:

    Baulmovia

    $$\text{Demand: } Q = 156 - 7\,P$$
    $$\text{Supply: } Q = -44 + 18\,P$$

    Bilandia

    $$\text{Demand: } Q = 320 - 10\,P$$
    $$\text{Supply: } Q = -20 + 10\,P$$

    a. In the absence of trade, what is the price of widgets in Baulmovia? In Bilandia? What quantity is produced in Baulmovia? In Bilandia?
    b. With free trade what is the one common world price for widgets? Which country exports widgets? Which country imports widgets? What is the volume of exports and imports?
    c. Manufacturers in the importing country have convinced the government to impose a tariff on widget imports of $4.50 a widget. What will happen to trade and the price of widgets in the two countries?
    d. What quota would have the same impact on trade?
    e. What factors might lead one to prefer a tariff over a quota?

2. Ricardia is a small country that produces wine and cloth. The production possibilities frontier for Ricardia is

    $$W = \sqrt{324 - C^2}$$

    where W = millions of barrels of wine and C = millions of bolts of cloth.
    a. Use a piece of graph paper. Label the vertical axis "wine" and the horizontal axis "cloth." Draw the production possibilities frontier.

b. Since Ricardia is a small country, it can export or import cloth or wine without affecting world prices. World prices are such that Ricardia can export one million barrels of wine for 750,000 bolts of cloth or it can export 750,000 bolts of cloth for one million barrels of wine. The government's chief economist argues that regardless of consumption preferences, Ricardia should produce 14.4 million bolts of cloth and 10.8 million barrels of wine. Do you agree? Why? (Hint: Consider what a graph of consumption possibilities looks like. For any production combination of wine and cloth, Ricardia's consumption possibilities are given by a negatively sloped straight line through the production point. The slope of the consumption possibilities line reflects world prices. A movement up the straight line to the left of the production point would imply exporting cloth in order to consume more wine. A movement down the straight line to the right would reflect exporting wine in order to consume more cloth. Exactly what Ricardia chooses to consume is a matter of preferences, but its choice is constrained by its consumption possibilities line, which in turn is determined by Ricardia's production choice and world prices for cloth and wine. Why does the production point 10.8 million barrels of wine and 14.4 million bolts of cloth offer the greatest consumption possibilities?)

STUDY QUESTIONS

1. Why do countries trade with each other? Why don't they try to be self-sufficient in the production of all goods?

2. What is the difference between absolute advantage and comparative advantage? (Use a per capita production possibilities frontier to illustrate your answer.)

3. Why do economists argue that a country with an absolute advantage in the production of all goods can still gain from trade if it specializes in a manner consistent with the law of comparative advantage? (Consider a two-good, two-country example.)

4. Why isn't it possible for all countries to improve their balance of trade by increasing exports and decreasing imports?

5. Why aren't a country's consumption possibilities limited by its production possibilities?

6. When considering a single commodity that is traded without tariffs or quotas, what are the two conditions that characterize equilibrium and determine world price and the location of production?

7. How are these conditions changed if the importing country imposes a tariff? A quota?

8. Use a demand-supply diagram to show an initial free trade equilibrium and how that equilibrium would be affected by a tariff or quota.

9. It is often asserted that for every tariff there is a corresponding quota in the sense of having the same impact on prices and production. Is this statement correct and if so what difference(s) would one policy make over the other?

10. How do you evaluate the arguments supporting strategic trade policies?

11. What is the role of trade adjustment assistance and why do many think it a necessary element of a policy that favors free trade?

12. What is the infant-industry argument? Do you believe it is ever a compelling argument? Why? Why not?

13. Some industries argue for trade protection on the grounds of national defense. Do you believe this is ever a compelling argument? Why? Why not?

14. "In order to increase the consumption possibilities of Americans, the United States should never prohibit dumping by foreign manufacturers." Do you agree? Why? Why not?

15. Why isn't it obvious to many economists that the United States should enact tariffs to level the playing field and protect American workers from unfair competition from low-wage foreign workers?

ECONOMICS IN ACTION

Jobs, Foreign Investment, and Free Trade

On June 14, 1993, *The New York Times* reported on the resolution of an issue that had divided some of President Clinton's top advisers: How far should the government go to encourage foreign-owned companies to build factories in the United States? The issue at the center was whether the expansion of an automobile factory in Tennessee, owned by the Nissan Motor Company, should be declared a foreign trade zone.

Designation as a foreign trade zone would allow Nissan to import auto parts and pay the 2.5 percent tariff for finished cars rather than the 4 to 11 percent tariffs assessed on individual auto parts. It was estimated the reduction in tariffs would save Nissan $20 a car or about $5 million a year.

The *Times* reported that approval of foreign trade zones had been routine in recent years. There are about 200 zones or subzones, including many auto assembly plants or refineries using foreign oil. Domestic auto makers have been among the biggest beneficiaries of such approvals. This time, however, objections were raised by American auto makers and by Mickey Kantor, President Clinton's special trade representative. The auto manufacturers argued that there were already too many car factories in the United States. Expansion of the Nissan plant could cause existing plants to close. Mr. Kantor appeared to argue against routine approval on the grounds its eventual approval could be used as a bargaining chip with Japan on other issues. There was also speculation that Mr. Kantor hoped to use disapproval of the foreign trade zone as a reason for American auto makers to support other elements of the President's economic plan.

On the other side, favoring approval were Laura D'Andrea Tyson, Chairwoman of the Council of Economic Advisers; Vice President Al Gore, former senator from Tennessee; and Ron Brown, Secretary of Commerce. Those supporting the foreign trade zone argued that

allowing foreign auto makers to expand production in the United States created more American jobs than importing fully assembled cars. Concern was also voiced that potential foreign investors could be scared off by a reversal of what had been seen as routine.

Nissan also argued that the foreign trade zone would help create U.S. jobs. "We certainly should not have a disincentive to build vehicles here," said Gail O'Sullivan Neuman, vice president and general counsel for the Nissan factory. Others speculated that Nissan was trying to protect itself from possible future trade restrictions and adverse changes in the exchange rate.

1. If you were one of the President's advisers what would you have recommended?

Chapter **19**

The International Monetary System: Order or Disorder?

LEARNING OBJECTIVES

After completing this chapter you should be able to:

- identify the factors that help determine a country's exchange rate under a system of floating exchange rates.

- distinguish between long-, medium-, and short-run factors that help determine the demand and supply of currencies.

- use a demand and supply diagram to show how changes in GDP, inflation, or interest rates can lead to an appreciation or depreciation of the dollar under a system of floating exchange rates.

- show, on a supply-demand graph, how fixed exchange rates can lead to a balance of payments deficit or surplus.

- explain why, under the gold standard, countries lost control of their domestic money stock.

- describe the options, other than changing the exchange rate, that were available under the Breton Woods system to a country wanting to eliminate a balance of payments deficit or surplus.

- explain why, under a system of fixed exchange rates, there was very little risk in speculating against an overvalued currency.

- explain how speculators can reduce the uncertainty exporters and importers face under a system of floating exchange rates.

IMPORTANT TERMS AND CONCEPTS

International monetary system
Exchange rate
Appreciation
Depreciation
Revaluation
Supply of and demand for foreign exchange
Floating exchange rates
Purchasing-power parity theory
Fixed exchange rates
Balance of payments deficit and surplus
Current account
Capital account
Balance of trade
Gold standard
Gold-exchange system (Bretton Woods system)
International Monetary Fund (IMF)
"Dirty" or "managed" floating
The European Exchange Rate Mechanism (ERM)

CHAPTER REVIEW

Meeting: President Richard M. Nixon and H. R. Haldeman, Oval Office, June 23, 1972 (10:04-11:39 A.M.)

> Haldeman: Burns is concerned about speculation against the lira.
> Nixon: Well, I don't give a (expletive deleted) about the lira...There ain't a vote in it.

> (Statement of Information: Appendix III, Hearings before the committee on the Judiciary,
> House of Representatives, Ninety-third Congress, Second Session, May–June 1974, page 50)

Soon after 1972, even American presidents paid attention to exchange rates. So should you. Even if you are never President, exchange rates are important for all Americans. Consumers are affected by the price of imports, and jobs for workers can be affected by the price of exports and imports. This chapter discusses exchange rates, that is, the price of one currency in terms of another. The discussion in the text covers the economic factors that determine exchange rates, the implications of attempts by governments to fix exchange rates, and a review of recent history focusing on the evolution of the world's current mixed international monetary system.

Discussions of international monetary arrangements involve a whole new vocabulary of fixed and floating exchange rates, current and capital accounts, appreciating and depreciating currencies and devaluations and revaluations. It may help you to keep the vocabulary straight

if you remember that most of the analysis of international monetary arrangements is merely an application of the supply-demand analysis originally introduced in Chapter 4.

(1) Find out how much it would cost, in dollars, to buy one German mark. This figure is the current dollar/mark _____ rate, expressed in dollars. Many newspapers now publish exchange rates on a daily basis. A student in Germany could do the same thing and get a price for dollars in terms of marks. If you both call on the same day you should both get the same price (ignoring sales commissions.)[1] If the dollar price of one mark increases, so that it takes more dollars to buy one mark, we say that the dollar has _____ relative to the mark. Alternatively, we could say that the mark has _____ relative to the dollar.

(2) Under a system of floating exchange rates, exchange rates will be determined by market forces of _____ and _____. Consider an example using two countries, Germany and the United States. The demand for German marks has three major sources:

>   (1)   the demand by Americans for German exports, such as cars, cameras, and machine tools;

>   (2)   the demand by Americans for German financial assets, such as stocks and bonds; and

>   (3)   the demand by Americans for German physical assets, such as factories and machines.

The supply of German marks also has three sources: the demand by Germans for American (exports/imports), American _____ assets, and American _____ assets. (Note that the demand and supply of marks has an interpretation in terms of the demand and supply of dollars. The demand for marks by Americans is simultaneously a _____ of dollars. Understanding this mirror-image aspect of exchange rates may help keep the vocabulary and analysis straight.)

(3) Under a system of floating rates, the equilibrium exchange rate will be at a level where demand equals supply. A change in any factor that affects demand or supply will change the exchange rate. For example, a sudden demand for German wines on the part of Americans would shift the (demand/supply) curve for marks. The dollar price of marks will (increase/decrease), a result economists call a(n) (appreciation/depreciation) of the mark in terms of the dollar. Conversely, a sudden demand for California wines on the part of Germans would shift the _____ curve of marks and would mean a(n) (appreciation/depreciation) of the mark in terms of the dollar. A simultaneous boom in the United States and recession in Germany are likely to lead to a(n) _____ of the mark in terms of the dollar.

(4) In the long run, the exchange rate between two currencies should be determined by comparing prices of traded goods according to the theory of _____

---

[1] In the United States you might get a price of 62.5 cents for one mark. The German student would get a price of 1.6 marks for one dollar. If x is the dollar price of one mark, then $1/x$ is the mark price of one dollar.

_____ _____. In order that its goods remain competitive on world markets, a country with a very high rate of inflation will see its exchange rate (<u>appreciate/depreciate</u>). In the medium run, a country that experiences an economic boom will find its imports rising and its exchange rate _____. In the short run, exchange rates will be affected by the movement of large pools of investment funds that are sensitive to differences in interest rates. Restrictive monetary policy that increases interest rates will attract funds, (<u>appreciating/depreciating</u>) the exchange rate.

Governments may try to peg the exchange rate. In fact, from the end of World War II until 1973, the world operated on a system of fixed exchange rates, established at the
(5) _____ Woods conference. At the time, it was thought that fixed exchange rates were necessary to stimulate the growth of international trade, so countries could reap the benefits of specialization according to the law of comparative advantage. Pegging an exchange rate is very similar to any other sort of price control and is subject to similar problems.

If, say, the Japanese government pegs the exchange rate at too high a level, the supply of Japanese yen will exceed the demand for yen, and Japan will experience a balance of
(6) payments (<u>deficit/surplus</u>). If the government pegs the rate too low, then (<u>demand/supply</u>) will exceed _____ and the result will be a balance of payments
_____.

A government pegging its exchange rate and faced with a deficit will need to use its
(7) holdings of international reserves, that is, gold or foreign currencies, in order to (<u>buy/sell</u>) its own currency. A country faced with a surplus will need to supply its own currency. As a result, it will find its international reserves (<u>increasing/decreasing</u>).

Under fixed exchange rates, most of the pressure for adjustment is placed on countries
(8) experiencing a balance of payments (<u>deficit/surplus</u>). If nothing else, such a country will eventually run out of international reserves. If a country does not want to change its exchange rate, other adjustment options include monetary and fiscal policies that (<u>increase/decrease</u>) interest rates, (<u>increase/decrease</u>) the rate of inflation, or induce a general (<u>contraction/expansion</u>) in the level of economic activity. Many of these adjustments occurred automatically under the gold standard as a balance of payments deficit led to an outflow of gold and a(n) (<u>increase/reduction</u>) in the stock of money.

A major weakness of the Bretton Woods system of fixed exchange rates was that deficit
(9) countries (<u>liked/disliked</u>) adjusting their domestic economies for balance of payments reasons rather than for domestic political and economic reasons. Another weakness was the special role accorded the U.S. dollar.

In recent years the world's major industrialized countries have operated under a mixed system of floating rates. Exchange rates are allowed to change on a daily basis in response to market forces. At the same time, many governments intervene by buying or selling currencies, hoping to influence the exchange rate to their advantage. Some have worried that floating exchange rates would be so volatile as to destroy world trade. However, market-determined prices need not be volatile, and importers and exporters can often relieve the
(10) business risk of changes in exchange rate by dealing with _____.

IMPORTANT TERMS AND CONCEPTS QUIZ

Choose the best definition for each of the following terms.

1. _____ International monetary system
2. _____ Exchange rate
3. _____ Appreciation
4. _____ Depreciation
5. _____ Devaluation
6. _____ Revaluation
7. _____ Floating exchange rates
8. _____ Purchasing-power parity theory
9. _____ Fixed exchange rates
10. _____ Balance of payments deficit
11. _____ Balance of payments surplus
12. _____ Current account
13. _____ Capital account
14. _____ Balance of trade
15. _____ Gold standard
16. _____ Gold-exchange system
17. _____ International Monetary Fund
18. _____ Dirty float

a. Value of currencies linked to the dollar whose value was linked to gold.
b. Price of one currency in terms of another.
c. Exchange rates determined in free market by supply and demand.
d. Difference between merchandise exports and imports.

e. Set of institutions that facilitate international movements of currencies.
f. System where exchange rates change in response to market forces, but with intervention by central banks.
g. International agency that extends loans for infrastructure to developing countries.
h. Amount by which quantity supplied of a country's currency exceeds quantity demanded in a given year.
i. Balance of trade involving purchases and sales of assets.
j. International agency that monitors exchange rate policies of member countries.
k. Reduction in official value of a currency.
l. Balance of trade in goods and services plus unilateral transfers.
m. System where currencies are defined in terms of gold.
n. Increase in the amount of foreign currency a unit of a given currency can buy.
o. Exchange rates set by the government.
p. Amount by which quantity demanded of a country's currency exceeds quantity supplied.
q. Idea that exchange rates adjust to reflect differences in the prices of traded goods.
r. Drop in the amount of foreign currency a unit of a given currency can buy.
s. Increase in official value of a currency.

BASIC EXERCISES

1. This exercise is designed to contrast the impact of similar events under systems of fixed and floating exchange rates.

Assume that the world is divided into two countries, the United States and France. Table 19-1 lists a number of events. Fill in the missing blank spaces in the table to analyze the impact of these events on (1) the dollar-franc exchange rate under a system of floating rates, and (2) the French balance of payments under a system of fixed exchange rates. Assume that each event takes place from an initial equilibrium that under fixed exchange rates entails neither a deficit nor a surplus. Figure 19-1 illustrates such an equilibrium at an initial exchange rate of 16 cents per franc.

TABLE 19-1

			Floating Rates	Fixed Rates
Event	Shift in Demand Curves for Francs (left, right, no shift)	Shift in Supply Curve for Francs (left, right, no shift)	Appreciation or Depreciation of Franc	Change in French Balance Payment
a. Federal reserve policy raises interest rates in the United States				
b. A change in tastes increases American demand for haute couture fashions from Paris.				
c. The U.S. economy enters a recession.				
d. Major labor strikes in France have resulted in a sudden increase in the (franc) price of French goods.				
e. A terrible freeze destroys French wine grapes and increase the demand for American wine.				

* Appropriate answers would be deficit, surplus, or no charge

FIGURE 19-1

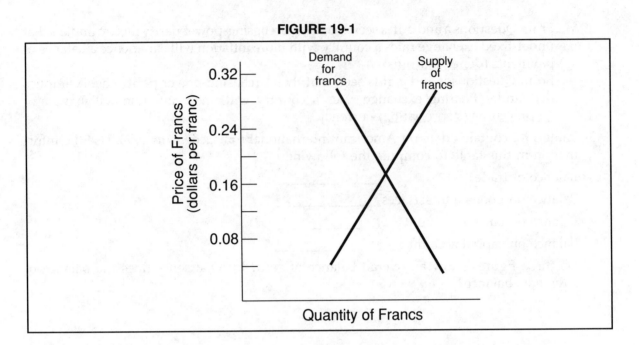

2. This exercise is designed to illustrate the theory of purchasing power parity.

Assume that the United States and France are the only suppliers of wine on the world market. Consumers of wine are indifferent between French and California wines and buy whichever is cheaper. Initially, the dollar-franc exchange rate is assumed to be 16 cents to the franc and California wine sells for $4.80 a bottle.

Ignoring transportation costs, the initial dollar price of French wines must be $4.80. Accordingly, we know that the initial franc price of French wine is _____ francs.

Assume now that inflation in the United States has raised the price of California wine to $7.20 a bottle, while inflation in France has raised the price of French wine to 40 francs. Based on this data, answer each of the following:
  a. If the exchange rate is fixed at 16 cents to the franc, what is the new dollar price of French wine? $_____ What would happen to the sales of French and California wines? What happens to the American balance of payments?
  b. If the dollar-franc exchange rate is free to adjust, what is the new exchange rate; that is what dollar price of a franc is necessary to equalize the dollar (or franc) price of both wines? _____ This change in the dollar price of a franc is an (appreciation/depreciation) of the franc and a _____ of the dollar.
  c. Assuming that the change in the price of wine is typical of the change in other prices, which country had the higher rate of inflation? _____

    d. From Questions a and c, it is seen that the purchasing-power parity theory implies that under fixed exchange rates a country with more inflation will experience a balance of payments (<u>deficit/surplus</u>).

    e. From Questions b and c, it is seen that the purchasing-power parity theory implies that under floating exchange rates a country with more inflation will have a(n) (<u>appreciating/depreciating</u>) currency.

3. Table 19-2 contains data on American international transactions in 1990. Use the information in this table to compute the following:

Balance of trade   _____

Balance on goods and services_____

Balance on current account   _____

Balance on capital account   _____

Do these figures show an overall balance of zero? In what sense does the balance of payments balance?

TABLE 19-2
AMERICAN INTERNATIONAL TRANSACTIONS
1990
(billions of dollars)

Line	Item	Demand for dollars (Gain of foreign currency)	Supply of dollars (Loss of foreign currency)
1	Exports	389.3	
2	Imports		498.3
3	Net military transactions		7.8
4	Travel and transportation (net)	9.0	
5	Net Income from investments and other services	49.8	
6	Private transfers		13.5
7	U.S. government transfers (nonmilitary)		20.4
8	Change in U.S. assets abroad		44.3
9	Change in foreign assets in the U.S.	71.0	
10	Change in the U.S. government assets	0.1	
11	Change in foreign official assets in the U.S.	34.2	

Source: Survey of Current Business, June 1993

SELF-TESTS FOR UNDERSTANDING

Test A

Circle the most appropriate answer.

1. The exchange rate between the American dollar and the French franc tells us
   a. how much gold each currency is worth.
   b. the dollar price of a franc and the franc price of a dollar.
   c. whether the French are running a balance of payments deficit.
   d. how many pounds each currency will purchase.

2. If an American can buy a Finnish mark for 20 cents, how many marks must a Finn spend to buy a dollar?
   a. 0.20 marks
   b. 1 mark
   c. 5 marks
   d. 20 marks

3. If the German mark appreciates relative to the British pound, then a mark will buy
   a. fewer pounds than before.
   b. more pounds than before.
   c. the same number of pounds as before.

4. If under a system of floating exchange rates the Mexican peso used to cost 33 cents and now costs 28 cents, one would say that
   a. the peso has appreciated relative to the dollar.
   b. the peso has depreciated relative to the dollar.
   c. there has been a devaluation of the peso relative to the dollar.
   d. there has been a revaluation of the peso relative to the dollar.

5. If the dollar price of a mark falls from 60 cents to 50 cents, one would say that the (There may be more than one correct answer.)
   a. mark has appreciated against the dollar.
   b. dollar has appreciated against the mark.
   c. dollar has depreciated against the mark.
   d. mark has depreciated against the dollar.

6. If the yen appreciates against the mark, then we know that the
   a. mark has appreciated against the dollar.
   b. dollar has also appreciated against the yen.
   c. mark has depreciated against the yen.
   d. yen has appreciated against the dollar.

7. Under a system of floating exchange rates, an increase in the demand for dollars by foreigners will cause a(n) _____ of the dollar.
   a. devaluation
   b. appreciation
   c. revaluation
   d. depreciation

8. Which of the following would cause an appreciation of the dollar? (There may be more than one correct answer.)
   a. An increase in American GDP.
   b. An increase in foreign GDP.
   c. A decrease in American interest rates.
   d. A decrease in foreign interest rates.
   e. An increase in inflation in the United States.
   f. An increase in inflation in the rest of the world.

9. Which of the following would cause a depreciation of the dollar?
   a. A decrease in American GDP.
   b. An increase in foreign GDP.
   c. An increase in American interest rates.
   d. A decrease in foreign interest rates.
   e. A decrease in inflation in the United States.
   f. A decrease in inflation in the rest of the world.

10. Under a system of floating exchange rates, which one of the following conditions will tend to depreciate the French franc relative to the German mark?
    a. An economic boom in Germany.
    b. A higher level of inflation in France than in Germany.
    c. An increase in interest rates in France.
    d. A sudden increase in German demand for imports from France.

11. Which of the following would lead to an appreciation of the franc relative to the mark?
    a. A recession in Germany.
    b. Less inflation in Germany than in France.
    c. An increase in French interest rates.
    d. A boom in France.

12. An economic boom is likely to mean (There may be more than one correct answer.)
    a. more imports.
    b. a depreciation of a country's currency.
    c. a balance of payments deficit under a system of floating exchange rates.
    d. an appreciation of a country's currency.

13. Purchasing-power parity theory says that
    a. only the volume of exports and imports determines exchange rates; interest rates have nothing to do with exchange rates.
    b. all countries are better off with a system of fixed exchange rates.
    c. adjustment of fixed exchange rates should be symmetrical between deticit and surplus countries.
    d. in the long run, exchange rates adjust to reflect differences in price levels between countries.

14. If inflation in Germany is at an annual rate of 2 percent and inflation in the United States is at 8 percent, then the purchasing-power parity theory suggests that in the long run the dollar price of one mark will
    a. increase at an annual rate of 8 percent.
    b. decrease at an annual rate of 6 percent.
    c. increase at an annual rate of 6 percent.
    d. increase at an annual rate of 2 percent.

15. In Question 14 above, one would say that the higher rate of inflation in the United States results in a(n)
    a. depreciation of the mark relative to the dollar.
    b. appreciation of the mark relative to the dollar.
    c. appreciation of the dollar relative to the mark.
    d. cross-subsidy of the mark by the dollar.

16. Assume that the mark—dollar exchange rate is fixed, that Germany and the United States are the only two countries in the world, and that inflation rates differ as described in Question 14. Which country will have a balance of payments surplus?
    a. The United States.
    b. Germany.

17. From an initial position of equilibrium under a system of fixed exchange rates, which of the following would lead to a balance of payments deficit?
    (There may be more than one correct answer.)
    a. A boom in the domestic economy.
    b. An increase in domestic interest rates.
    c. Domestic inflation in excess of inflation in the rest of the world.
    d. A devaluation by a country's major trading partner.

18. If the country of Zenon tries to fix its exchange rate at a level above that determined by demand and supply, it will likely
    (There may be more than one correct answer.)
    a. run a balance of payments deficit.
    b. run a balance of payments surplus.
    c. find its exports being priced out of world markets.
    d. see reduced interest by foreigners in investing in Zenon.

19. Which one of the following policies would not help to eliminate a deficit under a system of fixed exchange rates?
    a. Monetary and fiscal policies to raise the level of unemployment.
    b. A devaluation of the exchange rate.
    c. Monetary and fiscal policies to increase the rate of inflation.
    d. A change in monetary policy that increases interest rates.

20. If it takes 13 cents to buy one Swedish krona and 52 cents to buy one Dutch guilder, then how many kronor should it take to buy one guilder?
    a. $(.13 \div .52) = .25$.
    b. $(.52 \div .13) = 4.00$.
    c. $(1.0 \div .13) = 7.69$.
    d. $(1.0 \div .52) = 1.92$.

Test B

Circle T or F for true or false.

T F 1. If one mark used to cost 60 cents and now costs 40 cents, the dollar has appreciated relative to the mark.

T F 2. A pure system of floating exchange rates requires government intervention—purchases and sales of its own currency—in order to work properly.

T F 3. Under a system of floating exchange rates, a sudden increase in the demand for U.S. exports will lead to appreciation of the dollar relative to other currencies.

T F 4. Under a system of fixed exchange rates, a sudden increase in American imports would increase the American balance of payments deficit (or reduce the size of the surplus).

T F 5. Purchasing-power parity is a theory of the short-run determination of exchange rates.

T F 6. Under a system of fixed exchange rates, a country that attempts to peg its exchange rate at an artificially low level will end up with a balance of payments surplus.

T F 7. Today, world international monetary relations are based on the gold standard.

T F 8. A major advantage of the gold standard was that countries could control their own domestic money stock.

T F 9. The Bretton Woods gold-exchange system established a system of fixed exchange rates based on the convertibility of dollars into gold.

T F 10. Under the Bretton Woods system of fixed exchange rates, both surplus and deficit countries felt the same pressure to correct any imbalance in their balance of payments.

SUPPLEMENTARY EXERCISES

1. The Risks of Speculation Against Fixed Exchange Rates

Assume that in the mid-1960s you are treasurer for a large multinational corporation with 10 million British pounds to invest. The fixed official exchange rate vis-a-vis the U.S. dollar has been $2.80. At this exchange rate Britain has been experiencing large and growing deficits in its balance of payments and has been financing this deficit by buying pounds with foreign currencies. Britain's holdings of foreign currencies are running low, and there is a general feeling that Britain will have to devalue the pound. Exactly how large the devaluation will be and exactly when it will occur are uncertain, but given the history of chronic deficits, there is absolutely no chance that the pound will be revalued.

Complete Table 19-3 to measure the risks of speculating against the pound. (Changing from pounds to dollars and back again will involve transactions costs. Table 19-3 abstracts from these costs, which are apt to be small.)

What is the worst outcome?

As the talk of devaluation heats up, what are you apt to do? How will your actions affect the British deficit and the pressures for devaluation?

2. World Trade Under Fixed and Flexible Exchange Rates

Some observers worried that the introduction of a system of floating exchange rates would have adverse effects on the volume of world trade, as exporters and importers would have trouble coping with short-run fluctuations in exchange rates. Go to the library and look up data on the volume of international trade. (You might try data from one of a variety of international organizations, including the United Nations, the International Monetary Fund, or the World Bank.) What is the percentage change in the annual physical volume of trade since the establishment of current mixed system of floating exchange rates in 1973? How does the growth in trade compare with growth in world output, that is the sum of all countries' GDP?

TABLE 19-3

	(1)	(2)	(3)
Initial holdings of pounds	10,000,000	10,000,000	10,000,000
Current exchange rate	$2.80	$2.80	$2.80
Number of dollars if you sell pounds for dollars	___	___	___
Possible new exchange rate	$2.80*	$2.60	$2.40
Number of pounds following reconversion to pounds after devaluation	___	___	___

* This exchange rate assumes Britain takes other steps and does not devalue the pound

ECONOMICS IN ACTION
Hedging One's International Investments

The movement of exchange rates complicates the lives of companies and individual investors who by choice or necessity have to deal with international investments. Imagine that interest rates in Britain offer a better return than in the United States. Do you want to convert your dollars into pounds, invest in Britain, and then convert back to dollars? The higher interest return may look tempting, but any advantage of higher interest rates in Britain could be completely offset by an adverse movement in the dollar/pound exchange rate. For example, assume that a pound cost $1.60 when you invest to take advantage of a 10 percent interest rate in Britain compared to a 5 percent interest rate in the United States. What happens if at the end of the year, when you go to convert your pounds back into dollars, the pound has depreciated to $1.45 or appreciated to $1.75? As the example shows, changes in exchange rates can have a major impact on international investors and on the dollar value of international earnings of corporations.[1] Economists would say that these changes add to the variability and risk of international investments. If potential returns are sufficiently attractive, there is an incentive to learn how to manage the associated risk.

It is often argued that one should fully hedge international investments. That is, if you make an investment in Britain you should at the same time take other actions that lock-in the exchange rate you will use to convert your pounds back into dollars. While such actions mean you would not benefit from an appreciation of the pound, you would also avoid the loss that would accompany a depreciation. The use of future markets, that is dealing with speculators in foreign exchange, is one way to lock-in a particular exchange rate.

How important is it to hedge one's international investments? Economist Kenneth Froot argues that whether one should hedge international investments depends upon one's time horizon. Using almost 200 years worth of data on exchange rates between the dollar and the pound along with investment returns in the United States and the United Kingdom, Froot argues that hedging reduced the variance of international investments that were held for short horizons, e.g. one or two years, but that as one's investment horizon lengthened, there was less need to hedge international investments. How can this be?

Consider the following simple example. Assume that over longer time horizons, exchange rates tend toward levels defined by purchasing power parity, real interest rates are the same in the United States and Britain, and nominal investment returns reflect any differences in inflation. If inflation is higher in Britain, then nominal interest rates in Britain should be higher than in the United States. Note that nominal interest rates in Britain are measured in terms of pounds while in the United States they are measured in terms of dollars. If exchange rates are determined by purchasing power parity, the pound will depreciate at a rate that just offsets the difference in nominal interest rates. An U.S. investor would not be

---

[1]Changes in exchange rates are not just an issue for a system of flexible exchange rates. The system of fixed rates under the Bretton Woods agreement included long periods of stable exchange rates marked by sudden and often large adjustments of official exchange rates. If one of those large changes occurred when you had made an international investment, you could be much worse or better off, but usually worse.

disadvantaged by the depreciation in the pound and would receive no benefit from dealing with speculators who would incorporate the difference in rates of inflation into the future exchange rates offered investors. This view suggests that one should evaluate particular investments in the United States or Britain on their merits and that markets may work to minimize the risks associated with changes in the exchange rates if one is investing for the long term.[2]

How do businesses respond to the ups and downs of the dollar? A recent story in *The New York Times* talked about how Eastman Kodak and other companies deal with changes in exchange rates. These changes are of growing importance as American companies increase foreign operations. For example, in 1992 about 46 percent of Kodak's sales came from foreign countries. David Fiedler, director of foreign exchange for Kodak, reported that in the short term he uses financial hedges to protect against changes in exchange rates. Over the longer term he views questions of foreign exchange as a "business problem like any other business problem." That is, exchange rate risk is something that should be given careful consideration from the very beginning, when making decisions about markets, suppliers, and production sites. "Before 1988, Mr. Fiedler . . . often had to respond to currency swings within minutes after a phone call about foreign developments startled him from sleep. 'That's a real motivator to think of another way,' he said."

1. If you were to make a personal financial investment in a foreign stock market, in what market would you invest? How do you evaluate the exchange rate risks of your choice?
2. What strategies might business follow, other than financial hedges, to minimize the risks associated with international operations?

---

[2]Froot's findings are new and controversial. Measures of the returns one might have received in the past are no guarantee of what one will receive in the future. Even if over the long term one need not worry about movements in exchange rates, an investment that does poorly in either country will have been a mistake.

SOURCES: "Companies Learn to Live with Dollar's Volatility," *The New York Times*, August 31, 1992.

Kenneth A. Froot, "Currency Hedging over Long Horizons," Working Paper No. 4355, National Bureau of Economic Research, May 1993.

STUDY QUESTIONS

1. If you know the dollar price of a German mark, how can you figure out how many marks it takes to buy a dollar?
2. What is the difference between an appreciation and a depreciation of the dollar? Which is better for American tourists? For American exporters?
3. What factors would cause an appreciation of the dollar? What factors would cause a depreciation?

---

4. Is it possible for the dollar to appreciate against the pound and, at the same time, for the pound to appreciate against the dollar? Why?

5. What is meant by purchasing-power parity? How is it possible for exchange rates to vary from levels determined by purchasing-power parity?

6. How did the gold standard work to maintain fixed exchange rates?

7. What was the difference between the gold standard and the gold-exchange (Bretton Woods) system?

8. What is a balance of payments deficit? Is it possible to have an overall deficit under a system of floating exchange rates? Fixed exchange rates?

9. Under a system of fixed exchange rates, what policies might a country adopt to eliminate a balance of payments deficit? Surplus?

10. Who bore most of the burden for adjustment under the gold-exchange system, deficit or surplus countries? Why wasn't the burden of adjustment equal?

11. Under fixed exchange rates, balance of payment deficits reflect an overvalued exchange rate. The overvalued exchange rate increases the price of a country's exports. A devaluation would help to correct the balance of payments deficit by lowering the price of exports, increasing the demand for exports, and increasing employment in export industries. Yet most countries have resisted devaluation even when facing chronic deficits. What do you think explains this reluctance?

12. What steps might exporters and importers take to minimize the risk of currency fluctuations under a system of floating exchange rates?

13. Why is it said that under fixed exchange rates currency speculation was destabilizing, while under floating exchange rates it is likely to be stabilizing?

14. When would a country prefer a system of fixed exchange rates and when might it prefer a system of floating exchange rates?

15. What is meant by the term "dirty" or "managed" float?

Chapter **20**

Macroeconomics in a World Economy

LEARNING OBJECTIVES

After completing this chapter you should be able to:

- explain how an appreciation or depreciation in the exchange rate affects net exports.
- explain the J-curve and its relevance to an understanding of the impact of a change in exchange rates.
- use an aggregate demand—aggregate supply diagram to show how an appreciation or depreciation of the exchange rate affects GDP and the price of domestically produced goods.
- explain why the reaction of international capital flows to changes in interest rates works to offset the impact of changes in fiscal policy.
- explain why the reaction of international capital flows to changes in interest rates works to enhance the impact of changes in monetary policy.
- explain in what way government deficits and trade deficits are linked.
- explain how a change in the mix of fiscal and monetary policy affects macroeconomic variables such as GDP, real interest rates, prices, the trade deficit, and the exchange rate.
- evaluate the likely impact of proposals to reduce the U.S. trade deficit.

IMPORTANT TERMS AND CONCEPTS

Exports
Imports
Net exports
Closed economy
Open economy
Exchange rate
Appreciation
Depreciation
Trade deficit
J-curve
International capital flows
Budget deficits and trade deficits
$G - T = (S - I) - (X - IM)$

CHAPTER REVIEW

This chapter integrates the discussion of international trade and exchange rates of the last two chapters with the earlier discussions of income determination and fiscal and monetary policy. An economy that did not trade with any other economy would be called a **(1)** _____ economy. Today all industrial economies and most developing economies have extensive links with other economies through trade in goods and services and financial assets. Such economies are called _____ economies. These international linkages can affect important macroeconomic outcomes such as GDP and prices. A complete and rigorous examination of these linkages is the stuff of more advanced courses in economics, but with a few minor modifications we can use the model of income determination that we developed in earlier chapters to shed light on a number of important issues.

We start with a review of factors affecting the demand for exports and imports. As we saw in Chapter 8, the demand for exports and imports is influenced by income and prices. An **(2)** increase in foreign income will (decrease/increase) the demand for American exports and is an important reason why economic fluctuations abroad (are/are not) felt in the United States. Exports and imports are also influenced by changes in the exchange rate, these changes alter the relative price of foreign and domestic goods. An appreciation of the dollar makes foreign goods (less/more) expensive. The result is likely to be a(n) (decrease/increase) in American imports and a(n) _____ in American exports. Putting these two effects together shows that an appreciation of the exchange rate will lead to a(n) (decrease/increase) in net exports, $(X - IM)$. Similar reasoning shows that a depreciation of the dollar will lead to a(n) _____ in exports, a(n) _____ in imports and a(n) _____ in net exports.

A change in net exports that comes from a change in exchange rates is analogous to any other autonomous change in spending. It shifts the expenditure schedule and leads to a

(3) (movement along/shift in) the aggregate demand curve. More precisely, following an appreciation of the dollar, net exports (decline/increase), the expenditure schedule shifts (down/up), and the aggregate demand curve shifts to the (left/right). Opposite results follow from a depreciation of the dollar.

A change in exchange rates can also lead to a shift in the aggregate supply curve through its impact on the price of imported intermediate goods. An appreciation of the **(4)** dollar makes imported inputs (less/more) expensive. This result can be modeled as a(n) (downward/upward) shift in the aggregate supply curve. A depreciation of the dollar makes imported inputs _____ expensive and leads to a(n) _____ shift in the aggregate supply curve.

Once we understand the impact of a change in interest rates on international capital flows and on the exchange rate, we will have all the pieces necessary to examine the impact of changes in fiscal and monetary policy. We saw in Chapter 19 that an increase in interest **(5)** rates is apt to (decrease/increase) the demand by foreigners for American financial assets. This change in the demand for dollars should lead to a(n) (appreciation/depreciation) of the dollar. Tracing through the impact of this capital-flow-induced change in the exchange rate is the key to understanding how fiscal and monetary policy work in an open economy.

To review, consider a change in fiscal policy. A move to expansionary fiscal policy, say a(n) **(6)** (decrease/increase) in taxes, would shift the expenditure schedule (up/down) and shift the aggregate demand curve to the (right/left). With no changes in monetary policy (that is, no shift in the supply of money schedule), there will be a(n) (decrease/no change/increase) in interest rates. The impact of this change in interest rates on international capital flows will lead to a(n) (appreciation/depreciation) in the exchange rate. This change in the exchange rate will shift the aggregate demand curve to the (left/right) and shift the aggregate supply curve (down/up). The shift in the aggregate demand curve, induced by the change in the exchange rate, works to (enhance/offset) the original expansionary change in fiscal policy. The shift in the aggregate supply curve works to (lower/raise) prices and to (increase/decrease) output. If the shift in the aggregate supply curve induced by the change in exchange rates were large enough, it could offset the impact on output from the exchange-rate-induced shift in the aggregate demand curve. Evidence suggests that the shift in the aggregate supply curve is small and that, on net, the shifts in the two curves work to (enhance/offset) the impact of expansionary fiscal policy on output.

A move to restrictive monetary policy can be analyzed in the same way. The initial **(7)** effects will include an increase in interest rates that leads to a(n) (appreciation/depreciation) of the exchange rate. The impact of the change in the exchange rate will (enhance/offset) the original restrictive change in monetary policy.

Our equilibrium condition that $Y = C + I + G + (X - IM)$ can be manipulated to illustrate the important link between government budget deficits and trade deficits. Remembering that GDP equals disposable income plus net taxes and that disposable income equals consumption spending plus savings enables us to rewrite this equilibrium condition[1] as

$$G - T = (S - I) - (X - IM).$$

---

[1] This condition can also be written as $G + I + X = I + T + IM$. In terms of the circular flow diagram of Figure 7-1 in the text, this formulation says that injections must equal leakages.

If the government runs a deficit—that is, if the government wants more output than it can command through taxes—then either private savings must exceed private investment, $(S - I)$, or additional output must be forthcoming from foreigners—that is, imports must exceed exports. It is changes in income, interest rates, exchange rates, and prices that enforce equilibrium and the link between budget deficits and trade deficits.

The impact of a change in exchange rates on imports and exports usually takes some time. Economists refer to the lag in the adjustment of the balance of trade following a change

(8) in exchange rates as the _____ curve. Is the American trade deficit a problem? One's answer to this question depends upon whether one views capital inflows over the 1980s as a market response to extravagant spending requiring high interest rates in the United States to attract foreign capital or as the result of an autonomous increase in foreign demand for investment in the United States. Many feel that evidence on interest rates and consumption spending is more consistent with the first rather than the second view.

A number of suggestions have been made to reduce the trade deficit. Many argue that the United States should alter the mix of fiscal and monetary policy. According to this view,

(9) (contractionary/expansionary) fiscal policy and _____ monetary policy were responsible for the increase in the trade deficit during the 1980s. Reversing these actions, that is, a move to _____ fiscal policy and _____ monetary policy, could work in reverse and lower the trade deficit. Rapid economic growth abroad would increase American (exports/imports). Protectionism would lower imports, but retaliation by foreign governments could (lower/raise) American exports with little change in net exports. One also needs to consider the impact of protectionism on exchange rates. For any of these measures to work, the equilibrium condition described above, $G - T = (S - I) - (X - IM)$, shows us that a reduction in the trade deficit must be accompanied by a combination of lower budget deficits, higher savings, or lower investment.

IMPORTANT TERMS AND CONCEPTS QUIZ

Choose the best definition for the following terms.

1. _____ Exports
2. _____ Imports
3. _____ Closed economy
4. _____ Open economy
5. _____ Trade deficit
6. _____ J-curve

a. Domestically produced goods sold abroad.
b. Graph depicting response of inflation to changes in the exchange rate.

c. Economy that trades with other economies.
d. Time series graph depicting response of net exports to changes in the exchange rate.
e. Foreign-produced goods purchased domestically.
f. Economy that does not trade with other economies.
g. Amount by which imports exceed exports.

BASIC EXERCISE

This exercise is designed to review how the operation of fiscal and monetary policy is affected by interest-sensitive capital flows in an open as compared to a closed economy.

1. Table 20-1 is designed to help you review the impact of changes in the exchange rate on various macroeconomic variables. First, complete the column for an appreciation of the exchange rate. Then complete the column for a depreciation of the exchange rate. In each cell indicate how each variable changes, i.e. increases or decreases, shifts left, right, up or down, as appropriate. Be sure you can explain why each variable shows the change you have indicated. If the change in GDP and the price level seems ambiguous, see if you can resolve the ambiguity by assuming, as in the text, that any shift in the aggregate demand curve is greater than the shift in the aggregate supply curve.

TABLE 20-1

Macroeconomic Variable	Exchange Rate Appreciation	Exchange Rate Depreciation
Exports		
Imports		
Net Exports		
Aggregate Demand Curve		
Aggregate Supply Curve		
Real GDP		
Price Level		

2. Table 20-2 shows the impact on GDP and the price level of changes in fiscal and monetary policy. The completed upper portion of the table ignores any impact on exchange rates. Remembering that changes in interest rates are likely to influence the international investment of funds and hence the demand for dollars, complete Table 20-2 to determine whether capital flows offset or enhance these changes in monetary and fiscal policy. You should specify the change in interest rates; determine how the exchange rate is affected; consider the impact of the change in the exchange rate on GDP and prices; and, finally, combine your results from the change in policy and the change in exchange rates to determine the overall impact. Figure 20-1 may be helpful when completing Table 20-2.

3. What general conclusion can you draw about the effectiveness of monetary and fiscal policy in a world of interest-sensitive capital flows and flexible exchange rates?

TABLE 20-2

	Increase in G	Decrease in G	Open Market Sale	Open Market Purchase
Aggregate Demand Curve Real GDP	Right Up	Left Down Down	Left Down Down	Right Up
Interest Rate	_____	_____	_____	_____
Exchange Rate	_____	_____	_____	_____
Real GDP	_____	_____	_____	_____
Price Level	_____	_____	_____	_____
Overall Impact	_____	_____	_____	_____
Real GDP	_____	_____	_____	_____
Price Level	_____	_____	_____	_____

FIGURE 20-1

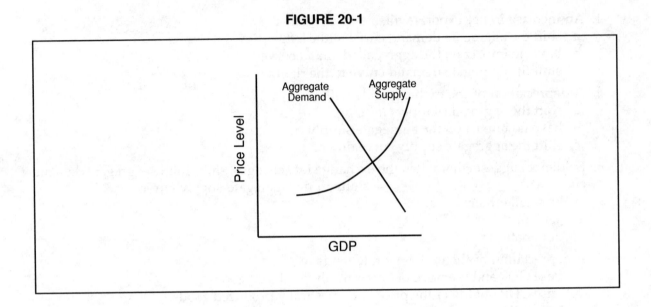

SELF-TESTS FOR UNDERSTANDING

Test A

Circle the most appropriate answer.

1. An appreciation of the exchange rate will make
   a. both exports and imports cheaper.
   b. exports more expensive for foreigners but imports cheaper for domestic citizens.
   c. exports cheaper for foreigners but imports more expensive for domestic citizens.
   d. both exports and imports more expensive.

2. A depreciation of the exchange rate will lead to
   a. an increase in exports and imports.
   b. a decrease in exports and an increase in imports.
   c. an increase in exports and a decrease in imports.
   d. a decrease in both exports and imports.

3. A depreciation of the exchange rate will lead to _____ in net exports.
   a. a decrease
   b. no change
   c. an increase

4. An increase in net exports will
   a. shift the aggregate demand curve to the left.
   b. have no impact on the aggregate demand curve.
   c. shift the aggregate demand curve to the right.

5. A depreciation of the exchange rate will
   a. shift the aggregate supply curve up.
   b. have no impact on the aggregate supply curve.
   c. shift the aggregate supply curve down.

6. Evidence suggests that when the exchange rate changes, shifts in the aggregate demand curve will _____ shifts in the aggregate supply curve.
   a. be smaller than
   b. just offset
   c. dominate

7. A depreciation of the exchange rate tends to
   a. raise GDP and the price of domestically produced goods.
   b. raise GDP but lower the price of domestically produced goods.
   c. lower GDP but raise the price of domestically produced goods.
   d. lower GDP and the price of domestically produced goods.

8. An increase in foreign GDP is likely to lead to
   a. a decrease in our exports.
   b. little if any change in our exports.
   c. an increase in our exports.

9. Higher foreign interest rates are likely to be followed by
   (There may be more than one correct answer.)
   a. an inflow of international capital.
   b. an increase in foreign investments by domestic citizens.
   c. an appreciation of the exchange rate.
   d. an increase in net exports.

10. An increase in domestic interest rates should lead to which one of the following?
    a. Capital outflow.
    b. Appreciation of the dollar.
    c. Increase in exports.
    d. Upward shift in the expenditure schedule.

11. An appreciation in the dollar vis-a-vis other currencies should lead to all but which one of the following?
    a. A decrease in exports.
    b. An increase in imports.
    c. A shift of the aggregate demand curve to the right.
    d. A downward shift of the aggregate supply curve.

12. A move to expansionary fiscal policy will lead to all but which one of the following?
    a. An increase in interest rates.
    b. An appreciation of the dollar.
    c. An increase in American exports.
    d. An increase in the American trade deficit.

13. A move to expansionary monetary policy will lead to all but which one of the following?
    a. A decrease in interest rates.
    b. An appreciation of the dollar.
    c. An upward shift in the expenditure schedule.
    d. An increase in inflationary pressures.

14. Taking account of interest-sensitive international capital flows means that in an open economy the impact of fiscal policy is
    a. smaller than in a closed economy.
    b. the same as in a closed economy.
    c. larger than in a closed economy.

15. Taking account of interest-sensitive international capital flows means that in an open economy the impact of monetary policy is
    a. smaller than in a closed economy.
    b. the same as in a closed economy.
    c. larger than in a closed economy.

16. The J-curve refers to
    a. What Julius Erving does with his body when he drives for the bucket.
    b. the delayed impact of higher rates of inflation on interest rates.
    c. the delayed impact of a change in the exchange rate on a country's trade deficit.
    d. the pitch that won the 1983 World Series.

17. In an open economy equilibrium requires that
    a. $G - T = I + S + X - IM$.
    b. $G - T = S - I + (IM - X)$.
    c. $G - T = I + X - S - IM$.
    d. $G - T = S - X - (I + IM)$.

18. If there is no change in the balance of domestic savings and investment, then any increase in the government deficit must be matched by
    (There may be more than one correct answer.)
    a. an increase in the trade deficit.
    b. a reduction in the equilibrium level of output.
    c. a capital inflow.
    d. a reduction in interest rates.

19. Which of the following would help to reduce the U.S. trade deficit?
    a. Higher government deficits.
    b. Increased domestic investment.
    c. Increased domestic savings.
    d. A decrease in exports.

20. An increase in the government deficit need not lead to an increase in the trade deficit if there is (There may be more than one correct answer.)
    a. an increase in private savings.
    b. a decrease in private investment.
    c. an increase in consumption spending.
    d. an increase in imports.

Test B

Circle T or F for true or false.

T F 1. International trade means that an economic boom in the United States is likely to lead to recession in the rest of the world.

T F 2. A change in exports has no multiplier impacts.

T F 3. A shift in the expenditure schedule coming from an autonomous change in domestic investment spending would be expected to have no impact on a country's trade deficit.

T F 4. A depreciation in the exchange rate is inflationary.

T F 5. A depreciation in the exchange rate should help to reduce a country's trade deficit.

T F 6. Under floating exchange rates, a country with a trade surplus will also experience a capital outflow.

T F 7. International capital flows make monetary policy less effective.

T F 8. International capital flows are unaffected by changes in fiscal policy.

T F 9. Increased protectionism may only lead to an appreciation of the dollar.

T F 10. The only way to reduce the trade deficit is by reducing the government's budget deficit.

ECONOMICS IN ACTION

Fixed or Flexible Exchange Rates for Europe?

As part of plans for a united Europe, the European Economic Community (EEC) countries were to adopt a single currency by 1996 at the earliest and 1999 at the latest. The development of a single currency was seen as an integral part of a united Europe and a natural evolution of the European Monetary System (EMS), established in 1979.

Under the EMS, member countries committed to maintain exchange rates within a fairly narrow band around established parities. While there were periodic adjustments of parities in the early years of the EMS, from 1987 through 1991 there were no parity adjustments. Many saw this record of stable exchange rates as a successful first step toward a single currency. Harmonization of macro policies were also important to the plans for a single currency. To join the single currency bloc, countries were to keep inflation below 3 percent per year and government deficits less than 3 percent of GDP. In addition, there were to be no exchange rate devaluations for at least two years. By the beginning of 1992, adjustments of exchange rate parities had been avoided for five years, but there was wide divergence in meeting the other two targets.

In the summer of 1992, the British pound, Italian lira, and Spanish peseta came under strong speculative attack. In all cases there was significant pressure for depreciation vis-à-vis the German mark. As each exchange rate reached the lower limit of the agreed upon trading band, governments were initially required to use their holdings of foreign exchange to purchase their own currencies but had to ask for help from other EEC countries in defending the established parities. In the end, the earlier parities could not be defended. The lira and pound left the EMS while there were adjustments of exchange rates withing the EMS for the peseta and other weak currencies. In the summer of 1993 there was similar downward pressure on the French franc. This time the result was a significant widening of the allowable trading bands.

The turbulence in exchange rates and financial markets left a number of observers unsure of the desirability of establishing a single currency in Europe. Those who had pressed for a single currency argued that integrated markets would work best if exchange rate uncertainty could be removed. They saw a single European currency as a boon to trade, commerce, and economic growth. However, experience in 1992 and 1993 showed the difficulty of sustaining fixed exchange rates when individual countries pursue divergent macro policies. In Germany there was a significant expansion of aggregate demand connected with the integration of East and West Germany. To minimize the inflationary impact of the increase in public spending, the Bundesbank had increased interest rates in Germany. The resulting flow of capital to Germany worked to appreciate the mark and depreciate other currencies.

A traditional defense to avoid depreciation would be to raise interest rates to increase the demand for your currency, although at the cost of restricting domestic aggregate demand. The risk of increasing unemployment made other countries reluctant to pursue this option. An alternative would be to accept the depreciation and be done with it. While depreciation solves the exchange rate problem and lowers the price of one's exports, it is likely to be seen as inflationary as it increases the cost of imported foreign goods. Depreciation would also admit the difficulty of maintaining fixed parities and thus question the desirability of attempts to move to a single currency. Concerns about the credibility of their commitment to fixed exchange rates led governments to resist exchange rate adjustments until the reality of market forces overwhelmed their ability to defend earlier parities.

As of this writing it is unclear whether the wider trading bands adopted in the summer of 1993 will be sufficient. Persistent differences in the rate of inflation across countries would

appear to require continual adjustments in exchange rates. Wider trading bands can help to accommodate temporary fluctuations in demand and supply but are not capable of dealing with a persistent trend in one direction. On the other hand, a commitment to fixed exchange rates requires that the most inflation prone economies take corrective action or their goods will be priced out of the market. It is this discipline on domestic macro policy that many find an appealing part of a commitment to fixed exchange rates.

1. What has happened to exchange rates between European currencies since the summer of 1993? What are the costs and benefits of continued efforts to establish a single currency as compared with a system of more flexible exchange rates? Do you think Europe should move to a single currency? Why?

SOURCE: "The European Community: Back to the Drawing Board," *The Economist*, July 3-9, 1993

STUDY QUESTIONS

1. What is the difference between an open and a closed economy?

2. How does an appreciation in the exchange rate affect net exports? What about a depreciation? Why?

3. How does a change in net exports, induced by a change in the exchange rate, affect the aggregate demand curve? The aggregate supply curve? Which effect is likely to be larger?

4. What is meant by the J-curve pattern of adjustment to a change in exchange rates?

5. Does an increase in interest rates lead to an appreciation or depreciation of the exchange rate? Why?

6. Consider a move to contractionary fiscal policy that reduces aggregate demand. What is the likely impact on interest rates, international capital flows, the exchange rate and net exports? Do these changes tend to enhance or offset the original change in fiscal policy?

7. Consider a move to expansionary monetary policy that increases aggregate demand. What is the likely impact on interest rates, international capital flows, the exchange rate and net exports? Do these changes enhance or offset the original change in monetary policy?

8. What is the link between government deficits and trade deficits? Under what conditions does an increase in the government deficit lead to an increase in the trade deficit?

9. Some have argued for a change in the mix of fiscal and monetary policy—easier monetary policy and contractionary fiscal policy—as a way to reduce both government deficits and the trade deficit. Would these changes have the desired impact? Why?

10. Why isn't increased protectionism a sure-fire way to reduce the trade deficit?

C h a p t e r **21**

Growth in Developed and Developing Countries

LEARNING OBJECTIVES

After completing this chapter you should be able to:

- distinguish between growth in total GDP and GDP per capita.
- describe what exponential growth is and explain why it usually cannot continue forever.
- explain why the composition of aggregate demand is an important determinant of the rate of economic growth.
- describe other factors that are important in determining an economy's rate of growth.
- describe the arguments for and against continued growth.
- distinguish between embodied and disembodied growth.
- discuss some of the important factors that impede the growth of incomes in LDCs.
- discuss what things LDCs can do for themselves to increase their growth.
- describe what role developed countries can play in assisting LDCs.
- explain what the World Bank is and what it does.

IMPORTANT TERMS AND CONCEPTS

Output per capita
Exponential growth
Social infrastructure
Exchange between present and future consumption
Embodied growth
Disembodied growth
Less developed countries (LDCs)
Growth rate in GDP vs. per capita income
Multinational corporations
Disguised unemployment
Entrepreneurship
Brain drain
World Bank

CHAPTER REVIEW

This chapter discusses some of the general issues concerned with economic growth: Can it continue forever? Is it desirable? What actions can countries take to influence their rates of growth? Economics cannot always offer definitive answers to these questions, but it can help you to think about the issues in a systematic fashion.

(1) Growth that occurs at a constant percentage rate for a number of years is called _____ growth. This snowballing effect, when projected into the future, seems to suggest doom for the human race. Simple extrapolations of population at current rates of growth lead to ridiculous conclusions. The clear implication is that growth cannot continue at current rates forever and that actual growth experience will be more a matter of economic choices than mechanical extrapolations.

(2) Many factors that are clearly important for growth are not well understood. Examples include _____, _____, and the _____ _____. Other factors influencing growth rates that countries *can* do something about, include accumulating more capital by higher levels of (<u>consumption/investment</u>) and devoting more resources to _____ and _____. Some new ideas and inventions require new machines before they can help increase output. Growth from these sorts of inventions is called (<u>disembodied/embodied</u>) economic growth. If new ideas permit more output from existing resources, the resulting growth is called _____ growth.

(3) In a full-employment economy, more of anything, including investment spending or research and development, requires less of something else. This reduction, which is necessary to release resources for an increase in investment or research and development, is the _____ cost of increased investment. In a full-employment economy,

resources for more investment would be available if current (<u>consumption/savings</u>) decreased and the amount of _____ increased.

The tools of economics cannot help you determine whether an economy should grow faster or slower; they can, however, identify the sources of growth and the consequences of more or less growth. In particular, a number of economists oppose zero economic growth on the grounds that a move in this direction would require extensive government controls and may seriously hamper efforts to eliminate poverty and to protect the environment. Solutions to these last two problems are likely to require more rather than fewer resources. Many feel that it is easier to reach a political agreement to devote resources to problems of poverty and the environment if total output is expanding rather than if it is not growing.

Concerns about economic growth are an everyday reality for citizens in developing countries. While it is common to develop lists of "the problems" of developing countries, it is important to remember that there is much diversity among these countries and that their problems are not all alike. Density of population shows a wide diversity among LDCs, as do recent gains in per capita incomes.

While income per capita increased in a number of developing countries during the 1970s, more recent developments have been less favorable, illustrating the fragility of recent growth trends. The world recession in the early 1980s had adverse impacts on a number of countries. High levels of external debt are a serious burden for some countries; there is evidence that recent growth has been accompanied by a worsening distribution of income; the rate of population growth remains high in many countries; and many LDCs have seen little if any increase in per capita income in recent years.

(4) As for narrowing the income gap with the developed countries, it should be remembered that growth in the developed countries (<u>has/has not</u>) stopped. Even if developed countries and LDCs show the same percentage growth in income, the absolute differences in incomes will (<u>increase/decrease</u>) due to the (<u>higher/lower</u>) base of the developed countries.

LDCs face many problems in their quest for higher incomes. A fundamental problem is the lack of physical capital. More capital would help to increase labor productivity. LDCs can accumulate more capital in either of two ways. They can try to get it either from domestic sources or **(5)** from foreign sources. The first option, domestic sources, would require (<u>more/less</u>) consumption in order to increase savings and investment.[1] This option will be (<u>easy/difficult</u>) for many countries because of their current extremely low levels of income. The second option, foreign sources, is not without its own risks. Profit-maximizing private businesses will clearly want as good a deal for themselves as possible. Mutual gain is still possible, however, especially if the LDCs insist upon the training of native workers for positions of responsibility and the development of social infrastructures, such as transportation and communication systems.

---

[1]We have seen earlier that $Y = C + I + G + X - IM$. If one wants to increase I and Y cannot be expanded, then reductions in C, G, or $(X - IM)$ will do. In an analysis of opportunities for growth, it is often useful to reclassify elements of G and X as either C or I. With respect to G, highways and dams would be _____, while bureaucrats and paper clips would be _____. With this reclassification, the only way to increase I is to reduce _____ or to get resources from abroad through an increase in _____.

---

(6) Population growth continues to be high for many LDCs primarily because of recent dramatic declines in (<u>birth/death</u>) rates. These declines appear to be the result of relatively (<u>inexpensive/expensive</u>) public health measures rather than the result of advancements in medical technology. High rates of population growth result in tremendous demands on a country to ensure that people do not starve. The experience of advanced economies suggests that birthrates may decrease as income rises. A lack of trained technical workers, extensive unemployment—especially disguised unemployment—a lack of entrepreneurship, and other social impediments to business activity, as well as extensive government interferences in markets, are additional problems facing LDCs.

What can the advanced economies do for the LDCs? They can help them accumulate both technical skills and physical capital. Training individuals from LDCs will add to the pool of technical skills for these countries if those receiving education return to their native countries. The fact that many of these individuals have not returned is referred to as the

(7) _____ _____. Aid in acquiring physical capital can be provided by long-term loans at preferential terms or by direct grants. Aid can be given by individual countries or through international organizations, drawing on the resources of many countries, such as the _____ Bank.

IMPORTANT TERMS AND CONCEPTS QUIZ

Choose the best definition for the following terms.

1. _____ Exponential growth
2. _____ Social infrastructure
3. _____ Embodied growth
4. _____ Disembodied growth
5. _____ Disguised unemployment
6. _____ Brain drain
7. _____ Multinational corporation
8. _____ Entrepreneurship
9. _____ World Bank

a. Educated individuals from developing countries who emigrate to wealthier countries.

b. Transportation network, telecommunications system, and schools.

c. Growth due to better ideas that can be implemented with existing factors of production.

d. Companies with operations in many countries.

e. The excess of savings over investment.

f. International organization that makes loans to developing countries to finance investments in social infrastructure.

g. Situation where more people are employed than the most efficient number required.

h. Starting new firms, introducing innovations, and taking the necessary risks in seeking business opportunities.

i. Innovations that require new capital before they can affect economic growth.

j. Growth at a constant percentage rate.

Table 21-1

Country	GDP (Trillions of dollars)	Income per capita
United States	$5.61	$22,204
Brazil		
Britain		
Canada		
China		
France		
Germany		
India		
Indonesia		
Italy		
Japan		
Mexico		
Spain		

BASIC EXERCISE

Complete Table 21-1 with your best estimates of total output and income per capita in 1992 for each of the countries listed below in terms of American dollars. Data for the United States is given as a starting point. Check the accuracy of your estimates in the answers section of the Study Guide.

SELF-TESTS FOR UNDERSTANDING

Test A

Circle the most appropriate answer.

1. If the objective of economic growth is an increase in individual material welfare which of the following is an appropriate indicator?
   a. Growth in total output.
   b. Growth in inflation.
   c. Growth in inventiveness.
   d. Growth in output per capita.

2. If something, say GDP, increases by the same percent each year, then the absolute increases in GDP will
    a. become smaller.
    b. stay the same.
    c. become larger.

3. Assume GDP grows at a constant percent each year. One would refer to this growth as an example of
    a. exponential growth.
    b. technical growth.
    c. disembodied growth.
    d. embodied growth.

4. While there are many factors that affect economic growth, economic policy is likely to be most effective in influencing which of the following?
    (There may be more than one correct answer.)
    a. Inventiveness.
    b. The work ethic.
    c. The level of investment spending.
    d. Research and development activities.

5. Which of the following is not an example of investment in social infrastructure?
    a. The construction of the trans-Amazon highway in Brazil.
    b. Substantial investments in public education in the United States.
    c. The development of Indonesian oil fields by American oil companies.
    d. Investments in public health to reduce the incidence of infant mortality.

6. Which of the following is the appropriate measure of the opportunity cost of increased investment undertaken to raise the rate of growth?
    a. The resulting increase in future consumption.
    b. The rate of interest.
    c. The present consumption goods that could have been produced with the resources used to produce the investment goods.
    d. Zero, because economic growth is really without cost.

7. An economy at full-employment can increase investment only if it reduces
    (There may be more than one correct answer.)
    a. consumption spending.
    b. government purchases.
    c. exports.
    d. imports.

8. Innovation
    a. is really the same as invention.
    b. can only be successful when there are large increases in investment spending.
    c. is another name for embodied growth.
    d. refers to putting inventions into practice.

9. Disembodied economic growth
    a. refers to increased output from reallocation of existing resources.
    b. has a zero opportunity cost because it requires only new ideas.
    c. has never been important in the real world.
    d. is likely to mean more resource depletion than embodied growth.

10. Skeptics of attempts to limit economic growth would agree with all but which one of the following?
    a. Economic growth provides resources to fight pollution without having to change current levels of consumption.
    b. Reducing poverty at home and abroad will be easier with greater economic growth.
    c. To reduce or stop growth would require elaborate and repressive government controls.
    d. The irony of economic growth is that it reduces personal satisfaction at the same time it increases the material possessions.

11. The recent record of growth in income per capita in LDCs shows
    a. greater growth during the 1980s than the 1970s.
    b. equal increases in all LDCs.
    c. slower growth during the 1980s as compared with the 1970s and with many industrial countries.
    d. substantial increases for all but a handful of LDCs.

12. Output per capita will increase whenever the growth rate of GDP _____ that of population.
    a. is less than
    b. is equal to
    c. exceeds

13. High rates of population growth in many developing countries are the result of
    a. recent dramatic increases in birthrates.
    b. recent dramatic declines in death rates.
    c. the application of advanced medical technology.
    d. the success of compulsory programs of birth control.

14. Reductions in death rates in many developing countries are for the most part due to
    a. advanced medical treatments for cancer that have been borrowed from industrialized countries.
    b. the adoption of relatively inexpensive public health measures.
    c. the efforts of Peace Corps volunteers.
    d. comprehensive programs of national health insurance in most developing countries.

15. Which of the following is not among the obstacles to high levels of income in the LDCs?
    a. Large rural—urban migration with dramatic increases in urban unemployment.
    b. Domestic savings rates that are so high they depress aggregate demand.
    c. A lack of entrepreneurial talent.
    d. Numerous well-intentioned government interventions that discourage the efficiency of private business.

16. For many LDCs the greatest contribution to economic growth is likely to be made by expanding
    a. general basic education.
    b. the number of college graduates.
    c. technical training.
    d. the use of direct controls to determine the composition of output.

17. Which one of the following is *not* likely to help LDCs achieve higher levels of income?
    a. Any increase in savings and investment that can be squeezed out of existing low levels of income.
    b. Central control of trade and investment.
    c. Agricultural research appropriate to the crops and climates of specific countries.
    d. Removal of impediments to innovation and entrepreneurial talent.

18. If a country tries to maintain an overvalued exchange rate, that is maintain the exchange rate at a level higher than would be sustained by demand and supply, the result will be to make
    a. imports cheaper and exports more expensive.
    b. imports more expensive and exports cheaper.
    c. both imports and exports cheaper.
    d. both imports and exports more expensive.

19. As a percent of GDP, foreign aid from the U.S. to developing countries is _____ that of many other industrialized countries.
    a. less than
    b. equal to
    c. greater than

20. Which one of the following has *not* been an important source of loans and grants for development projects in LDCs?
    a. The World Bank.
    b. The International Monetary Fund.
    c. The United States.
    d. The Soviet Union.

Test B

Circle T or F for true or false.

T F 1. GDP per capita will increase whenever total GDP increases.

T F 2. The fact that population growth has recently been exponential is a good reason to believe that it will continue that way forever.

T F 3. Zero economic growth would be easy to achieve.

T F 4. Zero economic growth would be an unambiguous gain for the environment.

T F 5. Increased investment spending leading to more capital accumulation is likely to increase the rate of economic growth.

T F   6.   Embodied economic growth refers to ideas and inventions that require new machinery.

T F   7.   Disembodied economic growth means that an economy can have higher rates of growth without having to sacrifice any current consumption.

T F   8.   For any year that the growth rate of income per capita in the LDCs matches that of the developed countries, the absolute difference in income will decrease.

T F   9.   Recently all LDCs have shared equally in increases in income per capita.

T F   10.   Historical evidence refutes the Malthusian law of population growth.

T F   11.   Research suggests that expenditures on technical training rather than general education are likely to have a greater impact on the rate of economic growth in LDCs.

T F   12.   Disguised unemployment is only a problem for developed economies and has little relevance for LDCs.

T F   13.   Unlike the United States, LDCs have not experienced any substantial rural–urban migration.

T F   14.   The only real constraint to growth in the LDCs is a lack of entrepreneurship.

T F   15.   In order to avoid the problem of default on loans, the World Bank makes loans only to developed countries, such as Britain and France.

SUPPLEMENTARY EXERCISES

1. The total volume of U.S. aid to LDCs is much greater than aid from other countries. However, the U.S. economy is much larger than other economies. How does the U.S. commitment to development assistance stack up when measured as a percent of national output? Has the volume of aid from all developed economies, both in total and as a percent of national output, been increasing or decreasing? What about OPEC countries and the former Soviet bloc countries? A good place to start to answer these questions is the library. *World Development Report* typically contains data on official development assistance from major industrialized countries and OPEC countries. *The United States Statistical Yearbook* is another source of data.

   Some observers argue that looking only at foreign aid is incomplete as a measure of a country's concern for others. These people suggest that in view of many multilateral defense agreements, that have been an important part of American foreign policy one must also consider military expenditures. What do you think of the argument? What is its quantitative significance? What does it imply at a time when superpower military tensions apperar to be diminishing dramatically? The *Statistical Abstract of the United States* is another place to start looking for data.

2. In 1950, the world's population was estimated to be 2.5 billion. From 1950 to 1990 it grew at an average annual rate of 1.9 percent to 5.3 billion. Assume that population has always grown at an annual rate of 1.9 percent. If we started with a population of two, how many years would it take for the world population to reach 5.3 billion? How long will it take for the world's population to double if it continues to grow at 1.9 percent per year?

3. Assume that growth policies were successful in raising the growth rate of income per capita in Mexico above that of the United States. Because of the initial higher level of incomes in the United States, $22,204 vs. $7,170, it would take a number of years for Mexican incomes to reach parity with those in the United States. Initially the absolute difference would increase even though the Mexican growth rate exceeds that of the United States.

Assume that the growth rate of income per capita in Mexico is 4 percent per year while it is only 1.5 percent per year in the United States.

   a. How many years will it take until income per capita in Mexico equals that of the United States? What would income be at that time?
   b. While the ratio of income per capita in Mexico to that in the United States will decline continuously, the absolute difference will initially increase. In what year would the difference in income per capita be greatest? What is the differential?

ECONOMICS IN ACTION
Understanding Economic Growth

What do we know about the growth experiences of different countries? In recent years much effort has gone into developing consisten measures of the economic performance of most countries in the world, many of which did not exist as separate nations until after World War II. A recent study by economists Stephen Parente and Edward Prescott used some of this data to look at the growth experience of 102 countries that had populations of at least one million in 1969 and for which data exists for the years 1960 through 1985. Looking at output per capita, Parente and Prescott find little variation in the range of disparity between the richest and poorest countries over time. The ratio of incomes in the five richest countries to that in the five poorest countries was about 29 to 1 in both 1960 and 1985. While this finding suggests that the distribution of income pre capita across countries has changed little, Parente and Prescott find that there were significant changes in the position of individual countries within the distribution. Some saw a substantial improvement in income per capita in both absolute and relative terms, while others experienced significant declines in income per capita.[1]

Is there a small set of factors that distinguish those countries with high rates of growth from those with low rates? In a number of cases, analysts have found important correlations

---

[1] The ten countries that had the largest declines in income per capita were Zambia, Mozambique, Madagascar, Angola, Chad, Liberia, Ghana, Zaire, Nicaragua, and Afghanistan, most of which experienced major military conflicts at some point between 1960 and 1985.

to explain the growth experience of particular countries but many of these findings are fragile. That is, conclusions as to what factors are important for economic growth are likely to change as the number of countries, the number of variables, or the time period of the study changes. One needs to be careful about premature generalizations from one or a limited number of studies. Over time, as the number of studies has grown larger and larger, some variables appear to be consistently correlated with high rates of economic growth. The ratio of investment to output is one such variable. Countries with a higher share of output devoted to investment tend to have higher rates of economic growth. Political and military instability appears to be correlated with lower rates of growth. There is some evidence of convergence in the levels of income across countries, although there is still wide disagreement about the exact form of convergence and the applicability of convergence among industrialized countries for less developed countries. Some economists argue that convergence depends upon education. A country with low incomes but an educated workforce would be expected to grow rapidly and catch up with similar countries. The immediate post-World War II experience in Europe and Japan would be examples of such experience.

Can we ever hope to find a small set of factors that will explain the growth experience of different countries? When thinking about this questions, it may be useful to remember the mathematical distinction between necessary and sufficient conditions. For example, increased investment in physical capital and increased spending on education may be necessary for higher rates of economic growth, but by themselves may not be sufficient if social and economic institutions are not supportive. Institutional factors that economists have argued can help to shape the impact of increased investment include the role of markets as opposed to central planning; incentives for entrepreneurs to create new businesses and adopt new technologies; the structure of government regulation; and so forth. Most of these institutional factors are difficult to measure but can have a significant impact on statistical correlations. The lesson that many economists draw from all this is not that economic analysis cannot explain growth rates, but rather that the way economic variables are likely to interact in a particular country will depend upon the institutions of that country. A country looking to change needs to think about both changes in important economic variables and the structure of social and economic institutions.

1. Pick a region of the world and go to the library to see what you can learn about the actual growth experience of the countries in that region. Try to find out such things as the proportion of output devoted to investment, the structure of educational opportunity and achievement, and the importance of international trade. Also find out what you can about social and economic institutions for these countries. Can you explain the growth experience of these countries compared with other countries? One place to start your investigation is *World Development Report*, an annual publication of the World Bank. Each volume contains detailed data on social and economic variables for a large number of countries.

SOURCES: Robert J. Barro and Jong-Wha Lee, "Losers and Winners in Economic Growth," Working Paper No. 4341, National Bureau of Economic Research, April 1993.

Stephen L. Parente and Edward C. Prescott, "Changes in the Wealth of Nations," *Quarterly Review*, Federal Reserve Bank of Minneapolis, (Spring 1993), pp. 3-16.

STUDY QUESTIONS

1. Why can we be reasonably sure that exponential population growth will not continue forever?

2. Can a country influence its prospects for economic growth by changing the composition of aggregate demand? If so, how? (What can a capitalistic society that relies on markets to allocate resources do to affect the composition of demand and output?)

3. How might the government influence important but intangible growth factors such as the work ethic, entrepreneurship and innovation?

4. Do you think that the United States should pursue policies that work to increase the rate of American economic growth? Why or why not?

5. What is the difference between embodied and disembodied growth? Can you think of examples of each?

6. Why do many observers argue that high rates of population growth have had a negative impact on the ability of LDCs to enhance economic well-being even if they add to the growth of GDP?

7. What are appropriate strategies for developed countries to adopt in order to enhance the growth prospects of developing countries?

8. What are appropriate strategies for developing countries to adopt in order to enhance their own growth prospects?

Answer Key

CHAPTER 1
Chapter Review

(1) information; value

Important Terms and Concepts Quiz

1. f	5. l	9. d
2. b	6. a	10. k
3. e	7. c	11. j
4. g	8. i	

Self-Tests For Understanding
Test A

1. c p. 3
2. a pp. 3-4
3. c p. 4
4. b pp. 4-5
5. a p. 5
6. d pp. 5-6
7. b p. 6
8. a pp. 6-7
9. c p. 7
10. c p. 8
11. d pp. 8-9
12. b p. 9

Test B

1. F p. 11
2. F pp. 15-17
3. T p. 7
4. T pp. 15-16
5. F p. 14
6. F p. 14
7. F p. 12
8. F p. 14
9. F p. 8
10. F p. 9

Appendix Review

(1) horizontal; vertical; origin
(2) vertical; horizontal; constant; positive; up; negative; no
(3) ray; 45–degree
(4) tangent
(5) contour

Important Terms and Concepts Quiz: Appendix

1. f	6. o	11. c
2. g	7. k	12. j
3. d	8. p	13. e
4. m	9. l	14. i
5. h	10. b	15. n

Basic Exercises: Appendix

1. a. 300
    b. increase; 500
    c. decrease; 200
    d. –50
    e. Slope equals vertical change divided by horizontal change or the change in salary divided by the change in the quantity demanded. Information about the change in the number of new Ph.D. economists demanded as salary changes is given the reciprocal of the slope. For example, the demand curve implies that a $1,000 change in salary will reduce the quantity demand by 20.

2. a. 9
    b. 10
    c. above
    d. non-economics

3. a. straight
    b. $5; the slope shows the change in total cost as output changes. In Chapter 5 you will learn that the slope of the total cost curve is called marginal cost.
    c. 1000; A business firm may have certain costs that it must meet regardless of the level of output. In Chapter 6 you will learn that this Y axis intercept is called fixed costs.
    d. The slope of the curve line declines as output increases to 10,000. After 10,000 the slope increases. This is a case where marginal cost decreases initially and then increases.

Self-Tests For Understanding: Appendix

Test A
1. b   p. 19
2. b   p. 19
3. c   p. 19
4. d   p. 20
5. a   p. 20
6. a   p. 20
7. 3; 1; 2; 4   pp. 20-21
8. A&E; C; B&D; none p. 22
9. d   slope = vertical change/horizontal change = (16-10)/(8-5) = $-^6/_3$ = –2
10. c   p. 21
11. b   p. 22
12. b   p. 22
13. b   p. 22
14. d   p. 22
15. c   p. 22
16. a   p. 24
17. d   p. 22
18. a   slope = $^2/_5$ = 0.4
19. b   p. 20
20. b   p. 24

Test B
1. F	p. 19		6. T	p. 22
2. F	p. 20		7. F	p. 23
3. T	p. 20		8. T	p. 22
4. T	p. 20		9. T	p. 24
5. F	p. 21		10. F	p. 24

CHAPTER 2

Chapter Review

(1) domestic; product; GDP
(2) inputs; outputs, free; private
(3) open; closed; closed
(4) inflation; real; per capita
(5) recessions
(6) production
(7) labor; 10¢; service
(8) proprietorship; partnership; corporations; mixed
(9) horizontal; vertical

Important Terms and Concepts Quiz

1. d	6. k	11. b
2. i	7. e	12. n
3. m	8. c	13. o
4. a	9. h	14. l
5. g	10. j	

Basic Exercises

1. a. No, increases in aggregate income due to inflation or population do not increase individual purchasing power.
    b. 8.1 times; column 3: 1,995; 3,521; 8,576; 16,177
    c. 2.1 times; column 5: 7,256; 7,588; 10,600; 15,304
2. 15.98; 28.47; 22.78; 22.08; 26.62; 28.90; 23.43; 26.28; 27.37; 33.10; 32.50
3. The graph in Figure 2-1a exaggerates the increase as it omits the origin. While there was a substantial increase in gold prices during the first half of 1993, the value of gold as an investment is by no means a sure thing. For example $10,000 invested in gold in 1980 was worth only $5,624 at the end of 1992. A similar investment in U.S. government securities would have been worth $27,599 by the end of 1992 while the value of a balanced portfolio of stocks would have grown to $54,520.
4. The trend line from 1968 to 1983 seems to tell a similar story; but, just as in the 1960s, the trend line does not mean that appropriate macroeconomic policy cannot lower the rate of unemployment.

Self-Tests For Understanding

Test A

1. a and d   p. 28
2. c   p. 28-29
3. d   p. 30
4. a   p. 33
5. d   p. 33
6. b   As it uses dollars of constant purchasing power, real GDP changes only if the volume of output changes.
7. c   p. 33
8. d   p. 34
9. c   p. 38
10. d   bread is the output
11. d   p. 36
12. c   p. 40
13. a   p. 40
14. b   p. 41
15. d   Imports are goods produced abroad and bought in America.
16. a   Exports are goods produced in America and sold in foreign countries.
17. d   p. 39
18. a   p. 44
19. c   p. 47
20. a   p. 45

Test B

1. T   p. 28
2. F   p. 34
3. F   p. 31

4. T   p. 29
5. T   p. 35
6. F   p. 35
7. F   p. 36
8. F   p. 36
9. T   p. 38
10. T   p. 40

Supplementary Exercise

1987 dollars:

Public: 1,030; 1,131; 2,043

Private: 4,267; 5,284; 10,765

Proportion of per capita real income:

Public: 13.6%; 10.7%; 13.3%

Private: 56.2%; 49.8%; 70.3%

CHAPTER 3

Chapter Review

(1) scarce
(2) opportunity cost
(3) scarce; specialized; fewer; more; more; consumption
(4) slope
(5) increase; increasing; specialized
(6) inside; inefficient;
(7) will

Important Terms and Concepts Quiz

1. g	8. s	15. h
2. i	9. f	16. d
3. n	10. q	17. o
4. r	11. p	18. k
5. m	12. b	19. t
6. j	13. e	
7. a	14. l	

Basic Exercise

1. a. 560,000; 40,000; rises; 120,000; continue to rise; specialized
    b. Point A is not attainable; point B is attainable; point C is attainable; on and inside
    c. Point B is inefficient. You should be able to shade a small triangular area above and to the right of point B out to and including a small segment of the PPF.
2. a. Catskill, the economy that produces the greater amount of capital goods will have the greater shift. That is, next year the PPF for Catskill should lies outside that of Adirondack.
    b. An economist would measure the cost of economic growth by the differences in the output of consumption goods or 120,000 loaves of bread, 400,000–280,000.

Self-Tests For Understanding

Test A

1. c   p. 57
2. c   p. 62
3. d   p. 60
4. d   p. 67
5. a   p. 60
6. b   p. 61
7. c   p. 60
8. b   p. 67
9. d   p. 61
10. d   p. 62
11. b   p. 65
12. b   On the PPF, output of computers must decline by 500.
13. b   Borrowing money would enable firm to pay for additional resources.

14. a   p. 61
15. b   Reflects economic growth.
16. c   More money helps a single firm buy resources. An economy's resources are given by its natural resources, population and capital.
17. c   p. 57
18. a   p. 70
19. b   p. 67
20. d   p. 68

Test B
1. F   p. 57
2. F   p. 58
3. T   pp. 61-62
4. T   pp. 65-66
5. F   p. 56
6. F   pp. 60-61
7. T   p. 67
8. T   p. 67
9. F   Any economic unit with limited resources will need to make choices.
10. F   Dollar bills are not a factor of production.

Supplementary Exercises
3. a. 300,000 cars; 1,000 tanks
   c. yes, it bows out.
   d. $^1/_2C^*$, $^1/_2T^*$ should be on straight line connecting C^* and T^*. Combination is attainable, lies inside frontier; inefficient, not on frontier as frontier bows out.
   e. 6 cars; 30 cars; 120 cars
   f. opportunity cost = (0.6)T cars; yes, opportunity cost increases as the production of tanks increases.
   g. new frontier lies everywhere outside the old frontier.

4. a. When $I = 1,600$ the sustainable level of $C = 10,292$.
   b. C drops by 400 to 9,892 and then rises to its new sustainable level of 10,574.
   c. The increase in consumption, 10,574 to 10,761, is less than in question b. Additional machines add to output but at a decreasing rate. This increase at a decreasing rate is an example of declining marginal productivity, a concept that is discussed in Chapter 6.
   d. There can be too much of a good thing. Additional machines allow for an increase in total output, but additional machines also increase the amount of output that must be allocated to investment in order to maintain the larger number of machines. With a large enough increase in the number of machines, the increase in investment needed to maintain machines swamps the increase in output available for consumption. Past this point, additional investment will actually lower the sustainable level of consumption. What is this critical point? In this problem, it depends upon the exponents on L and M in equation (1) and the rate of depreciation, assumed to be 8 percent. Ask your instructor for more details.

CHAPTER 4
Chapter Review
(1) price; negative; more; movement along; shift in

(2) price; positive; more; shift in

(3) demand

(4) $300; 4000; less; 6000; 2000; surplus; reduction; shortage; demanded; supplied; increase

(5) intersection; equilibrium

(6) demand; supply; movement along; supply; demand; demand

(7) maximum; minimum

(8) hard; auxiliary restrictions

(9) shortages; decrease

(10) high

Important Terms and Concepts Quiz

1.	k	7.	o	13.	d
2.	e	8.	p	14.	j
3.	g	9.	n	15.	b
4.	c	10.	h	16.	a
5.	i	11.	f		
6.	q	12.	m		

Basic Exercises

1. b. 40; 1100
   c. increased; 50; increased; 1200
   d. increase; decrease; 55; 1100
2. a. demand; right; rise; rise
   b. supply; right; fall; rise
   c. supply; left; rise; fall
   d. demand; left; fall; fall
3. a. 100; 100; neither, as ceiling exceeds equilibrium price
   b. 110; 80; shortage
      Price ceilings lead to shortages when they are less than the free market equilibrium price.
   c. 90; 120; surplus
   d. 100; 100; neither, as floor is less than equilibrium price
      Price floors lead to surpluses when they are greater than the free market equilibrium price.

Self-Tests For Understanding

Test A

1.	c.	p. 78
2.	a	p. 78
3.	c	p. 79
4.	d	p. 84 and 88
5.	c	p. 79
6.	b	p. 88
7.	a	p. 88
8.	a	p. 89
9.	d	p. 81
10.	b	p. 84
11.	c	p. 85
12.	a	p. 84
13.	a	pp. 89-90
14.	b, d	p. 90, cotton cloth is an input; skirts, pants and blouses may be related inputs
15.	b	p. 90
16.	b	pp. 86-87
17.	c	p. 83
18.	a	p. 96
19.	d	pp. 91-92
20.	b	p. 81

Test B

1.	F	The law of supply and demand is an empirical regularity, not a Congressional statute.
2.	T	p. 78
3.	T	p. 79
4.	F	p. 84
5.	F	p. 78
6.	T	p. 83
7.	T	p. 81
8.	F	p. 84
9.	F	p. 90
10.	T	pp. 91-92
11.	F	p. 96
12.	T	p. 91
13.	F	p. 93

14. F The increase in price and quantity comes from the movement along the supply curve following the shift in the demand curve.

CHAPTER 5
Chapter Review
(1) microeconomics; macroeconomics
(2) price; quantity; domestic product
(3) inflation; deflation; recessions; higher; higher; left; decrease; stagflation
(4) money; final; nominal; real; real; nominal; real; is not
(5) up; depends; risen
(6) inflation; stabilization; recessions; inflation

Important Terms and Concepts Quiz
1. p	7. q	13. g
2. h	8. l	14. k
3. e	9. b	15. c
4. i	10. n	16. f
5. m	11. d	
6. o	12. j	

Basic Exercises
1. a. c; d
    b. b; yes, 1929-1933
    c. a
    d. c
2. a. shift aggregate demand curve to left
    b. shift aggregate demand curve to right
    c. Real GDP will fall as aggregate demand curve is shifted to the left; prices will rise as aggregate demand curve is shifted to the right.

3. a. col (3): $600; $300; $225; $1,125
       col (6): $868; $416; $297; $1,581
    b. 40.5 percent
    c. $620; $320; $247.50; $1,187.50
    d. 5.56 percent
    e. The increase in real GDP is less than the increase in nominal GDP as the increase in nominal GDP includes both the increase in production and the increase in prices. The increase in real GDP is the better measure of the change in output. It is a weighted average of the increases in the output of hamburgers, shakes, and fries. The weights sum to one and reflect the relative importance of output in GDP for the base year, 1992 in this example.

Self-Tests For Understanding
Test A
1.	b	p. 105
2.	d	p. 105
3.	a	p. 105
4.	c	p. 108
5.	a	p. 108
6.	b	p. 109
7.	a	p. 110
8.	a	p. 109
9.	c	p. 109
10.	d	p. 110
11.	d	p. 110
12.	b	pp. 109-110
13.	a	pp. 111-112
14.	d	p. 109
15.	d	p. 108
16.	b	p. 108
17.	d	p. 118
18.	c	p. 119
19.	b	p. 114
20.	c	pp. 119-120

Test B
1. F p. 105
2. T p. 105
3. F Not if the decrease comes from a decrease in prices.
4. T p. 109
5. F If aggregate demand curve shifts to the left, prices will fall.
6. F p. 114
7. F pp. 113-114
8. T p. 118
9. T p. 119
10. F pp. 119-120

Economics in Action
1. The NBER committee dated the business cycle peak in July 1990 and the trough in March 1991.

CHAPTER 6
Chapter Review
(1) more; more
(2) cannot; partial; some
(3) potential; actual GDP
(4) is not; frictional; cyclical; structural
(5) discouraged; decrease; understate; understate
(6) frictional; increased; overstate
(7) real; the same; as; were unchanged
(8) different; less; more
(9) higher; nominal; real; inflation
(10) will; be unchanged; nominal
(11) usury; nominal; real; nominal; real
(12) creeping; galloping

Important Terms and Concepts Quiz
1. b	7. g	13. c
2. q	8. a	14. i
3. d	9. p	15. o
4. f	10. k	16. e
5. h	11. n	
6. l	12. j	

Basic Exercises
1. a. –0.7%; 0.21%; 2.32%; 1.07%; –3.69%; –2.50%; 0.91%; 0.46%; 2.7%; 0.68%; 1.38%; 2.55%; 2.71%; 6.91%; 5.03%; 4.07%; 3.97%; 3.57%; 4.89%; 2.92%; 1.65%.

   c. When actual inflation turns out to be much greater than expected, the difference between nominal interest rates and the actual rate of inflation may be negative.

   d. While the nominal rates were higher in December 1980, the actual real rate from December 1980 to December 1981 was lower than the real rate from December 1987 to December 1988.

2. a. $250,000; $5,250,000; $4,772,727; $5,750,000; $5,227,273. Borrowers gain at expense of lenders.

   b. $775,000; $5,775,000; $5,250,000; $5,225,000; $4,750,000. Both are treated equally.

   c. $1,000,000; $6,000,000; $5,454,545; $5,000,000; $4,545,455. Lenders gain at expense of borrowers.

Self-Tests For Understanding
Test A
1.	b, a, d, c	pp. 128-130
2.	a, b, d	p. 128
3.	a	p. 130
4.	c	pp. 125-126
5.	b	p. 126
6.	b	p. 129
7.	b	p. 130
8.	c	p. 130
9.	c	p. 131
10.	b	p. 137
11.	b	p. 137
12.	b	p. 137
13.	a	p. 137

14. c	p. 137
15. b	pp. 135-136
16. d	p. 139
17. c	p. 134
18. d	p. 143
19. a	pp. 132-133
20. c	p. 132

Test B

1. F Reduced hours, loss of overtime, and involuntary part-time reduce income for individuals counted as employed.

2. F	p. 128
3. F	p. 125
4. F	p. 131
5. F	p. 130
6. F	p. 126
7. F	pp. 129-130
8. F	pp. 136-137
9. F	p. 143
10. T	p. 141

CHAPTER APPENDIX

Important Terms and Concepts Quiz: Appendix

1. b	3. a	5. f
2. d	4. c	

Basic Exercises: Appendix

1. a. 2,500; 400
   b. $16,500 = 2,500 \times \$2.36 + 400 \times \$26.50$
   c. 110
   e. 10 percent
   f. $15,771 ($1,990); 5.1 percent
2. 1990 index, using 1991 base, 91.1. 1991 base implies inflation of 9.8 percent. The slightly lower rate of inflation reflects a larger weight on more slowly rising clothing prices when using the 1991 expenditure pattern.

Supplementary Exercise: Appendix

1. a and b. Insufficient information; for example, the price index for Canada for 1990 shows how 1990 Canadian prices compare to Canadian prices in 1982-1984, not how Canadian prices compare to those in other countries.
   c. Italy; West Germany

CHAPTER 7

Chapter Review

(1) demand; consumption; investment; government; exports; imports; net exports
(2) before; taxes; transfer
(3) more; movement along; shift in
(4) C; I; G; X; IM; less; decrease
(5) increase; marginal; larger; more; smaller

Important Terms and Concepts Quiz

1. g	6. l	11. e
2. d	7. b	12. m
3. h	8. n	13. j
4. c	9. a	
5. k	10. i	

Basic Exercises

1. a. .75; .75; .75; .75
   b. .9; .825; .8; .7875; .78
   e. slope of consumption function
   f. rays become less steep, that is their slope decreases. For straight line consumption function with a positive Y intercept, the APC will be greater than the MPC although the difference will be getting smaller as income increases.
2. a. $9,000; $39,000; $4,800,000
   b. .78; .9

  c. $12,750; $35,250; $4,800,000
  d. In this example, MPC is the same for the rich and poor. The rich reduce their consumption by the same amount that the poor increase their consumption.
3. C = 1,500 + .75DI
4. a. Estimated MPC = 3.6/4.0 = .9
  b. The estimate in a is greater than the slope of the consumption function. It overestimates the MPC because it includes the effect of the shift of the consumption function.

Self-Tests For Understanding

Test A

1. b pp. 151-152
2. b p. 151
3. d p. 154
4. b Circular flow diagram shows spending on newly produced goods and services.
5. b p. 152
6. d p. 152
7. c p. 160
8. a p. 162
9. c p. 162
10. b p. 156 and Appendix, Chapter 1
11. d pp. 163-164
12. a p. 160
13. b p. 160
14. c $\Delta C = MPC \times \Delta DI$
15. c $MPC = \Delta C/\Delta DI$
16. c Δ taxes $= -\Delta DI = \Delta C/MPC$
17. a $MPC = \Delta C/\Delta DI$. For 14, 15, 16, and 17, remember: $MPC = \Delta C/\Delta DI$. Each question gives you two numbers; you must solve equation for the third.
18. d p. 162

19. d p. 164
20. c changes in withholding affect the timing of when taxes are paid but do not change what a taxpayer owes. pp. 165-166

Test B

1. F p. 151
2. F p. 160
3. T pp. 155-156
4. T p. 160
5. T p. 163
6. T p. 164
7. F p. 162
8. T pp. 165-166
9. T p. 166
10. T p. 160

APPENDIX A

Important Terms and Concepts Quiz: Appendix A

1. d   2. c   3. a

Basic Exercises: Appendix A

1. $1,600; $3,200; $4,800; $6,400; $8,000
2. change in savings; $1,600; $1,600; $1,600; $1,600; MPS: .4; .4; .4; .4
4. APS: .13; .20; .24; .27; .29
6. DI/DI = C/DI + S/DI or 1 = APC + APS
 $\Delta DI/\Delta DI = \Delta C/\Delta DI + \Delta S/\Delta DI$ or 1 = MPC + MPS

APPENDIX B

Appendix Review

(1) final; produced
(2) exports; imports; produced
(3) income, do not; net national; depreciation
(4) value added
(5) taxes

Important Terms and Concepts Quiz: Appendix B

1. a   2. e   3. b   4. c

Basic Exercises: Appendix B

1. a. $2,200
   b. $1,700
   c. $1,700; wages = $1,200;
      profits = $500
   d. $500
   e. $1,200
   f. $1,700
   g. $1,700
   h. $1,700

2. a. $1,000; $2,100; $1,600; $4,700
   b. 0; $1,500; $3,200; $4,700

Self-Tests for Understanding: Appendix B

Test A

1. c   p. 172
2. c   p. 176
3. b   p. 172
4. c   p. 172
5. a   This year's GDP only includes goods produced this year. p. 172
6. d   pp. 176-177
7. d   Computers shipped to Japan are exports. p. 173
8. b   Computers from Japan are imports.
9. c   Social security payments are transfers. p. 173
10. d   p. 174
11. b   p. 175
12. c   p. 178
13. b   p. 178
14. c   pp. 177-178
15. a   p. 178
16. d   p. 176
17. d   p. 178
18. c   p. 172
19. c   p. 178
20. b   p. 175

Test B

1. F   p. 172
2. T   p. 176
3. F   p. 172
4. F   No effect on GDP. Value added by GM up. Value added by suppliers down.
5. F   p. 172
6. T   p. 176
7. F   p. 174
8. F   p. 178
9. F   p. 175
10. T   These are alternative ways to measure national income.

Supplementary Exercise: Appendix B

1. MPC = $50/\sqrt{DI}$; MPC declines as income rises. Thus consumption spending rises following redistribution from rich to poor as increase in consumption by poor is greater than decline in consumption by rich.
   $S = DI - 100 \sqrt{DI}$
   MPC + MPS = 1 and APC + APS = 1

CHAPTER 8

Chapter Review

(1) increase; increasing; decrease
(2) exports; imports
(3) intersection
(4) less; downward; lower; more; higher
(5) price level
(6) inflationary; recessionary

Important Terms and Concepts Quiz

1. d   4. g   7. i
2. f   5. j   8. e
3. b   6. a   9. c

Basic Exercises

1. e. $6,200
   f. 5,900; 6,000; 6,100; 6,200; 6,300
   g. Spending would be greater than output, inventories would decline, firms would increase output.
   h. inflationary gap, $200; recessionary gap, $300
   i. Expenditure schedule shifts up; $6,400; $4,700
2. b. $6,000
   c. $6,400
   d. aggregate demand curve
   e. negative
3. New aggregate demand curve should lie to the right of the aggregate demand curve in question 2.

Self-Tests For Understanding

Test A

1. b   pp. 182-183
2. c   pp. 184-185
3. a   pp. 184-185
4. a   Net exports = $X - IM$.
5. c   p. 185
6. c   p. 188
7. a, c, d, e, g   p. 188
8. c   p. 188
9. a   p. 188
10. c   p. 188
11. c   p. 191
12. a   p. 190
13. b   p. 190
14. b   p. 191
15. c   p. 194
16. a   p. 197
17. a   p. 194
18. c   p. 192
19. b   pp. 192-193
20. a, b, c The increase in the purchasing power of money-fixed assets shifts the consumption function and the expenditure schedule leading to a movement along the aggregate demand curve

Test B

1. F   p. 182
2. T   p. 188
3. F   p. 197
4. F   p. 190
5. T   pp. 192-193
6. F   p. 195
7. T   p. 194
8. F   pp. 196-198
9. F   pp. 192-193
10. T   pp. 192-193

APPENDIX A

Basic Exercises: Appendix A

1. 600; 700; 800; 900; 1,000; 1,100
2. Leakages: 1,900; 2,000; 2,100; 2,200; 2,300; 2,400
   Equilibrium income = 2,200
3. The intersection of the leakages schedule and the injections schedule; 2,200
4. Investment: steeper; no change; steeper
   Imports: flatter; steeper; no change
   Exports: affected by foreign, not domestic income
5. $S + T + IM = I + G + X$

APPENDIX B

Basic Exercises: Appendix B

1. $C = 1,850 + .5 (Y - T)$
   $= 1,500 + .5Y$
2. $C + I + G + (X - IM) = 3,100 + .5Y$
3. $Y = 3,100 + .5Y$
   $= 6,200$

CHAPTER 9

Chapter Review

(1) more than; autonomous; induced
(2) MPC
(3) consumption spending
(4) income; MPC
(5) smaller; international trade; inflation; income; financial
(6) do not; supply; autonomous; shifting; horizontal

Important Terms and Concepts Quiz

1. d   2. a   3. e   4. b

Basic Exercises

1. a. 5,600; 5,800; 6,000; 6,200; 6,400; 6,600; 6,800; equilibrium: 6,000
   b. 6,500
   c. 500
   d. 5; equilibrium level; income; autonomous spending
   e. .8
   f. $1/(1 - 0.8) = 1(0.2) = 5$
   g. slope expenditure schedule $= 200/250 = 0.8$
2. a. Total spending = 5,800; 6,000; 6,200; 6,400; 6,600; 6,800; 7,000; equilibrium = 7,000
   b. 500
   c. 5; it is the same as the investment spending multiplier.
3. less; autonomous
   a. 6,750
   b. –250
   c. fall
   d. 5
   e. the same
   f. It ignores effects of inflation, taxes, the financial system, and international trade.

Self-Tests For Understanding

Test A

1. c   p. 208
2. b   p. 208
3. d   p. 213
4. c   p. 210
5. a; c; e; g p. 213
6. c   See Figure 9-1 or 9-3.
7. b   p. 214
8. e   p. 220
9. c   p. 213
10. a   p. 213
11. c   p. 213
12. c   p. 220
13. b; d   Japanese imports from the United States are American exports to Japan.
14. c   p. 208
15. d   An autonomous increase in imports shifts expenditure schedule down.
16. b   p. 218
17. c   p. 218
18. a   p. 219
19. b   p. 218
20. c   pp. 217-218

Test B

1. F   p. 208
2. F   p. 208
3. T   p. 218
4. T   p. 213
5. T   p. 214
6. F   p. 218
7. F   p. 214
8. F   p. 215
9. F   pp. 217-218
10. T   p. 220

APPENDIX A
Basic Exercises: Appendix A

1. $Y = a + b\,(Y - T) + I + G + X - IM$

   $= \dfrac{1}{1-b}\,(a - b\,T + I + G + X - IM)$

   Multiplier $= \dfrac{1}{1-b}$

2. $\Delta Y = \dfrac{1}{1-b}\,\Delta a$

   $\Delta Y = \dfrac{1}{1-b}\,\Delta I$

   $\Delta Y = \dfrac{1}{1-b}\,\Delta G$

   $\Delta Y = \dfrac{1}{1-b}\,\Delta X$

   $\Delta Y = \dfrac{1}{1-b}\,\Delta IM$

APPENDIX B
Basic Exercises: Appendix B

2. 6,500
3. multiplier $= 500/125 = 4$
4. The multiplier is smaller because imports increase with income. The slope of the expenditure schedule $= 187.5/250 = 0.75$. Multiplier $= 1/(1 - 0.75) = 1/0.25 = 4$. Alternatively, the marginal propensity to import $= 0.05$. Multiplier $= 1/(1 - 0.8 + 0.05) = 1/(1 - 0.75) = 4$.

Supplementary Exercises: Appendix B

1. It ignores the multiplier.
3. b. Model should show change in income of 400 for multiplier of $4 = 1/(1 - MPC)$.
   c. Autonomous change in saving is necessarily a change in intercept of consumption function. Review Appendix A to Chapter 7 if necessary.

d. Larger MPC will mean larger multiplier; smaller MPC means smaller multiplier.

CHAPTER 10
Chapter Review

(1) increase; movement along; shift in; right
(2) steeper
(3) intersection; decrease; increases
(4) inflationary; is; inward; movement along; higher; lower
(5) less
(6) inflationary; supply

Important Terms and Concepts Quiz

1. c   2. e   3. a   4. d

Basic Exercises

1. a. increases; shift in; $6,200
   e. 95; $6,125
   f. Inflationary gap; increasing production costs would shift aggregate supply curve; 100 and $6,000
   g. no gaps
   h. recessionary gap; elimination of gap likely to be very slow; 90; $6,250
2. horizontal
   a. no
   b. At P^* aggregate demand would exceed aggregate supply. Prices would rise. The increase in prices would mean a movement along the dashed aggregate demand curve to the equilibrium, (Y_2, P_2), given by the intersection of the dashed aggregate demand curve and the solid aggregate supply curve.

The increase in investment
spending, which shifted the
expenditure schedule and gave rise
to the dashed aggregate demand
curve, will lead to an increase in
prices as part of the broader
multiplier process, reducing net
exports and the purchasing power
of money-fixed assets. The result of
the reduction in net exports and the
shift in the consumption function is
a downward shift in the
expenditure schedule (not drawn)
that partially offsets the
expansionary impact of the original
increase in investment spending
and reconciles equilibrium in the
income-expenditure diagram with
that of the aggregate demand–
aggregate supply diagram. That is,
to complete the analysis one would
need to draw a third expenditure
schedule between the solid and
dashed ones already shown in
Figure 10-4. We know from the
equilibrium determined in the
aggregate demand–aggregate
supply diagram that this final
expenditure schedule will intersect
the 45-degree line at a real GDP
level of Y_2.

3. s, m, –, –; m, s, –, +; s, m, +, +; m, s,
   +, –; s, m, +, +; m, s, –, +

Self-Tests For Understanding

Test A
1. b p. 229
2. b pp. 228-229
3. a change in the price level leads to
      a movement along the aggregate
      supply curve

4. a p. 233
5. c p. 233
6. a, b, c, d, e p. 237
7. d pp. 232-233
8. a p. 235
9. d p. 232
10. c p. 238
11. d An increase in G when there is a
       recessionary gap need not result
       in an inflationary gap. p. 235
12. a p. 241
13. c p. 243
14. b, d Net exports = exports – imports
15. a, c, d The increase in net exports
         leads to shifts on the demand
         side.
16. c Shift in aggregate demand curve
       leads to movement along
       aggregate supply curve.
17. d pp. 232-233
18. c A growing population shifts both
       curves every year.
19. d p. 246
20. c p. 246

Test B
1. T p. 228
2. T p. 228
3. T pp. 232-233
4. F pp. 239-240
5. T p. 243
6. F While there is a tendency to move
      toward full employment or
      potential output, there is nothing
      that requires the aggregate
      demand and supply to always
      intersect there.
7. F Equilibrium is determined by
      intersection of both curves.
8. T p. 238
9. F p. 238
10. F p. 244

Supplementary Exercises

1. $C + I + G + (X - IM) = 1,700 + .8Y - 5P$
2. $P = 340 - .04Y$ or $Y = 8,500 - 25P$
3. $P = 95$; $Y = 6,125$
4. $P = 90$; $Y = 6,000$
   New expenditure schedule:
   $C + I + G + (X - IM) = 1,650 + .8Y - 5P$
   New aggregate demand curve:
   $P = 330 - .04Y$

CHAPTER 11

Chapter Review

(1) fiscal; expenditure; demand; supply
(2) up; 1; 1
(3) are not; higher; permanent; propensity; less than; investment
(4) income; consumption; –; +
(5) up; variable; fixed
(6) less; smaller
(7) smaller
(8) MPC; smaller; smaller; flatter
(9) more; steeper
(10) consumption; MPC; less than; less; smaller
(11) increase; decrease; decrease; increase
(12) supply; increase

Important Terms and Concepts Quiz

1. d	3. f	5. e
2. c	4. b	

Basic Exercises

1. $6,000
2. $5,500
3. 2.5
4. $6,000
5. 2.0
6. The multiplier for a change in taxes is less than the multiplier for a change in government purchases.

7. No. The increase in GDP from the multiplier process increased tax revenues by $125, an amount less than the reduction in taxes that initiated the multiplier process.
8. $100; $125
9. $5,500; the multipliers are the same.

Self-Tests for Understanding

Test A

1. c Money supply is monetary policy decision. p. 251
2. d p. 258
3. b p. 258
4. a p. 251
5. c p. 252
6. b With fixed taxes $\Delta DI = \Delta GDP$ and in this case only C changes as GDP changes.
7. a With variable taxes $\Delta DI < \Delta GDP$ leading to a smaller change in C when GDP changes then in question 6.
8. d p. 251
9. c p. 252
10. a p. 258
11. b These changes leave disposable income unchanged.
12. b $\Delta Y = \Delta G \times$ multiplier, p. 259
13. a A reduction in transfer payments reduces disposable income and aggregate demand.
14. c pp. 257-258
15. b A reduction in income taxes makes the expenditure schedule steeper. pp. 254-255
16. b A change in any variable affecting demand except price will lead to a shift in the aggregate demand curve.

17. c As the multiplier for a change in taxes is smaller than the multiplier for a change in government purchases, it takes a larger change in taxes to offset the change in purchases. p. 257
18. c p. 260-261
19. d p. 263
20. b p. 265

Test B
1. F See comment to question 15, Test A.
2. T pp. 254-255
3. F Multiplier applies to any change in autonomous spending, i.e. vertical shift in expenditure schedule.
4. F p. 254
5. F p. 258
6. F p. 258
7. F pp. 260-261
8. T p. 258
9. F pp. 265-266
10. F p. 265

Supplementary Exercises
1. Income taxes are an important reason why Okun's multiplier is less than the oversimplified formula.
2. The tax multiplier is less than the multiplier for changes in autonomous spending.
3. The 1975 income tax rebate was a temporary tax change. The 1964 change was permanent.

APPENDIX
Basic Exercise: Appendix
1. $Y = 6,000$
2. No; Y declines by 25 to \$5,975; tax and spending multipliers differ. Deficit increases from 50 to 56.25

3. Multipliers:
$\Delta I = 2.5$; $\Delta Y / \Delta I = 1/(1-b(1-t))$
$\Delta G = 2.5$; $\Delta Y / \Delta G = 1/(1-b(1-t))$
$\Delta(X - IM) = 2.5$; $\Delta Y / \Delta(X - IM) = 1/(1-b(1-t))$
$\Delta T = -2.0$ (change in intercept)
$\Delta Y / \Delta T_0 = -\Delta Y / \Delta I = -b/(1-b(1-t))$

CHAPTER 12
Chapter Review
(1) barter; more difficult
(2) money; commodity; fiat
(3) M1; M2
(4) 1026.5; 3497.0
(5) lending; 900; reserve requirement
(6) 1/(reserve requirement); less
(7) smaller; excess; smaller
(8) contraction; no

Important Terms and Concepts Quiz
1. c	9. s	17. b
2. j	10. k	18. r
3. g	11. o	19. l
4. m	12. e	20. h
5. m	13. f	21. q
6. d	14. p	22. a
7. t	15. v	
8. n	16. u	

Basic Exercises
1. \$10,000; unchanged; col. 1: \$1,000; \$9,000
2. col. 2: \$1,000; \$9,000; \$10,000; \$1,000; 0
3. col. 3: \$9,000; 0; \$9,000; \$900; \$8,100; \$19,000; \$9,000
4. col. 4: \$900; \$8,100; \$9,000; \$900; 0
5. col. 5: \$8,100; 0; \$8,100; \$810; \$7,290; \$27,100; \$17,100

6. B: $9,000; C: $8,100; D: $7,290; E: $6,561; 0.1; $100,000; required reserve ratio.

Self-Tests For Understanding

Test A

1. b   p. 277
2. c   p. 278
3. a   p. 278
4. c   M1 includes cash in circulation. Vault cash is included in a bank's reserves. p. 218
5. b, d   p. 280
6. b   p. 281
7. c   p. 286
8. c   p. 286
9. d   p. 286
10. d   p. 287
11. c   p. 283
12. d   The increase in deposits offsets the reduction in cash in circulation.
13. c   p. 284
14. d   p. 292
15. a   9,000; net increase in money supply = deposit expansion – cash deposit.
16. a   p. 292
17. a   p. 294
18. d   100 ÷ (0.2) = 500, p. 292
19. a   Interbank claims lead to offsetting chains of deposit creation and destruction.
20. b   total reserves = required + excess = nonborrowed + borrowed.

Test B

1. T   p. 275
2. F   p. 278
3. T   p. 277
4. F   p. 277
5. F   p. 283
6. T   p. 284
7. F   p. 294
8. F   pp. 292-293
9. F   pp. 286-287
10. T   p. 286

Supplementary Exercises

1. 2,500; 1,500
2. Change in deposits = $[1/(M + E + C)]$ × (change in reserves)

CHAPTER 13

Chapter Review

(1) 1914; central; 12; Board; Governors; Federal Open Market; fiscal; monetary
(2) excess
(3) increase; larger; expansionary; required; contractionary
(4) securities; buys; increase; reduction; destruction
(5) moral suasion; higher; higher; discount rate
(6) more; fewer; more; larger
(7) right; demand
(8) decreases; increased; right; increased; left
(9) intersection; supply; right; increase; decrease; left; decrease; increase
(10) supply; demand; shift in; shift in; demand; supply

Important Terms and Concepts Quiz

1. b
2. h
3. k
4. e
5. j
6. f
7. i
8. a
9. d
10. g

Basic Exercises

1. a. decrease; left; contractionary; fall; rise
   b. increase; creation; right; expansionary; rise; fall
   c. less; decline; decline; left; contractionary; fall; rise

2. a. The scatter of points has a positive slope suggesting that an increase in the difference between the federal funds rate and the discount rate is associated with a larger volume of bank borrowing from the Fed.

    b. Remember that borrowing is a privilege not a right. The Fed is likely to use moral suasion to limit bank borrowing when the economic incentive from interest rate differentials gets large.

3. Note that when the interest rate differential increases, the ratio of GDP to money gets larger. That is, individuals economize on the use of money as the opportunity cost of holding M2 balances increases.

Self-Tests For Understanding

Test A

1. d   pp. 300-301
2. d   p. 298
3. c   p. 319
4. b   pp. 301-302
5. b   p. 302
6. d   pp. 302-303
7. c   Simple multiplier is determined by slope of expenditure schedule, e.g., MPC, tax rates, and slope of aggregate supply curve.
8. d   Shift of aggregate demand curve should reduce inflation, that is make prices lower than they otherwise would be.
9. b   p. 305
10. d   p. 313
11. c   Money supply schedule shifts to the right.

12. c   p. 306
13. d   p. 303
14. a, c   Both lead to variability in the deposit creation multiplier.
15. a   p. 310
16. c   p. 311
17. b   p. 308
18. a   p. 304
19. a, d   It takes time for an increase in investment to affect the aggregate supply curve. pp. 313-314
20. b   p. 318

Test B

1. F   pp. 301-302
2. F   p. 300
3. F   pp. 300-301
4. F   pp. 302-303
5. F   Reduction in reserve requirement shifts money supply schedule to the right, increasing M and decreasing R.
6. F   p. 306
7. F   p. 310
8. T   p. 308
9. F   Changes in monetary policy lead to shifts in the aggregate demand curve.
10. T   p. 318

Supplementary Exercises

1. a. 6,000; $C = 3,650$; $I = 1,350$; $G = 900$; $X - IM = 100$
    b. increases to 6,240
    c. In this model, equilibrium in the income–expenditure diagram depends on the rate of interest. The expenditure schedule is as follows:

    $C + I + G + (X - IM) = 650 + .6(5/6)$
    $Y + 1,710 - 30r + 900 + 100 =$
    $3,360 - 30r + .5Y$

The 45-degree line is $C + I + G + (X - IM) = Y$. Solving these two equations for one expression in Y and r yields

$$Y = 6{,}720 - 60r$$

Setting the demand for money equal to supply of money yields a second expression in Y and r.

$$Y = 20BR + 50r.$$

When $BR = 270$ then $Y = 2{,}400$, $r = 12$, and $M = 1{,}380$. The value of M can be found from either the demand for money equation or the supply of money equation.

d. Changing bank reserve shifts the second equation for Y and r. A little experimentation should show that bank reserves of 292 will yield an interest rate of 8 and a money stock of 1,480.

2. a. $1,500; $600
   b. $1,220.80; $698.87

CHAPTER 14

Chapter Review
(1) GDP; money
(2) nominal GDP; M; V; P; Y; velocity
(3) money; does not; nominal GDP; 100
(4) should not; opportunity cost
(5) velocity
(6) decline; increase; increase
(7) higher; increase; higher; demand
(8) monetary; fiscal
(9) higher; higher; left; right
(10) output; prices; steep; steep; flat
(11) automatic
(12) judgmental; are not
(13) need not

Important Terms and Concepts Quiz
1. e   4. b   6. f
2. c   5. a   7. d
3. h

Basic Exercises
1. a. V_1: 6.84; 7.17; 6.91; 6.84; 7.04; 6.89; 6.35; 6.16; 6.38; 6.64; 6.81; 6.58; 6.18
        V_2: 1.73; 1.77; 1.68; 1.65; 1.66; 1.63; 1.58; 1.58; 1.63; 1.66; 1.68; 1.67; 1.71
   b. Col. 3: 2,892.1; 3,266.5; 3,442.4; 3,671.0; 4,125.2; 4,631.5; 4,681.0; 4,732.6; 5,042.6; 5,383.9; 5,878.7; 6,333.2
        Col. 5: 2,964.6; 3,316.1; 3,480.6; 3,753.9; 4,096.7; 4,397.8; 4,539.9; 4,747.6; 5,158.8; 5,473.1; 5,700.6; 5,804.2
   c. Errors are highest when velocity changes. The greater variation in V_1 leads to larger errors for predictions based on M_1.
2. Each speaker is arguing that the demand for money has shifted to the right. In both cases the shift is consistent with the increase in M and r.

Speaker A is arguing that the shift in the demand for money derives from an autonomous shift in the aggregate demand curve to the right. A shift of the money supply curve to the left, an open market sale, would increase interest rates even further, inducing an offsetting shift of the aggregate demand curve to the left. With a bit of luck, the policy induced shift of the aggregate demand curve to the left would offset the autonomous shift in the aggregate demand curve to the right, and there would be no inflation.

Speaker B is arguing that there has been an autonomous increase in the demand for money. If there is no offsetting increase in supply, interest rates will rise, inducing a shift of the aggregate demand curve to the left. In this case the appropriate action would be to shift the money supply curve to the right and hold interest rates constant to avoid inducing a shift in the aggregate demand curve.

The appropriate policy response, whether to focus on M or r, depends upon the origins of the shift in the demand for money.

Self-Tests For Understanding

Test A

1.	c	p. 322
2.	b	p. 323
3.	e	p. 323
4.	a, b, d	p. 323
5.	a	p. 322
6.	a	The reduction in V means that the percentage increase in P times Y must be less than the percentage increase in M
7.	d	p. 324
8.	d	Quantity theory predicts that increases in M will increase nominal GDP, P times Y. It does not predict P and Y separately.
9.	b	This change should lower interest rates and reduce velocity.
10.	c	p. 328
11.	d	Increase in taxes would lower nominal GDP.

12.	c	pp. 325-326
13.	a, b, c, d	p. 329
14.	b	p. 330
15.	b	pp. 330-331
16.	a, b	p. 333
17.	a	p. 335
18.	b	p. 335
19.	c	p. 341
20.	c	p. 345

Test B

1.	T	p. 322		6.	F	p. 331
2.	F	p. 323		7.	F	pp. 331-333
3.	T	p. 327		8.	T	pp. 336-337
4.	F	p. 327		9.	F	p. 341
5.	T	p. 330		10.	T	p. 341

CHAPTER 15

Chapter Review

(1) spending; revenue; revenue; spending; deficit; surplus

(2) down; left; decline; decline; deficit; increase; decrease; accentuate

(3) will; will not

(4) small; without; small; large

(5) monetized

(6) foreigners

(7) investment; recession; war; crowding in; crowding out; high; out

Important Terms and Concepts Quiz

1.	c		5.	h
2.	g		6.	f
3.	b		7.	d
4.	e			

Basic Exercises

1. 6,250; 6,375; 6,500; 6,625; 6,750; equilibrium = 6,500
2. –25

3. surplus; 37.5
4. 6,125; 6,250; 6,375; 6,500; 6,625; equilibrium = 6,250; actual deficit increases to 87.5; no change in structural deficit
5. raise; lower equilibrium level of income.
6. lower; lower equilibrium level of income.
7. 146; 6,016.7
8. –175; 5,900

Note: Figuring out the correct answers to 7 and 8 is a bit tricky. With regard to 7, increasing the fixed component of taxes by 87.5 would eliminate the deficit if Y did not change. However, the increase in fixed taxes will reduce Y and result in a smaller net increase in taxes. Letting FT stand for the fixed component of taxes, one can find the necessary increase in fixed taxes by solving the following two equations:

$$\Delta\text{Deficit} = -\Delta FT - 0.25\,\Delta Y$$
$$\Delta Y = -\Delta FT\,[MPC/(0.5)].$$

The first equation shows how the deficit changes when the fixed component of taxes and Y change. The second shows how Y changes when the fixed component of taxes changes. The number 0.25 measures the responsiveness of taxes to income, and the expression $[MPC/(0.5)]$ is the multiplier for a change in fixed taxes in this model. Setting the change in the deficit equal to –87.5, one can solve for the necessary change in fixed taxes and the associated change in Y. A similar approach provides the answer to question 8, but note that there are some small but important differences in the two equations:

$$\Delta\text{Deficit} = \Delta G - 0.25\,\Delta Y$$
$$\Delta Y = \Delta G\,[1/(0.5)].$$

Self-Tests For Understanding
Test A
1. d   p. 356
2. a   p. 356
3. d   p. 359
4. c   p. 360
5. c   p. 361
6. c   p. 361
7. a   pp. 359-360
8. b, c   p. 357
9. d   p. 361
10. c   pp. 354-355
11. c   Monetizations means a further rightward shift of the aggregate demand curve along a steep portion of the aggregate supply curve. p. 369
12. d
13. a   pp. 362-364
14. a, b, c, d, e, f   pp. 375-376
15. b   A reduction in taxes would not reduce the deficit.
16. b   p. 376
17. d   p. 371
18. b   p. 371
19. a, b pp. 371-373
20. d   p. 371

Test B
1. F   p. 355
2. F   Depending upon the strength of private demand, a deficit or surplus may be required to insure that aggregate demand and supply curves intersect at full employment.
3. F   p. 364
4. F   p. 376
5. T   pp. 368-370
6. F   p. 359
7. F   pp. 365-366
8. T   p. 373
9. T   p. 373
10. T   p. 371

Supplementary Exercises

1. It is important to distinguish between deficits during periods of recession and deficits from deliberate increases in G or reductions in T. All of the examples come from periods when the economy was falling into recession.

   g. The ratio of debt to GDP should approach 0.72.

   h. As long as g is greater than τ and λ is greater than R, the ratio of debt to GDP tends toward $(1 + \lambda)$ $(g - \tau)/(\lambda - R)$. If g is less than τ, the government runs surpluses that eventually pay off the debt. If R is greater than λ, then interest payments on the debt are sufficient to make the national debt grow faster than GDP, and the ratio of debt to GDP grows without limit. If $R = \lambda$, the formula above will not work. Interest payments alone keep the ratio of debt to GDP constant. If in addition $G > \tau$, then the ratio of debt to income grows without limit.

   Is recent experience a case of adjusting to a lower value for τ and hence a larger, but stable, ratio of debt to GDP or is it a case of interest rates exceeding the growth of nominal GDP, $(R > \lambda)$, in which case there may be no limit to the ratio of debt to GDP? Would spending and tax policies remain unchanged if the ratio of national debt to GDP appeared to be increasing without limit?

CHAPTER 16

Chapter Review

(1) higher; negatively; Phillips; negative

(2) incorrect; inflationary; natural (or full-employment); vertical

(3) smaller; larger; higher; steeper

(4) vertical

(5) expectations; is not

(6) indexing

(7) increase; more

Important Terms and Concepts Quiz

1. h   5. c
2. e   6. i
3. a   7. b
4. g   8. f

Basic Exercise

1. purchase; decrease; decrease; increase; increase
2. 103

3. No; aggregate supply curve will shift up as long as output exceeds full-employment level of output; aggregate supply curve will continue to shift up and prices will tend to rise faster and faster.

4. a. 6,300; 106
   b. expansionary; 109
   c. restrictive; 6,100

Self-Tests For Understanding

Test A

1. d   p. 386
2. d   p. 391
3. a   p. 388
4. d   p. 394
5. c   pp. 395-397
6. a   p. 398
7. a   The aggregate supply curve shifts up whenever the cost of inputs increases.

8. c p. 399
9. d p. 404
10. a,c p. 401
11. d p. 401
12. b p. 402
13. a pp. 398-399
14. c pp. 398-399
15. d As any policy induced shift in the aggregate demand curve will mean a movement along the new aggregate supply curve, it is not possible to return to the original equilibrium.
16. c pp. 399-400
17. a pp. 404-405
18. a pp. 406-407
19. c p. 407
20. d p. 407

Test B

1. F p. 383
2. F Any shift in the aggregate demand curve, from whatever source, will affect prices.
3. T p. 391
4. T p. 394
5. T p. 395
6. F p. 398
7. T pp. 398-399
8. F Both monetary and fiscal policy would shift the aggregate demand curve along the aggregate supply curve with similar effects on prices.
9. F See comments to question 15, Test A.
10. F pp. 394-397

Supplementary Exercise

1. 440,000; $2,200,000; $440,000; profits up 10 percent
2. 440,000; $2,310,000; $462,000; profits up 15.5 percent
3. What happens if inflation differs from the announced target rate?

CHAPTER 17

Chapter Review

(1) more; more; demand; supply; out; increase
(2) is; 200
(3) convergence; faster; slower; are not
(4) need not
(5) no

Important Terms and Concepts Quiz

1. d   2. a   3. c

Basic Exercises

1. a. 2.7
   b. 7.2, more than twice as great.
   c. The concept of convergence suggests that major differences in the growth of labor productivity cannot be sustained for 100 years.
   d. 50 years, 7 months
2. a. 37,688
   b. 41,434
   c. No, labor productivity still increases but at a slower rate.
   d. GDP per capita increases at an average annual rate of 1.72 percent from $9,441 (23,900 × 0.395) to $19,350 (41,434 × 0.467). The average rate of growth of labor productivity over the same period is 1.32 percent per year.

   Numbers for this exercise were chosen to illustrate American experience over the period 1950 to 1992. See *1993 Economic Report of the President,* Tables B-2, B-29, and B-30. Labor productivity was measured as GDP per employee in the civilian labor force and the armed forces. Alternatively, and

---

more appropriately, one could measure labor productivity per hour of labor input. If average hours of work reported in Table B-42 for private nonagricultural industries is representative of average hours for all workers, labor productivity per hour of work increased at an average annual rate of 1.66 percent from $11.55 in 1950 to $23.09 in 1992. The rate of increase in labor productivity per hour of work is greater than the rate of increase in labor productivity per worker because average hours declined from 39.8 hours per week in 1950 to 34.4 in 1992.

Self-Tests For Understanding

Test A
1. d   p. 416
2. a   p. 416
3. c   p. 416
4. a   p. 418
5. c   see Chapter Review
6. a, b, c and d   help to determine the productivity of each member of the labor force. p. 416
7. d   pp. 416-417
8. b   pp. 412-413
9. c   p. 422
10. c, d   pp. 420-421
11. d   p. 429
12. a   p. 426
13. a, b   pp. 426-427
14. c   p. 419
15. c   p. 423
16. b   pp. 424-425
17. b   p. 425
18. c   pp. 420-421

19. b   pp. 421-422
20. a   p. 429

Test B
1. F   p. 419
2. F   p. 417
3. F   p. 420
4. F   p. 422
5. F   pp. 426-427
6. T   p. 420
7. F   p. 422
8. F   p. 422
9. F   p. 428
10. F   p. 429

CHAPTER 18

Chapter Review
(1) comparative
(2) scale
(3) comparative
(4) A; B; 8000; wheat
(5) 2000; 1200; cars; wheat
(6) demand; supply; exporting; importing
(7) tariffs; quotas; subsidies; price; quantity
(8) government
(9) low; do not; can
(10) adjustment
(11) defense; infant
(12) both the exporting and importing; comparative

Important Terms and Concepts Quiz
1. j	5. i	9. h
2. d	6. f	10. k
3. g	7. a	11. b
4. m	8. l	12. e

Basic Exercises
1. a.   Japan; Japan
   b. $^2/_3$; $1^1/_2$; Canada; Japan; Canada; Japan

c. Calculators; 1,000,000; 3,000,000; 4,000,000
   Backpacks: 1,500,000; 2,000,000; 3,500,000
d. 300,000; 450,000
e. 600,000 hours; 300,000 calculators; 200,000 backpacks
f. increase; 250,000
g. Calculators: 700,000; 3,450,000; 4,150,000
   Backpacks: 1,950,000; 1,700,000; 3,650,000
   The output of both calculators and backpacks has increased as compared to Question c.
h. Canadian backpack output would fall to 1,050,000. Japan would need to reallocate 1,350,000 labor hours. Total calculator output would fall to 3,625,000. This reallocation is not in line with the principle of comparative advantage. The opportunity cost of backpacks in terms of calculators is greater in Japan than in Canada.
i. There will be no change in total world output. Neither country has a comparative advantage. The opportunity cost of increased calculator or backpack production is the same in both countries.

2. a. India: $10; 1,000
      United States: $40; 600
   b. $20; production in India increases to 1200; production in United States decreases to 400; India exports, United States imports 400 shirts.
   c. United States: price = $30, production = 500; imports = 200
      India: price = $15; production = 1100; exports = 200
      United States; India; United States; India; decreased
   d. Tariff of $15

Self-Tests For Understanding
Test A
1. b p. 434
2. d pp. 435-436
3. b p. 437
4. d p. 440
5. a p. 441
6. b p. 441
7. d pp. 442-443
8. d p. 435
9. a p. 436
10. a pp. 438-439
11. c p. 443
12. a Export subsidies increase the volume of trade.
13. a p. 445
14. b p. 445
15. c p. 445
16. c p. 449
17. d Although domestic demand declines, a tariff induces a greater decline in foreign imports, allowing for an increase in domestic production.
18. c p. 448
19. b and d Higher prices hurt the users of computer chips—computer manufacturers and consumers.
20. c pp. 452-454

Test B
1. F p. 437
2. F pp. 434-435
3. F Trade should reflect comparative not absolute advantage.
4. T pp. 433-434
5. T p. 441

6. F   As world exports must equal
      world imports, it is not possible
      for all countries to increase
      exports without increasing
      imports.
7. T   p. 445
8. F   pp. 452-453
9. F   pp. 454-455
10. F pp. 455-456

Supplementary Exercise

1. a. Baulmovia: 8,100; Bilandia:
       17,150
    b. 12; Baulmovia; Bilandia; 100
    c. Baulmovia: price = 10;
       Bilandia: price = 14.5;
       Trade = 50.
    d. 50
    e. Tariff revenues accrue to the
       government. Tariffs do not protect
       high-cost foreign producers.
2. Production of 14.4 million bolts of
    cloth and 10.8 million barrels of wine
    allows Ricardia to choose from the
    outermost consumption possibilities
    line. Note that to be on the outermost
    consumption possibilities line
    Ricardia must choose to produce at
    the point where the slope of the
    production possibilities frontier equals
    the ratio of world prices.

Economics in Action

1. Tyson, Gore, and Brown prevailed.

CHAPTER 19
Chapter Review

(1) exchange; depreciated; appreciated
(2) demand; supply; exports; financial;
    physical; supply

(3) demand; increase; appreciation;
    supply; depreciation; appreciation
(4) purchasing power parity; depreciate;
    depreciating; appreciating
(5) Bretton
(6) deficit; demand; supply; surplus
(7) buy; increasing
(8) deficit; increase; decrease; contraction;
    reduction
(9) disliked
(10) speculators

Important Terms and Concepts Quiz

1. e	7. c	13. i
2. b	8. q	14. d
3. n	9. o	15. m
4. r	10. h	16. a
5. k	11. p	17. j
6. s	12. l	18. f

Basic Exercises

1. a. The demand curve may shift to
       the left if some Americans now
       find French investments less
       attractive. The supply curve shifts
       to the right as French investors
       are attracted by higher U.S.
       interest rates. With floating rates,
       the franc depreciates. With fixed
       rates, a deficit results.
    b. The demand curve shifts to the
       right. There is no shift in the
       supply curve. With floating rates,
       the france appreciates. With fixed
       rates, a surplus results.
    c. The demand curve shifts to the
       left as Americans import less. The
       supply curve might shift to the
       right if a recession leads to lower
       dollar prices of U.S. exports. With
       floating rates, the franc
       depreciates. With fixed rates, a
       deficit results.

d. The demand curve shifts to the left. The supply curve might shift to the right if French citizens import more. With floating rates, the franc depreciates. With fixed rates, a deficit results.

e. The demand curve shifts to the left and the supply curve shifts to the left as the increase in the price of French wine leads Americans and French to increase their demand for California wines. With floating rates the franc depreciates. With fixed rates, a deficit results.

2. 30

   a. $6.40. Sales of French wine would increase. Sales of California wines would decrease. The U.S. balance of payments would show a deficit.

   b. 18 cents; appreciation; depreciation

   c. United States (50 percent vs. 33 percent)

   d. deficit

   e. depreciating

3. Balance of trade = –109.0 (drawn after line 2)
   Balance on goods and services = –58.0 (drawn after line 5)
   Balance on current account = –91.8 (drawn after line 7)
   Balance on capital account = 61.0 (lines 9, 10, 11, and 12)

   If balance of payments accounts were accurate and complete, the balance on current account and the balance on capital account should sum to zero. For 1990 they sum to –30.9 billion. See text page 474 for a discussion of the statistical discrepancy in measuring international transactions.

Self-Tests For Understanding

Test A

1. b   p. 461
2. c   p. 461
3. b   p. 462
4. b   p. 462
5. b, d   p. 462
6. c   p. 462
7. b   p. 464
8. b, d, f   These factors should increase the demand for American goods or financial assets and, hence, the demand for American dollars.
9. f   b, c, d, and e should increase the demand for dollars. a should reduce the supply of dollars. f should increase the supply of dollars.
10. b   p. 466
11. c, d   p. 468
12. a, b   p. 467
13. d   p. 465
14. c   A 6 percent depreciation of the dollar is necessary to equalize the purchasing power of dollars and marks.
15. b   p. 466
16. b   Higher inflation in the U.S. increases supply of dollars as Americans demand less expensive German goods resulting in U.S. deficit and German surplus.
17. a, c, d   All should shift the supply of domestic currency to the right.
18. a, c, d   At the overvalued exchange rate, demand for Zenon currency would be less than under a system of floating exchange rates.

19. c p. 477
20. b Exchange rates should adjust so that, except for transactions costs, direct conversion between kronor and guilders costs neither more nor less than first converting into dollars and then into kronor or guilders.

Test B

1. T A depreciating currency buys fewer units of foreign currency; an appreciating currency buys more units of foreign currency.
2. F A pure system of floating exchange rates involves no government intervention by definition.
3. T p. 467
4. T An increase in imports would mean an increase in the supply of dollars by Americans. The shift in the supply schedule for dollars would increase a deficit or reduce any surplus.
5. F p. 465
6. T p. 471
7. F pp. 479-480
8. F p. 475
9. T p. 475
10. F p. 476

Supplementary Exercises

1. Col. 1: $28,000,000; £10,000,000
2. Col. 2: $28,000,000; £10,769,231
3. Col. 3: $28,000,000; £11,666,667
   If there is no devaluation, you are out only the transactions costs. If the pound is devalued, you stand to make a handsome profit. As the prospect of devaluation increases, there is a greater incentive to sell your pounds before their price falls.

Your efforts to sell pounds, along with similar actions by others, will increase the pressure for devaluation.

CHAPTER 20
Chapter Review

(1) closed; open
(2) increase; are; less; increase; decrease; decrease; increase; decrease; increase
(3) shift in; decline; down; left
(4) less; downward; more; upward
(5) increase; appreciation
(6) decrease; up; right; increase; appreciation; left; down; offset; lower; increase; offset
(7) appreciation; enhance
(8) J
(9) expansionary; contractionary; contractionary; expansionary; exports; lower

Important Terms and Concepts Quiz

1. a   3. f   5. g
2. e   4. c   6. d

Basic Exercises

1. Appreciation: Exports decrease; Imports increase; Net exports decrease; Aggregate Demand Curve shifts to the left; Aggregate Supply Curve shifts down; Real GDP decreases; Price level decreases.

   Depreciation: Exports increase; Imports decrease; Net exports increase; Aggregate Demand Curve shifts to the right; Aggregate Supply Curve shifts up; Real GDP increases; Price level increases.

2. Increase in G: Interest rate increases; Exchange rate appreciates; GDP and price level down, which work to offset the initial impact of the increase in G.

Decrease in G: Interest rate decreases; Exchange rate depreciates; GDP and price level up, which work to offset the initial impact of the decrease in G.

Open Market Sale: Interest rate increases; Exchange rate appreciates; GDP and price level down, which work to enhance the initial impact of the open market sale.

Open Market Purchase: Interest rate decreases; Exchange rate depreciates; GDP and price level increase, which work to enhance the initial impact of the open market purchase.

3. The impact of monetary policy is enhanced. The impact of fiscal policy is diminished.

Self-Tests For Understanding

Test A
1. b   p. 489
2. c   p. 489
3. c   p. 489
4. c   p. 489
5. a   p. 492
6. c   p. 494
7. a   p. 493
8. c   pp. 487-488
9. b, d p. 495
10. b   p. 495
11. c   The decrease in exports following an appreciation of the dollar shifts the aggregate demand curve to the left.
12. c   p. 495

13. b   The reduction in interest rates from the move to expansionary monetary policy leads to a capital outflow and a depreciation of the dollar.
14. a   pp. 495-497
15. c   pp. 497-498
16. c   p. 490
17. b   p. 501
18. a, c p. 501
19. c   p. 503
20. a, b p. 501

Test B
1. F   pp. 487-488
2. F   A change in exports, whether from a change in foreign GDP or a change in the exchange rate, is modeled as an autonomous change in spending with multiplier effects similar to those of any other autonomous change.
3. F   Autonomous shifts in investment spending affect interest rates, exchange rates, net exports, and the trade deficit in a manner analogous to changes in fiscal policy.
4. T   p. 493
5. T   p. 489
6. T   p. 496
7. F   p. 498
8. F   pp. 495-496
9. T   p. 505
10. F   p. 503

CHAPTER 21

Chapter Review
(1) exponential
(2) inventiveness; entrepreneurship; work ethic; investment; research; development; embodied; disembodied

(3) opportunity; consumption; saving

(4) has not; increase; higher

(5) less (footnote: *I*; *C*; *C*; *IM*) difficult

(6) death; inexpensive

(7) brain drain; World

Important Terms and Concepts Quiz

1. j	4. c	7. d
2. b	5. g	8. h
3. i	6. a	9. f

Basic Exercise

1. On May 20, 1993, *The New York Times* reported new international income comparisons from the International Monetary Fund using estimates of purchasing power parity to convert various national currencies into American dollars and avoid the transition fluctuations of exchange rates.

Brazil:	0.79	5,240
Britian:	0.90	15,720
Canada:	0.52	19,178
China:	1.66	1,450
France:	1.04	18,227
Germany:	1,25	19,500
India:	1.00	1,150
Indonesia	0.50	2,730
Italy	0.98	16,896
Japan	2.37	19,107
Mexico	0.60	7,170
Spain	0.50	12,719

Note the different rankings by total output and income per capita. For example, in terms of total output China ranks third, but in terms of income per capita it ranks twelth. Canada ranks eleventh in terms of total output and third in terms of income per capita.

Self-Tests For Understanding

Test A

1.	d	p. 510
2.	c	p. 512
3.	a	p. 512
4.	c, d	p. 515
5.	c	p. 515
6.	c	p. 516
7.	a, b, c	p. 516
8.	d	p. 517
9.	a	p. 518
10.	d	pp. 519-520
11.	c	pp. 523-525
12.	c	p. 525
13.	b	p. 528
14.	b	p. 528
15.	b	p. 529
16.	c	p. 529
17.	b	pp. 526-531
18.	a	p. 531
19.	a	p. 533
20.	b	As explained in Chapter 19, the IMF helps developed and developing countries with exchange rate and balance of payments issues.

Test B

1.	F	GDP per capita will decrease whenever the growth rate of population exceeds the growth rate of total GDP.
2.	F	pp. 512-514
3.	F	p. 520
4.	F	p. 520
5.	T	p. 515
6.	T	p. 518
7.	F	p. 518
8.	F	p. 524
9.	F	pp. 523-524
10.	T	p. 511
11.	T	p. 529

12. F   p. 530
13. F   p. 530
14. F   pp. 525-531
15. F   p. 532

Supplementary Exercises

2. 1,152 years; 294 days; 36 years; 302 days

3. The absolute difference in incomes would grow from its initial value of $15,034 to $17,303 in the 30th year. After that the absolute difference in incomes would decline until parity is achieved shortly after the start of the 78th year at an income per capita of $69,928.